# DELIVER US FROM EVIL

# Deliver Us from Evil

## THE RADICAL UNDERGROUND
## IN BRITAIN, 1660–1663

Richard L. Greaves

NEW YORK    OXFORD
Oxford University Press
1986

Oxford University Press

Oxford   New York   Toronto
Delhi   Bombay   Calcutta   Madras   Karachi
Petaling Jaya   Singapore   Hong Kong   Tokyo
Nairobi   Dar es Salaam   Cape Town
Melbourne   Auckland

and associated companies in
Beirut   Berlin   Ibadan   Nicosia

Library of Congress Cataloging-in-Publication Data
Greaves, Richard L.
  Deliver us from evil.
  Bibliography: p.   Includes index.
  1. Great Britain—Politics and government—1660–1668.
2. Radicalism—Great Britain—History—17th century.
3. Subversive activities—Great Britain—History—17th century.   I. Title.
DA448.G75   1986   941.06′   85-18772
ISBN 0-19-503985-8

Printing (last digit): 9 8 7 6 5 4 3 2 1

Printed in the United States of America
on acid free paper

TO ROBERT AND LILI ZALLER

# Preface

The restoration of the monarchy and a church governed by prelates in 1660 was neither the beginning nor the culmination of the defeat of the radicals. In retrospect we know that the radicals never again seized the reins of power once General Monck's forces secured London, but neither their ouster from the seats of authority nor the return of the king and his court crushed their aspirations. If 1649 or 1653 was the high watermark of their power and 1659 their Indian summer, 1660 signaled the redirection of their energies to focus less on their internal disagreements and more on their common animosity to monarchy, prelacy, taxes, and popery. In the end, however, their rebellions were few and futile: Lambert in 1660, the Vennerites in 1661, the northern rebels in 1663, and the Galloway insurgents in 1666. Other conspiracies, such as the Tong cabal in 1662, the Dublin plot in 1663, and the Rathbone plot in 1665, were smashed by the government before the radicals could take up arms. Other schemes, such as assassination plots and the theft of the crown jewels, likewise met with failure. Nevertheless, the relentless scheming—the discovery and prosecution of which was rendered far more difficult by the torrent of allegations and rumors of radical activity—was not only a destabilizing element but something that of necessity occupied the attention of officials ranging from the secretaries of state to local magistrates. Radical threats—real and imagined—fueled the drive for the repression of Nonconformists, heightened the concern for domestic security, and prompted the state to utilize a network of informers.

This book is the story of the "radical underground" from the eve of the Restoration to the collapse of the northern rebellion in 1663. It is a tale that winds by devious and sundry routes not only throughout the length and breadth of England but into Scotland, Ireland, the Netherlands, and Switzerland. I have, however, opted to relegate most of the Scottish material to the sequel to the present study, where it can be treated in the context of the events leading up to the Galloway rebellion. The sequel will carry the story of the radical underground in the three kingdoms from 1664 to the Declaration of Indulgence in 1672. Ultimately, I hope to track radical activities and ideas as far as the 1688 Revolution.

Biographical information on many of the figures in this study may be found in the *Biographical Dictionary of British Radicals in the Seventeenth Century*, 3 vols., ed. Richard L. Greaves and Robert Zaller (Brighton: Harvester Press, 1982–84), and in A. G. Matthews, *Calamy Revised* (Oxford: Clarendon Press, 1934).

It is always a pleasure to acknowledge the debts one incurs in writing a book. Much of the research for the present study was made possible by a fellowship from the American Council of Learned Societies under a program funded by the National Endowment for the Humanities. A delightful sojourn at the Huntington Library, which culminated in a memorable Christmas eve supper at the home of Robert and Beverly Middlekauff, gave me the opportunity to engage in daily discussions with Leland Carlson and to present the gist of my work to a receptive luncheon audience. Colin Davis shared his thoughts on the concept of "radicals," while Paul Hardacre provided detailed information on the size and composition of the Cromwellian army. Keith Sprunger has been especially helpful with his expertise on Puritans and Nonconformists in the Netherlands. For advice and support I would like to thank Geoffrey Elton, Christopher Hill, Geoffrey Nuttall, Richard Schlatter, Paul Seaver, Leo Solt, Ted Underwood, and Dewey Wallace. My debt is especially great to Sears McGee and Robert Zaller, whose critiques of the manuscript were invaluable. The staffs of the following libraries distinguished themselves by their courtesy and efficiency: the Public Record Office (Chancery Lane), the Bodleian Library, the Department of Manuscripts at the British Library, Dr. Williams's Library, and the Huntington Library. Nancy Lane has been delightful to work with as an editor, as has Rosemary Wellner, my associate editor. It is a special pleasure to thank my family for its continuing faith and support. This book is dedicated to Robert and Lili Zaller, whose abiding friendship, encouragement, and scholarship have enriched my life more than they know.

*Tallahassee*　　　　　　　　　　　　　　　　　　　　　　　　*R. L. G.*
*July 1985*

# Contents

DELIVER US FROM EVIL

# Introduction

The return of the monarchy in 1660 brought no cessation of revolutionary thinking or acting. Two decades of unprecedented political, social, and religious upheaval could not be eradicated by mere revival of kingly rule, the resurrection of the House of Lords, and the return of the state church to its prelatical overlords. The armies that had marched victoriously across England, Scotland, and Ireland were not smashed by royalist forces in 1660; on the contrary, they defeated themselves through indecision and the lack of generals with vision and political acumen. Some, moreover, willingly followed General George Monck down the road to a restored monarchy. What Charles II faced in 1660 were realms deeply riven by political and ecclesiastical disputes, weary of unstable governments and high taxes, and hungry for a return to stability. But there were also many who were unprepared to relinquish their hard-earned religious freedom or turn back their political and military authority to the country's "natural" rulers. These people, however, lacked a common bond to unite them into a force powerful enough to compel the king to negotiate. Agreeing neither in principle nor in practice, they had no leader capable of forging unity out of their diversity. Yet the Restoration was neither as easy nor as complete as it appeared to be in retrospect.

The revolution did not perish in 1660, but lived on in the words and deeds of the hosts of soldiers and sailors, officers and men, sectaries and republicans who found the Restoration regime wanting. The defeat of these persons in 1660 was not as exhaustive as the great historian of the radicals, Christopher Hill, once suggested.[1] No amount of penal legislation could eradicate dissent from the restored church, nor did the return of the Cromwellian officers and men to their traditional occupations quench their thirst for a government more responsive to their needs and aspirations. Some, in fact, frankly expressed a willingness to take up arms again to drive the scepter from the land. The more radical among them not only grumbled and schemed, but girded on their swords to fight for the Good Old Cause. But they never rebelled together. Despite the links that joined radicals in England, Scotland, Ireland, the Netherlands, Germany, and Switzerland, not once did the dissidents successfully concert their risings. Had they done so, they perhaps would have failed anyway, given the uncertain quality of their leadership and the diffuseness of their aims.

What the historian now so confidently knows about the situation in the first years of the Restoration was considerably less apparent to Charles II and his advisers. The radicals contributed to a sense of unease in the government that produced a major effort to enhance the internal security of the realm. The dissidents also kept alive the ideas and traditions of the Interregnum, though the pedigree of those ideas is difficult to trace, as Hill reminds us, because "they are the ideas of the underground, surviving, if at all, verbally."[2] But the "underground" can itself be traced, and with it the publications that came from its presses. This book is the story of that underground and of the government's efforts to cope with it. In ideological terms it is the saga of a pragmatic quest, however haltingly and imperfectly undertaken, for political and religious freedom.

## Radicals and Reformers

The concept of a "radical underground" is a conscious anachronism. Contemporaries indiscriminately used a variety of terms ranging from fanatic and disaffected to saint and godly in referring to the subjects of this book. It is, however, essential to utilize a category of discourse that enables us not only to understand the past accurately but simultaneously to communicate that knowledge to the present. As Colin Davis has aptly observed, because we live "in a diachronic relationship with our material, we naturally and necessarily wish to make diachronic observations both in order to make statements about a phenomenon over long periods of past time and to make statements about that past phenomenon intelligible in our own day."[3]

The modern term radical more accurately conveys the essence of what the men and women discussed in this book were trying to do than such terms as godly or fanatic. The judicious use of anachronistic terms is not only justifiable but essential if the historian is not to be a mere chronicler.

Elsewhere Robert Zaller and I have defined radicals as "those who sought fundamental change by striking at the very root of contemporary assumptions and institutions."[4] In theory a radical can be distinguished from a reformer, for a radical aims at nothing less than the replacement of the status quo by something new, whereas a reformer seeks its betterment. In practice the distinction is often more difficult to make, as proposals for reform take on colorations so drastic that they threaten to alter the status quo into something substantially different.

The radical's task, as Davis has argued, was essentially threefold. He first had to delegitimate the existing structure as inherently bad and therefore unacceptable in its entirety. Thus republicans advocated the abolition of monarchy, and sectaries the overthrow of the established church. Secondly, the radical had to legitimate a new structure, such as a commonwealth or a voluntary system of religion. Properly, whatever he utilized to delegitimate the old order—for example, the divine will, Scripture, traditions, force, or freedom—had to be used to establish the validity of the new. Finally, to be effective a radical had to provide for a transfer mechanism, a means of moving from the old institutions to the new. Ideally, the transfer mechanism had to be consistent with the principles enunciated to legitimate the new order.[5]

In political terms, few radicals had either the intellectual ability, the educational background, or the time to measure up to these standards. Whether in politics or in religion, the radicals were nevertheless reasonably clear on the broad outlines of what they opposed and what they wanted in its place. There was, however, no unified vision of a new order but a spectrum of views. One of the greatest weaknesses of the radicals was the absence of a commonly accepted vision of what the new order would be, and on what basis it derived its legitimacy. Lacking this unity, it was therefore impossible for the radicals to work out an effective transfer mechanism. The result was a dissident "community" loosely held together by common animosities: dislike of monarchy, hostility to prelacy, repugnance toward the persecution of Protestants, anger over taxes, concern about the potential loss of their estates, and fear of popery. To the extent to which radicals essayed to delegitimate the old order, they typically thought in terms of tyranny and ungodliness. Thus the new order had to be structured to conform to Scripture and to preserve traditional liberties. To achieve these ends the radicals thought primarily in terms of an insurrection, the details of which were never adequately worked out. Had any of the conspiracies succeeded in their negative functions— assassination of political leaders, seizure of strongholds, ouster of traditional authorities—they probably would have instigated a period of rampant confusion. Never did any conspiracy formulate a transfer mechanism that provided for the effective implementation of a new order. If any of the plots had succeeded in toppling the status quo, the resulting chaos might have led to a tyranny unhindered by traditional limitations rather than a free and "godly" commonwealth. Ironically, the contribution of the radicals to the goals they espoused is probably greater because their conspiracies failed. Their ideals were not sullied by actions that inadvertently might have given rise to despotism or to a reign of terror.

The importance of the radicals cannot be discounted because they failed to overthrow the old order. Their efforts and ideas stand as proof that the revolutionary tradition lived on well beyond 1660. That their significance has not been fully recognized is probably due to the incredible tangle of cabals, allegations, rumors, insurrections, and abortive attempts to revolt in the 1660s. In the end, they were all important to some degree, not least because they caused the government incessant concern. No alleged plot could be ignored, but neither could each one be exhaustively investigated. Only the radicals' inherent weaknesses saved the government from potentially explosive confrontations. In the end, only three risings got underway in the 1660s, the first of which was a rebellion by Thomas Venner and the Fifth Monarchists in London in January 1661. In the spring of 1663, Thomas Blood and his co-conspirators were stopped in Dublin on the eve of their revolt, but a potentially large-scale insurrection in northern England ensued that autumn. This could have become the most dangerous revolt of the period, though in the end it collapsed ignominiously. Had the Scots of Galloway rebelled then instead of three years later, England and Scotland might have returned to a state of civil war, particularly if the dissidents in London had also risen. In addition to these insurrections, there were other conspiracies, such as the 1662 Tong plot and the 1665 Rathbone plot, which the government discovered before the rebels could act. Other alleged designs proved wholly fictitious, being based on rumors, malicious accusations, or calculations of personal gain.

The Presbyterian plot of 1661 belongs in this category, but even so its consequences cannot be ignored. Regardless of the flimsy evidence adduced for the plot, the state responded with sweeping arrests, the Presbyterians were tarred with the brush of sedition, and the case for religious uniformity was strengthened.

Only when the insurrections, abortive plots, treasonable scheming, and baseless allegations are examined in context can their cumulative impact be fully understood. Previously, most historians have been content to study the insurrections and abortive "designs" essentially in isolation, which is neither how they occurred nor how the government perceived them. As new reports and allegations surfaced, they did so in direct relation to the plots and rumors that had preceded them. Separating fact from fiction was made all the more difficult because of the common threads running through both the real and the imaginary plots. Repeatedly, there were reports that the Tower and Windsor Castle would be seized, the king and the duke of Albemarle assassinated, the Long Parliament recalled, and the executed regicides avenged. There were, of course, variations on these themes; some designs, for instance, mentioned the burning of London.

The name most often cited in connection with the scheming was that of Lieutenant-General Edmund Ludlow, a committed radical, republican, and supporter of the sectaries. The other great hero of the radicals, Major-General John Lambert, launched an abortive insurrection on the eve of Charles' return and thereafter figured only occasionally in the wistful schemes of the radicals. Throughout the 1660s Lambert remained in custody while Ludlow was an exile in Switzerland. The active leaders of the radicals were men of lesser ability, typically former Cromwellian officers of virtually all ranks. The more prominent among them included Colonel Gilby Carr, Lieutenant ("Colonel") Thomas Blood, Captain George Elton, Colonel Henry Danvers, Colonel John Rathbone, and Lieutenant Nathaniel Strange. Danvers and Strange were also Nonconformist ministers, a reminder of the close links between political and religious radicalism. Those ties were reinforced by the fact that so many former Cromwellian officers were associated with Nonconformist congregations. It was therefore hardly surprising that royalists tended to think of sectarian conventicles as nurseries of sedition. In reality, the large majority of Nonconformist churches were not engaged in plotting, and many of their ministers defied the state only to the point of passively suffering imprisonment and fines. From the standpoint of the government, however, they and their followers

were still engaged in acts of disobedience to duly constituted authority. For that reason they remained objects of suspicion throughout
the period.

Thus dissident activity extended from open insurrection on the
one hand to a refusal to obey statutory regulations governing
religious behavior on the other. Those in the latter category were in
the gray area where radicalism shaded into reform. The spectrum of
radical activities also included utilizing the press to spread their
message. Despite the government's attempts to reimpose censorship,
radicals and reformers continued to publish their works throughout
the period. Their writings helped keep radical ideology alive and
fanned the discontent upon which conspirators fed. The press was
power, a fact only imperfectly perceived by the Restoration regime.
Often couched in religious terms, the radical message could be
conveyed from the pulpit or through books and pamphlets, and
from there it could be reinforced through the myriad irrepressible
discussions in taverns throughout the land. The revolution of the
1640s and 1650s lived on because the government failed in its efforts
to choke off the propagation of radical ideas, either in press or in
pulpit.

## The Radical Community

The difficulty facing the government stemmed not only from the
problem of sorting through the reports and allegations of cabals, but
also from the potential size and geographical diffuseness of the
radical community. The immediate problem concerned the fate of
the Cromwellian army. In July 1652 nearly 70,000 soldiers had been
in arms, though the number was reduced by February 1660 to
28,342. As late as September 1658, however, the figure had been as
high as 42,500 or 43,500. At the beginning of 1659, the number of
officers exceeded 1,700, of whom some 161 were colonels and
majors. In addition there were approximately 373 captains, 537
lieutenants, 537 cornets and ensigns, and 138 quartermasters. When
we add to this the number of officers who had previously resigned or
been dismissed, the result is a formidable body of men that must have
numbered more than 2,000.[6]

The king and his advisers, the Convention, and even the army
were substantially agreed that the latter had to be disbanded. As Lois
Schwoerer has demonstrated, within the Convention there was
distrust of a standing army, resentment of its cost, and concern for
the members' own liberties and power.[7] After the Convention sought

General Monck's advice in August 1660, a bill was prepared and finally signed into law on 13 September. It provided for disbanding all the army except for those units the king chose to retain and support out of his own funds. By the end of December only Monck's regiments of foot and horse remained, and they were formally reconstituted the following February.[8] Keeping track of the former officers and men was an almost insurmountable task, though some efforts were made. In June 1662, Chepstow, Monmouthshire was surveyed to ascertain how many persons who had borne arms in the garrison under Cromwell still lived there; the search turned up thirty-two men. That August parish constables in Staffordshire made an exhaustive effort to list all those in that county who had fought against Charles I or II; the resulting list contains the names of 1,329 officers and soldiers.[9] Normally, however, government agents contented themselves with providing only lists of suspects, among whom ex-officers were typically prominent.

The Nonconformist community varied considerably in its outlook on both religious and political issues. On the whole, the most moderate and certainly the largest of the Nonconformist groups were the Presbyterians, one wing of which was not radical. Led by men such as Richard Baxter and Edmund Calamy, both of whom served briefly as royal chaplains, these Presbyterians favored comprehension within a reformed Church of England. There was a roughly comparable group in Scotland willing to make their peace with the new regime. But in both countries as well as in Ulster and Rotterdam, there were Presbyterians who would brook no thought of compromise with either prelacy or the prescribed liturgy. It was this wing of the Presbyterians that on occasion evinced some willingness to engage in radical activity against the government. Of the 1,610 preaching licenses issued in 1672 under the terms of the Declaration of Indulgence, by far the largest number—939—went to Presbyterians, though this figure must be used with caution since the denominational labels were not always used accurately.[10] Presbyterians were particularly strong in Northumberland, Lancashire, Cheshire, Devon, Somerset, Bristol, and Carmarthenshire.[11]

The Congregationalists (Independents), though in some cases a part of the state church in the 1650s, eschewed the possibility of comprehension at the Restoration. Politically, they were potentially more dangerous than the Presbyterians, though their adherents were in general neither as wealthy nor as socially prominent. The Congregationalists drew heavily from the tradesmen, artisans, and tenant farmers, and they appear to have been especially popular with the old Cromwellian officers. In practice the Congregationalists varied sharply on political views. One wing, led by George Griffith and Joseph Caryl, was more moderate, and in April 1660 placed their faith in the Convention to achieve a just religious solution. Others, such as Philip Nye and Thomas Brooks, were prepared to support Major-General John Desborough's proposal to preserve the republic by the use of force.[12] Among the most radical of the Congregationalist ministers in the 1660s were Edward Richardson (the "doctor of plotters" who earned the M.D. degree at Leiden University in 1664) and the Scots John Forbes and Robert Ferguson. There were, however, relatively few Congregationalists in Scotland; their strength lay primarily in southern and central Wales, the Midlands, Essex, Hertfordshire, and Suffolk in England, and to a modest degree in Dublin. A total of 458 Congregationalists were licensed under the Declaration of Indulgence in 1672.[13]

The Baptists were a heterogeneous group. In addition to the two principal branches, the General (Arminian) and Particular (Calvinistic) Baptists, there were open-membership and communion Baptists, such as John Bunyan, who did not insist on adult baptism as a condition of church membership. A fourth group, the Seventh-Day Baptists, observed Saturday as the proper Christian sabbath. Their leader, Francis Bampfield, opposed radical political activity, but adherents of the General and Particular Baptists were divided on this issue. Two of the leading radical activists of the period, Paul Hobson and Henry Danvers, were Particular Baptist preachers. For the most part the Baptists were strongest among the lower social orders, and for that reason the government tended to be especially wary of them. At the Restoration there were approximately 130 Particular Baptist congregations and 110 General Baptist churches, but only 210 Baptists were licensed in 1672. Altogether the Baptists probably numbered between 20,000 and 30,000.[14]

The Fifth Monarchists were not a denomination in their own right but found disciples among the Baptists and Congregationalists. Their historian, B. S. Capp, estimates that they probably never numbered more than 10,000.[15] Advocates of a radical millenarianism, many Fifth Monarchists accepted the principle that it was the duty of the saints to overthrow the old order in church and state preparatory to the coming of the millennium. Of the three insurrections of the 1660s, they were responsible for the first, under Thomas Venner, and were implicated in the northern risings in 1663, as well as in some of the abortive schemes, such as the Tong and Rathbone plots. Their congregations seem to have been watched more carefully than other conventicles. Among the most active Fifth Monarchists were the Particular Baptists Nathaniel Strange and Henry Danvers and the Congregationalists George Cokayne and Thomas Palmer. Some of the Fifth Monarchists rejected radical political activity, preferring to contain their millenarian expectations in wholly spiritual forms.

The most radical of the sects, the Quakers, were paradoxically the least involved in militant activity in the 1660s. On the one hand their repudiation of any form of established church or formal ministry as well as of the sacraments made them anathema to conservatives, but the government was more concerned with their refusal to take the oaths, the test of political obedience. As the Quaker leaders developed pacifistic principles, the concern of the authorities ebbed. Nevertheless, in the early 1660s there were periodic reports of "fighting Quakers" allegedly involved in plots against the government. They caused more problems by their illegal publishing, disruption of church services, and refusal to take the oaths. Their greatest appeal was in northern and southwestern England and in the cities of London and Bristol, though they also made some headway in Scotland and Ireland. They must have numbered at least 35,000, and by early 1661 more than 4,200 were in jail.[16] Repeatedly imprisoned, they refused to be broken by penal legislation.

Outside England, political unrest and plotting were generally the most common where Nonconformity was the strongest. In Scotland, dissident Presbyterians were especially influential in the southwest, where the Galloway rising occurred in 1666. The problem areas in Ireland were Ulster, where the Presbyterians were in frequent communication with their colleagues in southwestern Scotland, and Dublin, the hub of Protestant political activity in the 1650s. A radical insurrection almost occurred in Dublin, and those involved had some contact with Ulster Presbyterians.

By way of contrast, there is no clear correlation in England between regions of Nonconformist strength and areas associated with insurrections, whether actual or abortive. The principal exception is London, to which most of the major plots had significant ties. The Venner insurrection and the Tong and Rathbone plots, for example, were based in London. Of the four shires most directly involved in the 1663 northern risings—Durham, Westmorland, Yorkshire, and Lancashire—only the last is notable as a center of Nonconformist strength. Moreover, the Presbyterians were prominent there, but they were not involved to any important degree in the northern risings. In Yorkshire the centers of Nonconformity were around Sheffield,[17] but the 1663 conspirators tended to be from the Leeds area to the north. The embryonic Tong plot, however, allegedly included conspirators in Kent, one of the strongholds of the General Baptists, and Essex, where both Congregationalists and Presbyterians were numerous. Two other counties—Dorset and Nottinghamshire—were areas of Presbyterian strength, but Leicestershire, Shropshire, Norfolk, and Durham did not have large numbers of Nonconformists. Nor was the Yarrington plot, which reportedly involved radicals in Worcestershire, Gloucestershire, Herefordshire, Warwickshire, and Staffordshire, linked to shires with marked Nonconformist appeal; only Staffordshire was a county with an important Presbyterian concentration. Conversely, counties where the Congregationalists were strongest—Bedfordshire, Cambridgeshire, Hampshire, Huntingdonshire, Northamptonshire, Hertfordshire, and Essex—were relatively free of major plotting. Only Essex was allegedly tied to the Tong plot. Apart from Bristol and Kent, the same thing is true of areas where the Baptists had their greatest success.

This discontinuity in England between areas of Nonconformist strength and centers of plotting suggests several things. First, apart from dissidents in the London area, the proclivity to radical political activity was greater among Nonconformists in areas where they were more heavily outnumbered. This implies that radical activity was to some degree a response to feelings of endangerment and insecurity. Where Nonconformity was relatively strong, there was less reason for recourse to extreme measures. Because the insurrections were planned for areas where Dissenters were relatively weak, as in Durham, Westmorland, and Yorkshire, their chances of success were diminished. Finally, again with the exception of London, a surprising amount of the radical scheming occurred in those parts of the country that had sided with Charles I in the Civil War. This too suggests an element of desperation by those who found themselves badly outnumbered.

## The Radicals and the Government

Faced with continuing hostility and plotting, as well as periodic outbreaks of radical violence, the government had no clear policy to deal with the threat. Nevertheless many of its actions were pro-active rather than merely reactive. Its policies, however, were shaped not only by the radical threat but also by the constraints placed on it by those conservatives who rallied around Gilbert Sheldon, bishop of London and then, beginning in 1663, archbishop of Canterbury. Sheldon must bear a heavy share of the responsibility for the repressive religious policies of the new regime. He and his colleagues successfully pushed for an exclusively episcopal state church, characterized by conformity to prescribed doctrine and the Book of Common Prayer, and then provided the legal means to suppress those who dissented in the statutes that constituted the Clarendon Code. Beset by inadequate finances, exclusive ecclesiastical interests, insufficient and unreliable military forces, and well-entrenched patterns of radical thought and organization, Charles II never realistically had a chance to reduce radicalism to an inconsequential murmur. He realized this more clearly than did Sheldon and his disciples, but "Anglican" exclusivism and hostility to the dispensing power combined to destroy the king's hope in 1662 for a policy of toleration. Had the royal proposal for an indulgence received parliamentary approval in 1663, much of the religious discontent might have abated, limited only by the extent to which Catholicism became obtrusive under the proposed new conditions. In the political sphere, the only effective counter to the republicans was a monarchy that made itself beloved among the people, but the hearth tax, the sale of Dunkirk, and the execution of Sir Henry Vane and the regicides mitigated against this.

The government's first measure to secure the realms was, of necessity, military in nature. In addition to disbanding the Cromwellian army, it had to resettle the militia, particularly by appointing loyal, effective officers and by increasing its efficiency. This task proved to be so unexpectedly difficult and frustrating that the militia's effectiveness was never fully assured in the 1660s. In February 1661, however, Charles did establish the Royal Guards, which numbered 3,200 men and 374 officers, a force substantially larger than its predecessors.[18]

The government adopted other measures to reduce the likelihood of a successful insurrection. Whenever reports of disaffection were particularly frequent, or when events approached that might incite radical activity, the Privy Council issued a proclamation ordering former military officers to leave London and Westminster for a stipulated time. The government also posted troops in London and other strategic sites when trouble was anticipated, as on 17 August 1662, the Sunday before the great ejection of Nonconformist clergy. In June 1662, using the Yarrington plot as justification, the authorities decided to prevent dissidents from seizing strategic sites by tearing down the walls and fortifications at Coventry, Gloucester, Northampton, and Taunton.

All of these measures were essentially "pro-active." So too was the government's decision to employ informers to infiltrate radical groups at home and abroad, and even monitor their conversations in the taverns and the streets. There was, of course, nothing new about this practice, for it had been utilized rather effectively by John Thurloe, Oliver Cromwell's secretary of state. In fact, both Thurloe and the regicide Thomas Scott, first chief of the intelligence service during the republic and Thurloe's mentor, left records of their activities that were useful to the Restoration government. At the beginning of the reign, both secretaries of state had £700 per annum for intelligence activities, an amount that was increased for Sir Henry Bennet in 1663 because of the northern plotting. Between 1668 and 1675, the total sum allotted for intelligence purposes grew to £4,000 per annum. Informers were also used by Sir George Downing, ambassador to The Hague, and assorted peers and magistrates, such as Sir Thomas Gower, the sheriff of Yorkshire, deputy lieutenant of the North Riding, and veritable watchdog of the northeast. As sheriff of the same county in 1662, Sir Thomas Osborne employed six informers at a retainer of £15 apiece in order to spy on disbanded Cromwellian soldiers.[19]

In general the informers were an unsavory lot who typically saw nothing wrong with egging radicals on to hatch seditious designs. Edward Potter, who worked for both Secretaries Nicholas and Bennet, thought it was his responsibility to "help . . . [the radicals] forward in any plot against [the] Government, and then reveal it."[20] The former Cromwellian John Bradley was instrumental in the development and then the discovery of the 1662 Tong plot. Pretending to be doctors, the informers Peter and John Crabb were particularly active in London.[21] A career in this occupation lasted only as long as one's cover could be protected, but the prospect of a secure government position followed. Bradley was awarded the post of king's messenger, while Edward Riggs was made a navy chaplain after informing on the exiles in the Netherlands. Stephen Harris, who spied on sectaries in Southwark, petitioned the king for an appointment as keeper of the White Lion prison.[22] There were, then, incentives for spies to uncover as much information as possible, even to the point of elaborating on and perhaps even manufacturing stories. Yet there was some limit to the use of false allegations since the informers' credibility and hope for reward rested at least to some degree on the overall validity of their information. They were most dangerous in their ability to distort and misinterpret conversations, sermons, and private meetings. Innuendo and guilt by association were commonplace in their reports.

Those in the highest levels of government were aware of this danger. The duke of Ormond once told the earl of Orrery that when allegations became too frequent, those who reported them should be "discountenanced, since their information must proceed from levity, a desire to ingratiate themselves, or from some worse design; perhaps from a desire to hurry people into Rebellion, by every day's saying they are so, and thereby giving them cause to believe, they shall always be suspected, and consequently always disquieted and in danger."[23] Charles too was inclined to be skeptical and at times personally interrogated suspected plotters. Yet given the size, the geographical diffuseness, and the depth of the hostility of the radical community, the government could hardly afford to forgo the use of informers without some form of professional intelligence network.

There was nothing innovative about the manner in which the state reacted to insurrections and alleged plots. Potentially dangerous persons (normally former officers) as well as other suspects were routinely imprisoned throughout the period. The most menacing dissidents, such as John Lambert, were secured in isolated castles and sometimes moved from place to place to prevent attempts to liberate them. Some escapes were successfully engineered, notably those of Colonel Henry Danvers and Captain John Mason. On the whole the authorities showed little inclination to execute radicals apart from the Vennerites, the Tong and Rathbone plotters, and the northern and Galloway rebels. Conventiclers faced imprisonment or fines, but the laws against them were never consistently enforced, at least in part because of their considerable numbers and the king's inclination toward toleration. The twelve years John Bunyan spent in prison were a striking exception, not the norm. Although such persecution failed to break the back of Nonconformity, it undoubtedly reduced the numbers of those who attended dissenting services. Similarly, the government's efforts to censor the press were only marginally successful. The strength of radical traditions was simply too deeply rooted to be destroyed by state policies.

## The Historical Perspective

The very nature of a radical underground poses special problems with respect to evidence. As one of the principal sources, informers' reports are particularly enigmatic because of the tendency of domestic spies to exaggerate, misinterpret, and even fabricate. Nevertheless, no informer could have maintained his employment unless there was some degree of reliability in his reports. These reports are indispensable in uncovering the story of the radical underground, though every attempt must be made to locate reliable corroboration for an informer's allegations before they can be fully accepted. Reports of magistrates and other officials are important, but they too can be of little use if they contain nothing more than hearsay and unsubstantiated allegations. Trial records are woefully slim, but where they exist they provide crucial information. Confessions and depositions are likewise valuable, but like trial testimony they are occasionally prone to be self-serving. One of the most solid classses of evidence is the arrest records, though they measure only suspicion and accusation, not proven guilt.

Among other types of evidence, newspapers are very helpful, even though as government-licensed publications they present a biased story. When, for example, the Act of Uniformity was implemented in 1662, the papers ran a steady stream of reports concerning how peaceful and obedient the people were. Of the various diaries and memoirs, that of Samuel Pepys is the best for chronicling the general flow of events. In comparison, John Evelyn demonstrated little interest in the activities of the radicals. Edmund Ludlow's memoirs, edited for the period 1660–1662 by Blair Worden, present a consistently hostile view of the Stuart regime as well as sharp skepticism with respect to allegations of radical conspiracies. Although he wrote the memoirs while exiled in Switzerland, Ludlow maintained contact with friends in England. Sir James Turner's memoirs, though bitterly hostile to the Galloway rebels who kidnapped him, provide one of the best sources for that insurrection. Sir John Reresby's memoirs are less useful for events in northern England than one would wish.

Most of the evidence for the workings of the radical underground comes, expectedly, from hostile sources. By virtue of its very nature, those who engaged in radical political activity could hardly afford to keep records. The letters of radicals that have survived were in most cases intercepted by the authorities and thus preserved. The bulk of the correspondence pertaining to radical activity, however, comes from the pens of royalists. In addition, the Venetian resident showed a consistent interest in dissidents, but the reports to his government tend to exaggerate radical activity. One of the best sources for the views of the radicals is the publications of the underground press, but they are of very limited use in untangling the assorted conspiracies.

The historiography of the plots and insurrections reflects both the problematical nature of the sources and the varying reactions to the Restoration monarchy. The earliest histories of the individual plots were usually anonymous and very pro-government. An exception is Andrew Yarrington's account of the plot that bears his name. Written two decades after the alleged conspiracy, the title of his book makes his approach abundantly clear: *A Full Discovery of the First Presbyterian Sham-Plot* (1681). The anonymous author of one of the accounts of Thomas Venner's Fifth Monarchist insurrection treated it in thoroughly reprehending terms, paralleling it to the Anabaptist fiasco in Münster.[24] The best contemporary account of the Tong plot, *A Brief Narrative of That Stupendious Tragedie* (1662), was composed by the state's chief witness and is both biased and self-serving. The story of the abortive Dublin conspiracy in 1663 is told from the Presbyterian perspective by Patrick Adair.[25] The first attempt to write a survey of all the major designs against the government was undertaken by Thomas Long, a prebendary at Exeter Cathedral, but the result is neither reliable nor particularly useful.[26] Easily the best of the seventeenth-century accounts is the general history of the Scottish historian Gilbert Burnet, bishop of Salisbury, but his relevance to the present topic is largely limited to Scottish affairs.[27] Archbishop Sheldon's onetime chaplain, Samuel Parker, bishop of Oxford, was no friend of the Nonconformists but nevertheless provides helpful accounts of some of the more significant radical activity. One of Parker's more interesting contributions is his fourfold typology of rebels as ex-Cromwellian officers, espousers of sedition, Rumpers, and evicted purchasers of crown and ecclesiastical lands.[28]

The eighteenth century produced three works of distinct interest to the historian of radical activities in the 1660s. Bishop White Kennet's *Register and Chronicle Ecclesiastical and Civil* (1728) draws extensively on documents of the 1660s, but is less interpretive than James Ralph's *History of England* (1744–46). Ralph was the first to attribute crucial significance to the conspiracies as a key to evaluating Charles II's reign: "According as these Plots were real or fictitious, or as they appear to have been contemptible or formidable, we must acquit or condemn this Reign."[29] Ralph was an astute critic of the evidence, concluding, for example, that the crimes attributed to the Tong plotters were highly improbable. Despite its pronounced

Presbyterian bias, Robert Wodrow's *History of the Sufferings of the Church of Scotland from the Restoration to the Revolution* is indispensable for the story of the disgruntled Presbyterian clergy as well as the Galloway rising in 1666.

The only modern historian to attempt an overview of all the major plots was Wilbur Cortez Abbott, whose two-part article in the *American Historical Review* in 1908–1909 is both tantalizing and perceptive. It was Abbott's thesis that a study of the radical tradition from 1660 to 1688 would "help to restore that sense of continuity between revolution and revolution which has been so long lacking, to the great detriment of a proper understanding of that period."[30] But the great Harvard historian never followed through on his article with a full-scale study. He did, however, write an interesting biography of one of the age's most intriguing radicals, Thomas Blood.[31] Maurice Ashley's semipopular and sometimes unreliable biography of John Wildman provides an overview of most of the major plots (sans documentation), but Ashley rather cavalierly dismisses most of them as exaggerations if not fabrications.[32]

Much of the best work on the radicals in the 1660s has been done in specialized studies. Early this century Champlin Burrage wrote a good narrative of the Fifth Monarchist insurrections, but the more recent study of the Fifth Monarchy Men by Bernard Capp allows the rising of Venner and his followers to be viewed in a broader historical and ideological context.[33] The northern risings in 1663 were briefly surveyed in journal articles by Henry Gee in 1917 and James Walker in 1934.[34] Walker also wrote a useful article on the intelligence service of Charles II and James II.[35] The account of the 1666 Galloway rising has been retold numerous times by modern historians, including a brief book-length narrative by Charles Terry in 1905, but he was more interested in the movements of the rebels than the causes and significance of their uprising.[36] No historian has treated the Galloway rebellion in the broader context of radical developments in England and Ireland as well as Scotland.

Restoration historiography still reflects the profound influence of T. B. Macaulay, who found little reason to concern himself with religious and political radicals. Within a few months of the Restoration, he argued, "there remained not a trace indicating that the most formidable army in the world had just been absorbed into the mass of the community."[37] The Restoration was, in the traditional view, an immensely popular event. The hostility against republican rule was such, as Richard Lodge asserted, that Charles' welcome was "apparently as unanimous as it was boisterously enthusiastic."[38] Recent historians have embraced a more realistic view of the Restoration, but nevertheless have been reluctant to attribute to the sectaries—apart from the Vennerites—anything more than "resigned political inactivity." Because the Restoration, according to J. R. Jones, "shattered the rationale as well as the morale of those who had vainly tried to prevent it," the godly accepted the new order in a quietist, submissive spirit as a manifestation of God's judgment.[39] Similarly, while recognizing the *idea* of a radical Nonconformist plot as a factor in politics until at least 1688, J. P. Kenyon insists that "all the Nonconformist sects after 1660 were imbued by a profound political quietism."[40] In order to arrive at a more accurate understanding of the Restoration era, the present study provides a full-scale account of radical activities in all three kingdoms and relates those activities to the broader world of Nonconformity.

# 1

# "An Antichristian Generation"

## RADICALS AND THE RESTORATION

The England to which Charles returned in May 1660 had suffered through two decades of war, unstable government, internal dissension, and frustrated hopes. Expectedly, then, the promised restoration of the traditional order was greeted with substantial enthusiasm in some quarters. May Day, according to Samuel Pepys, was marked with prodigious bonfires, bell-ringing, and toasts to the king's health by persons who kneeled in the streets. "Methinks," he wryly observed, it was "a little too much." By the 5th, he thought there was a greater contentment among the people than he had ever seen.[1] But this public expression of enthusiasm masked a strong undercurrent of deep-rooted hostility to monarchy in general and to the Stuarts in particular. The Venetian resident in England was clearly wrong when he informed the Doge and Senate in April that the desire for Charles was universal. Even Sir Edward Nicholas, buoyed by positive reports from Ireland and Scotland, seemed unconcerned in August about "the dying struggles of fanatics and sectaries."[2] Although some advocates of the Good Old Cause were ready to make their peace with the new regime, others fanned the smoldering embers of discontent for decades, hoping to ignite a revolutionary upheaval that would restore the republic, provide religious toleration for Protestants, and achieve social and economic reforms.

21

## Climate of Hostility

The themes of discontent that pervaded most areas of the country remained fairly constant throughout the 1660s. No refrain was more common than the old accusation that Charles was a bastard.[3] A Durham gentleman not only hoped that Charles would never be crowned for this reason, but expressed his disdain on several occasions by clapping his horse on the buttocks while exclaiming, "Stand up, Charles the third by the grace of God." Henrietta Maria was still reviled as "the Great Whore of Babilon" and Charles as the illegitimate fruit of her tryst with Henry Jermyn.[4] The duke of York was castigated as a rogue, while a Tynemouth gentleman allegedly asserted that the king had no follower "that hath a principle of God in him except Sir Ralph Hopton." Some found Charles no better than Cromwell, and typically worse. In the words of one Londoner, Charles was "a poore and beggerly King."[5] The disdain stemmed in part from the fact that he was considered a Scot and the beneficiary of a dubious Stuart succession, unlike Cromwell who won his position as a latter-day William the Conqueror. Calling for a divine curse to strike Charles, a Newcastle woman protested:

> What! can they finde noe other man to bring in then a Scotsman? What! is there not some Englishman more fit to make a King then a Scott?

Beloved only of drunken whores and whoremongers, Charles, she feared, would "sett on fire the three kingdomes as his father before him has done." For this, she hoped to see his bones hanging from a horse's tail and the dogs running through "his puddins."[6] Accusations of treasonous speech against the king were commonplace at the Restoration.[7] Among those charged were two London ministers, the Presbyterian William Jenkyn and the Congregationalist George Griffith, who like so many of their colleagues in the 1660s were suspected of seditious preaching in their private meetings. Some of the alleged accusations were clearly treasonous, often because they encompassed the death of the sovereign. One Londoner hoped to meet the king at the gallows, while another threatened to wash his hands in Charles' blood after running him through with a rusty sword.[8] Reflecting the hostility characteristic of many Cromwellian officers, Captain Southwood (or Southwold), formerly of Desborough's troop, reportedly boasted that if Charles "came in by fair means or foul, he would have his head off, and cut him as small as herbs in a pot." A Newcastle-on-Tyne man castigated Charles as a traitor and a rogue who deserved to be whipped from town to town until he reached London, where his skin should be "pulled over his Eares."[9] When an excise official in northern England was rebuked by a woman for demanding that the king be hanged as a rogue, he caustically responded: "Did you anoint him, did you take up your Coates & pisse upon his head to Anoynt him?" The man's superior, no less disrespectful, reportedly accused the bastard Charles Stuart of engaging in sexual relations with his own mother, the "whore" Henrietta Maria.[10]

Some of the hostility stemmed from fears that the return to Stuart monarchy would lead to Catholicism. In November a West Yorkshire man claimed that the trained bands as well as disbanded soldiers were flocking to Scotland in order to take up arms against the king, who had forsaken his oath to the Solemn League and Covenant, and was planning to impose popery. Animosity to Charles was frequently laced with religious fervor. Militant millenarianism inspired an ex-parliamentary officer, Wentworth of Bilsby, Lincolnshire, to proclaim that the saints would bind their monarchs in chains and their nobles in fetters of iron. In the aftermath of the Fifth Monarchist insurrection in January 1661, he was reported to the justices at Burwell, Cambridgeshire. The attorney Hugh Ayscough told the same justices that 300,000 men were prepared to overthrow the government, but hesitated because of doubts as to whether God had granted them the right to shed blood.[11]

Substantial animus was directed toward General Monck, whom Edmund Ludlow castigated as "that monster of mankind[,] the devill's great instrument in this chandge." An ex-lieutenant in Cromwell's Life Guards summed up the view of many of his comrades when he insisted that Monck should hang. A Wapping glazier who wanted to see Monck and Charles hang together reflected the sentiments of many radicals in London.[12] The City, according to Robert Blackborne, secretary to the Admiralty Committee in the 1650s, considered Monck "a most perfidious man, that hath betrayed everybody." It was a commonplace that Monck was a betrayer—worse, said one gentleman, than Jezebel herself. A fifteen-year veteran of Cromwell's army voiced the bitter frustration of men whose leaders had lost their stomach to fight for the Good Old Cause: "We would a fought it out to the last man before the Kinge should a com in."[13]

Out of such feelings came the belief—partly from hope, partly from conviction—that Charles would not reign long, if indeed there was even a coronation. "The king shall never be crowned," warned a northern laborer, "and, if hee is crowned, hee shall never live long."

In December 1660 a Canterbury shoemaker imbued with republican convictions thought the restored monarchy was "now almost att an end." A London woman gave Charles less than a year, a Yorkshire man eight, "and he might then prepare himself for the Lord." The end would come, predicted a woman of Great St. Bartholomew's, London, "in the kings meate."[14] It is worth noting that expectations of the imminent demise of Charles and the Stuart monarchy were typically not connected with eschatological visions but with visceral feelings of revenge. If the king did not flee soon, a Yorkshire laborer threatened, he would "die the sorest death that ever King died." For some, life after monarchy was no more than a return to the heady days of the republic.[15]

The loathing the Restoration induced in anti-monarchists is vividly manifested in vows to assassinate Charles or die in an attempt to keep him from the throne. George Keddell, who had once solicited signatures among his Kentish neighbors to have Charles I tried, declared himself ready to shed his own blood rather than see monarchy triumph. A Londoner claimed to prefer hanging rather than see Charles crowned, while a Brighton man was summoned before the assizes for saying, "A King! if I had but one batt in my belly, I would give it to keep the King out, for Cromwell ruled better than ever the King will."[16] In June 1660 Captain Cuthbert Studholme of Carlisle was arrested for threatening to run Charles through with his sword. The matter was deemed serious enough for witnesses to urge their town clerk to press government officials to increase the king's protection.[17]

Threats of personal violence to the king by ex-military men could not be lightly disregarded, particularly when they were uttered by ex-officers capable of enlisting former soldiers for their cause. One of the more serious cases involved Colonel Daniel Axtell, who supported Lambert's insurrection in April 1660, and had once threatened to put a dagger into the heart of anyone who exercised the powers of government as a single person. In July he warned that the king and the Privy Council would return the country to civil war by ruining the 300,000 people who had purchased crown, church, or delinquents' lands. The army in Scotland, he claimed, was corresponding with the London Presbyterians, and "in a very little tyme" the people "should see as fayre a day for it again as ever was in England, which a considerable member of the Councile of the Citty did assure him off." Monck, he predicted, would be "a pittifull fellow" in two or three months. When that time elapsed, however, it was Axtell who suffered, having been convicted of compassing the king's death; he was executed at Tyburn.[18]

Dissatisfaction with the Restoration was fanned by sectarian clergy. In his speech to the House of Lords on 13 September, the chancellor complained that the king was receiving frequent reports of seditious sermons, a problem that never abated throughout the 1660s. The Fifth Monarchist Richard Goodgroom, formerly a chaplain to Major-General Harrison, typified the recalcitrance of those who remained adamantly hostile. Imprisoned in the Tower in September 1660 for preaching seditiously to radical enclaves in Coleman Street and Bethnal Green, he was jailed again in October 1661. After his release in 1667, he resumed preaching, only to be arrested once more in July 1671.[19] The sort of fiery rhetoric that Charles faced from some of the pulpits is exemplified in a sermon by the Presbyterian John Milward, rector of Darfield in the West Riding. After warning his congregation in May 1660 that Charles would introduce popery and mandate the worship of images, he exhorted them to

> shew ourselves men, and gird every man his sword upon his thigh, and sheath it in his neighbour's bowell, for I doe beleive too many of us have Popes in our bellies. Let us feare the King of heaven and worship Him, and bee not so desireous of an earthly King, which will tend to the imbroileing of us againe in blood.[20]

The Presbyterian Zachary Crofton, the Congregationalist Thomas Jollie, and the Fifth Monarchist Wentworth Day were all accused of seditious preaching at the Restoration; Crofton was imprisoned in the Tower.[21]

Although some ministers indicated disapproval only by refusing to use the Book of Common Prayer, others were openly inflammatory. Nathaniel Jones, rector of Westmeston, Sussex, was briefly jailed for allegedly preaching that the king had broken the Covenant and forced the people to violate it. According to several parishioners of Newton Ferrers, Devon, the Presbyterian John Hill excoriated the king as a rebel and a traitor against the Commonwealth, maliciously preached against his right to the succession, and justified the execution of his father.[22] At a meeting in White's Alley, Coleman Street, an unnamed firebrand, referring to the Privy Council, prayed "that a spirit of variance might bee amongst them to confound them," and then prophesied that the saints would finally prevail. The Presbyterian Andrew Parsons, rector of Wem, Shropshire, spent three months in jail for comparing the devil to a king who spoke fairly until he gained his throne and then played pranks. Thirteen witnesses deposed that John Wesley, grandfather of the Methodist founder, called from the pulpit for God to "extirpate, root out, and confound the name of the Stewarts: for they were an Antichristian generation." Ominously he exhorted his followers that "God had a great work to do: And the meanest, and despised of men, should do it."[23] Most dissident clergy, however, were content to urge a policy of passive disobedience. A "factious combination" of radical clergy and ex-military men, as Bishop Morley of Winchester called them, encouraged the people not to conform, though with only mixed success. Morley told Hyde that hundreds in his diocese had conformed during his visitation. Sixty Lancashire ministers, including Edward Richardson (who was involved in the northern plotting in 1663), James Walton, Nathaniel Heywood, and William Cole (all soon to be ejected), petitioned Charles in December 1660, professing peace and loyalty, and requesting a repeal of the penal statutes concerning nonconformity. The General Baptist Henry Adis likewise asked for religious toleration, but promised that if Parliament "intermeddle[d] with the regulating of our consciences as to the worship and service of our God, . . . we shall not, by force of arms, nor the least violence, oppose them."[24] A petition from Lincolnshire Baptists expressed a similar attitude, while Baptists in the Maidstone jail were willing to acknowledge the king's authority in religious matters but not his right to impose the oath of supremacy. The Quakers too refused oaths but were willing to recognize Charles as rightful sovereign and not conspire against him. In November 1660 they offered to designate six male Friends in each county to pledge that their meetings would not involve plotting. Despite complaints about the Quakers (and Baptists) in Bristol refusing the oaths and a Quaker threat that Charles would be punished if he persecuted the Friends, the king freed approximately 700 of them in 1660.[25]

Although the climate of hostility at the Restoration was more pervasive and deep-rooted than is usually recognized, the radical community was clearly divided. By adopting a punitive and narrow settlement, the government missed the opportunity to calm a good deal of the apprehension and mitigate the acerbity that characterized the 1660s. A policy of comprehension for Presbyterians and indulgence for peaceful Dissenters might have effectively isolated militant dissidents and stripped away much of their potential base of support, rendering the possibility of a successful plot remote indeed. As it was, the reservoir of bitterness was a potentially valuable resource for militants to tap.

## Radical Activity and the Government's Response

John Lambert's escape from the Tower and abortive insurrection in April 1660 marked the transition from the death throes of the republic to the shadowy underground of plotting and rebellion. On the evening of the 10th he slipped down a rope, fled in a waiting barge, and went into hiding in the City. The Council of State issued a proclamation summoning him to surrender and offering £100 for his capture. Monck, who had already begun to purge the military of sectaries and other radicals, acted quickly to ensure the loyalty of the troops by promising arrears of pay for soldiers who stayed with their units. The Tower was secured. Nerves were already so jittery that three weeks before Lambert's escape the City had urged Monck to take up quarters in London until the new Parliament convened.[26] As Lambert picked up some support in Hull, Gloucester, Coventry, and Nottingham, it became clear to Pepys "that either the Fanatiques must now be undone, or the Gentry and citizens throughout England and [the] clergy must fall." Four troops of horse joined Lambert in a rendezvous at Edgehill.[27] The troops of Captain Robert Haselrig and Captain Timothy Clare were there, as were those of Colonel Matthew Alured and Major John Nelthorpe, though the latter two officers did not participate. At most, only one company of foot was involved.[28] Although Lambert sent agents to the regiments in England seeking support, he was hampered by the fact that Monck had aready dispersed them. Lieutenant Merry, who had served under Major John Smithson in Robert Lilburne's regiment, enlisted forty of Captain John Deverell's men to seize York, but Merry himself was apprehended by Colonel Hugh Bethell and his force dissipated.[29]

The regicide Richard Ingoldsby, who had lost his regiment at Richard Cromwell's fall and been restored to his command by Monck, was sent as a trusted loyalist to join forces with Northampton. Colonel Charles Howard was ordered to Worcester to prevent further defections and to watch Coventry, which Lambert hoped to garrison. Three companies of John Streater's men secured Coventry.[30] As a further precaution, the Northamptonshire trained bands were alerted, and the earl of Exeter made nearly a hundred horse available to Streater. Ingoldsby and Streater, having joined forces on Saturday evening, 21 April, caught up with Lambert's rebels some two miles from Daventry on Easter Sunday morning. With Lambert were Colonels Daniel Axtell, Ralph Cobbett, and John Okey, Lieutenant-Colonel Arthur Young, Major Richard Creed, and Captains Timothy Clare, Henry Clare, John Gregory, and Anthony Spinage.

Haselrig's troop was cornered before it could reach Lambert and its captain induced to switch sides.[31]

In the fields near Daventry, Lambert's men professed to fight in the name of Richard Cromwell, but a counterappeal to military authority prompted the desertion of Alured's troop. When Lambert's horse refused to return the brief fire of Streater's companies, Lambert and his officers vainly sought Ingoldsby's permission to leave, then turned in flight. Axtell, Okey, and Henry Clare escaped, but Lambert, Cobbett, Creed, Young, and the other captains were captured.[32] With relief, the earl of Northampton reported to Charles that Ingoldsby had crushed Lambert's "aspiring ambition, desperate and bloody designs in the growth." In the meantime, three of Lambert's cohorts, (Captain George?) Everard, Captain Nicholas Lockyer, and Captain Thomas Cradock failed to take Nottingham, which was defended by Captain John Sherman of Colonel Sanders' regiment.[33]

Before Lambert's defeat, Pepys had observed that the London "fanatics" were holding their heads high, but the collapse at Daventry temporarily dampened their enthusiasm. "Some clouds," the earl of Northampton observed on May Day, "still hang on the brows of some disgruntled persons: and I hope that God . . . will . . . blow them over without a shower." With Lambert back in the Tower, Pepys thought that "every man begins to be merry and full of hopes," but an Essex writer more perceptively pondered "this distracted nation."[34] Lambert's failure seems to have had little impact on his stature in radical circles, for his name continued to be invoked by plotters for years. To a Londoner that May, Lambert was more deserving of the crown than Charles, while a West Riding man openly hoped to see Lambert king. Hyde was informed on 4 May that the militants in the City and the army were still active, and the king himself warned Monck the same day to take care for his safety in the aftermath of Lambert's debacle. In turn, Charles was cautioned that "the despair of the late King's murderers may make them urge on fanatic spirits to attempts they themselves lack courage to undertake; religious zealots of whatever kind are more dangerous than impious people."[35]

The state in fact took the radical threat very seriously, and responded by detaining suspicious persons and instigating searches for hidden weapons, which were prevalent in the aftermath of the upheavals of the 1640s and 1650s. In late April sectaries suspected of complicity in Lambert's rising were placed under guard, and the following month Parliament directed magistrates to suppress all riots and unlawful assemblies. Even before Lambert's escape the authorities searched for hidden arms in the houses of such men as Captain John Crofts and the Fifth Monarchists Carnsew Helme and Anthony Palmer.[36] Loaded firearms were seized in the houses of London sectaries in late March. Four muskets, a carbine, a fowling gun, a case of pistols, two swords, a blunderbuss, some ten pounds of shot, several parcels of gunpowder, two daggers, and a suit of armor— all hidden away—were discovered in June in the possession of a Warwickshire man, who claimed he had forgotten he owned the weapons. The following month an apprehensive Secretary Nicholas requested a warrant to search the house of the Quaker William Woodcock, who lived in the precincts of the old Savoy Palace and reportedly had "arms hid under ground." Nicholas was even suspicious of a Yeoman of the Guard who had privately purchased gunpowder.[37]

A virtual arsenal was purportedly assembled by Major Brent, who by May 1660 had concealed some three hundred muskets as well as ammunition and long knives under the lime kilns at his house in Pickle Herring Street, across the Thames from the Tower. According to two informers, he hoped for an insurrection in which his weapons would "bee usefull for their own party." When he learned that his Southwark house would be searched on the eve of the king's return, Brent and his servants secreted the weapons at his house in Greenhithe.[38]

The policy of searching for and seizing the firearms of dissidents was extended throughout the kingdom that summer, as the lords lieutenant were instructed to confiscate all arms and munitions in the hands of disaffected or suspicious persons, and in addition to secure all forts and apprehend vagrants. The lords lieutenant were also ordered to see that the troops received regular training, though volunteers had to be organized and drilled separately. Adequate numbers of officers and men were to be maintained, and precautions taken to prevent disgruntled persons from assembling. As late as 3 September, the House of Lords, fearing that Baptists and Quakers in Northamptonshire were meeting seditiously as supporters of Lambert, ordered the sheriffs to prevent their gatherings. The mood of concern that prevailed among some royalists was summed up in a letter from Charles Lyttelton to Lady Hatton: "There are some who feare that, unlesse they regaine theyr creditt and interest by a warr, they shall not be able to maintaine those greate thinges they pretend to." Others were more confident, suspecting that "the mad zealots and the desperate persons of quality and estate" were few compared with those who welcomed the Restoration.[39]

In the wake of Lambert's abortive rising there was in fact substantial radical activity, much of it centering around the Fifth Monarchists. *Mercurius Publicus* reported that they had been acquiring saddles and arms and unsuccessfully trying to steal horses in mid-May for a rising. Fifth Monarchists and other "dangerous" persons were observed meeting in the houses of John Skinner and a Mr. Wilson of Bridge Court. In his diary John Nicoll noted the discovery of a plot to assassinate the king by a group of radicals that included Lieutenant-Colonel Abraham Holmes, who had defected from Monck in December 1659.[40] According to an unsubstantiated rumor, Baptists and other malignants allegedly contributed £200,000 to raise forces for the extirpation of monarchy. Another report indicated that fanatics in Portsmouth were dissuaded from rebelling only by the arrival of Colonel Richard Norton. Arrests of sectaries and other radicals continued and included persons apprehended in Fleet Street for speaking seditiously against the king.[41]

Some of the suspicion focused on Major-General John Desborough, who tried to flee the country. A forged letter to the radical London bookseller Livewell Chapman bearing the date 8 April 1660 was purportedly from his hand. It outlined a plot that involved such prominent radicals as Henry Vane, Colonel John Okey, who had participated in Lambert's rebellion, John Owen, who had been ejected from Christ Church, Oxford, in March, the regicide Hugh Peter, and the Welsh evangelist Vavasor Powell. Chapman was arrested on 2 May, but the state had been after him since 28 March. When Desborough was brought into London on the night of 22 May, he was jeered by boys who lined the streets, calling him "Phanatique, Phanatique."[42] The following month there were further suspicions of his plotting, primarily because he lived in close proximity to other ex-officers in Windsor Park. Among them were Major Michael Jenkins and Captain Southwood, who had threatened to murder Charles II; Jenkins and an associate were arrested. One of them may have been the alleged assassin who stood with an unsheathed sword near the king's closet on 28 June, but was apprehended by the sergeant-at-arms. Whitehall Palace was inadequately protected. On 25 July Captain Henry Clare, wanted for his part in Lambert's rising, was seen sneaking up the palace stairs. He was reportedly hiding in a Catholic's house, going about in disguise and threatening to "sheath his sword in the Kings blood . . . up to the Hilte."[43]

To the north, the alleged Sowerby plot unfolded in July and August. A group of about thirty ex-officers, sectarian ministers, and others met on 17 July in the house of Joshua Horton at Sowerby, four miles from Halifax. The group included Captain John Hodgson of Coley Hall near Halifax, Captain William Pickering, and the ministers Jeremiah Marsden, Thomas Jollie, Samuel Eaton, Henry Root, Michael Briscoe, Thomas Smallwood, and Christopher Marshall.[44] What transpired at the meeting could only be surmised, but the informer feared they were planning an insurrection. Certainly some of those present are known to have espoused views hostile to the government. In 1661 Smallwood was indicted for preaching that the restoration of the Church of England was a sign that the whore of Babylon was "rising and setting up." Marsden, who sometimes hid his bushy black hair with a wig and had a lisp, was to be involved in the northern plot in 1663, and the others suffered periodic imprisonment. Although Monck was not convinced that an insurrection was being planned, a commission was sent to investigate. The jury that heard the evidence returned a verdict of *ignoramus*.[45]

Sir John Armitage, who reported the Sowerby meeting to the king's secretary, linked this story to a report that he had received of a party of about one hundred well-armed horse that rendezvoused at Coley Hall before dispersing to Craven and Ripon. Hodgson was later arrested for treasonable words against Charles: "Your Kinge, your Kinge ere longe will have notheinge left to sett his crowne upon." For this offense he spent five months in York Castle.[46]

Arrests and rumors continued throughout the summer. A spurious report reached London in mid-August that rebels had seized Stafford and had risen in Scotland. Thomas Tillam, the Particular Baptist and Fifth Monarchist who had founded a church at Hexham, attracted the government's attention because of his travel between the north and London; his mail was intercepted and he was imprisoned in June. Colonel Henry Bradshaw, brother of the regicide, Captains Edward Alcock and John Griffith, and Major Edmund Wareing, brother-in-law of Major Richard Salway, had been arrested by July.[47] Although the republican Luke Robinson made a quick conversion to royalism at the Restoration, he was nevertheless expelled from the Convention and temporarily imprisoned. Ralph Constable of Selby sought a warrant for Robinson's arrest in July on the grounds that he was "inveterate formerly against his Majestie & continues in Rebellion and [is] at present lurking privately in London or the parts adjacent." Although Constable thought he might be scheming against the king, the former's motives are suspect, for he had recently been released from a three-year prison term for which he blamed Robinson. In September the Fifth Monarchist Wentworth Day was arrested for treasonable words.[48]

The general hostility among radicals to the return of monarchy and episcopacy was exacerbated by systematic efforts to punish the regicides. In May the House of Commons approved a resolution to secure those who had sat in judgment on Charles I, and both Houses subsequently ordered the seizure of the regicides' estates. The Bill of Indemnity, which received the royal assent on 29 August, totally excepted twenty-six living and four deceased regicides (Oliver Cromwell, John Bradshaw, Henry Ireton, and Thomas Pride). The estates of twenty other deceased regicides were made subject to fine or forfeiture. Nineteen other living regicides (who had surrendered) were excepted, but the act provided that, if attainted for high treason, they could be executed on the king's order only with the prior advice and consent of Parliament. Twenty-eight regicides and one alleged executioner were placed on trial in October, but only ten were sentenced to death.[49]

The outcome had been anticipated in sectarian circles. At a meeting in Wapping on 18 September, the preacher, who was probably the General Baptist and ex-Leveller Thomas Lamb, told his audience that only the blood of the regicides and other saints would satisfy the royalists. He called in advance for their judges and juries to tremble, "and as thou hast struck one stroke already in the family [of Stuart,] Lord strike another . . . that thy people have cause to rejoyce."[50] On the eve of the first executions, Thomas Scott warned that if the king "proceed[ed] to blood, will it not refresh the memory, and renew the argument of the quarrell in all Men's mouthes, which should be forgotten?" There was truth in what he said. Thomas Harrison "led the dance of that black Masque," followed by Scott, Axtell, John Carew, John Cook, Gregory Clement, John Jones, Francis Hacker, Adrian Scrope, and Hugh Peter. On the scaffold Harrison reportedly said that he would rise from the dead within three days and sit at the right hand of God to sentence his judges.[51] Although there were popular expressions of satisfaction at the executions, those who died became martyrs in the radical camp. John Simpson instructed his congregation that despite the condemnation of the regicides, their action was justified before God, "and that what they had don their Consciences did beare them witnesse that it was just and right." At year's end a Canterbury shoemaker who espoused republican tenets argued that Charles I had a fair and legal trial, and that the regicides had suffered wrongfully. Their deaths, said William Sedgwick, "revived a zeal, confidence and boasting of their cause."[52]

Because it created a radical martyrology, executing some of the regicides was a grave political miscalculation. Even less justifiable was the pointless exhumation and hanging of the corpses of Cromwell, Ireton, and Bradshaw in January 1661. The wiser course was the treatment accorded to John Lambert, who spent the rest of his days in captivity as a fading radical hero, or John Milton, no regicide but a prominent polemicist for the republic. If it is an overstatement to say with J. R. Jones that "the accelerated decline and early disappearance of the defeated republican and Cromwellian parties were ensured by . . . [the] avoidance of a harsh and general proscription," it is nevertheless true that a more general revenge by the royalists would have made the divisions in the country even worse. Charles and Clarendon recognized this. When efforts were made in June 1661 to bring the nineteen regicides who had surrendered to trial, the king informed Clarendon that "I am weary of hanging except on new offences; let it sleep. You know that I cannot pardon them."[53]

The threat of execution or substantial imprisonment as well as the search for a new base of operations led some of the radicals into exile, a move reminiscent in some respects of the Marian exile more than a century earlier. Ludlow used the fate of Carew and Scrope as the rationale for his flight to the continent, though in fact he left in August, well before the trials and executions. "The fickelness, instabillity and injustice of those in the House of Comons, in having so unworthily sacrificed Mr. Carew and Colonell Scroope to the lust of Nero" by excluding them from the indemnity "made me unwilling to put my life upon a moote point before such partiall persons." A proclamation for his apprehension was issued with the promise of a £300 reward, but the underground spirited him away. In exile he attained even greater stature than Lambert and was commonly regarded as the titular leader of the underground. Proclamations were also issued for the capture of Edward Whalley and William Goffe, who had already reached Boston, Massachusetts, on 27 July.[54]

Other prominent radicals were scattering as well, both to save their lives and to keep the movement alive. General Thomas Kelsey and the regicides William Cawley and Thomas Scott escaped to the Netherlands, but the latter was recognized in Brussels, surrendered to the king's resident, and was returned to England for trial and execution. Cornelius Holland and the regicide Colonels John Hewson and Valentine Walton, after narrowly eluding their pursuers, made their way to the continent, but Sir Henry Mildmay, who also sat on the regicide court, was captured and died a prisoner.[55] Captain Philip Thorp, whose arrest shortly followed Lambert's, fled to Holland when he was released on bail, but voluntarily returned in order to benefit from the indemnity. In contrast, Richard Rogers allegedly recruited men to go to Flanders from England to prepare to topple the monarchy. Understandably, Charles wanted the regicides in the Netherlands apprehended and returned to England, not least for reasons of safety. Sir William Davison and others sought to accomplish this, but were hindered by their need for the States' approval and the well-armed condition of their quarry.[56]

The search for leading radicals was accompanied by measures to secure the realm. As early as June 1660 Sir Richard Browne was commissioned to serve as commander-in-chief of the forces in London, with instructions to apprehend rebels and utilize martial law to repress insurrections or illegal assemblies. In September the king directed Sir Horatio Townshend to assume control of the government of King's Lynn, using sufficient horse and foot to secure the town, for "in this conjuncture ill affected Persons may endeavour to possesse themselves of such Places of Strength as may be most Lyable to a surprize."[57] The chancellor of the duchy of Lancaster was asked to remove six justices from the commission of the peace because of doubtful loyalty. On the eve of the first regicide executions, the earl of Northampton provided detailed instructions to Sir Richard Temple and Sir Henry Puckering to "have an eye on all disaffected meetings and prevent getting of armes into their [rebel] handes, and if necessitie require to use the power in our handes to prevent all ill designes." Arms and ammunition were to be taken from the malcontents and given to the trained bands. Upon sufficient cause, they were to secure the dissidents as well as all strongholds in times of imminent danger. The earl especially urged his deputy lieutenants and justices of the peace to "bee carefull to prevent all endeavours of any disaffected persons to seduce his Majesties Liege people."[58]

As in the 1650s, a special eye was kept on Baptists and Quakers as potential threats to the peace. In Sussex, Sir Humphrey Bennet, who complained that they were "in every corner" of the county, secured their leaders. Throughout the 1660s the number and activities of sectaries in Bristol caused concern, though a report in November that they were holding meetings of a thousand or two thousand was an exaggeration. Sixty-five Quakers were arrested at the home of Dennis Hollister, who had sat in the Barebones Parliament, and that number quickly grew to 190 as more detentions followed throughout the city.[59]

Nothing was more basic to control of the radicals than settling the military. A Bristol merchant warned Monck in the summer that he had knowledge of a plot by officers and soldiers in the London area to "hinder the sittings of this Parliament & settlinge the Militia." Rumors of such plots, as Lois Schwoerer noted, facilitated passage of the Disbanding Act on 13 September. Under its terms the king could raise as many troops as he required if he paid them. On the whole, the disbanding went very well, in part because the militia served as a deterrent to disruptive acts.[60] Secretary Nicholas was pleased that the army and navy "cry up and pray for the King, thus frustrating the last hopes of some old traitors." However, there were problems in early October with some of the regiments stationed in the more remote counties. Disenchantment among the disbanded increased by year's end, probably due to economic dislocation and the drift of the government's religious policy. A worried Lord Langdale told Nicholas in early January that "the multitude of Casheired officers & souldiers that are all over the Countrey [are] well provided with Horse & armes & long . . . to fall to there ould trades."[61] His concern reflected the government's discovery the previous month of a plot involving former military personnel.

## The White Plot

At the heart of the alleged new design was Major Thomas White, who had served in the army since 1648. A member of the West Indies expedition, he was wounded in Jamaica and had to return to England. At the Restoration he fled to Flanders, where he associated with the regicide Thomas Scott, but by early December he was back in London, hoping to restore his sagging fortunes. The government was first tipped off to his plans by Richard Warren, a veteran of Colonel Edward Rossiter's regiment.[62] White was imprisoned in the Gatehouse at Westminster no later than 12 December, and warrants followed for the arrest of suspected accomplices. His mistake, according to two independent accounts of the plot, had been an attempt to bribe a porter at the gate to Whitehall. Although the porter had served with White under Fairfax, he reported the bribe to Monck, and White went to prison.[63]

In the ensuing investigation the government focused on a meeting in early December at the Rose tavern in Tower Street. According to the testimony of John Hall of St. Giles', Cripplegate, White boasted that he would "pull the king from his throne" by St. Bartholomew's day and assassinate Monck before Christmas. Had his colonel permitted, he allegedly told Hall, he would have killed Monck and burned the capital when the general arrived in London. The City, he believed, would be the second Jerusalem. The crucial part of Hall's testimony concerned a piece of parchment White had showed to him containing the names of men involved in the plot. Hall was offered a commission.[64] When White was arrested, several "confus'd" lists were found in his chamber, though their meaning was unclear to authorities. Hall recalled that the scheme involved John Barkstead's lieutenant-colonel, John Miller. The examination of White confirmed his hatred of Monck, whose white star he threatened to pull from the general's cloak.[65]

The others who had been at the Rose tavern refused to corroborate Hall's story. Captain James Greenaway, who had served with White in Ireland, insisted that he had invited White to the tavern to mediate a monetary dispute between himself and Robert Rose, pursar of the frigate *Foresight*. Rose also claimed he heard nothing of a plot. A fourth witness, Robert Hull of Stepney, testified that White indicated he was pleased that he had received his arrears, which enabled him to "lye still all the Winter" and seek employment in the spring.[66]

On Saturday evening, 15 December, Sir Gilbert Gerard (or Gerrard), a Middlesex justice of the peace, ordered a series of arrests. The *Parliamentary Intelligencer* for 10–17 December listed forty names, adding that "many" others were also jailed. Of the forty, twenty-four were discharged almost immediately, having transgressed only by the accidental timing of their recent arrival in London. Among the sixteen people detained, the only person of prominence was Major-General Robert Overton, the former commander in Scotland, who was sent to the Tower. Accused of smuggling weapons into the capital, he claimed he had intended only to sell them.[67] As the arrests continued, the number of prominent names grew, among them Major-General John Desborough, Colonels George Payne, (William?) Walker, Jerome Sankey, William Rainsborough, and Unton Croke, and two men previously arrested in April, Lieutenant-Colonel William Allen and the Fifth Monarchist Hugh Courtney. A number of lesser officers were detained as well.[68]

The dragnet uncovered two caches of arms, which lent some credibility to the allegations. On examination, Colonel Rainsborough claimed that he had purchased forty cases of pistols for the militia, thirty-one of which were sent on the 15th to William Walgrave of Cripplegate to sell, the remainder being dispersed in the country. Blunderbusses, powder, balls, and "many Ensigns staves new shod" were found in Captain Blackwell's house. No less damaging was the discovery of a declaration against monarchical government in Captain Thomas Middleton's pocket. Although many private homes were searched, apparently nothing else of consequence surfaced.[69]

There is scattered evidence of associated radical activity far beyond the bounds of London. Lieutenant Thomas Gray, who once served with Monck in Scotland, was incarcerated at Derby on charges that he offered a horse, arms, and 20s. to a Kings Newton man if he would join the rebels. Gray confessed only to loaning him two or three guns.[70] Several persons in Lincoln were interrogated about the plot, though only (Christopher?) Marshall was formally accused. Observers noted the suspicious movements of Colonel Edward Salmon, a republican supporter of Lambert and Fleetwood the previous year, who arrived in Lincoln one December evening at 8 P.M. and left at 2 A.M. The activities of Colonel Matthew Alured, who had risen with Lambert in April, were also noted.[71] There was a report of active plotting in York and of the journey of Ensign (Christopher?) Dawson, a former Agitator and member of Overton's regiment, from York to Hull. In Wiltshire the disaffected "talke high still & saye they shall have a turne before Chrismas day & hop[e] to see all Cavaliers beg thair bread, & thair pulpitt men preacheth as high." Wiltshire authorities confiscated a barrel of gunpowder delivered to Humphrey Ditton, a "Commonwealth" man, in Sarum. Edward Shelton of Brentwood, Essex, who as bailiff had refused to proclaim Charles king, had a dozen men in arms on the 16th and more ready to join them. In his judgment the restoration of episcopacy and the execution of the regicides "would suddenly Cause a new war." Although Scotland "proves honest above expectation," some were convinced that the design included rebels in Ireland.[72]

The movement of disbanded troops from Hereford to Wapping may also be linked to the White plot. According to Captain Henry Leicester, who was sent to Hereford to replace Captain Green at the Restoration, most of Colonel John Birch's men had gone to Wapping. Green himself was accused of distributing the garrison's weapons to republicans, most of whom were undoubtedly ex-soldiers, for Leicester complained that Colonel Pury, Colonel Robert Harlow, and other ex-officers in the area were angry when he halted the disbursement. These arms must have been carried to Wapping by the disbanded troopers. When Leicester received word that one of Lambert's agents had approached the soldiers, he offered to go to Wapping in disguise to ascertain their intentions. Sir Orlando Bridgeman, who was instrumental in the prosecution of the regicides, apparently thought that Birch's ex-soldiers were linked to White's plot. Former soldiers were also reported en route to London from Salisbury, where one Baxter, a former agent of Cornet Joyce, had been stirring them up. Baxter allegedly asserted that "now [that] the Army was disbanded, wee shall see good sport as ever was, swords drawne againe." Some of the ex-soldiers echoed Baxter's enthusiasm and were acquiring weapons.[73]

Inevitably, the names of Lambert and Ludlow were quickly linked to the scheme. There was a rumor that Lambert was attempting to escape from the Tower by offering bribes. An intensive search was made for Ludlow, primarily in London, though magistrates wanted to look for him as far afield as Wiltshire. His wife's clothes were plundered and the lodgings of his brother-in-law, Lieutenant-Colonel Nicholas Kempson, were ransacked. Authorities even imprisoned one of his former servants in the Gatehouse for ten weeks, but Ludlow was safely in exile.[74]

Evidence of the conspiracy was sufficient to prompt the government to issue a proclamation on 17 December ordering all cashiered officers and soldiers to remove themselves at least twenty miles from London and Westminster unless they were exempted by the Privy Council or the Committee to Disband the Army. Guards had already been posted at Whitehall and throughout the City. When news of the plot reached Edinburgh, residents were required to give the names of guests to the authorities each evening, daily and nightly watches were posted, and two companies were ordered to stand guard. On 2 January, an order of the king-in-council prohibited meetings of sectaries at unusual times or in large numbers, and forbade them to leave their parishes to attend religious gatherings, supposedly because they conspired against the government. Two days later a second order directed the lords lieutenant in England and Wales to disarm factious persons and administer the oaths of allegiance and supremacy to them.[75]

Was there, in the end, a real plot? Wilbur Cortez Abbot passed over these December events in silence, while Maurice Ashley, after a brief overview, opined that no such plot was "anywhere near realization."[76] Some contemporaries were of the same mind: a Mr. Edwards confessed on Christmas day 1660 that "divers . . . are in doubt; & whether there was any such Plott att all I cannott Learn." A Canterbury surgeon reportedly accused Monck of fomenting the plot in order to start another war, but the surgeon denied it. Giles Horsington of St. Margaret's, Westminster, who had served with the parliamentary forces in Ireland, testified that he had heard of no plotting among the disbanded soldiers. Another ex-soldier, the Londoner Robert Brown, was arrested as he dined at Major

Mountford's house with Captain Hannibal Vyvyan (formerly of
Colonel John Fagge's regiment), but professed to have no intelligence of a design apart from "the common voyce of the people."
Ludlow's denunciation of the plot as a continued sham was scath-
ing.[77]

If the design was largely contrived by the government, what was
the motive? Ashley suggests that it was an excuse to imprison
Cromwellian officers who might have become the nucleus of a real
plot in the future, and that it helped set the stage for the election of
royalists to the Cavalier Parliament.[78] But the bulk of the arrests were
made in London, which in fact did not return the kind of men the
government sought.[79] Moreover, if the intent was to imprison
dangerous officers, it is odd that the government began releasing
them in a matter of weeks. Unton Croke, Thomas Middleton,
Colonel William Sydenham, John Shovell, and Robert Shaw were
bonded on 29 December, William Rainsborough on 7 February.[80]

It is, however, indisputable that Clarendon embellished such
evidence as there was in order to discredit the Cromwellians,
republicans, and sectaries. In a speech to the Convention on 29
December, he blamed the plot on discontent arising from the
regicides' execution. His account of the conspiracy owed more to
rumor than substantiated testimony. Ludlow, he averred, was expected to lead the fanatics, who had planned to surprise the Tower
and Windsor Castle. Now that their design had been uncovered, they
would wait until the rest of the army had been disbanded before
undertaking a "considerable Rising" in the west, the north, and
London (where they supposedly had 2,500 men).[81] But Clarendon
had to admit that after hours of questioning the suspects, Charles
himself thought some of those imprisoned were innocent. Despite
the overkill in Clarendon's address, he put his finger on a practice
that characterized almost all the scheming in the 1660s: "It is a vulgar
and known Artifice, to corrupt inferior Persons, by persuading them
that better Men are engaged in the same Enterprize."[82]

What the authorities unearthed was no organized plot, no insurrection planned for a specific time with designated leaders, but a
growing number of disenchanted men who had begun to gather
weapons and explore possibilities for an uprising.[83] To say, however,
that Clarendon was guilty of fictional elaboration is not to assert that
the plot itself was fabricated. The disaffected men and their weapons
were real enough. Secretary Nicholas, who was privy to whatever
information the government gleaned, summed it up best in his
reference to "the restless malice of the plotting traitors, who designed

to embroil the kingdom in new troubles."[84] The very process of disbanding the troops without adequate measures to secure their civilian employment throughout England virtually ensured that substantial numbers would drift to London and become a festering sore of unrest. There was a report on 19 December, for example, that members of Colonel Morley's and Colonel Ingoldsby's regiments were drinking—and probably griping—together in the capital. One observer aptly commented the following day that people agreed "some mischief was intended by reason that the heads of the Phanaticks from all parts of England were flocked thither."[85] The stories about the conspiracy in the newspapers and Clarendon's embellishments can only have served to focus more attention on the possibility of an insurrection, and in this sense the government's efforts were counterproductive. Although the allegations helped to discredit the dissidents, there is no evidence that the government had such a purpose in mind prior to the arrests. On the contrary, the arrests and early releases suggest a government that was understandably jittery in its first months of power, and which therefore responded overzealously at news of the alleged conspiracy.

## The Welsh Radicals

In Wales, radical strength was pronounced, thanks especially to the work of the Commission for Propagating the Gospel. This was an area where the Particular Baptists had been noticeably successful. Efforts to quash opposition to the Restoration concentrated on the Fifth Monarchist Vavasor Powell, the most prominent of the Welsh radicals, and his sectarian allies. Well known for his 1654 petition, *A Word for God*, which condemned the Protectorate, he was arrested in April 1660, at which time the focus of his work was in Montgomeryshire. There is no evidence that he was engaged in seditious political activity, but his theocratically oriented preaching clearly troubled the authorities. For nine weeks he was held in the Shrewsbury jail.[86] Following his release, Powell defied the orders of Sir Matthew Price, high sheriff of Montgomeryshire, by resuming his preaching. Price had already complained to Secretary Nicholas that Richard Price of Aberbechan "did countenance & incourage unlawfull & riotous Assemblyes, & was a great favourer of factious & seditious persons." The sheriff regarded Powell, "a most dangerous & factious Minister," and the knight Richard Saltonstall as his principal acomplices. On 18 July the Council ordered the arrest of all three.[87]

In the meantime, the commander of the militia in Breck-
nockshire, Colonel Henry Williams, received intelligence of a meeting at Llanthetty of seditious persons who came from the counties of
Monmouth, Glamorgan, Radnor, and Brecknock, ostensibly to hear
Jenkin Jones, an open-communion Baptist. Jones had served as a
captain under Major-General Harrison. Convinced that these men
had a "designe against the person of your sacred Majestie," and that
they opposed both the Restoration church and state, Williams
ordered two officers and twelve soldiers to disperse them. Em-
boldened by an audience of more than 500 persons, Jones defied the
soldiers, crying, "Fall on, & you that are strangers shift for your
selves." In the melée that ensued, some of the soldiers were wounded,
but the sectarian leaders fled to Jones' house where they eventually
surrendered. Among those captured were four of Jones' assistants.[88]

Jones had espoused the use of armed force in the Gospel's cause.
The saints, he told his followers, would rise before Michaelmas and
"have another turne." If the king "would not mind things hee should
not long Continue." Jones' people believed that the government
would be altered within the coming week, "and that they should bee
as highe as once they were before this government, by that time."
Jones was detained for a month in Carmarthen prison.[89]

To the north, in Montgomeryshire, Sir Matthew Price complained
that the sectaries were disregarding his warnings by holding meetings in late July. At Aberbechan they bragged that "they did nott care
who did forbid it; they would continue their meetinges as longe as
they lived." These were militant people, Price insisted, who gave each
other bread on the point of a rapier. Now they demanded the return
of the arms that had been taken from them, threatening to use force
to retrieve them. According to Price they already possessed numerous concealed weapons, including long knives, which had been
acquired for Lambert's insurrection and would be used if Argyll rose.
The sectaries were so numerous that the justices of the peace were
afraid to interfere with them. Powell, for instance, reportedly attracted 400 to his meetings in Radnorshire.[90]

Price ordered the arrest of Powell and Captain Lewis Price,
formerly a Commissioner for the Propagation of the Gospel, between 24 and 30 July. Other Powell allies were jailed too, with
Thomas Tudge and Henry Williams, Powell's protégé and successor
at the Newtown church, joining Lewis Price in the Welshpool jail.
Thomas Gwyn, a Brecknock gentleman, was imprisoned at Carmarthen with Jenkin Jones, and other Powell supporters were incarcerated at Bala.[91]

Sir Matthew Price thought he found further corroboration of Powell's seditious intent in an intercepted letter from Powell to Henry Williams, Lewis Price, and Tudge. Powell instructed them to "expect more sufferings or strange deliverance shortly." Their release, he said, was imminent, and he hoped they would leave quickly, "least the great stirs now in London may by the next post obstruct" their freedom. Powell himself had not yet been arrested when he wrote this letter, but Sir Matthew used it as evidence that he was planning an insurrection.[92]

On 29 August the Privy Council studied a petition from the high sheriff and justices of the peace of Merionethshire charging that Powell was a seditious sectary with a large, rebellious following in northern Wales. According to the petition, only those who swore against magistracy and ministry could be admitted to his congregation. The Council ordered the justices to investigate.[93] The complaint underscores Powell's leadership throughout the Welsh sectarian community and the concern he provoked among royalists.

By January 1661 Powell had been transferred from the jail at Welshpool to Shrewsbury, where Lord Herbert closely monitored his activities. On 24 January Herbert informed the earl of Carberry that he had intercepted a copy of Powell's tract, *Common-Prayer-Book No Divine Service*, along with similar pamphlets and letters under assumed names. Powell, he surmised, had been rightly imprisoned because "he cannot forbeare his endeavours to sowe division in the Church." The authorities also learned that Powell had the backing of the attorney Richard Edwards, a former Caernarvonshire justice of the peace, and that he continued to support imprisoned sectaries in Wales.[94]

Finally released in November 1667, Powell was only at liberty until about September 1668, when he was arrested a final time. He died at the Fleet prison in London.[95]

The fact that the radical movement in Wales was consistently less troublesome than its counterparts in England, Scotland, and Ireland was undoubtedly due in large measure to the fact that Powell had eschewed physical violence in the 1660s in preference for a fundamentally spiritual opposition. How much this was the result of his lengthy incarceration is difficult to ascertain, but it is worth noting that in both Wales and Bedfordshire, which also remained quiet, the leading Nonconformists spent long years in prison.

## Dissidents in Ireland

The unrest and plotting that characterized the Restoration in England were mirrored, though to a lesser degree, in Ireland. There the Protestant community was a reflection on a smaller scale of its English counterpart. Because the Presbyterians in Ulster and Scotland enjoyed particularly close ties, discontent in one realm typically infected the other. In mid-May 1660 a purported design was uncovered, but those involved were quickly dispersed and its leader, Colonel (William?) Eyres, was secured by Sir Theophilus Jones. There were rumors of further plotting in June, but again the authorities were on top of the situation and nothing materialized.[96]

During the summer attention shifted to the problem of ecclesiastical uniformity. The newly appointed lieutenant general, John Lord Robartes, was ordered to do everything possible to make the dissenting groups conform, short of endangering the peace. Although Bishop Kennet reported that the Ulster Presbyterians were preaching against the king, in general they remained loyal to Charles even as they defied his authority in religious matters at the local level.[97] In late August a bishop-elect observed, probably with exaggeration, that the Ulster Presbyterians "talke of resisting unto bloud, & stirre up the people to sedition."[98] Like the Remonstrants in Scotland, their devotion to the Covenant made them increasingly hostile to a regime uncommitted to its support, but in the beginning they were willing to confine their disobedience to religious matters. Once again, a tolerant ecclesiastical policy would have been an inducement to a more positive attitude toward the government.

By the autumn the sectaries and ex-Cromwellians were increasingly restless. In Dublin the Congregationalist Samuel Mather, minister of St. Nicholas' church, similarly indicated a willingness to accept the new government, though he preached two sermons critical of the Book of Common Prayer and episcopal polity. To the earl of Mountrath, who failed to distinguish between political and spiritual loyalties, Mather's remarks were conducive to sedition and tumult. Mather, however, insisted that it was his "judgment to render obedience to any Civil Government which God in his providence places over him." With his ministerial associates, he protested against William Bulkeley, archdeacon of Dublin, who was reasserting traditional authority through the archdiaconal visitations. Bulkeley accused Mather and his friends, who refused to cease preaching, of "tumultuary carriage." One of the most troublesome was Robert

Chambers, author of an allegedly treasonable book which was burned by the common hangman. Apparently no copies have survived. Although barred from the pulpit unless he recanted his work, Chambers refused to remain silent. When Mather too was suspended, he returned to England and settled at Burtonwood, Lancashire, as curate.[99]

Seditious activity was reportedly underway in Clonmel and other places in Munster by early October. Those involved—Colonel (Peter?) Stanley, Colonel Thomas Sadler, and others—were purportedly enlisting men in a conspiracy against the government. Mountrath launched an investigation that led to the arrest of Stanley and Sadler as well as Colonel Edward Warren and his brother, Major Abel Warren, and others. Disgruntled persons were also distributing books critical of Charles for not honoring his oath to the Solemn League and Covenant. Lieutenant-Colonel Finch, a royalist, sarcastically observed that those who disseminated such books were not doing it "out of any good will to his maiestie." Orders were given to secure those responsible.[100] Mountrath judged that such discontent would abate when the government was settled and the soldiers' arrears had been paid, but he underestimated the depth of both republican hostility and the religious convictions of the Presbyterians and sectaries. The Presbyterians made their demands known in "The Heads of the Intended Declaration," which linked the demand for payment of arrears to the establishment of a "pure" state church in keeping with the Solemn League and Covenant. They also demanded reaffirmation and restoration of the traditional liberties of the corporations in the three kingdoms and the return to each person of lands held in 1659.[101]

In county Down the Presbyterians were in an agitated state at year's end, partly because of their opposition to Dr. Jeremy Taylor, the bishop-elect, whom they deplored as a Socinian and an Arminian. After a committee was organized to prepare charges against him, four representatives were delegated to take the accusations to Dublin and then to London if necessary. The committee also urged Presbyterian clergy to preach vigorously against bishops and the Book of Common Prayer. One of them, Mr. Richardson (or Richeson), acquiesced with alacrity, even to the point of warning his congregation that the forthcoming persecution would be more dreadful than the Marian fires at Smithfield. Although Richardson exhorted his people to do nothing more drastic than acquire a Bible for each household, Mountrath was perceptive enough to recognize that the tone of the sermon inculcated hostility toward royal and episcopal government in the people. Convinced that the outcome could only be the exciting of factions and seditious behavior, he launched an investigation. Other ministers urged their followers to draw the sword rather than take the prescribed oaths of supremacy and allegiance, and warned that the bishops, with a service book "hatched" in hell, intended to impose popery.[102]

Mountrath was also concerned about the growing hostility of the Catholics, including increased activity by the priests. Orders were given to secure them, and those who persisted in preaching were jailed. Quantities of gunpowder were arriving from Scotland, prompting fears that the intended recipients might be Catholic. Although a report from Dublin in late October indicated that there was no longer "any noise of discontent," by mid-December a siege mentality was clearly developing. Against a background of Presbyterian unrest, particularly in county Down, and increasing Catholic activity, Mountrath and William Bury complained to Secretary Nicholas that they were "beset on all sides by parties" intent on disturbing his majesty's government.[103] The discontent continued to spread until it erupted in the Dublin plot in 1663.

## Scotland at the Restoration

Until August 1660, the government of Scotland was in the hands of four commissioners appointed by the republican government in London. Major-General Thomas Morgan, Colonel William Daniel, Colonel Philip Twistleton, and Molyneux Disney directed affairs from the time of their arrival in the second week of May until the Committee of Estates assumed power on 23 August. It was an unsettled summer. The Scots were sending copies of Charles' 1650–51 declarations to their colleagues in Ulster.[104] More alarmingly, the Venetian resident reported in July that Cardinal Mazarin had provided the Presbyterian clergy in Scotland with substantial funds to fan the flames of rebellion. "The idea is to kindle a fresh fire in these kingdoms, to which France will contribute all she can to divert the storms that menace her." Even before Lauderdale, Middleton, and their colleagues took control, dissidents were being arrested. Among them were Sir James Stewart, provost of Edinburgh, and Sir John Chiesley, both of whom were Protesters, as well as John Swinton, laird of Swinton, who had served Cromwell as a judge and counsellor and was now a Quaker.[105]

The task of those who assumed power in Scotland on behalf of Charles was rendered easier by the bitter division in the Presbyterian camp between Protesters and Resolutioners. Insistent that the Covenants were perpetually binding on the people, the Protesters were intolerant of any hint of compromise or of the exercise of power in the church by any but the godly. For their part, the Resolutioners, who formed the larger group, were hoping in 1660 to oust the Protesters from their parishes. From the king's standpoint, the more serious enemy was the Protesters, who demanded nothing short of Presbyterianism throughout Britain. The men who governed Scotland for Charles, however, were determined that no clerical authority, whether presbyterian or episcopalian, would establish primacy over lay authority.

When the new government took over in August, its first act was to strike at a group of Protesters who had come to Edinburgh to complain about the use of the Book of Common Prayer in the royal household and to petition the king to adhere to his Covenant obligations. Eleven men were arrested at the home of the collector Robert Symson as they were "subscribing a Paper tending to the disturbance of this Kingdom." Among them were James Guthry, minister of Stirling, and the Edinburgh pastors Robert Trail and John Strivling.[106] All but one were incarcerated in Edinburgh Castle. The Committee of Estates followed this up on 24 August with a proclamation banning unlawful meetings and seditious petitions and remonstrances.[107]

The crackdown on dissident ministers and their supporters continued throughout the autumn. In mid-September Patrick Gillespie, one of the leading Protesters, was interned in Stirling Castle, while Robert Row, minister at Abircorne, and William Wishart, pastor of Kinnell, were confined to their chambers in Edinburgh. On the 22nd the government issued a proclamation against all seditious railers, whether civil or ecclesiastical, in the hope of calming the troubled waters. They soon followed this with the arrest of Sir Andrew Kerr of Greenhead and Walter Pringill of Greenknow, who were imprisoned in Edinburgh Castle for aiding the Protesters and other seditious persons. Still, the Protesters refused to remain silent. When the minister of Rutherglen, John Dickson, used his pulpit to attack the Committee, he was committed to the Edinburgh Tolbooth in October. The same fate awaited Colonel William Osburne, a Quaker, the next month. One of the first Quaker missionaries north of the Tweed, Osburne had guided a party that included George Fox on a Scottish tour in 1657.[108]

The Committee of Estates, which sat when the Scottish Parliament was not in session, was particularly interested in examining prominent ex-Cromwellians. When six of them did not appear after being cited, they were declared fugitives on 10 October. Chief among them was Sir Archibald Johnston of Wariston, a prominent Protester who escaped to the continent. Colonel Gilby (Gibb) Carr, an "old kirk man," also fled, but had a long career of plotting and insurrection ahead of him. The others were Colonel David Barclay, John Hume of Kello, Robert Andrew of Little Tarbet, and William Dundas, a Cromwellian trustee. Carr and Barclay were reportedly in London associating with Robert Hodge and William Purves, "also deip complyeris with that traitour" Cromwell.[109]

Of the three kingdoms, Scotland had the best potential for a secure and peaceful future. The key was an ecclesiastical settlement that was comprehensive enough to embrace a substantial number of moderate Presbyterians. Although the nobility had once played a prominent role in replacing episcopalian with presbyterian polity, in 1660 they cooperated in the restoration of episcopacy when they realized that even the more moderate Resolutioners had every intention of continuing their attempt to dominate the nobility.[110] The major political leaders who might have rallied the disaffected, the marquis of Argyll and Johnston of Wariston, were powerless, Argyll in prison and Wariston in exile. Both would soon be executed, Argyll in May 1661 and Wariston in July 1663. With the single exception of James Guthry, the Protesters who had gathered at Edinburgh in August were eventually freed. Guthry was tried before Parliament and executed on 1 June 1661. Of the sectaries, only the Quakers had a meaningful following in Restoration Scotland, but they shunned radical political activity. After the withdrawal of the English army, Scotland was also left without a core of republican leaders. On 8 October a jubilant Secretary Nicholas informed Sir Henry Bennet that "happy order is taken to restrain the seditious turbulent Scotch ministry."[111] The optimism proved to be unfounded. The Restoration settlement in Scotland was too narrow, the convictions of militant Presbyterians too ingrained for lasting peace to be established. Charles' government was fortunate indeed that the leaders of the radical underground never successfully tapped the reservoir of discontent that extended throughout southwestern Scotland.

Thus although 1660 brought the re-establishment of monarchy and set the stage for the recovery of prelatical authority in the state church, the revolutionary tradition of the 1640s and 1650s, with all its rich diversity and self-contradictions, was far from dead. It was less a principled love of monarchy than a desire to preserve property and social order that made the Restoration so smooth. Moreover the hope of liberty for tender consciences that Charles so shrewdly—and probably sincerely—promised at Breda offered timely hope to those whose principal concerns included religion. The "saints" had bungled the task of ruling, if for no other reason than the fact that the images of the godly state were so heterogeneous as to doom any single form to failure. Some of the religious radicals themselves were prepared to accept the return of monarchical rule, assured in their faith that divine providence worked in mysterious ways. Others remained adamantly hostile to anything kingly, and it was a small group of these people who took up arms against the Stuart regime in January 1661.

# 2

# "A Door of Hope"

## FROM VENNER'S RISING TO
## NONSUCH HOUSE

Charles II had been on his throne less than a year, the coronation
ceremony still in the future, when the kingdom was rocked by a
violent insurrection. The number of rebels proved to be small, but
the rising confirmed the suspicions of conservatives who viewed
sectarian congregations as nurseries of sedition. Those who took to
the streets of the capital on a cold January evening were adherents of
the most violent of the sectarian groups, the Fifth Monarchists,
whose eschatological doctrine taught that Christ would return only
after the saints had seized civil and military power. "There is," said a
Fifth Monarchy tract, "a Kingdom and Dominion of the Church, or
of Christ and the Saints, to be expected upon Earth," and that
kingdom would be external and visible.[1]

This was an extreme manifestation of the millenarianism that had
been spreading in English Protestant circles for more than a century,
but which was not confined to those of radical persuasions. Like
other European millenarian groups, the Fifth Monarchists rejected
the present, evil world, longing instead for the one envisioned in
their chiliastic ideology. "How unbeseeming it were for the followers
of the Lamb, to comply in the least with the powers of the world, in
setting up their worldly kingdoms." In contrast to most millenarian
groups, some Fifth Monarchists were increasingly confident about
the means through which the new society would be established. The
wine-cooper Thomas Venner and his followers were on the thresh-
old of developing what Eric Hobsbawm has called "a doctrine

49

concerning the transfer of power," though unlike modern revolutionary movements they did not replace their chiliastic ideology with secular theory.[2] The extremity of their religious convictions was repugnant to many sectaries, whose attitude to the government was fundamentally submissive, even to the point of quietly suffering for their principles. Venner's rebellion was but one example of the extent to which the radical underground was riven by conflicting ideological principles, ranging from secular republicanism to militant chiliasm.

## The Vennerite Insurrection

Sunday, 6 January, was Epiphany. Charles had escorted Henrietta Maria to Portsmouth on the first leg of her journey to France, and most people prepared for a day of traditional celebration, replete with merriment and ale. Venner's plebian congregation gathered at their meeting house in Swan Alley, Coleman Street, where Venner, John Tufney, and Thomas Cragg preached. From the pulpit Venner thundered that it was time to fight for King Jesus. Although their numbers were small, the outcome would be sure, for "one should chase Ten, and Ten should chase a Thousand."[3] Swords, he cried, must not be sheathed until the monarchy—Babylon—had become "a Hissing and a Curse," with nothing left, "neither Remnant, Son, nor Nephew." Ensigns emblazoned "the Lord God and Gideon" had been readied along with a manifesto, *A Door of Hope: or, a Call and Declaration for the Gathering Together of the First Ripe Fruits unto the Standard of Our Lord, King Jesus.* Their plan was simple: England must be conquered first, and then the campaign would spread from France and Spain to the German states and beyond. Kings would be bound in chains, nobles in fetters of iron. There could never be a league with monarchists. The *Door of Hope* also called for reform of debt law, the abolition of primogeniture and capital punishment for theft, and the introduction of democratic government in guilds and towns.[4]

After nightfall Venner's landlord peered into the meeting room and observed the congregation wearing buffcoats and arming themselves with blunderbusses. With Venner, Giles Pritchard the cowkeeper, and Roger Hodgkin the button-seller in the lead, the rebels, numbering perhaps fifty, marched to the house of the bookseller Thomas Johnson near St. Paul's and there demanded the keys to the church. When he refused, they broke open a door, posted sentries, and then—after killing a man who declared his support for Charles

II—vacated the church because it was insecure. Pressing on, their battle cry was "King Jesus, and the heads upon the gates." Not only did they seek the regicides' heads, which were affixed to Westminster Hall and London Bridge, but they also hoped to retrieve their quarters from the London gates.[5] At St. Thomas Apostle's the "saints" confronted Lieutenant-Colonels Cox and Shepheard, who alerted the lord mayor, Sir Richard Browne. When the latter gave the alarm, some of the Fifth Monarchists scattered, chased by Browne, four halberdiers, and six swordsmen. The Vennerites fled via St. John's Wood to Kenwood, between Highgate and Hampstead. Around midnight two files of the trained bands tracked down thirty or forty of the rebels. When Venner's men asked whom the trained bands were for, they responded, "For God and King Charles," but the Vennerites retorted that they were "for King Jesus." After an exchange of shots that left two dead, the rebels retreated to Aldersgate, where they forced the watch. In White Cross Street they killed the constable and wounded others. Another group of rebels exchanged fire with two files of guards near Bishopsgate, forced them back, and then melted away.[6]

On Monday Albemarle dispatched Sir Thomas Sandys with a troop of horse and 200 of the duke of York's regiment of foot to search Kenwood. Night had fallen before the rebels were discovered near a gravel pit. Venner's men fired on the soldiers, but from too great a distance to be effective, and then escaped into the woods. Few prisoners were taken. On Tuesday Pepys heard rumors of "a head of Fanatiques that doth appear about Barnett," but discounted them. In the meantime Sir Richard Browne had had one of the meeting houses of the rebels pulled down.[7]

Early Wednesday morning the Vennerites were spotted in a lane near Leadenhall, where they made a stand between 5 and 6 A.M. After shots were exchanged, the rebels retreated, first to Little Eastcheap, and then after another stand to London Stone, where they dispersed. A second group of Fifth Monarchists, led by Venner himself, had gone to Maiden Lane where they hoped to kidnap the lord mayor, chanting "Now for Browne, Now for Browne." The mayor, however, was with the trained bands pursuing the first rebel party. Venner's group went next to the Counter gate to demand the release of prisoners. A group of trained bands and Life Guards caught up with Venner's gang in Wood Street, but the Fifth Monarchists "disputed as if they had a greater number and a better cause." Wielding a halberd, Venner personally killed three soldiers. Browne's men were reinforced by a party of twenty horse dispatched by Albemarle under the command of Colonel John Corbet. With nine of his horse, Corbet charged down Wood Street, breaking Venner's line of blunderbusses and clearing the way for the trained bands to attack. Venner was wounded, and four or five of his men went down with him. The rest were chased down Moor Lane to the London wall, where seven barricaded themselves in a house. Forcing their way in, the trained bands shot it out with the Vennerites, killing seven. The rebels, as Sir Richard Baker observed, had been "insensated to that heighth of Enthusiastick Valour."[8]

The fighting was over when the dukes of York and Albemarle, the earls of Oxford and Northampton, and Lord Fairfax rode into the City with 700 horse of the Life Guard. Londoners were in near panic, convinced that the rebels numbered at least 500, ten times their actual size. As Pepys moved through the streets he found the shops closed and people standing in their doorways bearing arms. The following day, at the urging of Gilbert Sheldon, bishop of London, the government issued a proclamation prohibiting all unlawful meetings and conventicles.[9] Worship services were banned unless they were held in parochial churches and chapels, or in private homes for residents only. The target was the sectarian community of Fifth Monarchists, Baptists, and Quakers. Magistrates were directed to search for conventicles and apprehend those in attendance. The proclamation reinforced a similar ban that had been made on 2 January in the context of the White plot.[10]

In the wake of the Fifth Monarchist insurrection, some forty persons were dead, about half of them rebels. Twenty-five more were apprehended in the fighting, and four others were known to have escaped, including the joiner Thomas Gibbs. The three leaders—Venner, Pritchard, and Hodgkin—were arraigned on the 17th, along with the shoemaker Robert Hopkins (a future Seventh-Day Baptist), the silk-weaver William Ashton, the brewer's clerk John Patshall (later involved in the 1663 plotting), and fourteen of their compatriots.[11] The two men who had preached with Venner on the 6th—Tufney and Cragg—were among the dead. The investigation was hampered by the obduracy of the prisoners. Not one, remarked Sir John Finch, would confess anything about his accomplices, "crying that they will not betray the Servants of the Lord Jesus to the Kings of the Earth."[12] Nevertheless there was sufficient evidence to convict all but four of the accused of murder and treason. Only Patshall, a career rebel, Hopkins, Richard Marten, and John Wells were acquitted. The others were sentenced to be hanged, drawn, and quartered. On the 19th Venner and Hodgkin were accordingly punished in Coleman Street, the latter calling for divine vengeance on the king, the judges, and the city of London. Venner too was unrepentant. By virtue of a modest royal clemency the others were hanged and beheaded, Pritchard and William Oxman (alias Orsingham) in Wood Street the same day. Nine more followed on the 21st. "They dyed resolutely," Sir John Reresby observed, "and unrepenting of their crime." Three rebels received reprieves.[13]

A nervous government filled the Gatehouse, Newgate, and the Counters with a host of additional suspects, including the Quaker William Devenham. Richard Culmer, "the fierie Demolisher of Churches and Chapels" who had wreaked such destruction at Canterbury, was arrested while he was riding on Chatham Hill en route to Coleman Street.[14] The Fifth Monarchist preacher Robert Malban, the astrologer William Lilly, the former agitator John Gladman, and Thomas Fitch, an M.P. in Richard Cromwell's Parliament and erstwhile governor of the Tower, were among the apprehended. So too were Colonels Matthew Alured, Nathaniel Rich, and William Packer, in whose regiment Gladman had once served. Colonel Francis Buffett was suspected of complicity but could not be found. By the 18th, some of those who had been jailed were released after pledging not to engage in any activity against the government.[15] Still the magistrates could not rest, for on the 19th they learned that dissidents were meeting daily at the Southwark home of George Tutchins. Having failed in Venner's attempt, he allegedly said, they would rise again on the next moonlit night, and this time would have the use of fifty-five barrels of powder stored at Deptford.[16]

There is evidence that some preparations had been made for the Fifth Monarchists to rise in other areas of the kingdom. Venner himself had been in Devon sometime between mid-December and the beginning of the insurrection. Seditious books were being shipped out of London, though the magistrates were seizing them from the carriers. The authorities arrested one man carrying two hundred letters from Fifth Monarchists to their brethren in London, promising to be zealous in the cause. They also found hundreds of arms in the possession of a Mr. Pierson, "that second *Hugh Peters*." Altogether, more than a hundred persons were arrested, including two "furious" ministers, the Fifth Monarchist Nathaniel Byfield and the Congregationalist Thomas Mall. Also jailed were Captain Henry Hatsell, the former admiralty commissioner for Plymouth, and John Searle, a Congregationalist ejected from the living at Rattery, Devon.[17]

At the opposite end of the country a party of 150 horse attempted to surprise Newcastle on the night of 9 January. According to one observer, most of those in the town who opposed the Stuart monarchy were merchants engaged in shipping "infinite quantityes" of powder and shot throughout the northern counties and into Scotland. There was fear that the disbanded soldiers were ready to join with the "phanaticks to raise a new war," and widespread belief that the present government could not last a year. In Lincolnshire there were reports of stirrings by the Baptists on the night of 6 January, when Venner rose. About the same time dissidents in Cheshire and Flintshire began to "troop together," some well equipped with arms and good horses. The Vennerites were known to be in correspondence with persons in Chester. To preserve order in this region the earl of Derby was dispatched to Chester to secure suspects, ban illegal assemblies, and seize seditious material that was being prepared for the press in London.[18]

When word of Venner's rising reached Oxfordshire, Viscount Falkland, the lord lieutenant, took command of a company of 250 volunteers. In the course of securing suspicious persons and searching their houses, Fifth Monarchist declarations were found. Falkland also arrested a number of Quakers, including Thomas Ellwood and Thomas Loe. Six or seven cases of pistols were found in the house of the Congregationalist, Dr. John Owen, at Stadhampton. In Warwick, authorities made a series of arrests between the 9th and 26th of January, concentrating on sectarian ministers and ex-officers, some of whom had served with Major Richard Creed, still in prison for his part in Lambert's rising. With them were imprisoned the Congregationalist pastor Thomas Worden and the Baptist ministers Thomas Gibbons, Richard Perkins, and Elias Clarke, in whose house weapons were found despite his denials. There is, however, no evidence to link these men to Venner's people.[19]

Throughout England, news of Venner's rising prompted increased surveillance. At Leicester the county gentry gathered to plan security measures. On the 14th they learned that many Baptists, some of whom had been officers under Lambert, were flocking to Earl Shilton. A party of horse was dispatched to arrest them and seize their weapons. Other dissidents were rounded up and their arms taken, but the mayor and aldermen of Leicester regarded them as lowly people. This was also the opinion of the earl of Denbigh with respect to those responsible for the "clouds of discontent" that appeared at Newnham in Gloucestershire. On the 19th "sectaryes of the forrest side" were reportedly flocking into Gloucester so fast that the townsfolk shut the gates, fearing that the town would be taken by surprise.[20] Authorities in Essex examined several suspects, but found only two worth detaining. One of them was Captain Laurence Moyer of Low Leighton, who allegedly deprecated the king as "that boy," and in whose house pistols, two barrels of powder, and a small cannon (or drake) mounted on a carriage were found. Officials also interrogated a Mr. Salmon concerning suspicious trips into Lincolnshire, which he denied. At Coventry the alarm was sounded on the evening of the 8th, and 300 volunteers were mobilized. Another 200 from the county joined them on Wednesday, giving the loyalists between 200 and 300 horse.[21] Arms were confiscated and suspects—especially Quakers—were secured. Similar measures were taken in Buckinghamshire, where Captain Draper was among those apprehended, and in Coventry, where the authorities secured Captain Owen, notorious for having pulled down the dean of Canterbury's chapel and part of his house, and the Congregationalist minister John Durant. At Newington Butts, just outside London, Captain Edward Short, a Congregationalist, had reportedly amassed nearly a hundred weapons to use against Charles "if occasion bee offred."[22]

In Yorkshire, Bristol, and Sarum, authorities looked closely at sectarian meetings, particularly those of Baptists and Quakers. A complaint from Wakefield on the 11th noted "great assemblyes" of these groups at which magistracy was denounced. Throughout the West Riding, Quakers went naked through the principal towns, crying "woe to Yorkshire." A request was made to Secretary Nicholas on the 12th for a proclamation directing Yorkshire magistrates to confiscate the weapons of persons believed to be associated with Venner's rising. This was underway by the 21st, when Sir Robert Hildyard expressed shock at how many fanatics actually were in Yorkshire. While searching for weapons at a Quaker's house in Holderness, officials discovered papers demonstrating that the Friends had "constant meetings & intelligence all over the Kingdome," including a register of their sufferings.[23] Bristol, complained a deputy lieutenant, teemed with Quakers and Baptists. On the 19th a great quantity of ammunition was found in an ironmonger's house, and more powder was intercepted en route from the Oxfordshire area. Three days later the justices of the peace came into the city with a volunteer troop of horse to compel the sectaries to take the oath of allegiance. The fourteen who refused were jailed. In Sarum about thirty Friends were incarcerated along with a number of former soldiers.[24]

Most of those who were apprehended undoubtedly had no contact with the Vennerites. This is also true of sectaries in Ireland

and Scotland, despite the unsubstantiated charge of an anonymous author that Venner's group corresponded with disaffected persons in those kingdoms. When news of Venner's revolt reached Scotland, the royal commissioner and the lord chancellor ordered those who had been involved with the Remonstrance and the Protestation to stay at least ten miles from the capital. On receipt of information that there were "sindry disaffected pepill" in Edinburgh, they doubled the guards and the watch. A proclamation dated 22 January prohibited meetings of Baptists, Quakers, and Fifth Monarchists as avowed enemies of authority. In Ireland the lord justices and the Council issued a similar proclamation the same day, but extended it to include Congregationalists, Presbyterians, and Catholics.[25]

It soon became apparent that the authorities had overreacted to the Fifth Monarchist threat, particularly with respect to unwarranted searches of private houses. Sectaries and moderates were noticeably upset. As early as the 11th, the Presbyterian minister Philip Henry, who would be ejected in October, correctly foresaw that Venner's insurrection "may give occasion to those that seek occasion to restrayn our libertyes hitherto indulg'd." Henry's own house was searched for weapons on the 8th of February, but none were found.[26] In retrospect, the Whig historian James Ralph aptly observed that "if Sedition was the Pretence, Oppression was always the Consequence." Predictably, Ludlow's reaction was the same. The government was aware of the abuses, and on 17 January the king issued a proclamation forbidding searches and seizures without a warrant unless an insurrection was in progress. This was not, however, intended to halt the searches but to legalize them. On the day the proclamation was issued, Secretary Nicholas informed Sir Henry Bennet that "orders are everywhere taken to disarm and secure the fanatics."[27]

Venner's rebellion made it easier for the crown to achieve its goal of establishing the royal Guards and settling command of the militia in the king. As Lois Schwoerer has demonstrated, however, the creation of the Guards was in Charles' mind some six months before the Vennerites rebelled, so that the insurrection did no more than facilitate plans that were already underway. Although, as Secretary Nicholas explained on 10 January, the rebellion involved inconsiderable numbers, "their taking and giving no quarter showed what might be expected from their barbarous rage, had they succeeded. The nation," he insisted, "is too sensible of their principles not to secure the public peace against them." On 14 February Monck dismissed his regiments of horse and foot at the Tower, only to reconstitute them on the spot as the Lord General's troop of Guards and the Lord General's regiment of Foot Guards.[28] In addition to these forces, the king and the duke of York each had a troop of Guards, and there was a regiment of horse under the earl of Oxford and two of foot under Monck and Colonel Russell. There must have been many who thought, as Stephen Charlton did, that the king had to have a stronger military because the sectaries were "leagued together in the plottings."[29]

## The Sectaries in Venner's Wake

The abortive Fifth Monarchist insurrection had an immediate impact on the sectaries. Nicholas was optimistic that the swift justice meted out to the offenders would have a salutary effect on others, but to hardened radicals the executed men acquired the status of martyrs.[30] For the most part, Congregationalists, Baptists, and Quakers were quick to condemn Venner, lending credence to the secretary's view that the only threat to the quiet of the realm was "the malicious continuances of some few fifth-Monarchy-Men, who are the worst of all Sectaryes."[31]

Twenty-five prominent Congregationalists, including Joseph Caryl, Philip Nye, George Griffith, Thomas Goodwin, and George Cokayne, co-authored *A Renuntiation and Declaration of the Ministers of Congregational Churches and Publick Preachers* in which they deplored Venner's rising as scandalous to the Christian religion. They were even willing to suggest a possible parallel with the notorious Münster sectaries. It was, they insisted, the duty of Christians to obey the lawful commands of magistrates, even if the latter were infidels. Such obedience was a matter of conscience. The ministers were insistent that meetings for religious worship not be used to plot the disturbance of "those States which *yet by Christ do Reign*."[32]

From the Baptists came a variety of addresses to the king. A group of some thirty Particular Baptists, which included William Kiffin, Henry Denne, and Francis Smith, submitted "The Humble Petition of Some Commonly Called Anabaptists," in which they denied having any communion with the Vennerites. A group of Baptist prisoners in the Maidstone jail protested their incarceration, the illegal entry into their homes, and the unlawful seizure of their goods and cattle. Civil authority, they averred, had no right to compel people's consciences. Other petitions disavowing Venner followed, one of which included such eminent radicals as Packer and Desborough. A group of Lincolnshire General Baptists of whom the most prominent was Thomas Grantham submitted three petitions protesting persecution, dissociating themselves from Venner, and promising to keep the peace.[33] Henry Jessey, a former Fifth Monarchist and now a Particular Baptist, hoped that Venner would insist that no Baptists took part in his uprising. In May, seven Baptists, among them the bookseller Francis Smith and the pastor George Hammond, pressed the king and Parliament for liberty of conscience for those who did not disturb the state. Entitled *Sion's Groans for Her Distres'd*, the appeal recognized magistracy as a divine ordinance, but held out the right to refuse obedience to commands that were contrary to scriptural precepts. One of Nicholas' correspondents accurately summarized the prevailing Baptist view when she noted that they were "Much ofended with the 5th Monarchey Men for there latte actions." Yet she had intelligence in early February that the Baptists expected aid from France in the spring because of the former league between Cromwell and Mazarin![34]

The Quaker reaction to Venner's revolt was typified by Thomas Ellwood's deprecatory reference to "that mad prank of those infatuated fifth-monarchy men." George Fox, Francis Howgill, Henry Fell, Richard Hubberthorne, and eight others expressed the Friends' position in *A Declaration from the Harmles & Innocent People of God, Called Quakers, Against All Plotters and Fighters in the World* (21 January). Those who schemed and rebelled were condemned as worldly. For Fox and his colleagues, it was wrong to utilize any physical weapon to establish Christ's kingdom, which had to be initiated by divine promise rather than might. As pacifists, these Quakers deplored the use of armaments as contrary to both the spirit and doctrine of Christ and the practice of the Apostles.[35]

Within a few weeks of the royal proclamation prohibiting meetings of Baptists, Quakers, and Fifth Monarchists, the prisons were packed. Some 400 Baptists and 500 Quakers were arrested in London alone, while throughout England the number of imprisoned Quakers soared to 4,230. So many sectaries were committed at the Croydon sessions for refusing to take the oath of allegiance that Sir John Maynard wondered where they could be detained. Some refused to swear on principle, others because the king had not taken an oath to preserve the laws. According to Maynard, the leader of the Croydon sectaries, Dr. Bradley, was allowed by the jailer to "imprecate destruction on the king, & all the Royall Line, in that which they call there devocion." The more militant sectaries would not be intimidated.[36]

In late January there were moves to release some of the sectaries, especially those who took the oath of allegiance. On the 25th an order of the king-in-council directed that Quakers in London prisons be released if there were no specific charges against them, and if they took the oaths of supremacy and allegiance.[37] Preachers and other leaders were excepted. But Quakers, of course, refused all oaths as a matter of principle, so the prisons remained full. There were 270 in the Lancaster jail in late March, and approximately 200 in Dorset prisons that spring. The government finally had to yield: On 11 May a proclamation decreed the release of all Friends in prison only for matters of conscience, including refusal to take the oaths.[38]

The government was also unsuccessful in putting a stop to sectarian conventicles with its January proclamation and the ensuing program of arrests. In February Fifth Monarchist meetings were discovered at the Maiden Head tavern in Piccadilly and the Shoreditch home of Robert Malban, who had been arrested earlier as a suspect in Venner's escapade. The prominent City merchant William Kiffin was among those apprehended that month. The problem was compounded by uncooperative clergy, such as Adam Martindale, vicar of Rostherne, Cheshire, who had not yet been ejected and who refused to read the government's orders banning unlawful religious meetings.[39]

Their professions of political obedience in the wake of Venner's revolt notwithstanding, the Nonconformists were adamant in insisting on their right to worship according to their consciences. A conventicle that met at Glovers' Hall in the City drew between 300 and 400 people on 10 March 1661. On the 31st, substantial numbers of Presbyterians, Congregationalists, Baptists, and Fifth Monarchists met in London. According to one informer, "the major part of [the] Citty of London were there." In the morning Robert Bragge, rector of Allhallows the Great, the Fifth Monarchist Anthony Palmer, and the former Fifth Monarchist John Simpson all preached in Bragge's church. Palmer's sermon stressed that the saints must expect to suffer, but promised that their deaths would be followed by their resurrection. Simpson too emphasized the theme of suffering. The Congregationalist Joseph Caryl followed with a sermon at St. Magnus the Martyr, and in the evening the people gathered at St. Antholin's, where the preacher exhorted them to die rather than pollute their consciences with "the superstition & prophanenesse of these tymes." Among those who were seen at these meetings was Colonel John Clarke, a friend of Desborough and former admiralty commissioner, as well as a number of former naval captains, who are "the instruments, why our Common seamen doe so flocke over for

Holland." The informer noted that money was collected at Allhallows and St. Antholin's, ostensibly for the relief of poor ministers, but he suspected (falsely) that the real purpose was to support a bloody insurrection to overthrow episcopacy. The report is a good illustration of the extent to which sectarian activity was thought to be linked to seditious plotting.[40]

The attitude of royalists toward the sectaries was never positive, but Venner's uprising and the continued association of former officers and soldiers with sectarian congregations exacerbated the problem. The tone of the government's position throughout the 1660s was set in Clarendon's speech to Parliament in May 1661. Seditious preachers, he complained, were not messengers of Christian peace but trumpets of war and incendiaries to rebellion. Preaching treason from the pulpit was worse than espousing it in the marketplace, hence the firebrands, he insisted, must be quenched.[41] The problem, however, was distinguishing between genuinely revolutionary ministers and parsons who repudiated the state church but disavowed rebellion. Discrimination, as we have seen, was made harder by the incautious accusations of informers, who had a financial stake in persuading government officials that the sectaries were seditious and had to be watched.

By August the Privy Council had received so much information about sectarian meetings and the dissemination of radical pamphlets that it ordered the lords lieutenant to be especially vigorous in settling the militia as a prelude to suppressing seditious activities. The Council specifically remarked on "the more then usuall confidence and presumption that at present appears in many of those who were active Instruments in the late times of Usurpation, and Tyranny." The sort of meeting that worried the councillors took place on 24 August, when nearly 300 sectaries assembled in St. Bartholomew's, London. By the time the magistrates arrived, all but ten men and thirty women had gone, but one of those they arrested was Major (Robert?) Cobbett. He and his confederates proclaimed to the magistrates that "they were not bound to obey the King when the spirit commanded the contrary."[42]

Despite the ignominy of Venner's failure, the Fifth Monarchy movement refused to die. On 27 August there was a Fifth Monarchy meeting at Norton Folgate, outside Bishopsgate. A month later two recently released Vennerites reportedly declared that "the King and his bishopps, were Riding post [haste] to their owne destruction." John Belcher, who did not support Venner because of unspecified differences, had become the principal preacher in the Coleman

Street meeting by September. He was a primary source of the informer Peter Crabb's intelligence in the 1660s, though perhaps not knowingly.[43]

One of the most notorious conventicles in the City met at Allhallows the Great, where Simpson, Jessey, and Hanserd Knollys preached every Monday, Wednesday, and Thursday, and where Anthony Palmer and Thomas Carter substituted in their absence. "Those that doe exercise there," according to the printer Richard Hodgkinson, "they doe first breed them to it, in a house at a Conventicle held in Anchor Lane every Sunday, where there are two Pulpitts putt up together for prophesying." Allhallows the Great was a showcase for proven sectarian talent. In early September the pulpit oratory stressed that God would fulfil his work of pulling down those who opposed his truth. A few weeks later Simpson made it the duty of God's people to overcome their enemies, eschewing fear in their determination to overturn everything contrary to God. Laurence Wise used the example of Daniel in the lions' den to urge the godly to be faithful, while another preacher warned them that the time in which to accomplish their work was short. Clearly the imagery of such preaching conjured up a bleak picture of Restoration England and was more conducive to the inculcation of an embattled mentality than the achievement of a quiescent reconciliation.[44]

In the months that followed, Simpson, Palmer, and Carter fed their listeners a steady diet of spiritual fortitude. Speaking on Revelation 3:20–21, Simpson promised triumph if the saints would "fight it out to the Last." They must be willing to lose everything material, to undergo incarceration, and to forsake those who conform to the established church. Daniel 2:35 provided Simpson with ammunition for his claim that Christ is a stone who will crush all the powers of the earth: The enemies of God's people "had Best have a care how they medell with any of his peopell" lest this stone crush them. With millenarian zeal Simpson used Acts 20:22–23 to proclaim the imminent end of the wicked, though they would not be overturned by might but by "the sperett of the saints mad[e] perfect. . . . Itt is your hour Christians[,] doe not feare." Palmer developed the same theme, praying for the time when Babylon would fall, never to rise again. In the meantime he exhorted his hearers not to countenance superstition or idolatry. There was solace, he said, in the fact that the enemies of God could not harm the saints. The Congregationalist Stephen Ford also preached at Allhallows in this period, taking as his theme the concept of the present as "the tyme of tryall." But none of the preachers at Allhallows was as provocative as Simpson, and for that reason a warrant for his arrest was issued on 29 November on the grounds of seditious and dangerous speech.[45]

While Allhallows the Great was the center of sectarian preaching in London, on virtually any Sunday a number of sectaries were preaching in the City and its environs. Edward Potter was kept busy providing Secretary Nicholas with the names of the preachers and the content of their sermons. On 13 October, for instance, he provided a synopsis of one of Simpson's sermons and then said simply that there were many other ministers who preached in a similar vein, including Matthew Meade and Thomas Woodcock. On other occasions he provided notes from sermons by such sectaries as William Kiffin and Laurence Wise. In his opinion the "Chief Ringleaders" responsible for fomenting dissatisfaction in the City included Simpson, Wise, Meade, Jenkyn, Woodcock, and Samuel Annesley. Another of Potter's ringleaders, Mr. Bareman, told a congregation at St. Thomas', Southwark, that those who called themselves "the Companies of Christ" were in fact the Antichrist and should be shunned. At St. Sepulchre's, Palmer developed the same theme, insisting that the saints have nothing to do with the clergy who replaced the ejected ministers. George Cokayne and Nathaniel Holmes were also kept under surveillance.[46]

One of the more mysterious preachers among the London sectaries was William James, whose meeting in a dark alley in Duke's Place was reported by John Crabb. James exalted the executed regicides Harrison, Carew, and Scott as martyrs whose blood was seed that would increase a thousand-fold. Their deaths were blamed on "the Redd Scarlitt whore, that hath baithed her self in the blood of the Saints, that God would give the murderers blood to drink." James seemed to hope for an insurrection when he prayed that God would "hasten the worke, and put itt into their harts whoe should bee their chief-man to carry on their design." For James, God was the great bookkeeper of justice who maintained exact records of how his people were treated. Any harm to them was an offense to God. Although much of the violent language was intended only in a spiritual sense, the cumulative effect was conducive to militant behavior.[47]

As persecution slowly deepened, some Presbyterians found spiritual kinship with the sectaries, into whose arms they were driven, especially after the collapse of the Savoy Conference in the spring. This development, which tended to discredit the Presbyterians, played into the hands of those who favored their exclusion from both the corporations and the established church. In Exeter, the Presbyterians and the Congregationalists drew closer through the efforts of their leaders, Thomas Ford and Lewis Stucley. "Their usuall Theames are to possesse the people that a famine or scarcity of the word is like to bee, & that they must doe as some Creatures, live on what they have laid up in summer." From Windsor Castle Lord Mordaunt complained that the Presbyterians in his region were preaching nothing but rebellion. "If they should continue heere," he fretted, "constant intelligence would bee sent out of the Castle to theire Crew."[48] Secretary Nicholas noted that the Presbyterians had become increasingly bold and insolent in London, and had begun to share churches and meeting houses with the Baptists and Fifth Monarchists, preaching a common message of imminent deliverance. What the Presbyterians did was all the more meaningful because they enjoyed some support among the higher social orders. Nicholas learned that in August Lord Massereene took a minister recently expelled from Ireland to preach in Jenkyn's church. Jenkyn himself at this point established a lecture at Christ Church, London, where he prepared his people for persecution.[49]

Reports of dangerous preachers filtered in from the counties. From Uffington, Lincolnshire, came word that the ejected rector, Henry Field, maliciously preached against the government. For this the Privy Council ordered his arrest, and he died in the Gatehouse at Westminster. At Lee, Kent, where the former City radicals George and Maurice Thompson had settled, Caleb Trenchfield, the ejected rector of Chipstead, Surrey, criticized the saints because they were less willing to "engage" or suffer than they once were. He exhorted them—in biblical language with obvious overtones—to "fight the good fight." Because Lee was only a few miles southeast of London, it was easily accessible to radicals from the City. On 1 October, a number of ex-Cromwellians were at Lee, including Colonels Robert Blount (or Blunt) and Thompson along with three other officers. The pulpit at Lee was open to virtually all comers. In the opinion of the informer Edward Potter, its congregation of more than a hundred would "prove as Dangerous to the government of England as any if They are not sudenly prevented." The minister at Lee, William Hickocks, contributed to such fears by preaching that the saints must be willing to die for God's cause.[50]

The sectaries posed threats to the public order in yet other areas. The bishop of Salisbury had a difficult time suppressing the ones in his diocese. At Shinfield, Berkshire, the vicar, William Cosins, had turned over his responsibilities to the Baptist William Stanley, a former judge-advocate in Colonel John Birch's regiment. Stanley, who claimed to "see the whore of Babylon come creeping in," told his auditors that the spirit of Antichrist reigned in England. When the bishop ordered him to desist from preaching in the parish church, he refused on the grounds that the majority of the parish had chosen him and still supported him. The recalcitrant Stanley summoned a force of sixty stout men, mostly from Reading, to back him. On 21 October the Privy Council finally resolved the ugly dispute by ordering the arrest of both Stanley and Cosins.[51] In nearby Reading, where Stanley lived, Christopher Fowler, vicar of St. Mary's, refused to read the Book of Common Prayer, but he was not ejected until the following year. Some of the deprived clergy were moving into the Kentish Weald, where, according to Sir Edward Hales, they "vented Abundance of seditious practices, on their new-Created Lecture Days." The area was a special worry because the people purportedly could arm as many as 1,000 men with only a day's warning.[52]

The disquietude over potentially seditious preaching increased in November with the trial of the Fifth Monarchist and Seventh-Day Baptist John James. Variously described as a weaver and a "Small-coal-man,"[53] James preached to a conventicle of some forty persons at Bullstake Alley in Whitechapel on 19 October. After speaking in the morning on Psalm 8:2, he was expostulating on 1 Corinthians 6:20 in the afternoon when a justice of the peace and a head-borough dragged him from the pulpit for allegedly making treasonable statements in his first sermon. Those in the congregation who refused the oath of allegiance were put in Newgate prison, where James himself was held.

On 14 November James was tried in King's Bench on a charge of plotting Charles II's death, preparing to levy war against the crown, and espousing a change of government. The indictment accused him of portraying the king as a bloody tyrant who was responsible for shedding the blood of the English saints at Charing Cross and of the Covenanters in Scotland. James had condemned the nobles too as blood-suckers, and, according to the indictment, prophesied that the death and destruction of the king were nigh. He regretted that the godly had not done more when they exercised power and bewailed the apostacy of the people for not fighting the Lord's battles more thoroughly. Although he pleaded not guilty, there were four witnesses against him, two of whom were valueless. According to one witness, James said of Cromwell "that every finger of his was a Champion," but James denied that he was Cromwell's advocate and insisted that he had opposed Oliver's usurpation. He did, however, admit to preaching that Christ was the king of nations and that the government of all kingdoms belonged to him. Moreover, he said, Christ "shall use his People in his hand as his *Battle-ax and Weapon of War* for the bringing in the Kingdoms of this World into subjection to Him." Although James regarded Venner's rising as a rash act, he felt some remorse for not having supported it. The jury found him guilty and on the 26th he was hanged, drawn, and quartered at Tyburn.[54] The severity of a sentence based on such shaky testimony was probably the result of a climate of opinion poisoned by reports of yet more plots.

## Underground Rumblings

Plots and alleged conspiracies were continuing occurrences thoughout 1661. The dust had hardly settled from Venner's rising when the Millenex plot was exposed in Cheshire. In a letter dated 18 January at Helsby, near Frodsham, the Baptist Richard Millenex appealed to a Quaker named Jellico to recruit men for an insurrection. Millenex claimed the rebels were already about 6,000 strong, though more were needed. He planned to come to Chester on the 24th, but in the meantime news of their progress was to be conveyed to Peter Deusbery and Randal Morgan. Claiming that in conscience he was struck with "the horrour of the design," Jellico gave the letter to the mayor of Chester, who passed it to the earl of Derby. The latter, after ordering the militia in Cheshire and Lancashire to stand ready, alerted the lords lieutenant of Derbyshire, Staffordshire, Shropshire, Westmorland, Cumberland, and the West Riding. Derby also detained a number of ex-Cromwellian officers, including Colonels Birch, Briggs, Robert Duckenfield, and Francis West, and Major Morgan. There is, however, insufficient evidence to support the existence of a plot of this magnitude.[55]

At the end of January royalists celebrated not only the quashing of Venner's uprising and the Millenex plot, but also the public display of the corpses of Cromwell, Bradshaw, and Ireton, which were dragged on sledges to Tyburn and hanged on a gibbet for thousands to see. Nicholas was clearly pleased with what to him was a manifest act of justice. By early February there was no news of radical activity in the London area, though officials reported that dissidents in Cheshire, Lancashire, and Scotland "are provideinge for the Springe." There were rumors at the same time that Ludlow had been seen in Wiltshire, ready to take command of an insurrection if Venner had been successful, and that he had since left for

Ireland. An intelligence report in March noted that a Deptford radical was expending funds to win supporters in the army, while another report of about the same date indicated that ministers in the west who were managing a design were corresponding with the Congregationalist Ralph Venning, lecturer at St. Olave's, Southwark, and had dispatched thirty-three agents throughout the country to "Crye up theire Covenant." Nevertheless, a mood of cautious optimism prevailed in royalist circles, though there was always an awareness, as the London auxiliaries expressed it, that "Men of Loose & dangerous principles" posed some threat to the kingdom's peace.[56]

The results of the City elections in March were a shock to some of the king's supporters. Feelings were running high among those who were concerned about the use of old statutes to enforce religious conformity as well as those who wanted a Parliament that would confirm the legality of the transactions for church lands during the revolutionary era. With cries of "noe bishops, noe Lord Bishops," the Congregationalists, Presbyterians, Baptists, and possibly even the Quakers joined forces to elect two Presbyterians, John Fowke and Captain John Jones, and two Congregationalists, Sir William Thompson and William Love. More conservative candidates were cried down and decisively beaten in the polling. Their supporters, according to an eyewitness, left cursing, and one courtier interpreted the results as a salutary warning to the bishops. For their part, the godly were enthusiastic, hoping that the forthcoming elections in the rest of the country would produce similar victories. The royalists in turn pondered delaying the election results. Although there was little support in the country as a whole for Presbyterians and Congregationalists, the election in the City signaled the presence of a sizeable number of people who were uninterested in restoring the bishops and the traditional liturgy. In the aftermath of the election, ministers opposed to prelacy, such as the Presbyterian Lazarus Seaman, were "mightily followed." Yet in Southwark, where there was a long-standing radical community, the Presbyterians, Congregationalists, Baptists, and Quakers, under the leadership of Colonel George Thompson and Captain Samuel Lynn, were unable to prevent the election of four conservatives. Once their defeat was apparent, the radicals drew swords and fought with the supporters of Sir Thomas Bludworth, one of the newly elected M.P.s. The triumph of the dissidents in London did not prove to be a harbinger of success in the rest of the country, for in the end only thirty-seven Presbyterians and Congregationalists were returned to the House of Commons in 1661.[57]

As attention turned to the coronation in April, Secretary Nicholas gathered information about possible radical attempts to disrupt the ceremonies. A set of undated notes that he endorsed was probably compiled at this time. In them reference was made to the universal expectation of a governmental change as well as "a generall desertion in point of affection in the middle sort of people in City & Country from the Kings interest." The notes expressed concern about the close ties of the sectaries and the Presbyterians, and observed that a sudden revolution was expected in Scotland. The growing number of conventicles and lectures was cited as a threat to the king's interests as well as the church's. But with the impending coronation, the most immediate concern had to be a report that numerous ex-officers and soldiers were coming into the City on the pretense of finding employment. It was undoubtedly this influx that prompted the secretary on 10 April to order the apprehension of fifteen ex-officers and soldiers if they were found in London. Thirteen of them were former officers, among whom were Major-General James Berry, the Fifth Monarchists William Allen, John Vernon, William Packer, Hugh Courtney, and Nathaniel Rich, Lambert's supporter John Gladman, Colonel Butler, Major Child, and Richard Salway, a former M.P. in the Long and Barebones Parliaments. Extant records indicate that some of these men were still in prison, perhaps suggesting that the government was contemplating their release.[58] Three days later the authorities issued a proclamation ordering all former officers and soldiers to leave the capital by the 19th and stay at least twenty miles away until 20 May.[59]

The usual diet of rumors and suspicious meetings fed concerns for the king's safety. There was a report in early March that Lambert was considering an escape, but the astrologer William Lilly persuaded him to ask the king for release on bail. According to an April rumor, City radicals had sent for Richard Cromwell. On the 12th there was a meeting at the home of Mr. Sampson behind the Exchange at which Captain (Samuel?) Poole and others were arrested and weapons confiscated. Poole and his friends were unresolved as to when to rise, but they contemplated an attempt to free Major-General James Berry and Major John Breman. Sampson reportedly would receive £10,000 to finance the design. Six days later there was a meeting near the Exchange at which John Desborough, Thomas Kelsey, and Lieutenant-Colonel Jeffrey Ellison (or Elleston) were allegedly present. Desborough and Kelsey, however, were in the Netherlands and almost certainly had not risked their lives by sneaking back into England to plot.[60]

There was also some disquiet about conditions in Bristol, where dissident aldermen such as Joseph Jackson and Robert Aldworth had not been ejected. Two ex-officers, Majors Samuel Clarke, a Baptist, and Henry Roe (or Row), a Quaker, were stockpiling arms. No less than eighteen barrels of gunpowder were found in Roe's house along with weapons and ammunition.[61]

To the north, there was an attempt to seize the magazine at Berwick on 22 April. A rebel party attacked the sentries at night, but fled when a shot was fired by one of the guards. Eighteen persons were subsequently arrested, though seven of them, all townsmen, were soon released on bail. Before the attack there were rumors that the disaffected planned to have a "joyful" day prior to the coronation. In Berwick as elsewhere, however, Charles' crowning passed without incident.[62]

In general, the summer of 1661 provided a relatively quiet interlude before the worrisome appearance of widespread rumors and suspected plots in the autumn. Secretary Nicholas informed the earl of Winchilsea in early May that the people were becoming increasingly affectionate toward the king and his government in all three kingdoms. If the secretary really believed that, he nevertheless continued to gather intelligence and to proceed with the confiscation of weapons. Security was particularly tight when the king left London.[63] In the process of searching houses, numerous weapons were discovered, some of them hidden under the ground. The political danger was serious enough to threaten the royal progress. Nicholas had one report that the dissidents had recently acquired 40,000 arms, excluding those previously concealed, and that the weapons were dispersed three and four to a house. There was a rumor in June that Colonel John Okey would return from the continent the following month, prepared to rise, and that Henry Danvers, who was consulting regularly with Clement Ireton and others, had agreed to "head a party." Conservatives were especially apprehensive about radical activity on 3 September, the anniversary of Dunbar, Worcester, and Cromwell's death.[64]

Allegations continued to filter in of seditious speech, which served as a reminder of the depth and extent of popular hostility to the new regime. A Leeds worker hoped that the rebels would disperse the trained bands like chaff before the wind, while in Dorchester Lieutenant Wadden and others threatened to hang those who had deserted the Good Old Cause to serve Charles. "Another course" would be taken with the royalists, "& that speedily." A Westminster shoemaker looked forward to serving in a rebel army of "brave boyes," adding that "if ever the ould army wear togather againe thay would never be fooled as thay have bine." Faced with such expressions, royalists understandably considered the people turbulent.[65]

The state of the army and the militia continued to be a source of worry. A loyalist in Wrexham, who considered his town the most factious in England, complained in September that the trained bands were still unsettled and the king's enemies not disarmed. A royalist lieutenant stationed in Grantham feared that despite a remodeling of the army, the soldiers might turn against their officers. As an added concern, Grantham's civilians and the Cromwellian army "understood one another very well." In London, rebel agents were reportedly dispensing money to discontented soldiers in order to win their support. Among the proposed solutions were an increase in the number of informants and major military reforms.[66]

The government's response to the continual allegations of disaffection and scheming was more surveillance and renewed arrests. The most active of the government agents in the summer of 1661, Peter Crabb and Samuel Wilcox, compiled lists of persons believed to be involved in treasonable designs. They included the usual collection of former officers such as Colonels Thomas Fitch, Francis West ("to act in Lancashire"), Francis Buffett of Somerset, Robert Bennet ("to act" in Devon and Cornwall), Weeks of Smithfield, Kiffin, Jerome Sankey, and Lockyer, Lieutenant-Colonel Robert Read, and Captain Jennings. The preachers suspected of seditious activity were Henry Jessey, John Simpson, and the Particular Baptist Edward Harrison, whose congregation met in Petty France, near Moorfields. The lists were unusual, however, in the names of prominent citizens they contained, such as the City aldermen William Webb and Timothy Wade, the former Speaker of the House of Commons William Lenthall, two former M.P.s, (John?) Lowry and George Thompson, Sir Thomas Allen, the merchant Benjamin Howland, and three City justices.[67]

Informers tried to keep track of who visited whom in the radical community, hoping thereby to disentangle the threads of any schemes. Praisegod Barebone called attention to himself by looking in on Vavasor Powell and Major John Breman in prison; Barebone himself went to jail in November. The prisons provided radicals with opportunities to explore their grievances at greater length, and often the security was slack enough to enable them to enjoy ample contact with the outside world. In August, September, and October Colonel Nathaniel Rich was at liberty to stay away from the Fleet prison for days at a time. John Bunyan was out of his Bedford cell long enough to make trips to London. Informers and jailers, however, could monitor radical activity by these goings and comings. In September Sir Edward Broughton, keeper of the Gatehouse at Westminster, compiled a list of thirty former officers who lived near Whitehall and another of nineteen ministers who allegedly were seducing the people. Nearly all of the officers were captains and lieutenants, though the list included Major Andrews. On the ministers' list were such prominent clergymen as John Simpson, William Kiffin, Anthony Palmer, Laurence Wise, and the Presbyterians Thomas Gouge and William Jenkyn.[68]

Some attention also had to be paid to ex-naval officers. At ports such as Plymouth and Dartmouth, "ould sea Captaines" such as Edward Blagg, John Jeffreys, Peter Mootham, and Nicholas Heaton, all of whom fought the Dutch in 1653, were known to oppose monarchy and episcopacy. There was also concern about officers still in the fleet who corresponded with the rebels, and thus could lead a fifth column if an insurrection began.[69]

As these reports accumulated, Westminster officials opted in late September to arrest some of the dissidents and to seize their horses. Among those taken into custody were Lieutenant Wadden of Bridport, Dorset, and Henry Field, the former for "treasonable matters," the latter for seditious speech. In early September a number of arrests were made in Wales, mostly of ex-officers such as Colonel Philip Jones, Majors Evan Lewis, Rowland Dawkins, and John Gawler, plus seven captains and a coronet. Rice Powell and John Price, former justices of the peace, were also imprisoned. The build-up of concern set the stage for the government's announcement on 21 October that a fresh conspiracy had been detected.[70]

## The Presbyterian Plot

The details of the alleged new conspiracy were rather murky. Pepys, in fact, thought there was no plot, "but only a pretence, as there was once pretended often against the Cavaleers." The aim of the purported cabal was to rekindle the civil war as the means to overthrow monarchy and episcopacy. Various reports indicated that there were either 3,000 or 6,000 men in London, "mainteyned by the Presbiterian Ministry," ready to rise. Another source placed the total strength of the rebels at 40,000 ex-soldiers.[71] Information received by the Venetian resident indicated that some of the rebels would come from Albemarle's own forces. The London dissidents were believed to be in contact with disaffected officers in Hertford—particularly Colonel

Henry Markham—who were replacing soldiers loyal to the king with radicals. With this revolutionary core they intended to surprise the Hertford garrison as soon as the insurrection was launched in London. Lambert was reportedly the mastermind, but Ludlow was also mentioned as the leader. According to the Venetian resident, the conspiracy was discovered a mere six hours before the scheduled uprising. At least one informant was convinced that "if they weare not nipt in the bud . . . they would carry it."[72]

There were suspicions that the plot extended as far afield as Leicester and Carlisle. Nicholas was informed that gunpowder camouflaged as clothware had been shipped to Leicester for use by rebels. In Carlisle Sir Philip Musgrave was confident that the cabal "did reach to within thes[e] walls," but he lacked sufficient evidence to press charges. He was especially distrustful toward a group of disbanded soldiers in the town, but could do little more than keep them under observation.[73]

The supposed design, which was based on flimsy evidence, provided the pretext for sweeping arrests in England and Wales. The government also took the precaution of ordering radical leaders transported to more secure locations—Lambert to Guernsey, Sir Hardress Waller and Colonel Ralph Cobbett to Jersey, Henry Vane to the Scilly Isles, Major-General Robert Overton to Chepstow Castle, Colonel Edmond Harvey to Pendennis Castle, and Colonel Robert Lilburne to St. Nicholas Island. The king directed the lord mayor of London to be more vigilant with night watches, claiming that too many feeble men were guarding the City and leaving their posts before daybreak.[74]

Most of the leaders of the reputed conspiracy were arrested at a meeting in London; among them were Colonels William Packer, John Streater, Timothy Wilkes (currently a captain under Albemarle), and William Kenrick.[75] The former M.P. Henry Neville was arrested in Berkshire. In some places the authorities discovered substantial quantities of arms, particularly at Winchester and Hadley in Hampshire. Although Sir Michael Livesey had already fled to the continent, some of his associates were secured and lost their weapons. Chief among them was Captain May, as "Ill principled a phanatique, as is possible." Their offense was providing hospitality to ex-soldiers, meeting together, looking cheerful, enquiring about the news, and manifesting an unwillingness to conform to "the Civill, Military, or Episcopall power." Other purportedly dangerous ex-officers were closely watched. They included Lieutenant George Kadwell, who had served with Colonel Kenrick, Captain William Dunke, who bragged that he had been the first to draw a sword against Charles I, and Captain Andrew Tucker, who had weapons hidden in his hay and twenty horses. It was impossible, of course, to imprison all the disaffected, but officials clearly hoped, as one lieutenant put it, that by punishing "one in a tribe," the others would be cowed into submission.[76]

The Presbyterian plot was in fact no more than a fabrication based on suspicions and allegations. But given the experience of the previous uprisings by Lambert and Venner, the government was in no mood to take chances. In the end the real significance of the putative design was the added impetus it provided for the attempt the following month to exclude Presbyterians from the corporations. There is insufficient proof, however, to charge the government with inventing the plot in order to smooth the way for passage of a corporation bill.

## The Yarrington Plot

On the twelfth of November, Sir John Packington, an M.P. and justice of the peace for Worcestershire, informed his lord lieutenant that a "suddaine riseing of the Presbiterian and factious party" could be expected, based on two letters he had received several days earlier and had forwarded to Secretary Nicholas. He had already alerted the guards and arrested many suspects, but he was afraid the design extended throughout the country.[77] The letters in question were brought to him by Richard Churme of Winchenford, a village some six miles northwest of Worcester. Churme claimed he found the letters in a country lane where they had been dropped by a blond-haired man wearing a gray coat with a green cloak around his shoulders. Both letters were from Anne Ba., with the addressees being Captain Andrew Yarrington (or Yarranton), a specialist in iron and canals, and Ambrose Sparry, rector of Martley, Worcestershire, and a former member of the Worcestershire Association.

The contents of the two letters implied the existence of a plot, though in reality it was yet another fabrication. The letter to Yarrington noted that an oath had been taken on 1 November, begged him to come at an appointed time, and asked him to inform others of the date and place of the meeting. Mr. Ba. reportedly could not delay, having had little rest for a fortnight. The letter also mentioned a shortage of funds. Perhaps the real clue to these vague comments was Mrs. Ba.'s statement that "I pray for the Gospell and the fatall blows to our advarsaris fayle not." The letter to Sparry acknowledged that he was anxious for "them" to proceed and should therefore send money. Mrs. Ba. told him that the company had been increased to 300, asked him to speak with Mr. Osland and Mr. Baxter, and referred him to Yarrington (who had been to her house) for further details, including the names of those who had been sworn. She indicated that she had "sent to" Hereford, Gloucester, and Worcester, presumably for support and probably with the latest information. Their friends in Shrewsbury also had been informed of "the day." Finally, she looked ahead to happier times, hoped their business would soon be completed, and advised Sparry to burn her letter.[78] One of the two men referred to in this document was the Presbyterian Henry Osland (or Oasland), curate of Bewdley, and like Sparry a former member of the Worcestershire Association. Mr. Baxter is usually taken to be the eminent Richard Baxter, ejected vicar of Kidderminster. Kidderminster's proximity to Bewdley (where Osland was) suggests such an identification; yet after his ejection in 1660 Baxter spent most of his time in the London area, particularly at Acton, Middlesex. Moreover Baxter was one of ten Presbyterians selected by the king to be a chaplain-in-ordinary, and thus hardly the sort of man inclined to plot. There were two other Baxters in Worcestershire, the brothers Benjamin, ejected as rector of Upton on Severn in 1660, and Stephen, rector of Harvington until his ejection in 1662.[79] In Yarrington's account, written twenty years later, he refers to Richard Baxter, despite the fact that he was one of the least likely candidates for scheming in the country—which was precisely Yarrington's point.

Packington sent the secretary these letters along with Churme's account and depositions from two other persons. The depositions were dated on the 8th, the day Packington received the letters. The two witnesses deposed that Yarrington claimed he had a commission to cure people of the "simples," and that he said there would be more news very shortly. They also testified that Colonel Turton's man said there would be a rendezvous at Edgehill on the night of the 9th involving Lambert's forces and some men from Worcestershire.[80] By the time this information was forwarded to London, the 9th had passed without any rendezvous.

In his report, Churme provided an account of an unidentified gentleman who approached Sparry on the 10th to inquire if he read the Book of Common Prayer in his services. When Sparry responded negatively but was fearful that he might soon be coerced into doing so, the gentleman replied that "if this wicked King doe Raigne as he begins I hope I shall see his head cut of[f] as his fathers was; then there will be noe King noe Bishops noe Common prayers."[81] There was, however, nothing in this story to support the existence of a plot.

Some corroboration came from Gloucester, where officials intercepted a letter to Captain William Neast from a Tewkesbury man named Jones who was then in London. The letter contained information similar to that found in the missives of Anne Ba.: reference to an oath taken on 5 November, to a company that now numbered 300, to the need for money, and to the expectation of "a glorious day, and a fatall blowe to the Adversaryes." The royalist who reported this also referred to the appearance of armed groups of disbanded soldiers for a week or two at a time. In his opinion "the godly . . . [were] preparinge for a darke time in expectation of a glorious appearance or Risinge sometimes in Herefordshire."[82]

Further evidence of a conspiracy was sent from Coventry to the earl of Oxford by William Jenkins on 13 November. Jenkins claimed he had located evidence that the rising was general, but he provided no particulars. Coventry, he asserted, was very "factious and of that Arrogance that if there be not a sudden Course taken with them, they will attempt any thing." He was particularly apprehensive about the strength of the Presbyterians and sectaries. As the details of the alleged plot were investigated, authorities learned that a rising was scheduled in Lichfield on the night of 21 November. Rebels would set fire to the town in three or four places, and while the 300 foot were containing the blazes the rebels would seize weapons, secure the soldiers, and begin a march through the country.[83] Captain Henry Stone, Lieutenant George Hill, and Thomas Sheppard of Walsall were arrested, as was an unidentified man carrying five letters in a cipher unknown to the magistrates. Officials also examined a man who claimed he overheard four armed and mounted men near Fisherwick, Staffordshire, say that in the shire towns "they had more friends then enimys & armes for them." One remarked that they had "friends enough in the house" of Commons, to which a companion added that he knew of a castle where they could obtain 5,000 arms.[84] The reports from Coventry and Gloucester reinforced the government's belief that Yarrington was indeed involved in a general conspiracy.

Yarrington's version differs sharply from the official account. In order to persuade Parliament and king to accept an act of uniformity that would exclude "every Puritan in the Kingdom" from the state church, he charged, a group of clergy and laymen contrived the plot. Supposedly it involved some sixteen counties. Yarrington accused Packington of writing the Anne Ba. letters and having a neighbor deliver them to Mr. Cole at Martley. Cole gave them to Churme, who passed them back to Packington, claiming they were dropped by a Scottish peddler headed toward Colonel John Birch's house. The packet contained letters directed to Yarrington, several of which were from ministers. One was supposedly from Richard Baxter, who promised to supply a large body of armed men. Another was from Sparry, who claimed he had £500 to give Yarrington. Maurice Ashley is inclined to believe Yarrington's profession of innocence, but it is odd indeed that Yarrington's description of the letters in the packet does not match the documents submitted to Secretary Nicholas by Packington.[85] If there was a letter in Richard Baxter's handwriting that was clearly seditious, one must wonder why it was neither mentioned by Packington nor dispatched to London.

Very early on the morning of 9 November Yarrington was arrested, as were Sparry, Henry and Edward Osland, Colonel Turton, Major Easthopp, Captain (Thomas?) Wells, who lived near Bethnal Green, and "scores" more. According to Packington, four of these men—Sparry, Henry Osland, Turton, and Easthopp—were with Yarrington when he was arrested. When the trained bands in Worcester dispersed after ten days, all but Yarrington, Sparry, the Oslands, and Wells were discharged.[86]

Yarrington also provided an account of the discovery of kindred plotters in Oxfordshire. According to the captain, the town clerk of Oxford, Matthew Martin, passed a letter to the mayor that he had received from a stranger. In it was a list of 111 men who were to receive instructions to be in arms the next Wednesday night. The letter went on to say that 200 armed men would come to Oxford, and "you know who doth Command them." Dr. Daniel Greenwood, the ejected principal of Brasenose College, allegedly told a barber named Combs to get "his Party of Scholars" ready. The unnamed author of the letter had likewise instructed Hickman—probably Henry Hickman, fellow of Magdalen College until his ejection in 1661—to prepare his men. Similar plans were made by Dr. John Owen, the former vice-chancellor, Henry Cornish, ejected as canon of Christ Church the previous year, Dr. John Conant, rector of Exeter College, and a Mr. Fogge. At the specified time, the scholars were supposed to meet in the garden of Dr. Christopher Rogers, principal of New Inn Hall. The addressee was directed to send blunderbusses and give the bearer £5 "out of Stock." There was even a mysterious request to be remembered "to the six Men unnam'd," possibly a reference to a revolutionary council that purportedly sat in London and directed the affairs of the underground. The author of the letter indicated that five counties would rise that night, the password being "God is the Word."[87]

The mayor, according to Yarrington, informed Lord Falkland of the discovery. Because some of the 111 on the list were serving in Falkland's company of foot, while others too were known to be loyal, Falkland only had the militia guard the town for two days. The mayor himself thought the plot was a fabrication.[88] Indeed it was, but whose? The letter supposedly given to the mayor of Oxford is not in the State Papers. Falkland's reaction was strikingly different from what happened in Worcester. Although some initially laughed at accounts of the Yarrington plot, Packington took it seriously from the beginning, which was obviously the safer course. Alarms were sent out and neighboring towns—especially Gloucester and Shrewsbury—were put on guard. As far away as Wiltshire, the towns were placed in a defense posture, illegal meetings were banned, and disaffected persons were secured and prohibited from corresponding with other dissidents. Copies of Anne Ba.'s letters were sent to Henry Coker at Warminster, Wiltshire, and he was also told of a design to burn Worcester, where three men were arrested with fire balls in their pockets. He was convinced that such plots were the work of persons who refused to conform to the Church of England. Bristol too was placed on alert. At Derby a company of horse and two of foot were called out, and the rest of the foot went to Chesterfield and Bakewell, but the militia was dismissed after three days.[89]

Packington told his story to the House of Commons on 20 November, with support from other members, including those from Oxfordshire and Staffordshire. The following day the Commons asked the Lords to join with them in requesting that the king issue a proclamation ordering all "suspicious and loose persons" to leave London and Westminster for a suitable time. The proclamation followed a week later, as all cashiered soldiers "of the late usurped powers" were ordered to leave the London area by 4 December and not return before 24 June 1662. They were also prohibited from wearing arms, a provision the Privy Council directed the deputy lieutenants to enforce. At least one ex-officer, Captain Thomas Elliot, was jailed in Newgate for refusing to leave London.[90]

The end of this tale is not much clearer than the beginning. Yarrington claimed he was released in April 1662 and went immediately to London to tell his story to the earl of Bristol. The Privy Council thereupon ordered the deputy lieutenants of Worcestershire to appear before it to render an account, which they successfully did. Yarrington claims he was once again arrested for high treason and taken to London, where Bristol procured his release. Against this account must be placed a letter dated 29 May 1662 from the deputy lieutenants to Secretary Nicholas indicating that Yarrington had escaped from the Marshalsea in Worcester. Two days later, the sheriff of Worcestershire, Thomas Wilde, informed the secretary that Yarrington had gone to London where he was meeting with dissidents. A warrant for his arrest was issued on 3 June. Nearly three weeks later three justices of the peace in Surrey notified Nicholas that he had been captured, apparently in Southwark, and was being sent for examination. Yarrington, they added, was pleading that the king had ordered his discharge.[91]

Yarrington's account, written at a distance of twenty years and for propaganda purposes in the exclusion crisis, is essentially a case of self-pleading. Time and emotion undoubtedly colored the tale he told. From his vantage point in exile, Ludlow too believed that the Yarrington plot was a sham and perpetrated by those who forged the Anne Ba. letters.[92] Ludlow was probably correct. The Yarrington plot, at the core of which was allegedly a group of Presbyterian ministers with no record of seditious political activity, followed on the heels of the October Presbyterian plot, which itself had no solid evidential foundation. The rumors of October provided the inspiration for the accusations of November. However, the villain was very likely not the Packington of Yarrington's tortured story, but a neighbor of Sparry's, who knew the minister and his colleagues well and was familiar with the style of spiritual discourse they used. The probable motive, as Edmund Calamy suggests, was Sparry's reproof of his neighbor for adultery.[93] The plot, however, was sufficiently believable—at least for a time— precisely because the Presbyterians and their sectarian allies were already known to be critical of the government's religious policy and hopeful of better conditions in the near future. The association of ex-officers and soldiers with the Presbyterians and sectaries only deepened the suspicions of royalists, setting the stage for accusations of the kind made against Yarrington. Reports of designs from Coventry and Gloucester, again based on flimsy evidence, suggested the reality of a projected general uprising, and the government responded accordingly. As reports of plotting spread, the effect was multiplicative. Rumors and allegations, whether substantive or not, fed each other, creating an onerous task for the authorities in sorting fact from fiction.

## The Nonsuch House Plotters

Five days after Packington recounted the story of the Yarrington plot to the House of Commons, the government began arresting radicals who frequented Nonsuch House, a food and coffee establishment in Bow Street, Covent Garden. Operated by John Wildman's friend, William Parker, the house had been the headquarters of the Commonwealth Club in the late 1650s. Because republicans still met there, Nonsuch House attracted Nicholas' attention. From a neighbor he learned that those who visited the house included Wildman, Praisegod Barebone, Sir John Lenthall, Henry Neville, James Harrington, Colonel Edward Salmon, and Major Haynes, as well as the royalist postmaster-general, Colonel Henry Bishop, and his clerks.[94] This, however, was no more than an excuse for further surveillance.

Suspicion deepened when the widow of Major William Smith reported that two clerks of the post office had illegally tampered with the mail in her inn at Hounslow on the night of 24 November. After they spent two hours examining the mail, possibly looking for informers' reports, they instructed the carrier to say nothing of what had transpired. When Nicholas learned of this, he moved at once on the 25th to have Barebone, Harrington, and Samuel Moyer arrested on charges of treason. Harrington's warrant charged him with high treason for conspiring to change the government "and for that purpose contriveing and designeing to meet and assemble att sett and appointed times and places, and meeting and assembling accordingly." The following day Harrington, Wildman, Haynes, and John Ireton were incarcerated in the Tower. Warrants followed for Colonel Salmon on the 29th and John Portman, the Fifth Monarchist and former secretary to the Generals at Sea, on 5 December.[95]

From the interrogation of the suspects by members of the Privy Council it is possible to reconstruct what the government thought had occurred. In essence, a design to alter the government had supposedly begun in March with discussions for the forthcoming parliamentary elections. A group of twenty or more, including Harrington, Wildman, Ireton, John Fowke, and William Love, met at an alehouse in Covent Garden, where Harrington allegedly spoke for some thirty minutes on the need to restore the Long Parliament or bring in a new one. A subsequent meeting attended by Barebone, Haynes, Moyer, Portman, Neville, and Wildman in St. Martin's le Grand reportedly pursued this idea; those in attendance took an oath of secrecy. In August there was another conference, this time at the King's Head near Butcher Row, where Neville, Wildman, and Sir

Robert Harlow purportedly discussed the restoration of the Long Parliament, a petition to terminate the excise, and opposition to a standing army. A subsequent gathering at Millbank, with Harlow, Neville, Wildman, and a Mr. Pretty present, again reportedly discussed an oath of secrecy and agreed to continue meeting as a private committee. From this group, the government believed, an invitation was sent to certain disbanded officers and purchasers of crown lands to meet in London by 10 December. Their design allegedly included an "attempt" on Monck and seizure of the gates of the City. Officials also suspected these men of being in contact with the Spanish ambassador.[96]

Secretary Nicholas was not unduly concerned about what the government had learned. "All things continue well and quiett here," he wrote to the earl of Winchilsea on 5 December, "notwithstanding the inveterate malice of the phanaticks."[97] In good time, he thought, Parliament would effectively deal with them. On the 11th a delegation from the House of Commons, after informing Charles that members had received letters from nearly every county regarding a universal conspiracy, urged him to defend the kingdom from the rebels. Clarendon thereupon presented an account of the plot to the House of Lords on the 19th. Based on intercepted letters as well as communications from several parts of the country, the chancellor announced that the king believed "divers discontented Persons are endeavouring to raise new Troubles, to the Disturbance of the Peace of the Kingdom."[98] Clarendon was stretching the truth, for the only letters in the State Papers that the government intercepted appear to be those allegedly by Anne Ba.

The two Houses appointed a joint committee to examine Clarendon's evidence and report after the Christmas recess. According to his version of the plot, the rebels had a committee of twenty-one, with three persons representing each faction: the City, the Long Parliament, the Commonwealthsmen, the Rump, the dispossessed purchasers of crown lands, the disbanded officers, and the sectaries. Harrington and Wildman were part of the Commonwealth contingent. With the exception of the Long Parliament's representatives, the others reportedly met regularly and also established a select committee of seven to carry out the design. An oath of secrecy was supposedly taken. Five members of the committee of seven had been arrested by the 19th, according to Clarendon.[99] They must have been among the eight prominent radicals recently apprehended: Barebone, Harrington, Haynes, John Ireton, Moyer, Portman, Salmon, and Wildman.

After Parliament resumed sitting, Clarendon provided further details of the conspiracy, noting in particular that a list of 160 ex-officers had been found on Salmon when he was arrested. Their plan was allegedly to gain control of Bristol, Coventry, Shrewsbury, and other towns in late January, launching the insurrection with a series of assassinations. From his anonymous informer, a member (he said) of the committee of twenty-one, Clarendon claimed he also learned that the regicides in exile were receiving encouragement from foreign princes, stockpiling armaments, and corresponding with dissidents in England. Another informant reported that rebels in Huntingdon, pretending to be Quakers, were riding at night in substantial numbers. As a precaution Albemarle stationed two troops in Coventry and a like number in Shrewsbury.[100]

According to Ludlow, who presumably got his information from correspondents, the parliamentary committee's inability to find substantial evidence of the Nonsuch House plot led to widespread skepticism among even "the greatest cavaleers." Once again, such evidence as the chancellor accumulated was inadequate to demonstrate the existence of a major conspiracy, at least in a court of law, though he had no qualms about manipulating the allegations for the government's benefit. There was, however, just enough substance in the accusations to provide the state with an excuse to keep the principals interred for years. Harrington was detained on St. Nicholas Island near Plymouth to prevent his release on a writ of habeas corpus, and Salmon was still a prisoner at Castle Cornet in Guernsey in 1671. Portman remained in prison in 1667, the year Wildman was finally released after detention on the Scilly Isles (with Ireton) and at Pendennis Castle in Cornwall.[101] Moyer too was freed in 1667. In sharp contrast Barebone was out in July 1662, which may suggest that he was Clarendon's informer among the inner circle.

Rumors were fairly widespread that the plot was a vehicle to establish a professional army. According to Pepys, Clarendon seized upon the conspiracy "to raise fears in the people, [and] did project the raising of an army forthwith, besides the constant Militia, thinking to make the Duke of Yorke Generall thereof." While Parliament did not go that far, it did approve the use of troops to ensure the safety of Coventry and Shrewsbury, request the trial of Lambert and Vane, and push ahead with the bills for religious uniformity and the corporations. In his opening speech to the Cavalier Parliament, the king had referred ominously to "many wicked instruments, still as active as ever, who labour night and day to disturb the public peace." The Presbyterian, Yarrington, and

Nonsuch House plots seemed to corroborate his concern and undoubtedly helped pave the way for smoother passage of the Corporation Act on 19 December.[102] There is no substantive evidence to accuse the government of fabricating the plots, but it showed no reticence to use the rumors and allegations for its own purposes.

## Radical Traces

While the government was investigating the Yarrington and Nonsuch House plots, there were numerous reports of other radical activity, centered as usual around ex-officers and sectarian preachers. One of the fullest accounts of radical activity in late 1661 was provided to Secretary Nicholas by Captain William Pestell on 28 November. From his sources Pestell learned of Fifth Monarchist activity in Yorkshire, Durham, Yarmouth, and Devonshire. Preachers such as Christopher Feake, John Belcher, Carnsew Helme, Anthony or Thomas Palmer, and John Canne were reportedly traveling from county to county to "blow up the Coales of rebellion." Their disciples met at the home of the wealthy brewer, Mr. Andrews, of the Limehouse, where Belcher had recently visited. Their scribe, accountant, and treasurer was William Medley, Venner's son-in-law, who was assisted by the scrivener Thomas Coates and the widow, Mrs. Harding, "a very violent woman." Pestell also told the secretary that Captain Owen Cox, another Vennerite, had a ship laden with 350 barrels of powder and seventy pieces of ordnance at Sandwich, though he had recently been arrested for seditious language. Pestell dispatched an informant to the Netherlands to obtain more knowledge about the exile community.[103]

About the same time, the government received further intelligence in the form of a list of suspicious ex-officers and sectarian ministers in London. According to an informer, such men were "the most probable to be acting and contriving mischief and . . . are the most dangerous in respect of the turbulency of their Spiritts, the decay of their fortunes, the disappointment of their aspireing ambitions[,] their experience in Armes, and their reputation amongst the Soldiers of the Late disbanded Army." Many of the latter were reportedly in London with their horses and arms prepared to revolt. On the list were such names as Colonel Packer (imprisoned in October), Major-General Kelsey (an exile in the Netherlands), Colonel Philip Twisleton, Colonel Henry Danvers, Captain Richard Deane (former treasurer-at-war), Lieutenant-Colonel Jeffrey Ellison, the Fifth Monarchist Captain Thomas Buttevant,

Captain Henry Hedworth (implicated in the 1654 Overton plot), and Captain Richard Burnell, who had served in Ireland. The same list included the names of four Fifth Monarchists, "men of violent spiritts and dangerous principles as to government": Cokayne, Feake, John Rogers, and John Clarke. Mention was also made of Barebone and the General Baptist Jeremiah Ives. A separate list recorded the names of eight cashiered officers in London, among them Colonels Richard Ashfield and John Mason, and Majors Thomas Johnson and Richard Salway. The Major Baines on the list was possibly Captain Adam Baynes.[104]

Reports from the counties fueled suspicion. From Hampshire Sir Robert Mason asked Nicholas for a commission to search for suspicious papers because "there are some contrivances hereabouts of daungerous Consequence." On 11 November a Wrexham man reported that in Denbigh "Blood-thirsty men . . . are bewitched for Rebellion." The informer Edward Potter sent word to Sir Edward Broughton on the 20th that former officers were going among the numerous dissidents in Essex, Suffolk, and Norfolk, where the fanatics supposedly had the best horses in the county.[105] The same week the state decided to proceed capitally against a man who spoke treasonably against the king at Salisbury. In Oxfordshire a group of Baptists was arrested on the 24th because seditious words were used in their meeting. On the night of the 21st two men stopped one of Lord Falkland's lieutenants; when he told them he was "for God & king Charles," one of the men, after retorting that he was "for God & Greene Sleeves," shot the lieutenant. Another of Falkland's men found a suspicious letter in the bag of a Devon carrier. The movements of the Particular Baptist minister Paul Hobson also attracted suspicion: After his return to Durham he and Thomas Lomes were arrested by the bishop, but were soon bailed. When the deputy lieutenants wanted to interrogate Hobson in November, he fled to London.[106] He may have already been establishing the contacts that led to the Northern plots in 1663.

Nicholas believed that yet another conspiracy had been detected in late November. The lord lieutenant for Derbyshire, the earl of Devonshire, had arrested Captain Robert Hope, a member of Colonel Robert Lilburne's regiment in the 1650s, as well as his sons because of an allegedly seditious letter written to them by William Clare. The secretary ordered Devonshire to apprehend Clare and confiscate the papers of the Hopes along with letters addressed to a Mr. Bennet. Directions were also given for the arrest of Colonel Hawksworth and other notorious persons.

There was also a reported plot in Lancashire about the same time. What little is known about it was taken from a letter found in Preston indicating "that the surprisall of 5 [justices?] that were there would render the whole county unto the enemies hands." Roger Lawrey was believed to be involved because he admitted knowing some of the schemers. Squadrons of horse were called out to protect the county. Authorities may have thought that the suspect letter related to the Yarrington or Nonsuch House plots.[107]

There was some awareness at Westminster of the danger of imprisoning the innocent, though this was not allowed to impede investigations of suspicious persons. On 31 December Nicholas ordered the deputy lieutenants of Northumberland to examine such individuals in order to discover any incipient designs. Four days later, however, he had to direct the deputy lieutenants in Here-fordshire to look more carefully at purportedly seditious correspondence because Charles believed that the accused were victims of malice.[108]

One of the clearest examples of forged evidence was a letter that implicated the Particular Baptist William Kiffin. Nicholas received the letter in question on 9 October, but it was dated 25 December 1660, at Taunton, Somerset. The letter was supposedly written by Colonel Francis Buffett to Nathaniel Crabb, a London silkthrower. In it the author prophesied that "all the sonnes and daughters of Beliall will be destroyed, for we doe intend to venter our lives, to bee assisting unto you all, & to as many faithfull Brethren as are under the hands of Tyranny." He went on to condemn the king for his unfaithfulness, especially in breaking the Covenant. Jessey, Kiffin, John Griffith, and their friends were exhorted "nott to drawe backe their hands from doing the Lords worke; for it is said by the Lord, that one shall frighten a thousand." In practical terms, the author urged the saints to amass as much powder and weapons as possible before Easter 1661. Monck and other members of the Council examined Kiffin, who staunchly professed his innocence. When he was questioned by Lord Chief Justice Foster, Kiffin satisfied him that the letter was a forgery because of inconsistencies in the dating. Kiffin, Jessey, and Griffith were released.[109]

The possibility that charges against former military personnel or sectarian clergy could be grounded on nothing more than a forged letter or a malicious accusation should have induced a healthy skepticism in the minds of government officials. The king, in fact, seems to have been less willing than his advisers to accept some of the stories, and Pepys was even more dubious. But the greatest skeptic (for different reasons) was Ludlow, who deeply resented the linking of his name to repeated plots. Wrongfully blaming the authorities for most of this, he bitterly wrote in exile that "as they contynued their old trade of scoffing at religion, and the professours thereof, so of carrying on their mischeiveous designes by lyes and fictions."[110]

There were traces of radical activity too in the post office, a potential source of powerful opposition, particularly in its early years. Because of his expertise in matters of intelligence and his financial suport for Colonel Henry Bishop, the postmaster-general, John Wildman exercised substantial influence in the post office at the Restoration. He and his friends were in a position to monitor the flow of intelligence throughout the country, which occasioned complaints by concerned conservatives. There were objections in 1660 and 1661 about the presence in the postal service of such dissidents as Cornelius Glover, a former servant of Hugh Peter, the Leveller Thomas Chapman, and the Baptist Clement Oxenbridge. In the judgment of Humphrey Cantell, postmaster at Newbury, various members of the postal service were "ill affected to the government," and none, he said, had taken the oath of allegiance by December 1660. Cantell also complained that Wildman, Oxenbridge, and a Baptist named Thompson were employing and firing persons at will. The postmaster on the Isle of Wight, a "schismatical knave" who had been appointed by the Rump Parliament, was suspended by Colonel Walter Slingsby when packets were mishandled.[111]

Some of the attention attracted by the post office in 1661 was due to dissatisfaction with Bishop, but there were also complaints about dissidents who continued to hold positions. There was even an accusation that Bishop was under Wildman's control. Sir Edward Hales complained to Nicholas that he could not obtain sufficient intelligence because of a postmaster named Gilpin, "an Ill principled and disaffected person."[112] Although Marsh, the postmaster at Preston, was not a royalist, authorities nevertheless discovered a letter in December of 1661 that revealed a plot. Nine Yorkshire gentlemen pushed for the removal of William Browne, postmaster at Wakefield and a former soldier in the parliamentary army, on the grounds that he was "Like to disperse the Intelligence of fannaticks & malecontents." The problem dragged on, and in May 1662 Sir Philip Musgrave complained to Nicholas that many "dishonest hands" in the post office "still continue who have evel will to Sion.[113]

Considering the importance of controlling the flow of intelligence, it is odd that the government was so remiss in its leisurely purge of the postal service. When loyalists were in charge, the radicals had to resort to alternate means of communication. By April 1661, it was no longer safe to use the London post office, hence most letters were directed to Zachary Standard in Bear Lane. For special communications they reportedly relied on a network of thirty messengers who stayed only at friends' houses and never longer than one night at each place. The government had a loyalist in the post office at Northallerton, Yorkshire, who monitored the correspondence between four Scottish clergymen and residents of the Berwick area. In April 1662 the postmaster at York, who had the king's permission to open the letters of suspected persons, reported that he had found information about "the Presbyterian design."[114] But it was not until May 1663 that the government issued a proclamation giving all postmasters six months to produce a certificate of conformity to the Church of England or be dismissed. The proclamation also prohibited anyone but the addressee from opening a letter without a warrant from a secretary of state. The same month Secretary Bennet directed mayors and other magistrates to arrest anyone carrying letters for hire without a license from the postmaster general.[115] By the time these regulations went into effect, the government had navigated through the dangerous waters of the Tong and Dublin plots and was in the midst of the unfolding crisis in the north.

Although 1661 began with the violent insurrection of the Vennerites, the rest of the year passed with little more than a steadily rising river of allegations and rumors. The coronation was not disrupted, nor did the radicals take up arms to champion their cause. They did, however, stockpile weapons and meet regularly to share their fears and aspirations. The failure of the Savoy Conference (5 April–23 July) to reach an accommodation between advocates of episcopacy and presbyterianism was a harbinger of future trouble, as the ranks of Nonconformity swelled considerably. When Convocation approved the revised Book of Common Prayer on 20 December, the stage was set for the reimposition of uniformity by Parliament in the spring of 1662. As the dark clouds of religious persecution began to build on the horizon, manifestations of popular discontent quickened. Rumors of radical scheming, however, played into the hands of those who advocated a narrow religious settlement and thus ironically facilitated the triumph of a narrow Anglican exclusivism.

# 3

# "The Glory Is Departed"

## RADICALS AND THE GREAT EJECTION

### Restless Spirits

The discontent that contributed to the government's skittishness intensified throughout 1662, especially as the country moved toward a narrow religious settlement and the honeymoon period of the new ruler ebbed. The 1650s began to look rosier as memories faded, and there were pronounced sentiments favoring both republicanism and the house of Cromwell. When a group of diehards at Taunton, Somerset, drank a toast to Colonel Richard Buffett (or Bovett) in July, they proclaimed that "Olde Dicke should be old Dick still: and that they would bee for the old Olivers Creation, and things weare not as they would bee, but ere longe they should bee."[1] Reflecting on the Protectorate, a Westmorland man opined that it had been such a time of peace that it would be worth decapitating all kings in order to return to such days. In the North Riding a yeoman was cited in the quarter sessions for claiming that Cromwell and Ireton were as good as the king. Referring to Charles II, a Somerset man warned in August: "Lett this younge Rogue take heed that his head be not cutt of[f] as his fathers was."[2] It is hardly surprising that some of Secretary Nicholas' correspondents cautioned him that the "ill humours" that disturbed the kingdom in the 1640s and 1650s were still very much in evidence.[3]

The government busied itself confiscating arms and searching for suspects. Concerned about meetings of armed dissidents near

Deptford in January, the king directed a constable with a band of volunteers to seize all concealed weapons in Blackheath Hundred. In March, London authorities discovered that the grocer Thomas Bone had some twelve pounds of powder and six of bullets hidden in his garret. Bone not only had ties to the Fifth Monarchist preacher Anthony Palmer, who told him "thes times cannot last long," but was also sending provisions to men incarcerated in the Tower for treason.[4] So jittery were some loyalists that they were suspicious even of the monthly collections taken up by the Quakers to support their religious work. These collections as well as their missionary work, according to two of Joseph Williamson's informers, "may give to[o] great an opportunity to malicious dissatisfied spiritts, through such like pretences to effect their dangerous designes."[5]

Among those whom the authorities tried to apprehend in 1662 was the Fifth Monarchist John Portman, who had instigated a riot in Newgate prison in April 1661 and had subsequently demanded vengeance on those responsible for Thomas Harrison's execution. John Alured the younger, son of the regicide and a veteran of service in Ireland, was arrested in February because he refused to leave London and was observed lurking around the palace. Timothy Roberts, vicar of Barton, Westmorland, was arrested in March simply because he refused to use the Book of Common Prayer and administer the Lord's supper, but he was a man of thoroughly radical views who associated with the Fifth Monarchists in 1663 and endorsed political violence in 1665.[6]

Manifestations of discontent took many forms. At Macclesfield, Cheshire, dissidents cut the king's arms from his proclamations. In June three women and two men broke into the parish church at Ashford, Middlesex, where they spoke contumaciously against the government and the Book of Common Prayer.[7] There was a similar occurrence at Beverley, Yorkshire the previous month, when the people tried to force open the chancel doors to prevent the minister from officiating. Their favorite was the Presbyterian Joseph Wilson, a man condemned by conservatives as "factious and seditious in his practice in what concernes the civill Government and schismaticall as to the Ecclesiasticall." The strength of the dissident community in London was reflected the same month when over 2,000 people attended funeral services for the Fifth Monarchist Cornet Wentworth Day, who died while a prisoner in the Gatehouse. Among the mourners, who ranged from Presbyterians to Quakers, were Joseph Caryl, Thomas Brooks, Robert Bragge, and Edward Pearse.[8]

Unwittingly, the government fanned the embers of discontent by its treatment of prominent radicals. In late January the Uxbridge Baptist Goody Roberts reportedly averred that there would be a plot to revenge "this bloud that was suddainly to bee spilt." The desire to avenge the executions of radical leaders was also at the root of discontent in Colonel Henry Washington's regiment, where dissidents were "fully resolved to try one bout" against the Restoration regime.[9] The leaders were corporals in contact with ex-soldiers. The informant who gathered this information, Richard Blackburn, subsequently learned from Roger Butters, a former parliamentary soldier, that he and nineteen other ex-troopers in Aylesbury had planned to rise the previous Christmas but were discovered. They still met, however, ready to raise a troop of experienced horse in an hour's time. At the end of February, Secretary Nicholas ordered surveillance on one Norton, a former member of Cromwell's Life Guards, who had come from Gainsborough to London with a message from ex-officers to the effect that conspirators would act as soon as the king had gone a good distance from the City. Nicholas took special note because Norton passed his message to a former servant of Lambert's.[10]

In addition to those who died the previous October, John Barkstead, Miles Corbet, and John Okey were hanged, drawn, and quartered at Tyburn on 19 April. When the king subsequently learned that Okey's relatives were preparing a large funeral, he ordered his remains privately interred in the Tower and an investigation of those who planned the obsequies. According to Ludlow, the 20,000 people who gathered for the funeral were angered when the sheriff forced them to disperse. (The bishop of Derry estimated the crowd at a more modest 5,000.)[11] The sectaries were drawn closer together when they responded positively to a request from Sir Henry Vane and John Lambert to set apart a special day of prayer on the eve of their trials. As Vane was transported to Tower Hill for his execution on 14 June, cries of support rang out from the people who lined the route. Vane's status as a radical martyr was enhanced by the publication soon after his execution of *The Life and Death of Sir Henry Vane*, which included a sonnet of tribute by John Milton.[12]

Executing radical leaders intensified dissident hatred. Incensed that the regicides and Vane had been "barbarously murthered," Major Clayton allegedly declared that "if we had but knowne that the times would have come to this pass," more soldiers would have joined forces to assist Lambert. Former Cromwellian officers were now ready to help in the counties, he averred, adding that there were thousands of discontented persons. A Lancashire yeoman reportedly talked extravagantly of the rebels' ability to raise an army of 30,000 to 40,000 to punish the king, who deserved to die, particularly because of Harrison's execution.[13] There was also a report that Praisegod Barebone, Colonel Mills (John Mill?), Alderman Timothy Wade, Humphrey Primale, and many other sectaries and Presbyterians in the London area, as well as former officers in northern and western England, were engaged in a design to impose judgment on Charles and his Council because of their "tyrannizing and the shedding the blood of the people of God." The regicides, said a Nottinghamshire gentleman, were honest men; he could have added that the government had made some of them into martyrs.[14]

Even without the punishment of the radical leaders, there was ample cause for unrest in 1662 over such matters as fresh taxes and high food prices. But one of the most irksome of the government's actions was the decision to sell Dunkirk, a source of pride when the Cromwellians acquired it. Now some swore that "Oliver would have sold his great Nose rather than Dunkirk."[15] Yet from the government's perspective, selling Dunkirk not only improved relations with France and reduced expense but eliminated a source of some radical strength. In September 1661, for instance, Lord Rutherford had complained of "the malignant humors of the old ill principled officers" in Dunkirk, who hoped to prevent the king from asserting mastery in the town. One of those whom Rutherford wanted to cashier at that time was Major Francis Conway, who purportedly spoke derogatorily of Charles in the marketplace.[16] As late as August 1662, on the eve of Dunkirk's return, Rutherford complained to Nicholas that there were still sectaries in the garrison, and asked that no one be permitted to come from England without a pass for fear that Dunkirk might otherwise become a den of thieves. He apprehended two brothers, one "ane old levelling Rogue," who were accused of writing scandalous material intended to instigate a revolt in the garrison. One brother confessed, but the Leveller was hanged despite his protestations of innocence. The king himself recommended the replacement of Brown, the muster master, because of his record of supporting rebellious activity.[17] Returning Dunkirk to the French was a convenient means to resolve the problem of festering discontent in an enclave across the Channel, though the state's considerations were not limited to this factor alone.

As a rule, those who viewed the Restoration regime with disdain were disenchanted on both political and religious grounds. At Gloucester, a man who denounced king and Parliament alike as fools likewise railed against the prelates. A good deal of the hostility toward the king was in fact based on religious considerations, particularly a hatred of prelacy and popery. John Pyne of Curry Mallet, Somerset, reportedly charged the king with establishing Catholicism, while a Middlesex man asserted that "if the Kinge did side with the Bishops, the divell take Kinge and the Bishops too."[18] All of this bred a spirit of defiance, as typified by Colonel William Stroud's boast to the deputy lieutenants of Somerset that he would never conform to their orders or to the rule of bishops.[19] For those of similar persuasion, one alternative was exile, typically in the Netherlands.

## The Exile Community in 1661–62

The government first began to demonstrate serious interest in the activities of the exiles on the eve of the coronation. In March 1661 Secretary Nicholas provided John Wright, an agent of Sir William Davidson, with a warrant to apprehend convicted traitors in Amsterdam and expressed a particular interest in designs timed for the coronation. There was a report the same month that John Desborough and other English refugees were holding weekly meetings at Sédan in which they prayed for God to avenge the blood of his servants and overthrow the tyrannical Stuart regime. According to Colonel Joseph Bampfield (or Bamfield), a government spy, Desborough, Ludlow, and other officers were willing to head a party of rebels. In May exiles were responsible for printing papers attacking the oath of allegiance. Thomas Tracey and three other Great Yarmouth men were arrested for smuggling the papers into England, where they were distributed by Quakers.[20]

A more systematic attempt to acquire intelligence about the exiles began with the appointment of Sir George Downing, a former preacher in Colonel Okey's regiment and scoutmaster-general under Cromwell, as ambassador to the Hague in June.[21] "A crafty, fawning man," as Bishop Burnet aptly described him, Downing "was ready to turn to every side that was uppermost, and to betray those who by their former friendship and services thought they might depend on him." One of his responsibilities was to keep track of the exiles, and for this purpose he had special funds for intelligence gathering. Beginning in February 1662 he expended approximately £1,000 a year in this endeavor. His counterpart in Brussels, Sir William Temple, also paid out substantial sums to gather information throughout the Netherlands and the German states. Among those he watched was Desborough.[22]

Downing's first task was to track the movements of the regicides until they could be apprehended and returned to England. The work was complicated by the growing number of refugees, the tendency of the regicides to move from place to place, and their spread into other states. When one of Downing's agents reported in July that Miles Corbet had gone to Germany, he added that the exiles were "going to strange places, where they may not be discovered."[23] The same month John Hewson reportedly intended to leave Rotterdam for Strasbourg, where John Okey had been spotted. Ill health, however, kept Hewson in the Netherlands, and he died in Amsterdam. By the fall Corbet and Cornelius Holland, a member of the regicide court, were spending most of their time at Zwolle and Kampen, northeast of Amsterdam, but they maintained regular contact with Abraham Kicke in Delft. When Downing discovered this, he offered Kicke £200 apiece for the apprehension of the two and threatened him with ruin if he failed. Okey, Corbet, and three of their fellow regicides—Valentine Walton, John Dixwell, and Sir John Barkstead—settled at Hanau, near Frankfurt.[24] To deal with them, Downing suggested to Clarendon on 1 November that "the King should authorize and send some trusty person to kill them." Clarendon responded with an offer of help from Lieutenant-Colonel John Griffith, but thought the king would never order the regicides' assassination.[25]

In the meantime, Downing employed his agents to learn as much as possible about other dissidents in the Netherlands. Coronet George Joyce, a prominent advocate of Charles I's trial, and Lieutenant-Colonel Paul Hobson were seen at Rotterdam in June. Hobson was there with the Fifth Monarchists Thomas Tillam and Christopher Pooley as part of their effort to elicit support to establish a godly community in the Palatinate. Hobson preached to the Congregationalists in Rotterdam under the guise of being the physician Dr. Love, but the trio returned to England in late July. Another prominent radical in Rotterdam was Edward Dendy, sergeant-at-arms to the committee of safety in 1659.[26] One of Downing's clerks compiled a list of dissidents and their Dutch contacts. Among the names were those of Captain Timothy Clare, who had fought in Lambert's rising, Major Richard Wagstaffe, the Congregationalist John Collins, formerly one of Monck's chaplains, Captain John Mason, and the Congregationalist William Greenhill, wrongfully suspected of complicity in Venner's rising. Another list was compiled in February 1662 of "the most disaffected Englishmen now in Amsterdam." They were accused of supporting the regicides, corresponding with dissidents in England, and castigating the English church and monarchy. The list contained the names of twenty-three men, mostly merchants, artisans, and professionals. At least some—Charles Goodhand, Henry May, Nathaniel Arnold, and probably Francis Prince—were affiliated with the Congregationalist church in Amsterdam.[27]

As early as July 1661, Downing spoke with Jan De Witt, the *de facto* head of the Dutch government, about the necessary authority to arrest the regicides, but it was not until the following March that a fit opportunity presented itself. In December Barkstead had informed Kicke that he and Okey would secretly come to Delft in late February or early March, but Kicke passed the letter to Downing, who in turn informed Clarendon. When Downing learned of Barkstead and Okey's arrival on 4 March, he applied to the Estates for a warrant. On the 6th De Witt procured it for him, and that evening Downing directed the arrest of Barkstead, Okey, and Corbet at Kicke's house.[28] Although De Witt obtained an extradition order from the Estates, the magistrates at Delft, encouraged by their counterparts in Amsterdam, balked at releasing the prisoners. Moreover, two Englishmen in Rotterdam (probably the merchants Dawson and Welch) offered lucrative bribes if the regicides were allowed to escape, forcing Downing to counter with bribes of his own. The prisoners denied their role in the trial of Charles I and insisted that they were Presbyterians who planned to invest £10,000 to establish the clothing industry at Delft. The wives of General Thomas Kelsey and Colonel John White tried to aid them, but the Estates ordered the magistrates to release the prisoners to Downing on the 13th. Within a week they had been taken to England and lodged in the Tower. To cover his expenses, Downing received £1,200 from Clarendon. Barkstead, Corbet, and Okey, as we have seen, were executed at Tyburn on 19 April "before an immense crowd."[29]

As Downing turned his attention to the pursuit of other regicides and dissidents, Clarendon gloomily remarked that "Amsterdam and the other towns will not be easily trusted again by their friends here." Still, he wanted Downing to press ahead with the work. On the 28th Downing reported to Clarendon that the regicides Valentine Walton, Daniel Blagrave, and Sir Michael Livesey were in the Hanau region, while Ludlow had recently been seen in Geneva. Kelsey and John Turner, a dyer at Delft, were reported to be "active underhand." There was renewed activity in the exile community in August, when 400 pairs of pistols were discovered at Breda, allegedly en route to Quakers in England. The same month Kicke reported that Desborough and White had gone to Germany. Late in the year, various suspects in the Tong plot, especially Thomas Cole, Edward Radden, and Mr. Spurway, sought refuge with the exiles.[30]

The Scottish community in the Netherlands also grew in this period as a stream of exiled ministers made their way abroad, primarily to Rotterdam. The minister at Airth, James Simpson, arrived in the autumn of 1661. For refusing to observe the anniversary of Charles I's death and take the oath of allegiance, John Livingstone was banished in December 1662; he died in Rotterdam nearly a decade later. The minister at Newmills, John Nevay, banished the same month for refusing the oath, also went to Rotterdam, as did the Edinburgh pastor Robert Trail.[31]

Some exiles rejected the Netherlands as a place of refuge, it being, as Ludlow insisted, "a country which depended so much on England as I knew they did upon the account of trade," and therefore unsafe for exiles. The regicides William Cawley and John Lisle were with Ludlow in Geneva when news of the betrayal of Barkstead and Okey arrived. For reasons of security the three moved to Lausanne. There they were joined by Dendy, Holland, the regicide William Say, Nicholas Love, who sat on the regicide court but did not sign the death warrant, Andrew Broughton and John Phelps, both commissioners on the court, Colonel John Biscoe, who had supported Lambert in 1659, and Slingsby Bethel, a critic of both the protectorate and the monarchy. In the autumn of 1662, Ludlow, Lisle, Cawley, Say, Love, Bethel, and Holland moved to Vevey on the shores of Lake Geneva for greater safety, leaving Dendy and Broughton in Lausanne. Phelps and Biscoe traveled between the Netherlands and Germany.[32]

At Vevey, Ludlow and his friends enjoyed the protection of the Bern government. Ludlow's mail, addressed to friends and landlords, was rarely intercepted as it came by ordinary post via Lyons and Geneva. Through his letters he kept abreast of events in England, and became increasingly bitter about the association of his name with conspiracy after conspiracy. Yet his sympathy clearly lay with the Nonconformists. Among those he admired were Edward Bagshaw, Henry Jessey, Vavasor Powell, Praisegod Barebone, and Thomas Brooks. Nevertheless, he opposed premature rebellion, convinced "that when the Lord's tyme is come we may up and be doing." In the meantime he advised the Nonconformists to do no more than "endeavour to wynne" their enemies to their own spiritual persuasion. Ludlow was a far cry from being the head of all the conspiracies, as Bishop Parker charged, though the mere evocation of his name seems to have inspired some radicals and contributed to the government's nervousness.[33]

From the government's standpoint, the existence of an exile community was not wholly negative. By its very nature it provided an alternative to disobedience for those who refused to accept the political and religious policies of the Stuart monarchy. But an exile community could only be an effective safety valve if it was shorn of those who could provide strong, militant leadership and who had the potential to influence foreign governments against the Stuart state. For these reasons as well as the more obvious desire to avenge the execution of Charles I, Clarendon and his master demanded the apprehension of the exiled regicides. The 1662 Anglo-Dutch treaty, which provided for the return of regicides in the Netherlands and the banishment of other rebels within twenty-eight days of an English request, gave Charles, at least in theory, the power to deprive the principal exile community of its leaders. Beyond this the government could not go. Given the commerce between the two states and the impossibility of closing the borders, any attempt to choke off relatively free movement was out of the question. The authorities could and did watch for shipments of illegal weapons and literature, and they tried to keep track of the movement of the more important dissidents. When Hobson, Tillam, and Pooley returned from the Netherlands in July 1661, for example, their arrival at Lowestoft, Suffolk, was duly observed.[34] The very existence of an exile community provided the disaffected with opportunities for some of their leaders to rendezvous as well as a place to print surreptitious publications and a general haven from persecution and arrest. As the government proceeded to implement Parliament's program of religious uniformity, the community of exiles offered a welcome alternative to those who preferred emigration to suffering or rebellion.

## To St. Bartholomew's and Beyond

The ejection was made more embittering by the unrealized hopes of the spring. In April the struggle in the House of Lords to accommodate those who in conscience refused to wear the surplice and use the sign of the cross in baptism raised the prospect of a compromise. The lord chancellor even supported a move not to force men of tender consciences to renounce the Covenant. For a time the Presbyterians in particular were hopeful, but with the passage of a narrow Act of Uniformity their mood quickly changed. The Venetian resident informed his government that the Act "causes a great stir in England

and Scotland, chiefly among the Presbyterians," while the French ambassador concluded that the Act inspired conspiracies, especially by the more fanatical groups who remained unintimidated.[35] In fact, however, the Presbyterians appear to have done little more than consult with each other as to whether to conform. At Bolton, Lancashire, for instance, over twenty ministers met in June to explore their options. The bishop of Lincoln probably reflected the view of most prelates when he remarked that many clergy would conform out of "worldly interests."[36]

As the country moved closer to the great ejection, religious tensions increased. "A storme appears," wrote one of the godly, "which should teach us to cast off any weight least we sink in it & cling to each other." Conventicle activity and provocative—sometimes inflammatory—preaching were a continuing problem in this period. Edmund Calamy was so worried by what he observed that in March he pleaded for moderation "lest the Gospell [be] quite lost."[37] The state was already prosecuting dissident clergy on charges of seditious preaching. For castigating the polity of the Church of England as popish and superstitious and for blaming the government for inciting the people to "Will-worship," Henry Field, the ejected rector of Uffington, Lincolnshire, was arrested in the autumn of 1661, fined £500 in King's Bench, and committed to the Gatehouse, where he died in 1662. For a sermon preached in October 1661, Andrew Parsons, rector of Wem, Shropshire, was accused the following May of seditious preaching, fined £200, and imprisoned.[38] In June the Presbyterian Elias Pledger, rector of St. Antholin's, London, reportedly preached that those who governed England followed the "divelish dictates" of Machiavelli and enforced human traditions in divine worship, including prescribed ceremonies and "dead" homilies. The congregation reacted by lamenting the impending ejection of the godly clergy and murmuring against the government. There were fears that England had entered into an age of apostasy.[39]

As radical activity intensified in the spring, the king directed Sir Richard Browne to commit suspicious persons to the Tower. On the same day (18 May), several prominent radicals were placed under closer guard. Major-General James Berry and Major John Breman were secured in the Tower, while Colonel William Packer and John Gladman were transferred from the Fleet to the Gatehouse. On the 19th the chancellor warned the House of Lords that the republicans were an enemy within who sought to "overthrow and abolish the Law, which they know to be their irreconcileable Enemy." He was also critical of those who used religion as a cloak for their political designs, adding that they were encouraged "from Abroad," presumably meaning the exile community.[40] Sir Henry Bennet urged the king to secure London with troops and to take suitable precautions to prevent disorders throughout the country, particularly while the militia remained unsettled. He was especially worried about the potentially explosive impact of the Act of Uniformity and the collection of the hearth tax. Commencing on the 20th or 21st, the royal Guards and City militia were in fact in greater evidence, making Pepys give credence to the rumors of plots that were circulating.[41]

The earliest of the suspected spring cabals was uncovered in March or April, shortly before the Act of Uniformity was passed. Its leaders were reportedly Colonel John Biscoe (who joined Ludlow at Lausanne in October) and Captains Warham, Burell (Richard Burnell?), Wise, and Flud. Supposedly they had agents throughout England and Scotland, and met at the house of the mayor of Leeds. The same informer kept an eye on Richard Cromwell, voicing suspicion that a tenant of Colonel Edward Whalley's in the Isle of Ely might have received letters from him.[42]

One of Nicholas' informers reported on 2 June that the Fifth Monarchist Nathaniel Strange, disguised in a white cap and long beard, was holding a conventicle in Trinity Lane, London, where he hoped "to bring there designes to some Action." A warrant for his arrest was issued the next day, and another followed on the 6th for the apprehension of the Congregationalist Laurence Wise for seditious and dangerous speech. Nicholas also learned of a meeting in Southwark at which the king was referred to as a beast. Strange apparently eluded arrest, for on 11 July Nicholas ordered Sir William Tyringham to apprehend Strange "of Aylesbury." A warrant for Major Clayton's arrest had been issued on the 3rd. The government had also taken the precaution on 22 June of issuing the usual proclamation ordering cashiered officers and soldiers to leave London and Westminster by the 26th and not to return before 24 December.[43]

Illegal religious meetings were a commonplace in the London area, making some form of *de facto* toleration a virtual necessity. Nevertheless, Edward Potter tried to keep Nicholas informed of such meetings. In July Potter formulated a list of eleven seditious preachers that included Henry Jessey, George Cokayne, Thomas Carter (who had lectured at Westminster Abbey, Allhallows the Great, and St. Michael's, Crooked Lane), and Joseph Cobb, lecturer at St. Thomas' Hospital, Southwark. The king directed the lord mayor in

May to commit those who met illegally and held fasts without proper authorization. He was especially concerned about the meetings at Allhallows the Great and St. Giles', Cripplegate, and the participation of Lieutenant-Colonel Maurice Kingwell, Major George Fiennes (both of whom had served under Sir Robert Harley at Dunkirk), and Major John Hinton of Lord Rutherford's regiment. Following passage of the Act of Uniformity, the Presbyterians and Congregationalists convened a large meeting at St. Bartholomew's the Great, where they celebrated the Lord's supper and appointed a fast, after which, according to an informer, "there will be som villonnous designes."[44]

Prosecution of illegal religious activity increased in the London area in late spring and summer. The Socinian John Biddle and seven others were arrested at a meeting in the City and sent to Newgate. On 6 June Nicholas ordered the justices of the peace in Southwark to suppress conventicles and report to the Privy Council. At one of these conventicles the justices arrested approximately 100 people who had "tumultuously" gathered. The dragnet eventually led to the arrest of such prominent sectaries as the Fifth Monarchist Thomas Dafferne, the Baptist John Griffith, and the Quaker Henry Fell. John Sturgeon, a Westminster grocer who was apprehended in the summer, may have been the Fifth Monarchist of the same name. Most of those detained were yeomen, clothworkers, artisans, and shopkeepers—the middling sort—but their number also included William Ralph, a gentleman of St. Martin-in-the-Fields.[45]

In Kent the conventicle at Lee continued to cause concern. Among those in attendance were Colonels Robert Blount and Thompson along with "many" gentry, but Potter thought they would remain peaceful as long as their worship was not disrupted. In early June three militia captains reported that "dangerous ill affected" Baptists and Quakers were meeting daily, often at night, and must be suppressed. Every Sunday two hundred or more Baptists met in Cranbrook, and among them were "many strange faces," suggesting a wide appeal. There were also meetings at night in private places. At one conventicle 150 Quakers were present.[46]

To the west, Joseph Crabb, vicar of Netherbury with Beaminster, Dorset, was accused of having "generally poisoned" his parishioners "with his factious & Schismaticall Sermons & discourses." At least forty indictments were brought at Exeter in March against nonconforming ministers who refused to use the Book of Common Prayer, while others, already ejected, were cited for teaching sedition in private houses and endeavoring to start another civil war.[47] Legal harassment failed to stop them; in June the bishop of Derry observed that the Presbyterians in Exeter were preaching nothing but "dangerous" doctrines and complaining about their persecution. Early in July a group of "loose principled people" was dispersed and their leaders jailed when they refused the oaths of supremacy and allegiance. Among other things they were spreading a false rumor about an impending imposition on brass and pewter as well as a mandatory contribution from every woman for her apron strings. The case provides a ready illustration of the way sectaries utilized economic grievances and rumors to foster discontent.[48]

Elsewhere sectaries were so active in Yorkshire that in July the king directed Buckingham to arrest the Congregationalists Jeremiah Marsden and Christopher Nesse, and to suppress all disorderly meetings. At Malton fourteen men were presented at the quarter sessions on 15 July for riotous assembly "under colour of performing an act of religion." The potential for violence inherent in the religious disputes was clearly manifest in Guernsey, where the dean had to be protected by soldiers as he traveled from parish to parish. Before the year was over, however, the lieutenant-governor thought all conventicles on the island had been suppressed.[49]

Although the Quaker leadership eschewed violence in the Restoration era, the Friends were still suspected of militant schemes and were incarcerated in substantial numbers. Edward Burrough counted nearly 250 Quakers in Newgate, Bridewell, Southwark, and New prisons.[50] When Catherine of Braganza arrived in England in May, the Quakers were falsely accused of plotting to kidnap her "that so a couler may be had for the securing of them; under which pretext many honest men were clapt up." George Fox, who distinguished between peaceful Friends and potential revolutionaries, interpreted the Quaker Act signed by Charles in May to apply only to those who plotted rebellion. At the Exchange on 15 August, Pepys heard about some Quakers who had been arrested for planning to blow up the White Lion prison in Southwark, where they were being held. In fact some eighty Friends had been imprisoned there on the 3rd for attending a conventicle, though there is apparently no evidence to substantiate the rumor Pepys heard. As a rule, the Quakers were content to warn of impending judgment and to refuse the prescribed oaths.[51] Nevertheless, the evidence for the 1660s indicates that some Quakers did not follow their leaders in adopting pacifism.

During July Nicholas pieced together the outline of another plot. From the informer William Williamson he learned that ten of those allegedly involved were City men worth £100,000 apiece. The dissidents pondered whether to return the Barebones, Richard Cromwell's Parliament, or the Rump, finally deciding on the last. Their plan was to prepare the people by disseminating seditious pamphlets, and then to rise after troops had been dispatched to quell an anticipated rebellion in Scotland. According to another informer, the Commonwealth men and cashiered soldiers were coming into London in preparation for an insurrection. If Lambert was scheduled to die, they planned to engineer his escape and make him their leader. William Williamson, however, thought the republicans would not rise until the Presbyterians rebelled, because the latter were more numerous, more zealous, and wealthier. The republicans, he said, were planning a meeting in July to discuss their options if there was a "transportation before the presbyterians be toucht."[52] Further corroboration of a plot seemed to come from a letter by one J. L., a member of (John?) Griffith's congregation, to Sir Robert Wallop, who had helped Ludlow escape to the continent but was now in the Tower. The letter, dated 13 April, urged Wallop to be steadfast and "leave the rest to God whoe in His owne best time will make a way to escape." Ten days before this letter was passed to Nicholas, a warrant was issued for the arrest of Ludlow, who was thought to be in England, and Sergeant Edward Dendy. Taking no chances, at month's end the government placed troops in the castles at Chester and Shrewsbury to prevent any disturbances. A few days later the Venetian resident informed his government that the Presbyterians were fishing in troubled waters, hoping to renew the old conflict in England and Scotland.[53]

Bristol and Somerset were one of the focal points of radical activity in the summer. On 12 July two Somerset justices of the peace reported to Nicholas that they had discovered "a generall designe," as manifested in part by the refusal of dissidents to pay taxes. From an examination of a Taunton man, the justices learned that John Ellett of the same town disclosed plans for a general rising across England, with each of the four sections of the country purportedly having 7,000 rebel foot and 4,000 horse. They allegedly planned to "hew in peices" any sheriffs who opposed them, and expected the support of most of the militia. Their leaders were supposedly Vane's son and Henry Cromwell, but they also expected the marquis of Argyll to invade England with a Scottish army. Proclamation of liberty of conscience was part of their mission. Further information was provided by John Heathfield, whose source was James Hurd, a former officer under Colonel Nathaniel Rich and Captain John Barker. According to Hurd, Colonel Richard Buffett and his brother

Francis had 600 to 700 men ready to fight, while Major Colbourne had another 300. Moreover, the rebels claimed to have access to 2,000 weapons and £2,000. The scheme called for Colonel Buffett to join dissidents in London, where the rebellion was supposed to start. Hurd even insisted that Ludlow had returned to England "to head their party." The design was discussed, according to Hurd, at a meeting in Taunton attended by twenty ex-officers. In addition to the Buffetts and Colbourne, the alleged leaders were Captain Quarle, (John?) Pyne, Colonel Nathaniel Whetham of Chard, Captain Barker, and a Mr. Scut of Poole.[54]

Convinced of the likelihood of a rising, the deputy lieutenants of Somerset and Dorset, supported by Lord William Herbert, persuaded the king to authorize the arrest of suspicious persons and secure Taunton with the militia. Troops were also dispatched to Axminster. One of the Buffetts, Colbourne, Barker, Quarle, Pyne, and others were apprehended.[55] Two Somerset justices hoped to apprehend more conspirators at the Bristol fair, where the trained bands were ordered to stand guard by the deputy lieutenants of Bristol. On 6 August, however, the Somerset justices reported failure at Bristol because their agent was suspected. Nevertheless many in the southwest had been imprisoned for speaking about "the Suddaine Chainge of the present Government," though Hurd escaped.[56]

In the north too there were ominous reports of plotting throughout the summer. Significantly, concern was mounting that even the Presbyterians were becoming a threat to engage in radical political activity as a consequence of their exclusion from the corporations and the established church. There was a request to garrison Chester because the Presbyterians were so numerous in Cheshire, Lancashire, Shropshire, Staffordshire, and northern Wales. Supposedly they could raise 7,000 to 8,000 foot and 500 horse in three days because of their resolution and discipline. Presbyterian "firebrands have such power, not onely over the comon sort of p[eople] of theire perswasion but alsoe the Gentry & Nobility, that they can Leade them to what they please." According to the author of this anonymous report, the Presbyterians were discontented because of their exclusion from commissions of the peace and other official positions, as well as their dislike of the church's liturgy. The Presbyterian gentry in particular were reportedly holding numerous private meetings, and on 15 July Colonel Richard Kirkby noted that he had received word of a rebellion in Lancashire.[57]

What Kirkby learned was perhaps related to the investigation of a purported design for a rising in the north on 28 August by the Nonconformists and the Scots. There were accounts of secret meetings and "much riding in the night" by dissidents. Lancashire ministers were reputedly "very Confident, and high in their Language, little Lesse then Treason." Lord Fauconberg ordered Sir John Morley to keep a special eye on Tynemouth, Northumberland, because its deputy governor continued to employ a sectarian chaplain and many Cromwellian soldiers. The trained bands were accused of being refractory, and in any case the alleged plotters intended to disarm them. Fauconberg also observed that the gunsmiths were unusually busy preparing arms.

Some of the information was gleaned from William Hallas, a Baptist and former sergeant in Arthur Haselrig's regiment, who was promised the rank of captain in the rebel forces. Hallas told his story to two Cowsby men whom he apparently hoped to recruit on his way from Hull to see the deputy governor at Tynemouth, an old acquaintance of his.[58] When news of the suspected rising reached Shrewsbury, Francis Lord Newport, whose information indicated that the projected date was as early as 22 July, ordered suspicious persons secured. Major Richard Salway was lodged in Shrewsbury Castle, and Newport thought his brother-in-law, Major Edmund Wareing, should also be apprehended. On 10 August, however, Clarendon ordered Salway's release in the absence of any evidence against him. In mid-August, Sir John Morley and Colonel Edward Villiers, who were in touch with Lord Middleton in Scotland, were still investigating at Newcastle. Morley intended to secure the town, while Villiers was considering similar actions at Tynemouth Castle.[59]

Because of the suspected plot the government opted on 16 and 17 July to instruct all lord lieutenants and their deputies to arrest the most active dissidents and require the others to find sureties for their behavior. By late August Nicholas pieced together enough information to believe that the conspirators intended to assassinate Charles and seize the Tower and Windsor Castle on the 22nd or 23rd. Fairfax, he thought, would be the principal general, with Ludlow commanding in the west. Among the others allegedly involved were Sir George Booth, Sir Edward Massey, Major Lee, Colonel Pyne, Cornet Billing (a Quaker), and Cromwell's surgeon Mr. Hill.[60] But the 22nd and 23rd passed without incident, and on the 30th Nicholas concluded that the rumors had been without foundation, the work of "subtle" Presbyterians who hoped to instigate the sectaries to rise and then procure for themselves a royal dispensation from the Act of Uniformity. Indeed, as early as 23 July Sir Thomas Ingram discounted the alarms of a design on the grounds that no one of substance would participate, and the "giddy commons" would "stir but to their destruction."[61]

On 17 August many London ministers preached their farewell sermons, with some predicting a famine of the Word and an end of the Christian world. They preached, said one observer, "with great Temper." The mood of the Nonconformist community was aptly reflected two months later by Humphrey Davie (or Davy): "The Candlesticks are removed, the Glory is departed, & evill come upon the people of God, to the utmost." Pepys, remarking on the dissatisfaction in London, fully expected the country to "fly a- pieces" if the bishops did not replace the ejected men with good ministers.[62]

Altogether, A. G. Matthews has calculated that 1,760 ministers and 149 men at the universities and schools were ejected in England and another 120 ministers in Wales. Of the English ministers, 695 had been ejected in 1660, and another 936 followed in 1662. (The date of ejection for the remaining 129 is not known.) The largest number of 1662 ejections came in Devon (73), Essex (66), Yorkshire (52), Suffolk (50), and London and Westminster (50). In the end, more Commonwealth and Protectorate clergy conformed than were removed. In the diocese of Canterbury, for example, 100 of 140 clergy conformed in 1662; in the diocese of Winchester 140 of 184.[63]

Scattered outbreaks of violence characterized St. Bartholomew's day, 24 August. At St. Matthew's, Friday Street, where Henry Hurst had been ejected, young people derisively cried "porridge" to protest the Book of Common Prayer, than seized a copy, stomped on it, and ripped it up. According to the authorities, the violence was limited to no more than two churches and was not the work of parishioners but fanatics "raked together from both sides of *London* Bridge."[64] The Venetian resident, however, reported that in some London churches the congregations rioted, tearing robes, destroying copies of the Book of Common Prayer, dragging intruded ministers from the pulpits, and singing indecent and derisory songs. Increase Mather was informed that in many places the people took the Book of Common Prayer out of the churches and kicked it up and down the streets. In contrast, Ormond learned from one of his correspondents that the London parishioners behaved with decorum on the 24th. Although conservatives appeared to play down the disturbances, the trouble was in any case short-lived, for at the end of September Pepys was surprised that the ejections had been accomplished more peacefully than anticipated.[65]

The relative calm with which the ejections were greeted was due both to a general unwillingness of Presbyterians and Congregation-alists to resort to violent action in a purely religious matter and to the government's precautionary measures. On the 17th, according to John Evelyn, the state posted guards in London to forestall any violence inspired by the farewell sermons. The government took no chances when it received information concerning a rising in London at the end of August. For three successive nights, many citizens were apprehended.[66] One of those arrested, Henry Jessey, asserted that he had informed the lord mayor as well as Major-General Richard Browne as soon as he received news of the intended insurrection, but he disclaimed any knowledge of the rebels' identity. Another suspect, Lieutenant-Colonel Kiffin, had boasted on the 19th that he would command 700 men. Referring to the king, Kiffin reportedly said that "the People of God could never doe the Lords worke untill the Scarlett whore [Charles] was stabbed and that it might bee easely done in his owne bedchamber."[67] In the end, there was neither an assassination attempt nor an uprising in London in 1662, but certain themes of the conspiratorial talk of the summer—such as the assassination of the king, the attempt on the Tower, and the involvement of Ludlow—were incorporated into the Tong plot in the autumn.

Rumors of disturbances by Presbyterians and Congregationalists in early September prompted the authorities to commit suspicious persons to prison. A carefully orchestrated campaign was conducted in the *Kingdomes Intelligencer* to persuade the people that the transition had been accomplished peacefully, and that the Nonconformists were both few in number and socially "inconsiderable."[68] Reports to this effect were published from such places as Gloucester, Northampton, Chester, Norwich, Dorchester, and Durham. From the Isle of Wight came word that there were only two Nonconform-ists among the island's twenty-six parochial livings. The official account clearly depicted a country that was calm. Bishop Morley surmised that in any case the wealthy and powerful lay Presbyterians would not undermine the government on behalf of their ministers for fear of losing the benefits of the Act of Indemnity. Conservatives became less apprehensive of the Presbyterians because, as Daniel O'Neill informed Ormond, "those ministers that most threatened fire and sword, finding the zeal of their congregations vanish in sighs and words, now cry out against their credulity and their own folly."[69]

Although most of the Nonconformists eschewed violence and illegal protests, they refused to cease preaching. On St. Bartholo-mew's day itself, those in the pulpit included Zachary Crofton,

Thomas Manton, and William Blackmore, ejected rector of St. Peter's, Cornhill. On the 14th of October the king blamed "the bold abuses & extravagances of Preachers in the Pulpit" for inflaming "the sad distempers & confusions" that were plaguing the country. He castigated many clergymen because they inculcated in their audiences an evil opinion of their governors "by insinuating feare & jealousies" with a view to fomenting rebellion. This indictment was dispatched to the archbishops with directions to prohibit preachers from meddling with such matters as the differences between subjects and princes, the polity of the state, or limitations on royal power. Charles also instructed the prelates to enforce attendance at church, to require licenses to preach, and to forbid preaching on such deep points of divinity as free will and predestination.[70] It was an impossible order.

The royal will notwithstanding, conventicles continued unabated—and so did arrests. A calendar of inmates in the New prison includes the names of twenty-seven persons committed between 7 September and 7 December for attending conventicles or "keepinge of a preechinge howse." No less than eighty-five persons were jailed in London on 10 December for refusing the oath of allegiance. At month's end, approximately 280 Nonconformists were in Newgate and the Gatehouse; the king was willing to free them if they would take the prescribed oaths and provide security. His concern was not theology but practical obedience. Sometimes those who frequented conventicles were armed.[71] In late September authorities in Norwich dispersed about 200 persons gathered for illegal worship and seized their weapons. Officials at Plymouth feared a Baptist insurrection in October after they arrested nearly fifty of them at a conventicle; the Baptists subsequently refused to swear not to take up arms against the king. Bishop Ward undoubtedly reflected the opinion of many conservatives when he complained that the Nonconformist clergy were "gnaweing at the root of Government & religion, and to that purpose have many secret meetings & conventicles."[72]

From time to time the authorities called out the trained bands to deal with the threat posed by conventiclers. A week after St. Bartholomew's, the bands stood watch in London, their presence necessitated in part because letters revealing a conspiracy had been seized. In late October Secretary Bennet ordered Lord Lovelace, lord lieutenant of Berkshire, to suppress conventicles in that county, using military as well as civil power if necessary. About the same time Bristol magistrates were utilizing the militia to prevent disturbances. In the absence of the lord lieutenant of Worcestershire, the king

ordered his deputies to call out the militia to prevent unlawful
assemblies. At least some of the sectaries monitored militia movements and took appropriate action to evade apprehension. In early
November a friend of Thomas Palmer, ejected rector of Aston-on-
Trent, Derby, warned him of a military crackdown on Nonconformists in Kent. Although he wore a disguise, Palmer (who offered "some
resistance") and thirty of his followers were arrested at Egerton, but
some 170 others escaped.[73]

At the request of the lord mayor, a troop of horse and a company
of foot moved into London in late October and were responsible for
the arrest on the 26th of approximately 160 Quakers and 140
Baptists. Among those arrested was Thomas Ellwood, Milton's
reader, who was held for some three months in Bridewell and
Newgate. The arrests were the direct result of new rumors of a
plot.[74] That autumn magistrates broke up Quaker meetings and
arrested Friends from Yorkshire to Southampton. The king, however, was unenthusiastic about jailing Quakers and other Nonconformists. In August he ordered the release of sectaries in London
and Middlesex imprisoned for illegal assembly if they professed their
obedience and had not been indicted for refusing the oath of
allegiance. Three months later the Council offered to release Friends
who promised not to take up arms or plot against the king.[75]

The persecution of Nonconformists was undertaken primarily for
reasons of state, not theology. The government was far less concerned with religious ideas than the capacity of conventicles to serve
as nurseries of sedition. There is a germ of truth in Bishop Kennet's
observation that the government was more inclined to tolerate the
Quakers than other sectaries because most Friends espoused pacifism. Nevertheless, the state, because of the political implications,
had difficulty coming to grips with the Quaker refusal to take oaths.
There was also some concern that conventicles left the parish
churches "quite deserted," and that Nonconformists were inclined
"to scorne the friendly admonitione and perswasion of the Civill
magistrate . . . and to bidd defyance to his power."[76] In August fear
that such defiance might lead to militant action prompted the bishop
of Durham and his deputy lieutenants to secure Raby Castle, for
sectaries in the area were loyal to the late Sir Henry Vane. When the
authorities heard reports of ejected ministers such as Edward
Bagshaw referring to Charles' countenancing of "halfe-faced Popery" and of the supremacy of the Long Parliament to its Cavalier
cousin, they were naturally apprehensive.[77] This wariness provided
the context for the interminable reports of anti-government plots

that continued throughout 1662. The state had to be constantly alert to sort out the false rumors from information pertaining to genuine conspiracies. The narrow religious settlement only added to the ranks of the disgruntled and thus to the potential base of support for a violent endeavor to change the government in church or state. The authorities aborted one such attempt at year's end when they crushed the Tong conspiracy.

# 4

# "That Stupendious Tragedie"

## THE TONG PLOT

The ejection of Nonconformist clergy in 1662 was undeniably a major provocation to the dissidents. Coupled with the exclusion of Nonconformists from the corporations, the ejection clearly signaled the strength of those opposed to compromise, and as such created a greater community of interest among those barred from the centers of governance and worship. In practical terms this expanded the recruiting base for those who espoused radical political schemes and thus compounded the government's problem of tracking radical activity. In the aftermath of the great ejection there were numerous rumors about alleged schemes, but nothing of substance until the authorities got on the trail of the Tong plotters in London late in the year. Discovered while still in the embryonic stage, the Tong plot entailed an ambitious scheme for a widespread insurrection to topple the Restoration regime and the supporters of exclusion in church and state. The discovery provided the government with an excellent opportunity to probe the nature and extent of the radical underground, but in their nervousness in the aftermath of the ejection they bungled their chance.

## A Harvest of Discontent

The government was noticeably apprehensive at the approach of 3 September, the anniversary of Cromwell's victories at Dunbar and Worcester as well as his death. Special precautions were taken to

109

prevent disruptive acts by his former supporters, including the arrest of suspected dissidents throughout the country. Lieutenant-Colonel (Adam or Robert?) Baynes was incarcerated in the Tower on the 2nd for seditious practices. A warrant for Lieutenant-Colonel Abraham Holmes' arrest was issued on the 13th, with instructions that he be taken before Secretary Nicholas.[1] According to the Venetian resident, by 5 September many malcontents had been jailed, and though the Presbyterians were outwardly peaceful, in secret they were adding "fuel to the fire." An intercepted letter from the Cheshire dissident John Wilson to Henry Lawrence, former lord president of the Council of State, observed that the Presbyterians were "disgusted" with recent events, but Wilson also noted that "if great men may be creditted we shall be able to worke our selves out of the bryers very shortly." Both men were arrested.[2]

At Leicester, supporters of the ejected aldermen joined forces with the sectaries "to offer a publike indignity to the Church." On a late September Sunday they forced the church doors open, defaced the sacramental vessels, and stole the surplice. The rioters apparently had political as well as religious ends, for the election of a new mayor had been scheduled to follow the service. Further north, there was a report at month's end of companies of men ranging in size from twelve to twenty en route to Scotland, and of Scottish efforts to purchase or steal as many good horses as possible. Newcastle sectaries maintained regular contact with the Scots, heightening royalist apprehension. Nicholas, however, played down the reports of dissident activity, blaming the sectaries for inventing such tales to scare the people.[3]

Manifestations of discontent were rampant in the autumn, much of it directed against Charles. "A pox on all the Kings," sneered a Middlesex housewife, for "she did not care a t[urd] for . . . a Kinge in England, for she never did lie with any." At the Winton assizes one John Richards read lines of verse denouncing both the monarch and persons of quality, while the London alderman Samuel Lewis was accused of uttering scandalous words against Charles.[4] The duke of Buckingham's porter, Thomas Fauster, allegedly "hoped ere long to trample in Bishops and Kings blood," and claimed he could raise between 2,000 and 3,000 men for that purpose. When examined on this charge, he pleaded inebriety, a defense that became increasingly common. Pepys reported widespread discontent in London, stemming at least in part from hostility toward the bishops and tales of a royal bastard. A Leicestershire man (who subsequently pleaded drunkenness) prophesied that the people would dethrone Charles unless he eased their taxes.[5]

Religious considerations continued to be at the core of much of the disillusionment with the government, whose overthrow was expected imminently. According to Pepys, some of the sectaries were convinced that the world would end on 2 December. For others, fear of popery loomed large. The attorney William Poulsen (or Poulson) of Ware, Hertfordshire, was arrested for opining that all England would soon be Catholic, that the king frequently attended mass, and that a cardinal would soon arrive in the country.[6] Another man refused to take an oath of allegiance because he thought Charles "might bring in papists." In November an anonymous letter was found in a Preston street describing a conversation concerning a papist plot to massacre Protestants on St. Andrew's day, but the letter was probably a hoax intended to inflame anti-Catholic hysteria.[7]

Out of such feelings came defiant expressions of insurrection. Because Charles had broken his pre-coronation promises, thousands, according to one dissident, were ready "to sheath our swords in the Bowells of him & his Councile," for "you cannot expect to have any thing of good so long as Jezabill & her whoredome raigns." A Dorset man, who thought all M. P.s were rogues, gave Charles no more than five years to reign, but a Wiltshire resident expected 40,000 men to be in arms against the king that autumn. In late October there was in fact a report from Cheshire concerning unusual purchases of horses, mysterious nightime rides, and "running up & downe as we did at our Riseing in 1659."[8]

More ominous were reports of plotting throughout the autumn. Warrants were issued on 1 October for the apprehension of Major Pitts and Oliver Lambert, both of London, and an Enfield, Middlesex man. On the same day a warrant was dispatched to confine Richard Newbury to the Gatehouse on charges of treason. The Walley plot, which unfolded in September and October, aimed to assassinate the king when he returned from Hampton Court to London. The brewer Robert Walley, "a stout man," allegedly outlined the scheme to Lieutenant Smith, who had served under Ludlow, but Smith tipped off the authorities. Walley, he claimed, had planned a rendezvous of his party of horse at Shoreditch and Mile End. Before Walley was arrested, he helped a prisoner escape from the Marshalsea. On 29 October the informer Peter Crabb claimed to have knowledge of an assassination plot directed against the king by men disguised in plush jackets with feathery plumes. Charles, he insisted, should be cautioned to beware of both his company and his food. In addition to Walley, the other conspirators named by Crabb were the former lord mayor Sir Thomas Aleyne, alderman Timothy Wade (who had been suspiciously inquisitive about court activities), the "Parliament man" (George?) Thompson, a Mr. Harrison of Harrow Alley, and possibly Colonel Kiffin. Additional information obtained by John Bincks, an informer for the earl of Pembroke, may be related to this scheme. According to Bincks, the Baptists and Presbyterians had the support of some of Albemarle's foot and intended to seize the weapons in the Artillery House, though the rising would not occur until the Guards had left London.[9]

The Walley plot was based on little more than the disgruntled remarks of London malcontents. After examining a number of imprisoned suspects who were probably associated with this scheme, Sir George Carteret concluded that there had not been "any great plotting among them, though they have a good will to it." Because the social status of the schemers was so inferior, he found no cause for alarm.[10]

Reports of another conspiracy came from the southwest, where the surgeon Edward Gerish of Broughton Gifford, Wiltshire, a critic of the bishops, claimed that he had knowledge of a design from Edward Buckle of Frome, Somerset. According to his story, a rising was tentatively scheduled for 13 October, but "Parliament"—probably an allusion to the Rump—supposedly had directed the schemers not to act until they received word of an insurrection in London. Ludlow reportedly would command rebel forces in the west and "an other as good as hee in the North." Horses and arms were in readiness. Gerish claimed that Buckle, an associate of Colonel William Eyres, the former Leveller, and William Trehearne, also of Frome, offered him a command in the rebel forces. Buckle and Trehearne denied the allegation, though Gerish's wife provided some corroboration of her husband's account.[11] The thrust of Gerish's story suggests that he had picked up some information concerning the scheming that subsequently became known as the Tong plot.

## The Tong Plot

The first conspiracy in Restoration England since Venner's rising for which the death penalty was imposed was the Tong conspiracy. But unlike either the Vennerite insurrection or the Dublin plot of 1663, the very reality of the Tong conspiracy has been challenged from the seventeenth century to the present. Predictably, Ludlow charged the government with manufacturing the scheme in order to disarm its critics and divert attention from its own cruelty, immorality, and corruption, as well as the unpopular sale of Dunkirk. According to Ludlow, Major-General Richard Browne and unnamed others channeled weapons and money to the former Cromwellian John Bradley and other ex-officers to encourage them "in this pretended design." Nearly a century later, James Ralph sarcastically observed that the scheme called for the seizure of the Tower and Windsor Castle, the deposition of the king, and the restoration of the Commonwealth, "all which mighty Things were to be perform'd by Six of the meanest of the People, unaided and uncountenanced, either by the Grandees at home, or any Sovereign State abroad." More recently, Maurice Ashley reiterated this skeptical judgment, insisting that no one who studies the evidence can seriously believe that a "grandiose conspiracy" existed. At most, he argues, there was "vaguely treasonable talk and vaguer treasonable plans."[12]

In contrast, sources close to the government gave specific details of the plot. The anonymous author of *A True and Exact Relation of the Araignment, Tryal, and Condemnation* of six of the conspirators outlined the state's case, while its chief witness, William Hill, recounted his story at length in *A Brief Narrative of That Stupendious Tragedie*. In his history of the age, Bishop Samuel Parker, claiming to write from the court record, accepted the official account of the conspiracy. Wilbur Cortez Abbott was less certain, but essentially gave credence to the state's assertion because of substantial outside testimony, the scaffold admissions of some of the plotters, and the suspicious language found in the letters of Archibald Johnston, laird of Wariston, and the London merchant Gavin Lawry.[13]

The evidence is not sufficient to support the claim of a well-organized conspiracy, but neither is it paltry enough to justify the skepticism of Ludlow, Ralph, and Ashley. The best brief assessment of the plot was made as early as 19 November 1662 by one of the principal secretaries of state, William Morice, who acknowledged the reality of the conspiracy but deemed it "an inconsiderable design, not formed nor any determinate way agreed on to execute it." Those involved, he opined, were lowly persons who lacked the necessary means to accomplish their ends and thus quit in despair. "But the very thought and design and debate will forfeit the lives of seven or eight of them," while many others fled.[14] If anything, the plot was more serious than he judged, as new evidence subsequently was discovered. The Tong conspirators indeed engaged in seditious discussions with a view to instigating an uprising, and in examining their options they embraced certain ideas already spreading throughout dissident circles. Those who investigated the design found that these common links, such as the references to Ludlow or the preparation of a revolutionary declaration, provided suspicious if highly tentative links between Tong's group and the broader community of the disaffected throughout the country.

Crucial to the government's case was the espionage work and testimony of William Hill and John Bradley. Hill, whose father had been a supporter of the Good Old Cause and a member of the Herefordshire committee, had studied at Merton College, Oxford, and graduated B.A. According to Anthony Wood, he was ejected at the Restoration. For his services in uncovering the plot, Hill received a benefice in Gloucestershire. His account of the cabal, though incomplete and somewhat self-serving, is the fullest exposition of what supposedly transpired. Bradley had once served as a messenger for the Cromwellian Council of State, and more recently distributed money to unemployed ex-officers. For his assistance in bringing the conspirators to justice, he was appointed a king's messenger.[15] In addition, the crown was aided by one of the schemers who turned state's evidence, Edward Riggs, a former chaplain to Admiral Robert Blake. After Riggs' ejection as vicar of St. John's in the Isle of Thanet in 1660, he became a clerk in a London brewery. He was arrested in October 1662 and taken before the king on the 29th. Sir John Robinson advised him to seek favor from Secretary Bennet by making "large" disclosures, and in December he made a formal confession. Released on bail in April 1663, he subsequently engaged in espionage against exiles in the Netherlands. He returned to England in 1664, but was killed two years later while serving as a navy chaplain.[16]

According to Bishop Parker, the authorities first learned of the plot on 15 October 1662. It was probably at this point that they delegated to Bradley the responsibility of ferreting out the full intentions of the schemers, for he was working with them by the 20th. Hill, who had arrived in London by the 12th, met four days later with Captain John Baker of East Smithfield. Once a member of Cromwell's Life Guards (a position he owed to the regicide Hugh Peter), Baker had been expelled from John Cotton's church in New England for blasphemy and atheism, and now supported himself as a knife-grinder. According to Hill, Baker told him that the "Rogues" at Whitehall would be slaughtered within a few weeks, and that he himself hoped to kill the king in order to deliver the country "from the Tyranny of an Outlandish Dog." On the 20th Baker introduced

Hill to Riggs, Bradley, and James Hill, a cloth drawer in Coleman Street. At this time Baker disclosed more of the plot to William Hill. There was, he claimed, a council of six "elected by general consent" whose duty it was to manage a design to overthrow the king, Albemarle, the lord chancellor, and Major-General Browne.[17]

The following day Hill met again with Riggs, Baker, Bradley, and James Hill, who were accompanied by James Hind, a ship's gunner, and Captain (Arthur?) Brown, a former naval officer who lived in Wapping. Riggs boasted that he had been invited to sit on the revolutionary council but had declined due to the pressures of his brewery business. Claiming to be in contact with the Fifth Monarchists, he explained that his task was to persuade all the Nonconformist groups to support the scheme. Despite expressions of sympathy for the conspirators' goals, the Presbyterians allegedly demurred. Riggs promised more details to Hill after his meeting with Lieutenant Nathaniel Strange, but he did offer that council members wore disguises, never met in the same place twice, and kept their identity secret from all but two (unnamed) persons. At this juncture Hill conveyed the information he had gleaned to Major-General Browne.[18]

From Riggs, William Hill claimed to have discovered that several months earlier a Southampton man—almost certainly Thomas Cole—offered his services to Nonconformist churches in London "with a new Model of Government for their Saintships, when they had rooted out the *Amorites* from amongst them; and also a Plot for them to act, whereby they should ease themselves from the Government of that Antichristian thing called Monarchy." The revolutionary council, however, rejected this scheme as well as older proposals of Sir Henry Vane. Disillusioned, the Southampton man sold his estate and emigrated to Holland, though the council, according to Riggs, dispatched a minister named Rogers to bring him back along with any ex-army officers willing to join them. The Dutch themselves had allegedly been targeted as potential supporters in September according to Samuel Goodwin, a member of the London Baptist church of John Sallers (or Sallows), a compass maker and an associate of Tong's. Sallers reputedly told the informer Peter Crabb that "severall Eminent Bretheren of the gathered Churches" had been sent to the Netherlands to negotiate a pact. Under its terms the Dutch would aid the rebels with shipping and ammunition in return for the fisheries and exemption from customs and excise fees.[19] If such a mission was undertaken, nothing came of it, for the idea of such a pact would have been anathema to the Dutch government.

This was probably nothing more than one of the options discussed by the dissidents.

If there was in fact a revolutionary council of six, the sources do not agree on its composition. The principal authorities for the existence of the council are William Hill, Riggs (via Hill), Sergeant George Phillips, a London yeoman and member of the trained bands who was subsequently executed for his part in the conspiracy, and Richard Tyler.[20] Testifying under oath during the conspirators' trial, Hill could name only five council members: Colonel Henry Danvers, Phillips, Cole of Southampton, the Congregationalist minister Philip Nye, and Captain John Lockyer (or Lockier). To some extent Hill may have based his list on the information of Riggs, who also cited Danvers, Nye, and Lockyer. The others, according to Riggs, were Lieutenant Nathaniel Strange, the Congregationalist minister Anthony Palmer, and Captain George Elton, one of the most active dissidents in the 1660s. Elton and Nye also appeared on Phillip's list, along with Captain Thomas, a coppersmith of Shoe Lane, Captain Spurway of Tiverton, Devon, Dr. Ward of Southwark, and Edward Radden (or Raden, Raddon, Rawdon), a former post office employee who now lived near Exeter.[21] Tyler's list was identical except for the inclusion of a minister named Jones in lieu of Nye. If the council was real, the variation of names may be the result of mistaken assumptions, deliberate deception (particularly by Phillips or Tyler), shifting membership, or confusion of the inner circle with a larger council of forty to which the council of six was supposedly subordinate. There is, however, no reliable evidence that the larger council existed. The council of six allegedly supervised a band of agitators who maintained contact with the shires and were accountable only to the council. It was also apparently responsible for the selection of former Cromwellian colonels to command the rebel forces, which would purportedly be composed primarily of Fifth Monarchists, Baptists, and "fighting *Quakers*."[22]

In a meeting on the 23rd with Riggs and Hind, Hill learned that preparations had been completed to seize Windsor Castle, in whose region the dissidents claimed to have 500 men. The contact with the Windsor garrison was Thomas Tong (or Tonge), a distiller and tobacco merchant at Tower Ditch who claimed that Tyler recruited him for the design. According to Riggs and Hind, Tong conveyed a letter to the council of six from sergeants at Windsor professing fidelity to the scheme. After his arrest, Tong cited Sergeant Thomas Seabrooke and the gunner Silas Seabrooke as his Windsor agents, the "Right Boys," but both men denied the accusation, suggesting that

Tong might have been attempting to "make his disigne . . . the more taking in the apprehension of his Confederates."[23]

Riggs further assured Hill that the conspirators enjoyed substantial support in the London area, primarily because of the backing of the Nonconformist congregations, whose "Money did fly." In addition to providing funds, these churches, Riggs extravagantly claimed, could raise between 12,000 and 20,000 men. He particularly singled out the Congregationalist Thomas Brooks as a minister who recruited men and raised funds in his church. In contrast, William Kiffin "and the Churches" were criticized for not providing money earlier so that the rising could have occurred in 1661. There was supposed to be a cache of arms in a warehouse in Crutched Friars near the Tower, with 500 weapons already in the hands of those too poor to purchase them.[24] Powder was allegedly provided by an East Smithfield chandler named Ward, who concealed it in baskets covered with white sheets. From a Cheapside potter named Baker, who once served in Colonel Okey's regiment, Hill learned that twenty-three or twenty-four Cheapside potters were prepared to rebel. An unnamed lieutenant who formerly exercised a naval command was reportedly lodged in the Wheatsheaf and had 500 men ready to revolt. He allegedly stayed with Lambert's butler, who ran a victualing house near Charing Cross and continued to communicate with his master. Riggs later confessed that they expected Lambert to escape from Guernsey and "head a party" once the revolution was launched. Taking no chances, the government instigated additional precautions to ensure Lambert's confinement, though the lieutenant-governor of Guernsey knew of no correspondence between Lambert and the ill-affected.[25]

Hill was also told by Riggs about supporters in Dorset and Kent. There were purportedly 400 "Assistants" in the former shire, and several cases of pistols had been shipped to them. Riggs named Colonel William Kenrick, who had been arrested as a suspect in the 1661 Presbyterian plot, as the leader of the Kentish rebels. The authorities subsequently discovered that William Brooke, who had fought in the parliamentary army, was his liaison with the London schemers, notably Tong and Lieutenant Francis Stubbs, a cheese merchant.[26]

On the 24th Hill, Riggs, Bradley, and Captain Baker met at the Feathers tavern in Fish Street. Hill had previously asked for enough weapons to arm thirty men, but he was now informed that Tong had vetoed his request unless he became "a Church member"—that is, a sectary. Hill and Riggs thereupon went to the Exchange, where

Sallers explained that between 500 and 600 weapons had been distributed the previous night, but that forty men had been turned away without arms. More weapons were expected for the magazine at Crutched Friars within three or four days. At his trial, Sallers testified that his information about the distribution of arms, with which he was not involved, came from a Mr. Watshet (or Watlot, Walshutt) of Mark Lane.[27] That more than 500 men received weapons in a single night in London is, however, most improbable.

On the night of the 24th, Riggs, Stubbs, Bradley, Baker, Hind, Hill, and Ward the chandler gathered at Tong's house to discuss strategy. Tong reported that Elton told him of Lieutenant Strange's arrival from the country the previous night after a mission on which he communicated with agents and provided for horses. Tong also noted that he had personally met with Captain Leigh (or Lee), who asserted that the revolutionary council intended to act imminently. To this end, Tong added that he had bribed members of the Tower garrison to open a back gate and allow the rebels to storm in with blunderbusses.[28]

Bradley, Hill, and Tong met at Rigg's house on the 25th. Presumably from Tong came an announcement that the commanders had been appointed, with Ludlow as their general, and that Captains Alban Spencer and Samuel Taverner (or Tavernor), who had served as governors of Walmer and Deal Castles respectively, had assured the council that they could surprise their erstwhile bastions. Riggs claimed to know the man who would help oversee the assault on Whitehall and would direct the insurgents to its treasury. No quarter would be given to those at Whitehall, Worcester House, St. James', and Somerset House; Monck and Browne in particular had to die. Copies of a letter describing a popish plot to assassinate the king and massacre Protestants were distributed at the meeting. The intent was to spread the letters around the country on the eve of the rising to provide a pretext for the rebels to arm themselves. The government subsequently learned that the plotters intended to distribute some 5,000 copies of the letter.[29] Dated at "Yexford, Suffolk," on 31 October 1662, the letter stated:

> *Sir*, Out of the respect which I bear to you in particular, and to the Protestant Party in General, I give you notice of this Passage. About a fortnight since, a woman, which you must be ignorant where, who had it from a Correspondent of the Papists, that they intend to make use of their Army (which all the World sees they have provided) against *Al-hallows* Eve next; It was thought good therefore, in as prudent [a] way as may be, to give notice to our Friends in remote Parts, that they may do what Piety to God, Loyalty to their Prince,

Love to their Country, and self-preservation should direct them: Sir,
I call the Eternal God to witness, that this is not to Trepan, to put a
Trick upon you, but a sober truth; And also Communicated to a
Justice of the Peace, and by him to the Privy Council; and what the
issue of it is I have not heard, I hope you will inquire, and tell us.[30]

According to Hill and Parker, the letter caused sufficient alarm in
Worcestershire and Warwickshire for magistrates to arrest Catholics.[31]

Several other items of interest were revealed at the meeting on the
25th. According to Tong, Strange had made another trip to confer
with associates in the shires and was due back that night. The date for
the rising was to be whispered in the Nonconformist churches the
following day. Reputedly, many new blunderbusses had been man-
ufactured, and altogether the cabal now claimed enough equipment
to outfit 2,000 horse. Riggs reported that Captain Leigh had pressed
them not to inquire into rebel connections in Ireland, which was the
council's responsibility. Hill now learned the identity of yet another
minister who was supposedly involved—the Congregationalist and
Fifth Monarchist Carnsew Helme. By the 27th Hill had seen the
weapons provided by Tong and Hind, and he learned that Captain
Brown had sold his ship in order to fight with the insurgents.[32]

There was growing confusion among the conspirators by the
28th. Riggs and a Baptist chandler and fruit seller named Beazley (or
Biersley) told Hill that the council had dissolved preparatory to the
rising, that 2,000 horse had arrived in London, and that the rebellion
had nevertheless been postponed from its originally scheduled time
the following night. It is certain only that 2,000 horse did not arrive
in London. On the evening of the 28th, Hill, Riggs, Beazley, Stubbs,
the feltmaker Nathaniel Gibbs, Captain Thomas, and three others
met. Gibbs apprised them that the council would meet the next
morning in order to reschedule the insurrection for All Hallows Eve,
a more propitious time.[33]

In addition to the meetings at which Hill was present and for
which his account is the primary source, there were allegedly other
gatherings to discuss the plot. According to Tyler, sessions took place
at Lunn's lodgings in Duke's Place near Aldgate, and other discussions may have occurred at Captain Foster's house in Leadenhall
Street. Elton was there with Richard Richard (or Richaut), who
admitted knowing Foster but not Tong.[34] Foster, however, insisted
that he had never heard Elton speak of a plot. Phillips too admitted
going to Foster's house, but only to discuss ships.[35] The authorities
also were interested in a meeting at John Ward's house in Redcross

Street at which Captain Timothy Cotes, Captain Faircloth, John Jackson, and John Whitehall were present, but these men could not recall whether Baker attended. The spy Bradley accused Gibbs, his servant John Lock, and Beazley of meeting together, but Lock would admit only that he knew Beazley. Once the arrests had begun, the authorities interrupted a meeting in the silkweaver Howard's house in George Alley, where they found weapons. Those present included the Baptist gunsmith Thomas Franke (who defiantly proclaimed that he would rather hang than inform on his friend Elton), Franke's son, the shoemaker James Johnson, Robert Luke, and Watshet, who was linked to Sallers.[36]

Disagreement over details of the proposed insurrection resulted in poor organization. Tong, Elton, Cole, and Leigh purportedly met frequently to discuss the attack but failed to reach an agreement. Various proposals were put forward to deal with the king, including an attempt to seize him at Camberwell on one of his biweekly visits to Henrietta Maria at Greenwich, or during one of his hunting expeditions. Thomas Fleet, who was subsequently imprisoned in the Tower, admitted hearing Riggs and Stubbs discuss an attack on Charles while he was hunting, and volunteering to "gird on his broad sword" to assist. Baker was accused of offering to serve in a band of fifty responsible for capturing the king as he rode through London. At his examination Baker testified that Tong was prepared to assassinate Charles if he reviewed Sir John Robinson's regiment. Baker himself allegedly offered to lure the king out of his coach in order to give Tong a better shot.[37]

There was debate too over the best way to attack Whitehall. One proposal called for a party to go by way of the gate in St. James' Park, while another would send one group down Charing Cross Road and a second via the Cockpit. Tong argued against the Charing Cross route because of gun emplacements at the bottom of the road, preferring instead to use King Street and approach Whitehall through a private garden and backstairs, a route known to Baker. The latter confessed that two royal Guards who had served in Cromwell's Horse Guards would provide entry. Likewise, Stubbs admitted that Riggs had a friend in the palace who was willing to let the conspirators in to seize Charles and Albemarle provided the rebels could raise 500 horse and 500 foot soldiers. The plotters were agreed on the need to act in such a manner that Browne could not use the trained bands against them. It was Phillips' responsibility to persuade members of the bands to support the rising.[38]

Tong concerned himself primarily with the Tower, which he

intended to secure himself by bribing members of the garrison to provide entry. John Spung, a Chancery clerk imprisoned in the Tower for his suspected role, testified that the rising would occur as soon as the Tower was delivered into rebel hands by lieutenants in its garrison. Another proposal called for conspirators to go to the Tower dressed like mariners, feigning to have accounts to make up. Tong also thought access might be had if a party of men followed Robinson's coach into the Tower. The dissidents schemed to seize the Guildhall treasury, confiscate the weapons in the Artillery Ground, and possibly even put London to the torch. The plotters expected at least one frigate to defect to their cause.[39]

Hope for some naval support rested largely on an overt attempt to demand reforms of interest to sailors. A formal paper was drawn up to this end, possibly by Cole, from whence it went to Tong and Riggs. It called for exemption from customs for sailors on all commodities valued under £10. There was also a proposal to provide sailors whose ships were "cast away" with funds (paid out of customs) to aid their homeward journey. The proposal also called for better efforts to ensure that sailors did not have to beg or starve.[40]

A general declaration was prepared in favor of a commonwealth. The rebels proposed to recall the Rump, excluding only those members who had deviated from the basic principles of the Good Old Cause, including republicanism. New members would be elected to bring the Commons up to full strength. The authors may have been influenced by Leveller ideas, for they wanted parliaments elected annually, with the franchise as well as the right to sit in the Commons restricted to republicans. The House of Lords, like the monarchy, would be abolished, and it would be treasonable for Parliament to restore the monarchy, the House of Lords, or government by a single person. The rebels also proposed to end the payment of salaries out of public funds. In the area of religion, the radicals wanted liberty of conscience for Protestants and the abolition of episcopacy and the Book of Common Prayer. To disturb the lawful meetings of religious groups would be treasonous, nor could Parliament impose anything against the consciences of the people. So long as Parliament did not violate any of these fundamentals, it would be an act of treason to disrupt its sessions.[41]

On 28 October Hill, who had been apprising Major-General Browne each night of the cabal's activities, was ordered by Browne and Robinson to accompany soldiers to apprehend Tong, Riggs, Hind, Stubbs, and others. More arrests ensued, including those of the brothers Thomas and Silas Seabrooke, John Sallers, Nathaniel

Gibbs, and the Fifth Monarchist John Venner, a Whitechapel ivory-turner.[42] The dragnet extended beyond the bounds of those directly implicated in the plot as a jittery government relentlessly pursued suspects. Among those sent to the Tower on suspicion of treason were the Baptist Richard Pilgrim and Colonels Philip Twisleton and Robert Swallow. Secretary Bennet personally wanted to interrogate Captain Thimbleton, who had once served in Roger Sawrey's regiment, John Gregory (alias Smith), a Southwark leather dresser and dyer who was probably the Captain Gregory who fought in Lambert's rising, and any disaffected persons who met at the house of a Mr. Methall in Kensington, where arms and seditious papers were allegedly kept.[43]

In the meantime, from the shires the government had been accumulating reports of radical activity linked to the Tong cabal. As early as 23 October 1662, rumors of a general rising surfaced in Dorset.[44] Thomas Rapson of Sherborne testified the following day that he had learned of a rising scheduled to occur before the 28th in which 20,000 men would be engaged in London. According to Rapson, the ex-soldiers in Sherborne would support the insurrection, though at the time only forty or fifty in the town had enlisted. One of the Dorset conspirators, John Lambert (not to be confused with the general), implausibly thought Lord Fairfax and Sir George Booth were also involved. Rapson told his story to Francis Bampfield, the ejected vicar of Sherborne, who encouraged him to speak to a justice of the peace. Security measures were immediately implemented in Dorset, and deputy lieutenants in the surrounding counties were called together to coordinate their efforts. Pepys heard the reports on the 26th and observed soldiers securing London the same day. There was even a report that the Tong plotters had sent weapons to Dorset rebels.[45] Further investigation revealed that 1,000 horse had allegedly planned to rendezvous at Clifton Wood, near Sherborne, on the night of the 28th, preparatory to moving through the county "to Cut the throats of the Kings friends." Ludlow, "that old Grande Rebell[,] was to Comande them." A report from Sherborne on 2 November indicated that only four persons, none of them leaders, had been arrested. In Devon, however, Captain John Coplestone, sheriff of that county in 1655, and a man erroneously identified as Major General Desborough were apprehended. This may have been a reference to Captain Nathaniel Desborough, arrested near Pendennis Castle in Cornwall no later than 2 November.[46]

In Kent attention focused on Colonel William Kenrick, who was linked to the Tong cabal by Riggs. Kenrick was reputedly in close communication with dissidents in Canterbury, who were "very high & insolent, and threattin all persons that have been any way loyall." More important, the rebels hoped to surprise the castles at Deal and Dover. Tong allegedly told Tyler that thirty or forty "servants" of Sir William Lockhart, former governor of Dunkirk, would support the plot, while Riggs himself boasted that he would lead the attempt on Deal, where he had previously served as a preacher. Suspects were consequently detained in both towns, and a search was made in the Shepway Lathe for weapons belonging to "factitious and seditious spirits."[47]

Elsewhere, dissidents associated with the Tong group were allegedly prepared to act. According to Hill, risings were planned for Leicestershire, Mansfield, and Nottingham. Near the latter a supply of bullets and powder was confiscated from the house of Captain John Garland of Lenton, formerly a member of Colonel Okey's regiment. Colonel Templar reputedly had between 2,000 and 3,000 men ready to fight in Essex, while 200 horse were supposedly standing by in Bristol. Authorities in Somerset arrested various persons who confessed that they had engaged to revolt, and signs of unrest were evident in Shrewsbury.[48] Colonel Edward Rossiter reportedly was preparing to gather 1,500 men at Stourbridge Fair and march them to London. John Chapman of Norwich, who condemned the tyrannical company of "Lowsy Bishopps" and called for vengeance on those who executed the regicides, was imprisoned in the Tower for encouraging the Tong conspirators.[49] In the north, Sir Philip Musgrave, who was especially alert to dissident rumblings, informed Williamson on 3 November that the Congregationalists were suspiciously placing their lands in trust and holding "their heads as high as ever." He too had picked up hints about the work of the revolutionary council in London and its use of agents to disperse "intelligence" to supporters in the shires.[50]

As the plot unfolded, the government intensified its efforts to track down Ludlow. Reports of his sighting became increasingly prevalent in late 1662, though he never left Switzerland. Nicholas had a report that he was seen in Westminster in June, and in October he was supposedly observed at Somerset House in London. On the 24th the Venetian resident noted that Ludlow was in the London area planning a fresh rising. As the resident later observed, he was thought to be "the most active of the fanatics able with his counsel, activity and money to encourage evil humours and renew the dissensions in England." By November Ludlow's secretary had been arrested, though he confessed nothing.[51] A party of six men who departed the country on a French fishing vessel on 5 November was thought to include Ludlow, thus prompting an investigation by the earl of Northumberland. Another sighting the same month placed Ludlow in the Canterbury area wearing seaman's clothes and carrying a counterfeit pass.[52] Colonel Thomas Culpeper (or Culpepper), who was also searching for Colonel Kenrick, dispatched several parties of horse and foot to pursue Ludlow and instructed the governor of Dover Castle to watch the coast in order to prevent his escape.[53] By the 27th, however, Culpeper was convinced that Ludlow had left the country by way of Deal, possibly with the assistance of a pass provided by John Boys of Betteshanger, a supporter of the late Richard Culmer, the notorious iconoclast. Culpeper and Vincent, however, did arrest Captain (Matthew?) Cadwell, Adcock of Hythe (who was taken to the Tower and interrogated by Bennet), and the Quakers Luke Howard and John Harrison. Kenrick was imprisoned in the Tower on 22 November. Ludlow, however, continued to concern the government: In February 1663 Lord Hawley received a warrant to search for him in Somerset.[54]

At the Old Bailey on 11 December 1662, the state brought Tong, Phillips, Stubbs, Hind, Sallers, and Gibbs to trial. Only Hind pleaded guilty, though Phillips confessed that he knew about the conspiracy and failed to report it. Additional testimony was provided by William Hill and Bradley, both of whom acknowledged their role as *agents provocateurs*. Although the prosecution admitted that the accused were only agitators and not responsible for the basic planning, the case was pressed on the grounds that there were four witnesses against Tong and two against each of the others. The jury found all six guilty of high treason, and on 22 December Tong, Phillips, Stubbs, and Gibbs were executed at Tyburn.[55] Before his death Tong confessed that he had been in the presence of others who contrived the plot, and that he had joined them because as an ex-army man he considered their cause worthy. He denied, however, that he personally intended to assassinate Charles. Phillips, Stubbs, and Gibbs admitted only that they were aware of the design and failed to report it.[56]

Four days after the trial, Baker was examined in the presence of the king, who had interrogated other prisoners as early as late October. Much of what Baker now confessed was nothing more than hearsay, including a rumor that Ludlow had been seen at Gravesend en route to London, and that the regicides William Goffe and Edward Whalley had been taken from New England to Scotland on a Dutch ship. Captain Brown, he also said, had told him that Vice-Admiral William Goodsonn (or Goodson) was "a sure man." More reliable, perhaps, was Baker's testimony that Smith and Kentish of the royal Guards told him that they would provide the rebels with access to Whitehall. But Baker did the most damage by reporting a conversation with Captain Robert Johnston, who had served as an officer in Manchester's regiment and subsequently in Cromwell's Life Guards.[57]

Clearly intent on saving his own neck, Johnston described a network of radicals that extended as far afield as Scotland, the Netherlands, and France. According to Baker, Johnston informed him that if the English did not rise soon, the Scots would revolt first. Johnston in turn characterized Baker as a liar whom he had met accidentally, and insisted that he had told Baker only that the Scots were as discontented as the English. Baker, he asserted, had outlined a scheme "for the delyverance of his brethren from the Yocke & Slaverie of Monarchie," and had even boasted that "if hee could have met the King in battle fields, hee could have found in his heart to have washed his hands in the Kings heart Blood." As Johnston understood the plot, the conspirators were preparing to assault Whitehall Palace, Somerset House, and the lodgings of Clarendon or Albemarle when Tong was betrayed. Nevertheless, Baker said they were ready to try again, having formulated their declaration, appointed their officers, and prepared for a new Parliament. The plotters, according to Johnston, considered including him in the cabal, but some found him "too strait-laced to joyne with them." In any case he claimed that he was too scared to join such a conspiracy, though in his confession to Bennet he also averred that he doubted the plot was real.[58]

As he poured out his story, Johnston implicated a wide circle of dissidents, at the hub of which were the Nonconformist John Caitness, Archibald Johnston, laird of Wariston, the London merchant Gavin Lawry, and Colonel Gilby Carr. The government was especially interested in interrogating Caitness, but Captain Johnston warned Bennet that his friends "will not Easily tell one of Another, because they are church members, & relations, the most of them."[59] One of those closest to Caitness was the Particular Baptist William Kiffin, with whom Caitness and Johnston regularly met at coffeehouses in Eastcheap for "general" discussion. Caitness was also friendly with the Congregationalist George Cokayne, whom Johnston claimed not to know very well, and Captain (Richard?) Williams, whose house Caitness visited. Johnston thought that

Caitness might have fled to the Netherlands to join Desborough and Lieutenant-Colonel Jeffrey Ellison (or Elletson), for the three were "old acquaintance[s] from the begining, they three knowes one Anothers hearts." A "great favorite" of Desborough's, Edward Radden, an alleged member of the revolutionary council of six, was also a friend of Caitness.[60] According to Captain Johnston, he, Caitness, Radden, and the Congregationalist James Forbes met near Cheapside, but Johnston was excluded from their private discussion. Forbes, a Scotsman who had been ejected as preacher at Gloucester Cathedral in 1660, was himself on good terms with the Fifth Monarchist Carnsew Helme, a "wittie projecting man." Johnston thought Forbes had been "Much deluded" by such suspicious preachers as the Congregationalists Philip Nye, Thomas Goodwin, John Owen, John Loder, Thomas Brooks, and Jeremiah Elborough, preacher to the Merchant Adventurers in Hamburg.[61]

Another of Caitness' intimates, Gavin Lawry, a merchant in Sherborne Lane, was a link to both Colonel Carr and Wariston.[62] According to Johnston, Lawry aided Wariston's flight from London via Dover to France after Johnston intervened on his behalf. Lawry subsequently denied the charge, but admitted knowing Johnston, Wariston, and Wariston's wife. He also acknowledged meeting with Lieutenant Calvert, who had been committed to Newgate for seditious designs on 16 December, some four days earlier. Johnston accused Lawry of corresponding with William Dundas, who had escaped after being attainted of high treason, and Wariston's friend John Scooler (or Scouler) of Rouen. Scooler accompanied Wariston and his wife on a trip to Hamburg, where she met with Elborough and several English and Scottish merchants to discuss the plight of Nonconformists.[63]

While in exile Wariston relied on his wife for news and books. He particularly wanted works by the Congregationalist John Owen and the early Stuart Puritans Paul Baynes and Robert Bolton, as well as more recent writings on the "consolation of afflicted persons." She also sent him the speeches of the regicides and books dealing with the Solemn League and Covenant. In addition, she urged Caitness to assist her husband, and considered Carr ungrateful because he refused to live abroad with the laird.[64] According to Captain Johnston, Lady Wariston's letters to her husband were often written in cipher by Lawry, though at her examination she refused to provide a key. Johnston himself admitted writing letters for her (under the alias John Turner) to Wariston, using a cipher only for the personal names. But the letters, he claimed, contained only news, business matters, religious affairs, and the places where her husband's papers were deposited.[65]

Colonel Carr, with whom Lady Wariston also corresponded, was living in Blackfriars in December 1661, but kept in regular contact with affairs in Ireland. At a meeting in Blackfriars, Carr apprised Johnston of Irish discontent, and at Carr's request Johnston arranged for him to meet with Lawry. Carr also hoped to talk with Wariston and the Scottish ministers James Simpson and Robert MacGuire (or Macguaire) about Argyll's papers and certain public matters, but Wariston had fled by that time and Carr failed to catch up with him in Holland. According to Johnston, Carr wanted this meeting to pursue "a reconciliation of severall interests" preparatory to an uprising.[66]

Wariston, captured at Rouen by Alexander Murray on 4 January 1663, was returned to England on the 24th. At his examination he denied any knowledge of conspiracies during the preceding six months.[67] Andrew Kennedy (or Cannady), who was imprisoned on a charge of concealing high treason, admitted sending Wariston's letters to Scooler, but claimed to know of no letters to the laird other than those from his wife. Despite the efforts of Lauderdale, the Scottish secretary of state, and Wariston's own offers of submission, he was executed on 22 July. In his gallows speech, he reaffirmed his adherence to the Solemn League and Covenant and urged other covenanted persons to continue working for that cause.[68]

In the aftermath of Wariston's capture, the government held another trial concerning the Tong plot on 21 February 1663, at which time Baker and Philip Gibbs, Nathaniel's brother, were charged with treason as "chief" conspirators.[69] Gibbs had been arrested in January at the house of the factor William Pardoe (or Pardo) in Warwick Lane, where he had gone to settle his estate prior to fleeing overseas.[70] Found guilty of treason, Gibbs and Baker were executed at Tyburn two days later.[71]

The search for other conspirators continued, as Bennet issued a warrant on 17 February for the apprehension of Elton, Danvers, James Hill, and William Prior (or Pryor). Elton was not caught until early July at which time he was sent to the Tower. Cole, Spurway, and Radden fled to the Netherlands.[72] The Scottish minister Robert Ferguson, whose career marks him as one of the period's inveterate rebels, had been arrested on suspicion of treason in January and interrogated by Bennet, probably in connection with the Tong plot. Warrants were issued the same month for the apprehension of Nathaniel Strange, whose name had been linked to the Tong

plotters, Quartermaster-General John Vernon, a prominent Fifth
Monarchist, Captain Charles Hooker, and Colonel Robert Barrow, a
supporter of Fleetwood and Lambert in 1659.[73] But the government's quest to unravel more of the plot was overtaken in 1663 not
only by fresh discoveries of new conspiracies but by an abortive revolt
in Dublin and an uprising in northern England.

The Tong plot, crushed in its embryonic stage, never became
potent enough to mount a serious threat to the government. Of this
there can be no question. Ludlow charged that between 500 and 600
individuals were seized on the pretext of plotting, but the arrests
probably only approached this number if one counts the Nonconformists apprehended for religious violations. The number of executions was relatively small, presumably because Charles did not
want a bloodbath. This, in effect, was suggested by the Venetian
resident, who observed that the king did not want to embitter the
people by severe punishment or "confound them by making known
the magnitude of the crime."[74] At most, the revolutionary council of
six was an informal cabal of whom the shadowy Elton and possibly
Danvers were the most likely members. Although Tong was not one,
he confessed to attending a council meeting at the Wheatsheaf.
Despite the constant evocations of his name, Ludlow was involved
only as an inspiration and hope.[75]

The Tong plot had clearly developed into something more than
a loose network of disgruntled persons. By suppressing it before it
had a chance to mature, the authorities—skittish in the aftermath of
the great ejection—missed an opportunity to strike a major blow at
the radical underground. The ideas the plotters were exploring
became the basis for subsequent scheming in 1663, and those of the
Tong plotters who eluded arrest provided a direct link with the
northern conspirators. In effect the Tong plot became the prototype
for subsequent major designs, with the nucleus being a City-based
revolutionary council linked to affiliated cells in other parts of the
country. But such a plan demanded organization, leadership, and
resources which the radical community lacked, and thus its ambitious
scope was a fundamental cause of radical failure.

In practical terms, the plot provided the state with the opportunity to explore various byways of the underground before it confronted the more serious threats of 1663. Although it failed to utilize
such an opportunity to strike hard at the radicals, the government at
least began to untangle some of the underground's dark mysteries.
With respect to the radicals themselves, some of those monitored in
connection with the Tong plot, such as Gilby Carr, Henry Danvers,

and Nathaniel Strange, subsequently engaged in seditious activity. It is probable that their association with the Tong plot, however tenuous, steeled their determination to force major changes in the government, even as the state became increasingly aware of their potential as rebels. The Tong plot also motivated the government to step up its efforts to increase the internal security of the realm, and it provided Charles with a fresh opportunity to offer an indulgence to Nonconformists and Catholics. Opposition to an indulgence among conservatives, however, was undoubtedly strengthened by the Tong cabal.

## Security and Indulgence

In late June 1662 the government began to take more forceful steps to secure the realm. Justifying the new policy by referring to the Yarrington plot of the previous year, Charles ordered the demolition of the walls, gates, and fortifications at Coventry, Northampton, Gloucester, and Taunton Castle in Somersetshire.[76] To garrison these places adequately, he contended, would be inordinately expensive as well as an inconvenience to the citizens. The task of demolition was entrusted to the lords lieutenant, with the king bearing the expense. The stones salvaged from the operation were granted to those who did the work or to other local inhabitants. Charles permitted part of the castle at Northampton to remain in order to serve the needs of the justices of the bench.[77]

Progress was so slow and disaffection so pronounced in Somersetshire that in mid-July Charles approved the decision of justices of the peace to place their companies in Taunton and to secure suspicious persons. In this context he not only ordered the arrest of Colonel (Richard?) Buffett and Captain Quarle, but gave his justices virtually a free hand to establish order: "What you shall doe in the further prosecution & discovery of this designe, & in suppressing all violent & Rebellious Spiritts, will not only be approved but warranted by his Majestie." In October Charles and Secretary Nicholas directed the deputy lieutenants in Somersetshire to press ahead with dismantling Taunton Castle and to settle the militia.[78]

There was, in fact, mounting concern in 1662 with the state of the militia. Writing to the M. P. Sir Edward Seymour, John Kelland actually welcomed rumors of plots in order to prompt the shires to get on with the task of readying their forces. Given the fact that so many members of the trained bands were disaffected persons, he favored "a considerable force" of reliable horse in each county.[79]

Kelland's outlook illustrates how royalists could take advantage of dissident activity as well as related rumors to press for the reorganization of the militia. To suggest, however, that the government itself fostered such rumors to this end is to overlook the very real concern the authorities manifested over the state of the country's internal defenses. Parliament had passed a Militia Act the preceding year, giving the king sole command of the militia as well as all other "forces by sea and land" and the forts. The act was confirmed in 1662 and 1663. The problem lay not in the need for more legislation but in the slow pace of acquiring trustworthy and effective personnel, and in the fact that the lords lieutenant and their deputies were not wholly responsive to the crown's wishes. The king's power of sole command was never effectively translated from theory into practice.[80]

The difficulty was perhaps most acute in Lancashire and Cheshire. Because the region was among the more disruptive, units had to be ordered into Chester as well as Shrewsbury, Shropshire, in the summer. Nevertheless in September the Lancashire and Cheshire militia were still in unsatisfactory condition due to the lack of deputy lieutenants. On the 9th and 23rd and again on 7 October 1662, Nicholas indicated the king's displeasure and his desire for an expeditious remedy to the earl of Derby. But according to one Cheshire royalist, even this action would be of little use because "the generality of the People, of which the militia must consist, . . . [are] vehemently infused with the Principles of disobedience to king & church, & are still soe kept by these preachers in their dayly conventicles."[81] Thus the repression of conventicles was tied to the need for a reliable militia.

Fear of designs by dissidents in Bristol forced the government to dispatch the duke of Ormond in September to settle the militia there, and in October the king, worried about the Wiltshire militia, ordered the earl of Southampton to have his deputy lieutenants keep a close eye on malcontents. Reorganizing the militia did not always achieve the intended results, for in the North Riding the changes meant that men were drawn from greater distances and could not be mobilized swiftly. Sir Jordan Crosland complained to Bennet of "how little saifety there is in these dull trained-bands."[82]

The discovery of the Tong plot incited greater efforts to expedite the militia settlement. On 31 October the Privy Council instructed the lords lieutenant to act with dispatch to get the militia ready and to direct their deputies to search for and confiscate weapons and ammunition in the possession of suspicious persons. The deputy lieutenants were also to post watches on the highways, disarm those who traveled with "unusual Armes" or at unseasonable hours, and arrest individuals who could not give a suitable account of themselves and their loyalty to the government. There was a sense of frustration as well as urgency in the king's directive to his lords lieutenant the following day: "The aforesaid danger is made most manifest & notorious by the profest disobedience & dissatisfaction which many discontented & mutinous spirits doe daily avow against the Government, and whom no Lawes how severe soever have hitherto been able to restraine from tumultuous & seditious meetings."[83] Charles directed the lieutenants to levy and disperse the £70,000 authorized by Parliament for the militia. On 3 November the deputy lieutenants in London ordered their captains to complete their company rolls, taking special care to ensure that each of their men was trustworthy, and to muster the companies for the administration of the oaths of allegiance and supremacy. The following day the deputies authorized their officers to employ their forces to suppress any insurrection and to assist constables in apprehending persons at unlawful meetings.[84]

As news of the Tong plot spread, special measures were taken to secure various towns and castles. At Exeter the governor, Sir James Smith, raised a company of foot at his own expense in a single day, clad them in red coats, and posted them to defend the castle and town until the trained bands could relieve them. In Chester too the mayor moved quickly to appoint a competent guard to protect the town. London's mayor commanded his constables to arrest those who attended illegal assemblies, especially the preachers and ringleaders, and to seize all arms and ammunition in the possession of factious persons. As soon as news of the plot reached Yarmouth, the watch was doubled and the post placed under observation; letters of suspected persons were opened by Sir Thomas Meadows in their presence.[85] Sir John Packington followed the same course in Norwich. In Devon the deputy lieutenants used the militia to secure Exeter and Plymouth, and one took direct command of Exeter Castle. Portsmouth too was secured, but the king was worried about the ports in general, especially Deal, because suspicious persons passed in and out of the country too easily. In early December Charles sent orders for the governor at Deal to prohibit ships from giving passage to unlicensed persons. Security was also responsible for the government's decision on 10 November 1662 to transfer the Fifth Monarchists Richard Goodgroom, John Portman, and John Rye from London to the castle at Hull, and Captain Bradshaw to the same castle from Nottingham.[86]

In addition to providing the motivation for improved security, the Tong plot offered the king an opportunity to reassess an earlier plan for an indulgence to benefit Nonconformists. On the eve of St. Bartholomew's day many Nonconformists had anticipated some form of toleration. When rumors of an indulgence reached Manchester, for example, "many Ministers that intended not to Preach fell to their work which caused great joy in many Congregations." Fearing an outbreak of violence if some toleration was not provided, Major-General Browne persuaded Clarendon to support an indulgence. But in the Privy Council the bishop of London, Gilbert Sheldon, successfully opposed the idea, even threatening noncompliance. For added measure, the bishop of Winchester informed Clarendon several days later that key officers in the London militia were threatening to lay down their commissions if the Presbyterians were tolerated.[87]

By December, Charles concluded that circumstances had sufficiently changed to warrant a fresh attempt to provide an indulgence. The Tong plot had highlighted the unsettled state of the militia and suggested the likelihood of future conspiracies directed against the monarch. Securing the realm would be not only expensive but politically costly for a government already unpopular because of taxes, the sale of Dunkirk, and religious repression. In the few months since St. Bartholomew's day it had become apparent that penal laws, instead of breaking the back of Nonconformity, were feeding the discontent. Honoring the promise at Breda of liberty to tender consciences might drive a wedge between the more moderate Nonconformists and those dissidents determined to overthrow the regime. Having faced the threat of a genuine insurrection, royalists presumably might be more amenable to a policy of modest toleration. Because Charles' real goal was to broaden his base of political support as much as possible—to be as comprehensive as feasible—he opted to extend the indulgence to Catholics. Curiously, his own officials had committed two priests to the Gatehouse for saying Mass only six days before he announced the new policy.[88] The decision to include the Catholics in the indulgence may therefore have been made very late or kept secret from some members of the government.

The declaration issued on 26 December 1662 took care to head off, insofar as possible, criticism of the king's proposal. On the explosive issue of the Catholics, Charles was adamant that blood would not be shed for religious reasons, a principle basic to his government. For the Catholics he proposed a *via media*, providing some relief from the penal acts but stopping short of full religious toleration, including public services of worship. This much, he said, they deserved, but he refused—rightly—to equate this step with favoring popery. With respect to the Tong plot, he expressed regret that some of his subjects had had to die for their treason, but declared that their infidelity would not dissuade him from faithfully executing the provisions of the Act of Indemnity. It was a shrewd appeal by Charles to the thousands of former Cromwellian officers and men, hoping to calm their apprehension that a general crack-down might ensue. Given the number of former officers arrested in the context of the Tong plot, such an assurance was necessary. The king also insisted that the Guards who had been raised were only to ensure his safety and were not the prelude to military or arbitrary rule. They did, however, number 3,200 men and 374 officers in 1661, making them more numerous than previous ceremonial Guards. Nevertheless, it is essential not to read this declaration through the perspective of the 1680s, for in 1662 the intent was clearly to achieve a policy of comprehension coupled with enhanced security. Charles was less interested in the religious convictions of people than their loyalty to the crown. In September he made it clear that he wanted the Corporation Act enforced in Bristol to ensure the city's allegiance, and nine days before his declaration concerning the indulgence he directed the lord mayor of London to assure the election of common councilmen whose loyalty was above suspicion. Sufficiently persuaded of the king's intent, the Privy Council approved his attempt to obtain parliamentary sanction for the indulgence.[89]

When a bill to implement the indulgence was introduced into Parliament in February 1663, however, it ran into intense opposition despite Clarendon's support. In the House of Commons the critics concentrated on three themes: (1) the bill would lead to popery; (2) an indulgence would bring an increase in the number of sectaries; and (3) the bill would recognize a prerogative in matters of religion that the king no longer enjoyed. Opposition was so strong that the bill was dropped in March. The wisdom of the king's policy with respect to toleration was defeated by the narrow interests of men determined to restrict the emoluments of power in church and state to themselves. Such proponents actually increased the likelihood of extreme action by dissidents deprived of any reasonable hope for toleration, though by pushing their enemies into more radical courses the advocates of exclusivism made it easier to tar them with the brush of sedition. Simultaneously, however, repudiation of the bill was a sharp and necessary rebuff to royal efforts to have Parliament recognize the king's dispensing power. By confusing the two issues, Charles doomed whatever chance he might have had to win limited toleration, at least for Protestants. Dashing the hopes of Nonconformists, whose expectancy one royalist described as "impudent," the advocates of exclusivism fed the mounting discontent that erupted in the insurrection of 1663.[90]

# 5

# "The Horrid Conspiracy"

## THE DUBLIN PLOT

Following the proclamation of Charles as king in Dublin on 14 May 1660, two key issues provided the basis for future disruption. The first of these involved the settlement of lands among a host of claimants ranging from royalists and former Irish rebels to the Cromwellian settlers currently enjoying possession. On 30 November the king issued an ill-advised declaration confirming the holdings of soldiers and adventurers who had possession in May 1659, with the exception of church lands, property acquired by decree in a Cromwellian court, and lands of persons who had opposed the Restoration. But Charles also promised that those who deserved the return of their property would not suffer. Loyalist officers who had fought for Charles I before June 1649 were to receive preference in their claims to the houses they had lost in walled towns. Similarly, dispossessed Protestants who had not rebelled were given precedence in their claims over soldiers and adventurers, but the latter groups were promised compensatory land. Catholics who had not rebelled in 1641–43 could reclaim their confiscated estates, even if they were in the possession of soldiers and adventurers, but in return they had to relinquish the lands they had received in Clare and Connaught. Such were the principles upon which the king's commissioners were to operate.[1]

In practice, the commissioners were beset with hopelessly conflicting claims. A 1662 Act of Settlement based on the 1660 royal declaration solved nothing, but in 1665 an Act of Explanation allowed one-third of the lands of soldiers and adventurers to be confiscated to help meet other claims.[2] In the end, the Catholics suffered the greatest injustices, but two overlapping groups of Protestants were also disgruntled: those who thought too much had been conceded to papists, and those who were dispossessed of their lands, whether to satisfy royalists, Anglican ecclesiastics, or Catholics.

The second disruptive issue involved the religious settlement at the Restoration. Charles' government adopted a policy of *de facto* toleration toward the Catholics, which alarmed Protestants in Ireland and England alike. Presbyterians and sectaries were likewise disturbed by the restoration of a narrow episcopal polity in the church, which was placed under the control of John Bramhall, archbishop of Armagh and primate of Ireland. Five days before the consecration of new bishops on 27 January 1661, the lords justices and Council issued a proclamation prohibiting unlawful meetings by Catholics, Presbyterians, Congregationalists, Baptists, and Quakers. Offenders were to be detained and bound over to appear at the assizes or sessions. According to the proclamation, recent assemblies of these groups were characterized by speakers who were "not afraid to speak evil of Dignities, and to cast dirt in the face of the lawful Magistrates, . . . and to inveigh against the known Laws of this Realm."[3] In May the Irish Parliament approved a declaration—which ministers were required to read aloud—calling on all subjects to conform to episcopalian polity and to use the prescribed liturgy. On the 29th, Parliament also issued an order for the public burning of the Solemn League and Covenant. In the meantime the bishops had begun the task of expelling incumbents who lacked episcopal ordination. Jeremy Taylor, responsible for the dioceses of Down and Connor and Dromore, was especially zealous, declaring no less than thirty- six parishes vacant in a single day.[4] As in England, the decision to re-establish a narrowly episcopalian state church exacerbated tensions, broadened the basis of discontent with the new regime, and contributed to political unrest.

## Irish Nonconformity

The policies of the Restoration regime made Nonconformity a more serious problem in Ireland than it should have been. A number of Cromwellian ministers sought to retain their positions in the state church, though not all were willing to pay the price of episcopal ordination. There was, nevertheless, a reservoir of good will toward the restored monarchy by many clergymen who were not Episcopalian. On 1 January 1661 a group of these Cromwellian clerics informed the earl of Orrery that "their is [not] the least Coullor or pretence for any who make the word of God their rule, to bee found in the least disobedience much less secrett ploteings or open resistance against a setled goverment, exercised by an undoubted lawfull authority." Even the Ulster Presbyterians, who were adamant in their refusal to countenance either episcopal ordination or the Book of Common Prayer, were preparing a remonstrance in September in the hope of getting Charles to grant them concessions to exercise their faith in light of their loyalty to him during the 1650s.[5]

The prelates and their allies worked to prevent any concessions and to insist on episcopal ordination. As early as February 1661, the earl of Orrery informed Secretary Nicholas that "we doe . . . every day gaine ground of the nonconformists & Phanatticks, for we give no Indulgence to any."[6] Although the non-episcopalian clergy had friends working in London on their behalf, John Parker, bishop of Elphin, was also there, pressing the case for an exclusive church with Bishop Sheldon and Ormond, both of whom had the king's ear. Michael Boyle, bishop of Cork, urged Archbishop Bramhall to have the bishops in northern Ireland watch the Presbyterians in order to head off any direct appeal to the king. Boyle himself had already warned Charles that any concessions to the Presbyterians would be prejudicial to the settlement of the Irish church.[7] As in England, the narrow interests of the prelates mitigated against a more comprehensive state church and thus of better prospects for domestic tranquility.

The return to a policy of exclusivity in religion caused a problem with conventicles. In the fall of 1661 the bishop of Derry was trying to stamp out illegal assemblies at Ballykelly and Limavady, where Presbyterians allegedly were going to the services in arms and speaking of an imminent rising. By early October he had routed them from their meeting places, only to find that they convened in the woods and hills. The threat of indictments brought most of the Presbyterians at Strabane into line, but in 1662 the bishop still anticipated trouble in Derry itself.[8] In July the former chaplain of the regicide Miles Corbet, a Mr. Smith, was arrested while conducting worship at a conventicle in Londonderry. Troops broke up a meeting outside Dublin in November at which 500 "Quakers and Sectaries" were allegedly present. "One Col. Ludlow and one Col. Desborough" were supposedly there, but this portion of the report was clearly erroneous. Altogether some 259 Quakers were imprisoned in Ireland in late 1660 and 1661.[9]

The Nonconformists posed a security problem. The episcopalian clergy pressed the lords justices in April 1662 to draw up a list of the "most dangerous seducers" and make them conform or banish them. In a broader context, there were fears that the Nonconformists undermined the defense of the kingdom. Because thousands in Ulster refused adherence to the episcopalian church, the lords justices were afraid to arm them, even for defensive purposes. The earl of Orrery worried that Nonconformists and Catholics would cause serious trouble if the army was withdrawn in an emergency, particularly since he expected the settlement of episcopacy in Scotland to drive both Catholics and Presbyterians into Ireland.[10] There was, moreover, uncertainty with regard to the army itself because so many of its men had served in the Cromwellian forces. Ormond hoped eventually to purge the army of all who did not accept the established church, but this required sufficient funds to pay arrears. By February 1661 the £20,000 that was provided was enough only to reduce the supernumerary horse and dragoons. Ormond moved slowly in replacing questionable officers, though he expressed himself pleased with the rate of progress by the end of 1663. He justified his decision on the grounds that many of the Cromwellians had in fact worked for the Restoration in 1660 and thus proved their loyalty. Their refusal to join in the radical plotting of the early 1660s proved him correct.[11]

## Years of Disaffection

The two years that preceded the Dublin conspiracy in the spring of 1663 were characterized by concern on the part of the authorities with spreading discontent, Nonconformist militancy, and contacts between dissidents in the three realms. Although Whitehall did not want the lords justices and Council in Ireland to prohibit travel and trade between Scotland and Ireland, it instructed them in March 1661 to apprehend "any dangerous or seditious persons" traveling between the two countries. Among the radicals thought to be in Ireland that winter were the regicides Edmund Ludlow and Thomas Wogan, though neither in fact was in Ireland after the Restoration.[12]

The government's concern with allegations of scheming and disaffection in England during the summer of 1661 extended to Ireland as well. On 31 August Secretary Nicholas directed the lords justices to take special care to discover any plots and secure those involved. On Orrery's recommendation, the corporations in Munster were purged of dissidents, and the earl of Mountrath urged a similar policy toward Connaught, particularly in light of his earlier difficulties with disaffected officials in Galway. As in England, there were problems too with radical publications.[13] In November the people of Ulster were "affrighted out of their wits" by the prodigies depicted in *Mirabilis Annus*, which the bishop of Clogher regarded as nothing short of treasonous. The same month Orrery recommended that Archbishop Bramhall seek out the author of a libelous pamphlet, for "such little seeds, if not rooted out, often bring forth quantity of ill fruit." In December 1662 Ormond decided to have Secretary Bennet investigate any suspicious publications believed to originate in England. Early the next year the authorities intercepted a letter apparently composed by Nonconformists in Ireland that Elizabeth Calvert was to have printed in London. Ostensibly written by a Catholic, the letter was clearly intended to inflame anti-popish hysteria, in part by talk of "Crush[ing] the fannatick officers by Peiling theire Rind, and Imprisoning some of the leading men" as part of a plan to make the army Catholic.[14]

The stockpiling of arms and ammunition was a further cause of consternation. Despite frequent prohibitions on the import of gunpowder and munitions into Ireland without license as well as orders that such substances be turned in to authorities, the dissidents remained defiant. On 10 October the lords justices and Council therefore issued a new proclamation, giving unauthorized individuals possessing powder until 10 December to surrender it without penalty. A further proclamation, dated 7 November, banned all but designated persons such as M.P.s and military personnel from using or wearing firearms as they traveled or from taking weapons into garrisons. As justification, the proclamation noted that disaffected persons were buying and wearing firearms more than usual.[15] Suspicious people were subsequently disarmed, especially in Derry, where both men and women had threatened the bishop. By December the problem was so pronounced that both houses of the Irish Parliament asked the lords justices to secure all dangerous persons and to prohibit any Catholics or malcontents from living within any walled town or fort without a license. Not until 1 October 1662, however, did Ormond and his Council instruct Orrery to remove such individuals from the Munster garrisons.[16]

By mid-1662 Secretary Nicholas had informers working in Ireland to apprise him of dissident activity. According to one report the radicals boasted that they were 20,000 strong and under the leadership of Sir Bryce Cochrane (or Cockram), an Ulster Presbyterian, Colonel Robert Duckenfield, a Cheshire Congregationalist and former Cromwellian officer, Colonel Jerome Sankey, previously arrested in connection with the White plot, and Marshal-General Richard Lawrence, a Baptist who had supported Lambert in 1659. One of their number, Captain Clerk, was in correspondence with dissidents in London. Another report indicated that the English malcontents in Ireland were ready to "withstand" Ormond if he tried to repress them, adding that they expected little opposition because a number of soldiers had been sent to Portugal.[17] In November the authorities arrested various dissidents, including someone identified as Major Desborough, Captain Oland, and one of Ludlow's kinsmen, all of whom were taken at a private meeting near Dublin on the 9th. Lieutenant-Colonel Nicholas Kempson (or Kempston), Ludlow's brother-in-law and probably the man arrested on the 9th, and Philip Alden, who subsequently became an informer, were imprisoned in Dublin Castle the following day.[18]

Unrest over religion and the land settlement had Ormond and Orrery very edgy in early 1663. Never, Orrery told Clarendon, had the English in Ireland been as disgruntled as they were now. Although the commissioners of claims had as yet issued few decrees, they had made numerous enemies of those who feared the confiscation of their estates. Wherever an Irishman was restored to his land, Ormond complained, reports were rampant that the king favored Catholics and Irish rebels. Charles himself urged his commissioners to remain impartial despite "severall threats, & disrespects used to you, by some turbulent & unquiet persons, to discourage or at least byase you."[19] Ormond was hopeful that the unrest would not lead to rebellion, especially because insufficient funds prevented him from keeping the army in a state of readiness. He suggested to Clarendon that the government threaten to arm the Irish to suppress disturbances and thus cow the rebellious English and Scots, but he clearly intended this to be no more than a threat. As he told the king in February, the military was so ill prepared that it was impossible to predict how far a rising might succeed.[20] Ormond had cause to worry, for a plot to surprise Dublin Castle and kidnap him was already underway.

## The Dublin Plot

The government received advance notice of a conspiracy to seize Dublin Castle from the attorney Philip Alden, a former Cromwellian, a dealer in forfeited estates, and allegedly an agent of Edmund Ludlow's. By early 1663 Alden was in the employ of Colonel Edward

Vernon, who had put Alden in his debt by interceding on his behalf with Ormond. On 6 January Alden divulged to Vernon that a revolutionary committee composed mostly of members of the Irish Parliament was meeting in Dublin to launch an insurrection in the three kingdoms. At Vernon's behest, Alden told his story to Ormond, who insisted that he continue spying and report regularly.[21] The attempt on the castle was originally scheduled for 9 or 10 March, but the cabal moved the date up to the 5th to coincide with the assignment of Sir John Stephens' company to guard duty. A sergeant and fifty men of Stephens' company were reputedly pledged to rise, supplied with arms and powder from a local depot. Alden learned of the new time too late to help the government, but Ormond had been tipped off on the 4th by a soldier whom Lieutenant Turet, one of the plotters, had tried to recruit. When the conspirators learned that they had been betrayed, some fled.[22]

There was no doubt in Ormond's mind that the plot was real, and this was confirmed by additional information from Orrery in Munster and from others in Leinster and Ulster. Repeated interrogations, however, did not lead to anyone more prominent than Captain William Hulet (or Hewlett). The inability to learn more, Ormond warned Bennet, was "an argument of our greater danger."[23] He was equally frustrated that they could not obtain enough evidence to procure a conviction even against Hulet. Most of those arrested were former English soldiers now working as tradesmen. Orrery told Clarendon they were Fifth Monarchists, but there is insufficient data to evaluate this charge. The government in any case had difficulty finding evidence to prosecute them.[24] It suspected the involvement of Colonel Henry Pretty (or Pritty), former governor of Carlow, who fled from Limerick in an armed ship that had ostensibly been preparing for a voyage to Brazil. Pretty remained at large until mid-May, when his ship was captured among the Aran Islands off Ireland's west coast. There was a rumor that Ludlow had escaped with him, but he was neither on the ship nor anywhere near Ireland.[25]

News that the plot had been discovered brought some relief, quieting "the mindes of most men in this Kingdome." The authorities responded to the design by stepping up security measures, especially in Munster. Orrery finally acted on Ormond's instructions of the previous October to have disaffected persons removed from the garrisons unless they conformed by 23 June 1663.[26] He purged "fanatics and needless papists" from Waterford and Limerick, and then ordered the mayor of Cork to expel "the most dangerous sort of fanatics." Orrery also took the precaution of making certain that none of his soldiers were linked to the Dublin plot.[27]

As early as April the government was aware that the abortive March conspiracy had been revived. One of Ormond's spies had been dispatched to Tipperary, Waterford, and Kilkenny to recruit dissidents, and Major Alexander Staples and a Colonel Wallace had reportedly joined the conspirators. Colonel Vernon informed Bennet on 6 April that this time Ormond would refrain from reacting too soon, preferring instead to "gather it when it is full rippe."[28] Vernon called Bennet's attention to Stephen Charnock, a former chaplain to Henry Cromwell; Charnock had reported to Irish radicals that "they warr soe Hampered in England that they could not stir till the Eyce was broken, either in this place, or Scott Land." They had "generally rejected" Cromwell as their general but "did not possitively refusse Ludlow for their designed Captaine."[29] Bennet had also been warned about Charnock by Lord Inchiquin, who believed that Charnock was in Ireland to encourage conspiracy. Ormond therefore informed the king on the 8th that a new design was in progress "by the same kinde of people" responsible for the March plot. He was still sensitive that he had learned so little about the first cabal, though he was adamant that it had been real because of confessions by those in custody and "the unusuall meetings & prepareations . . . about the same tyme in severall partes of the Kingdome." Interestingly, however, he was not sure of the trustworthiness of Alden.[30]

Ormond bided his time, determined to let the conspirators proceed so far that he could make examples of them. His goal was to apprehend them in the act of seizing the castle. By the 16th he had learned that so many were engaged that the rebels themselves believed someone would betray them to the authorities, but they had gone so far in their planning that they were determined to press ahead. Ormond's information indicated that they had allies in England and Scotland, though the latter would not rise until the insurrection was underway in Dublin. "If those here will begin they shall be seconded in both the other kingdomes." Despite the danger, Ormond was convinced he could safely delay making arrests, especially since he received information on radical activity almost hourly. To act precipitously, he said to Charles, would risk letting the conspirators escape the death penalty and live to scheme again. Ormond took the precaution on the 19th of ordering the governors of Londonderry, Galway, and Carrickfergus to use diligence to discover persons involved in the plot and to ensure sufficient security to protect their garrisons.[31]

On the morning of the 20th Ormond received a reasonably full outline of the plot from Sir Theophilus Jones, who had been approached the previous day at Lucan, west of Dublin, by Colonel Alexander Jephson, M. P. for Trim. What Jephson told Jones, however, was an account of the scheme flawed by lavishly inflated numbers, presumably in the hope of persuading Jones of the inevitability of success. Jephson, whose regiment had fought in Ireland in the 1640s, allegedly offered Jones command of a revolutionary army of 20,000 once the insurrection succeeded. According to Jones, Jephson—appealing to English interests—claimed the rebels were certain of their ability to seize Dublin Castle, Cork, Limerick, Waterford, and Clonmel. Some 15,000 Scots excommunicated by bishops in the north were reportedly ready to join them. There was enough money in Dublin, Jephson asserted, to pay the army's arrears in full, and he thought the funds might have come from the Netherlands. There were 1,000 horse in Dublin, he claimed, and as soon as the castle was taken and a flag raised, Sir Henry Ingoldsby, the former governor of Limerick, would declare for them and bring an additional 1,000. The rebels intended to seize Ormond but do him no harm. Jephson's responsibility was to secure the earl of Clancarty and Colonel Fitzpatrick. Six ministers had been assigned the task of patrolling the streets of Dublin to ensure that no looting occurred during the rising. According to Jephson, thousands of copies of a declaration had been printed that claimed the rebels were acting to secure the English interest in all three kingdoms. The English would be confirmed in the possession of the Irish estates they held on 7 May 1659 and the church would be established in accord with the principles of the Solemn League and Covenant. Such demands reflected no more than the concerns of moderate dissidents, and lacked, for example, the truly radical call for a republican government. As soon as Jephson left, Jones recorded the substance of the conversation and informed Ormond the following morning.[32] Still, Ormond did not arrest the rebels.

Although Jephson's version of the plot was grossly exaggerated, the conspiracy itself was real enough. On the 20th three congregations—two Presbyterian and one Congregationalist—gathered to seek divine blessing on the scheme. That evening Lieutenant Thomas Blood and his brother-in-law, the Presbyterian minister William Lecky (or Lackey, Lackie), James Tanner, formerly a clerk to Henry Cromwell's secretary, and Major (or Lieutenant) Richard

Thompson, who once served under John Otway (or Ottoway) and was deputy provost-marshal of Leinster, dined together at the White Hart in Patrick Street. After dinner they were joined for a discussion of the plot by Philip Alden, Captain Browne, Colonel Alexander Jephson, and two men from Trim. William Skelton arrived in Dublin that night with six horse to join the insurrection, but this apparently only raised the total number of horse to a paltry ten. Lawrence, one of the men from Trim, nevertheless urged them to act, despite the fact that the original plan called for 120 horse (not the 1,000 claimed by Jephson).[33]

According to the scheme, as the state later pieced it together from prisoners' accounts, six rebels, including a Dublin shoemaker named Jenkins, would enter the great gate of the castle between 6 and 7 A.M. the next morning in the guise of petitioners. As they moved toward the back gate leading into Ship Street, a band of eighty to one hundred foot would take up positions outside the gate. On signal, a rebel disguised as a baker was to spill loaves of bread as he entered the gate, enabling the six petitioners to jump the distracted guards and allow the foot to pour into the castle. While the foot secured the castle gates and the weapons' storeroom, the horse were to move through the city, dispersing any groups of soldiers and securing the town gates and the suburbs, crying all the while, "A free Parliament and an English interest."[34] After securing Dublin they planned to march north to join forces with the Ulster Scots. The rebels, however, found themselves shorthanded in the face of increased security forces. Expecting an additional 500 officers and men to arrive in Dublin in a week, they postponed the insurrection.[35]

After hearing about 4 A.M. on the 21st that the rising had been delayed, Ormond dispatched parties to arrest the conspirators, of whom two dozen were initially taken. Copies of the proclamation were seized, at least one of which was in Blood's handwriting. The lord lieutenant issued a proclamation the same day announcing the discovery of "mischevious Contrivances for renewinge bloody Confusions throughout this Kingdome," and directing the presidents of the provinces and the magistrates to arrest any persons who were involved.[36] The seriousness of the conspiracy was underscored by Colonel Vernon, who correctly observed that "many persons of Quallity & Carraige [were] conscerned in this bussinesse," though it was an exaggeration to think that "the Generallity of all the Olde Rebell English officers, and Scotts ware ingaged in it." Concern was increased because of the presence of malcontents in the army.[37]

Of the twenty-four men originally apprehended, six were ex-officers: Colonels Thomas Scott, son of the regicide, and Edward Warren, "a zealous Presbyterian," both of whom had served under Henry Cromwell in Ireland; Colonel Alexander Jephson; Captains Theophilus Sandford and John Chambers, who also had served under Cromwell; and Major (or Lieutenant) Thompson. At least six others, all troopers, had military experience. Two others were ministers, the Presbyterian William Lecky and the Congregationalist Edward Baines, formerly a pastor at St. Patrick's, Dublin, and a chaplain to Henry Cromwell. Among the rest were the informer Philip Alden and the Scottish merchant Thomas Boyd (or Bond) of Dublin.[38] However, some of the principal suspects escaped, forcing Ormond to issue a second proclamation on the 23rd that offered a reward of £100 for their apprehension. Among those named were nine more ex-officers, including Colonel Gilby Carr, Major Abel Warren, and Lieutenant Thomas Blood, and two more ministers, Robert Chambers (or Chambrey), who had been in trouble in 1660 for publishing a treasonable pamphlet, and the Presbyterian Andrew McCormack (or McCormick) of Magherally.[39]

By mid-June some seventy prisoners were in custody. Those who thought the conspiracy was no more than the work of a few petty malcontents were wrong, as were those who thought the plot was a government fabrication. Colonel Vernon may have been exaggerating when he reckoned that fully 30,000 persons in Ireland would have joined the rising had the castle been seized, but the reservoir of anger among the 'new' English as well as the Scots was sizeable enough to have made the situation explosive.[40] Untangling the full story initially proved to be difficult, and in late May Ormond determined that sufficient evidence to prosecute could only be obtained if some of the accused were pardoned. The lord lieutenant and his secretary, Sir Paul Davis, did most of the interrogating, and by mid-June they were hearing many confessions.[41]

The core of the conspiracy was a revolutionary committee of six members, of whom five were former officers: Colonel Robert Shapcote, an attorney, Majors Abel Warren and Richard Thompson, Captain Theophilus Sandford, and Lieutenant Thomas Blood. The others were the merchant Thomas Boyd and possibly the informer Philip Alden.[42] They had considered placing the command of their forces in one man, but finally opted to establish a council of officers that would include Edmund Ludlow, Henry Cromwell, Sir Richard Ingoldsby, Sir Theophilus Jones, Colonel Gilby Carr, Sir Edward Massey, Sir John Skeffington, Lord Massereene, and Sir Audley Mervin.[43] It was Jephson's attempt to recruit Jones, of course, that provided Ormond with crucial last-minute information about the plot. Such a council would have been a potent force indeed, though in fact it was never a realistic possibility. Ludlow was in Switzerland; Massey was a royalist who had actively helped restore Charles; Ingoldsby had already shown his colors by crushing Lambert's rising; Massereene, though a friend of the Presbyterians, was no revolutionary; and Cromwell had quietly retired. Only Carr was a hard-core dissident, but even his interests were fundamentally religious in nature. That such men were even considered underscores the fact that the plot was not essentially antimonarchical but a move to preserve Protestant and English interests in Ireland.[44] There were, it is true, some among the rebels who wanted to assassinate Charles and Ormond and establish a republic, but Alden's assertion that they prevailed is erroneous.[45] Only with the support of moderate dissidents did the conspiracy have any chance of success, and that meant focusing on land and religion, not the overthrow of monarchy.

As Ormond pieced together the story of the conspiracy, he learned that it had initially been conceived by Blood around early September 1662. About Christmas time Blood and Lecky had gone to Ulster to solicit Scottish support, meeting first with the Presbyterian ministers John Greg, John Hart (or Heart), and Andrew Stewart as well as Captain James Moor of Killinchy. After discussing such issues as prelatical usurpation and the increase of popery, they made it clear to Blood that they would do nothing unlawful or prejudicial to royal authority. Despairing of support in Down or Antrim, Blood and Lecky went to Lagan and Armagh, but in the end they found support only from the Presbyterians Andrew McCormack and John Crookshanks.[46] By the beginning of January, Blood and Lecky were back in Dublin, where they met with Colonel Shapcote and Major Thompson at Boyd's house to recount their trip to the north and explain their plans for a rising. When Boyd met Blood and Lecky about 10 February, he learned that Shapcote had backed out of the plot, though he promised not to reveal it. But Captain John Chambers had joined the cabal and was seen on several occasions in Blood's company.[47]

In early April Blood recruited James Tanner, showing him a letter from Stephen Charnock, which Tanner interpreted to mean that Henry Cromwell would soon be in Ireland to head the rebels. Charnock himself had arrived from England about 1 April and met in Dublin with Blood, Tanner, and Colonel Alexander Staples. At that meeting Blood announced that the attempt on the castle would take place in May. Staples subsequently went north to raise more support among the Scots and to secure Londonderry. Once Dublin Castle was in rebel hands, his plan was to take the field in the north. Having previously commanded the garrison in Derry, Staples knew soldiers there who were loyal to him.[48]

The secret meetings and preparations continued apace in May as the projected date of the rising neared. Blood and Lecky met with Thompson, Boyd, and Sandford in mid-May, at which time Lieutenant-Colonel More joined the plot. Another meeting was held on the 17th in the Dublin home of Colonel Edward Warren, at which Thompson, Tanner, Captain Browne, former governor of Liverpool, and John Chamberlain, a Dublin brewer, were present. The main subject of discussion was whether Thompson would command a party of horse that would help seize the castle or join Warren in securing the city itself.[49] Some of the other leaders left Dublin to take up their assigned positions elsewhere. Staples was already in the north. Carr and More went to Ulster, while Warren's brother William was at Trim to recruit soldiers. John Chambers agreed to raise a party in county Louth, which Foulke would lead to Dublin. After a visit to Dublin to check on preparations, McCormack returned to Ulster, though the cabal had expected to hear from him before the attempt on the castle was made. A group of dissident ex-officers in Munster who had served under Ludlow was also believed to be part of the conspiracy. Among them were Lieutenant-Colonel Nicholas Kempson (or Kempston), Ludlow's brother-in-law, and Colonel Solomon Richards.[50] The collapse of the plot on the night of 20–21 May defused whatever risings might have erupted in Ulster or Munster.

The man who allegedly conceived the plot,[51] Thomas Blood, escaped, fleeing initially to Presbyterian friends in Antrim. From there he hid among the Irish in the hills of Ulster, pretending to be a priest. Using aliases and disguises he also went into county Wicklow, where he renewed his correspondence with other radicals. There were fears that he might attempt to assassinate Ormond. Carr too escaped, going via Scotland back to the Netherlands, where he had been early in 1663. The ministers McCormack and Crookshanks fled to Scotland, where they eventually fought in the Galloway rising in 1666. Charnock escaped to England, took the alias of Clark, and renewed his association with the stationer Thomas Littlebury of Little Britain, London.[52]

Several score individuals were arrested and some confessed. Apprehended in the north by Sir Arthur Forbes, Major Staples insisted that he had written to him about the plot some two weeks before his arrest. Forbes eventually supported Staples' claim and urged that he be pardoned. The king, however, initially refused a pardon on the ground that Ireland needed examples of justice rather than mercy, but after spending a year in prison Staples received it. Charles initially felt the same way about Colonel Shapcote, though letters on his behalf from loyal subjects were apparently behind the king's decision in 1664 to grant him a pardon as well.[53] Thomas Scott and Theophilus Sandford not only confessed but testified against their compatriots, for which they were eventually pardoned in 1666. Robert Chambers remained in hiding until the autumn of 1669, when his wife negotiated a pardon in return for his providing security.[54]

The king wanted some swift and severe examples of justice, but only on those for whom there was sufficient proof. Ormond was of the same mind, and was ultimately disappointed that so few rebels were executed. Yet he too was concerned that the evidence be meticulously accumulated because "the prisoners are to well friended to want advice."[55] This did not stop him, however, from brushing aside the scruples of some of the judges and pressing ahead with a trial. On 25 June Lecky, Jephson, Edward Warren, Thompson, and John Chambers were arraigned at the bar of King's Bench.[56] Tried the first week in July, Lecky was the first to be found guilty, but he feigned madness, crying "out the divell was with him & what would they doe if he should confesse the whole plott & . . . [screaming] out as if he had beene really mad." He also blasphemed God and professed to be Jesus Christ.[57] Because of this display, his sentencing was deferred. Thompson, Jephson, and Warren were found guilty and sentenced to death, but proceedings against Chambers were delayed. According to Colonel Vernon, Thompson, Jephson, and Warren were penitent and recommended that officials closely watch the Presbyterians because they had engaged to act in all three kingdoms.[58]

Jephson, Warren, and Thompson were taken to Gallows Green to be executed on 15 July. On the scaffold, Jephson blamed his death on the Catholics, condemned "Church Papists who make a shew of the Protestant Religion," and asserted that the plotters intended no harm to the king, the duke of York, or Ormond. Warren too attributed his death to the papists, denied that he had committed treason, and defended the justice of their cause. Although God's government "be now in the Dust," he proclaimed, "yet not long since it made the Mountaines of the Earth to tremble and terribly shooke the Cedars of Lebanon and will againe revive till all the Enemies of it are dealt withall. . . ."[59] Thompson, however, acknowledged his offense, blamed Blood for seducing him, and professed his loyalty to the king and the Church of England. All three were hanged, but Thompson's confession saved him from being beheaded like the others.[60]

In prison Lecky continued to feign insanity. One report indicated that only a matter of days before the execution of his compatriots he "knocked out his owne braynes."[61] In November, however, he escaped from Newgate prison disguised as a woman after two friends filed off his irons. He was captured a day later as he left his hiding place in the hollow of a wall over Little Thomas Court. The escape was used as proof that he was no longer insane, and he was executed in Dublin on 12 December. A rumor that Blood was on his way to rescue Lecky made the crowd of 2,000 panic. Even the executioner temporarily fled, leaving Lecky on the scaffold with a rope around his neck, but all to no avail; the sentence was executed that day.[62]

Another of the principals, Philip Alden, feigned escape from prison in June with the covert assistance of Colonel Vernon, the intent being to preserve his credit with the radical community, particularly since he was supposed to be in communication with Ludlow. So carefully was the escape arranged that the constable of Dublin Castle was dismissed on the grounds of carelessness. Either in the expectation that the radicals were reading the mail or in a deliberate attempt to preserve Alden's cover, Vernon's letter of the 19th to Joseph Williamson urged him to secure the "villain" Alden if he came to Whitehall.[63] In England Alden worked as an undercover agent for three years before he was finally suspected in 1666. He subsequently retired to Ireland where he had the benefit of a formal pardon and a pension of £100 per annum.[64]

The Dublin plot posed special problems because of the involvement of several members of the Irish Parliament. In that body (now prorogued), feelings had been running very high against the commissioners, even to the point of contemplating their impeachment. Although some of the conspirators, according to Vernon, insisted that their design was "wholy presbyterian" and had been initiated "long before the Commissioners suites," he rightly observed that "this hasty Running of theires into Rebellion was much forwarded by the Commishioners proseedings."[65] Ten M. P.s were initially arrested for suspected complicity in the plot, and Ormond was persuaded that they were the principal contrivers.[66] In the end, no less than eight M. P.s proved to be conspirators: the barrister Robert Shapcote, M. P. for Wicklow, whom Ormond regarded as a leader in the House, Alexander Staples, M. P. for Strabane, Thomas Boyd, M. P. for Bangor, Abel Warren, M. P. for Kilkenny town, Thomas Scott, M. P. for county Wexford, John Chambers, M. P. for Ardee, and John Ruxton (or Roockston), also M. P. for Ardee. The eighth member, Alexander Jephson, was executed. When Parliament resumed sitting in the autumn of 1665, both Houses condemned the conspirators, and the Commons expelled the seven M. P.s who had been implicated and incapacitated them from sitting again. None of the seven chose to appear to defend himself.[67]

Ormond also had to deal with the fact that dissidents in Ireland were in regular contact with their counterparts in Scotland and England. Orrery was convinced that the Ulster Scots would not rebel unless they had "stronge Confederates in Scotland, to make them do it." He sent the king the names of messengers dispatched by the Dublin conspirators to Scotland. His agents also came across copies of a letter from Bristol containing an "ugly Libell" that were circulating among "Phanatticks" in county Tipperary. One of his informers told him that the Dublin conspiracy had supporters in all three kingdoms, and that "many" had come to Ireland to assist. Among them were Major John Browne, who had once served in Oliver Cromwell's regiment, and Captain Browne, the former governor of Liverpool, who was in fact linked to the Dublin cabal. The former was imprisoned in Limerick by Orrery. On the basis of such reports the king asked Ormond for further information on contacts between the Dublin plotters and dissidents in the other realms. The government also dispatched orders to the Scottish chancellor on 16 June to bar entry to all passengers coming from Ireland and to notify Ormond of any persons in Scotland who threatened the peace in Ireland.[68] When Sir Philip Musgrave returned to Carlisle in June, he learned that on the eve of the plot there had been unusual movements of soldiers between Ireland and Scotland as well as increased conventicle activity, all of which sounded suspicious. By August Bennet surmised that the conspirators had been in correspondence with English radicals, who "had bragged of there hopes" for the rising. There had even been a mysterious and probably unfounded report from Chatham in June of men leaving for Ireland and of a plot to burn the ships of the royal navy at their docks.[69] Although extant evidence is not sufficient to confirm any sizeable movement of dissidents between Ireland and England or Scotland, it is certain that radicals in the three realms as well as on the Continent were in touch with each other.[70] Under the circumstances it was imperative for Ormond to step up security measures.

## Securing the Realm

The condition of the military in Ireland was such that the government had little confidence in its reliability. The army was behind in its pay, staffed in part by officers who were absent or of dubious loyalty, and generally unsettled after the upheavals of the 1640s and 1650s. Although the government had ten days in which to ready units to deal with the anticipated Dublin insurrection, Colonel Vernon observed that only six troops could be trusted, and they were so poor, he claimed, that 180 rebel cavalry men could have beaten them. To Secretary Bennet he recommended that six or seven of the most unreliable troops of horse be disbanded and the savings be used to bring 200 trustworthy horse from England.[71] Ormond himself complained to Bennet that his greatest problem was insufficient money to pay the army. To compensate, he opted to reduce troops of horse to forty-five common troopers and companies of foot to sixty common soldiers. With the resulting savings he hoped eventually to raise the pay of the men and thereby reduce their desire to leave the service. Bennet approved partial disbanding and favored the idea of buttressing the forces in Ireland with reliable men from England. When Orrery accordingly reduced his forces in Munster, most of the dismissed men went home cheerfully.[72] Obtaining new recruits from England, however, proved to be difficult. On 20 June the lord lieutenant made a request for 500 foot and about 100 horse to distribute among the existing forces, but he did not want higher officers because this would require displacing officers already in Ireland. Although Albemarle complained that he did not have that many reliable men in his own army, the plan moved ahead. In late August Pepys and Sir William Penn, commissioner of the navy, discussed sending Ormond 500 soldiers. The lord lieutenant was adamant that he would accept them only if the cost was not borne out of his own Exchequer, and accordingly £1,100 was provided by the government in London.[73] In the end, more and more men were needed.

To deal with the problem of military discipline, Charles ordered Ormond on 6 June to formulate and implement a code of martial law in keeping with former precedents "for the restraining of all vicious, licentious and mutinous disorders" among his troops. Ormond, however, protested that in peacetime martial law was inadequate to inflict either corporal punishment or death on an offender, and, with Strafford's fate in mind, he could not "easily sign a warrant for it." Instead he preferred that appropriate rules to govern the army in peacetime be established by an act of the Irish Parliament.[74]

On 16 June Ormond reacted to the Dublin conspiracy by decreeing that all untrustworthy persons be disarmed and that concealing firearms was an offense. Because so many people would be employed in carrying out this task, he expected some of the dissidents to receive enough advance notice to secrete their weapons. In county Dublin only prelates, peers, privy councillors, judges, magistrates, and active soldiers were allowed to retain their arms. Ormond's decision met with the approval of both the king and Orrery, and the work proceeded apace.[75] Yet Ormond subsequently confessed to Charles that in taking up the firearms and securing suspicious persons he had acted without legal authority. What undermined this policy in practice, however, was the periodic threat of a Catholic uprising, which necessitated that English Protestants have recourse to weapons. On 5 August 1663 Ormond restored the right to bear arms to those who had taken communion in the Church of Ireland in the preceding six months or who had the lord lieutenant's approval.[76]

Other measures were proposed to enhance security, but none could substitute for a thorough resettling of the army. Bennet suggested to Ormond that he demolish some of the garrisons to prevent their falling into rebel hands in the event of an uprising. Orrery relied on informers both in the army and among the disaffected English and the Irish to keep him posted on incipient trouble. In the face of renewed Irish plotting in the spring of 1665, for instance, he instructed his forces in Munster to allow no armed persons to enter the garrisons, to prohibit markets in the towns, and to watch strangers who moved into garrisons. Orrery's difficulty with new recruits, many of whom spoke mutinously when their pay was as much as six months overdue, was probably typical.[77]

While acknowledging the problems with the military, Ormond was defensive about his own efforts to improve their dependability. In a memorandum dated 9 December 1663 he noted that a number of officers had been replaced, and that few remained who were untrustworthy. The problem of the officers was complicated by the fact that many were members of Parliament, so that proceeding against them too severely would create opposition in the Irish House of Commons. As long as they retained their commands, Ormond felt reasonably sure that they would support royal interests. He was also operating on the principle that those who had promoted the Restoration should not be displaced. On the whole, the lord lieutenant was convinced that his policy of gradual military reformation was justified by success, the Dublin conspiracy notwithstanding. There was, he insisted, insufficient appreciation of the fact that enough disbanded officers and soldiers remained in Ireland to constitute a good army and thus a potent threat to his government.[78]

The menace of the Dublin plot also persuaded Ormond to strike hard at selected Nonconformists. On 16 June, the day he ordered untrustworthy persons disarmed, he and the Council directed the presidents of the provinces to arrest all ministers suspected of involvement in the conspiracy or of seducing the people from obedience by their preaching, any bonds to the contrary notwithstanding. Ormond felt that as long as Nonconformist clergy lived in Ulster, the people would not embrace the established church and Ireland would be endangered. Although he lacked sufficient evidence to convict the Nonconformist ministers of complicity in the conspiracy, he found their general threat to the public peace sufficient grounds for apprehending many of them. At that point, however, he did not know how to proceed inasmuch as they could not legally be held in prison or banished. Shipping them back to Scotland would not prevent their return, nor would requiring them to post security keep them from freedom of movement among the population. The king resolved this dilemma by instructing Ormond to keep the most dangerous clergy in prison, moving them around as necessary in order to prevent their release on writs of *habeas corpus*, and to release the others on bond.[79]

Ormond attempted to distinguish between Nonconformists who were generally supportive of the conspiracy and those who "utterly declined any Conjunction in soe Traiterous a designe." Although a temporary indulgence announced on 30 April had not produced uniformity, the lord lieutenant and his council extended the indulgence from 29 June to 24 December, excluding only ministers who attempted to dissuade people from conforming. The practice of imprisoning factious clergy and bonding those who agreed to leave the kingdom was balanced against this offer of indulgence, the ultimate aim of which was ecclesiastical uniformity. Yet Ormond was hesitant about allowing them to leave Ireland without royal approval, knowing that most would go to Scotland or England and there be a source of trouble. Keeping them in prisons "remote from their aquaintance[s] & former habitations," however, required government expense because so many of the clergy were poor.[80]

Ormond's doubts were justified, for on 4 August Bennet ordered him not to allow the bonded clerics to leave for England or Scotland because their relative anonymity in those countries would facilitate their ability to spread "seditious" doctrines. The king, however, was willing for Ormond to continue jailing the factious clerics. Ormond protested that in Ireland "men were more prepard to receive their disloyall doctrine then either in England or Scotland by reason of the losse of the estates some were possessed & thought themselves sure of, & the apprehensions of very many others that the case will be theirs." Freeing them on bond while allowing them to remain on the island, he argued, would only make them martyrs. In any case, many of them ordinarily traveled back and forth between Scotland and Ireland. Having said his piece, however, he agreed to keep the bonded clergy in Ireland.[81]

Some indication of what this meant for the ministers is provided in the account of the Presbyterian pastor from Carncastle, Patrick Adair. Because Adair, Andrew Stewart, and William Semple had been in Dublin about six months before the rebels were ready to rise, Ormond suspected them of complicity and ordered them arrested and brought to Dublin. Lord Mountalexander interceded for Stewart and Lord Massereene for Adair, though the latter was confined at Dublin in Massereene's house for six months. Semple was not imprisoned but had to provide security. In June 1663 the government had the Nonconformist clergy in counties Antrim and Down apprehended. Those in Antrim, who were taken to Carrickfergus and detained in private houses for approximately two months, were twelve in number. When Ormond offered them freedom if they left Ireland, three departed. Massereene interceded on behalf of another.[82]

Seven Nonconformists from Down, all Presbyterians, were imprisoned in Carlingford Castle. Two of them—Andrew Stewart of Donaghadee and John Greg of Newtownards—were subsequently taken to Dublin, where Stewart confessed that they had met with Blood and Lecky. Although Greg was kept close prisoner for some nine months, Stewart became ill and received the freedom of the city on a bond of £1,000 after five or six weeks of confinement. Another Presbyterian in county Down, Henry Livingstone of Drumbo, was also taken to Dublin for interrogation. The Presbyterian William Jack (or Jacque) of Aghadoe in county Kerry was believed to have been involved in the plot but apparently was not arrested. Others, such as the Presbyterian Michael Bruce, escaped to Scotland before they could be apprehended.[83]

The attack on the Nonconformist clergy was only temporarily successful. The Presbyterians of Antrim and Down were deprived of their spiritual leaders, yet these men had not demonstrated any real proclivity to revolutionary activity. Nor does the support in the north for the Dublin conspiracy appear to have been extensive, though the authorities in fairness could not safely have ignored the potential for violence in Ulster. The government had more to fear from the former officers and soldiers, particularly those whose lands were threatened by the royal commission. In fact, some of the zeal with which the conspiracy was prosecuted can probably be attributed to a desire for the rebels' lands. Among the more attractive estates were those of Staples, Abel Warren, and Blood, worth £500, up to £500, and £100 per annum, respectively.[84] The unusual interest in the lands of the accused underscores the hopelessness the government faced in achieving a just land settlement satisfactory to royalists, former Cromwellians, and the Irish. The conjunction of religious and economic interests in Ireland created a volatile situation that was only compounded by the problems inherent in the army. That the government of Charles II survived in Ireland was due less to its policies than to the unwillingness and inability of either the native Irish—mostly docile after the Cromwellian conquest—or the ex-Cromwellians and Ulster Scots to mount a full-scale insurrection. Perhaps Colonel Vernon was right in thinking that Ormond's men could not have defeated 180 rebel horse in May 1663, but no matter how pervasive the discontent, the conspirators failed to forge a meaningful union between radicals determined to topple the entire regime and less militant men whose limited aims were confined to toleration for Protestants and security for their estates. With that failure, the hopes of the dissidents in Ireland received a severe blow.

The defeat of 1663 did not, however, destroy the radical movement in Ireland. Dissidents there were sympathetic when English rebels rose later in the same year. By early February 1664 the informer who first tipped off Orrery about the Dublin conspiracy reported new scheming by those who feared they were about to lose their lands. For leadership they looked to Colonel Daniel Abbott, who had lost some of his lands but still retained 1,253 acres and was a suspect in the 1663 plot, Captain Chesterfield, an innkeeper near Dublin, and Colonel Unton Croke of Clonmel, who had correspondents in the Waterford area and had been arrested in 1660 in connection with the White plot. These men had contacts with dissidents in England using Captains Browne and Philips as their messengers. According to Orrery's source, they met frequently at the house of a Dublin apothecary named Dobson, and the earl therefore recommended that Ormond have them placed under surveillance.

Interestingly, the dissidents in Ireland did not trust Philip Alden any longer. As of early February they had not resolved on another conspiracy, and Orrery thought a favorable land bill might dissuade them from radical action.[85]

Confirmation of continuing radical activity in Ireland came from Sir Bryan Broughton of Beaudesert, Warwickshire, who knew of the messengers that kept dissidents in Ireland and England in touch. Radicals in Ireland purportedly urged a revolutionary council in London to decide whether the rising should be launched in England or Ireland. They preferred Ireland because "the English are timorouse and slowe so that its thought it will bee long before they will bee redie for action." In February 1664 the disaffected in Ireland were wary of Ormond's soldiers, but by early March they were convinced they outnumbered the duke's men and were "resolved to fall on there if the London councill approves."[86]

In the meantime the royalists in Ireland were keeping a wary eye on the Nonconformists. An agent of Viscount Conway reported in February 1664 that Andrew Stewart and Henry Livingstone (or Leviston) were collecting funds to aid John Greg to speed his release. These men were linked to John Gordon, who had recently visited Andrew McCormack, and Lieutenant Montgomery of Ballymackelly. McCormack was being hidden by friends in Antrim—probably the same ones who hid Blood. The surreptitious movement of Nonconformists between Ireland and Scotland continued despite government efforts to curtail it. Late in 1664 McCormack, Blood, and Carr, all of whom had fled the island, were reportedly back in Ireland, but further investigation raised doubts and pointed instead to the arrival of Alexander or John Read. An attempt to apprehend Read, Michael Bruce, and Henry Hunter, all Presbyterians, failed in December. There was a report the same month that a Glasgow merchant had smuggled 300 firelocks of Dutch manufacture into the Lagan region.[87]

Although the radical community continued in Ireland after the 1663 debacle, it never again mounted a serious threat to the government. A harsher land settlement might have stirred them to more vigorous action, but there was still the fundamental problem of the disparity between their aims and the more restricted ones of those whose primary goal was religious toleration. Religion alone proved to be an insufficient motive to rebel. Yet the Presbyterians in Ulster refused to submit to an episcopalian state church; encouraged by their continuing ties to their co-religionists in Scotland they persevered over an administration that proved powerless to crush them. By generally eschewing repeated attempts to topple the government, they enhanced their status as victims of persecution and thus made it virtually impossible for the state to suppress them.

# 6

# From Derwentdale
# to Kaber Rigg

## RISINGS IN THE NORTH

The events that disrupted Ireland in the late winter and spring of 1663 paralleled the beginning of an extraordinary period of radical activity in England that culminated in the autumn with an insurrection in the north. The English dissidents, however, were plagued by inept leadership and incompetent organization, as manifested by the problems of the Derwentdale conspirators. Yet neither the collapse of the Derwentdale and Dublin plots nor government pressure deterred the radicals in the summer and early autumn of 1663. Fired by religious zeal, loyalty to the Good Old Cause, and dissatisfaction with the tenor of the Stuart regime and its policies, the dissidents displayed a striking resilience. As they intensified their plotting, the authorities responded by increasing the use of informers, arresting more and more suspects, calling up the militia, and finally turning some of the dissidents against their cohorts.

## Radical Traces and False Leads

The government's effectiveness in dealing with the ceaseless plotting was undermined not only by inadequate security forces and funds but also by the confusing tangle of schemes, real and imagined. The Tong plot blurred into the plans for the northern rising, and to complicate matters even more there were simultaneous reports of surreptitious radical activity from one end of the country to the other.

159

In the course of unraveling the Tong plot, the authorities failed to unearth dissident units that operated in Bristol and Somersetshire. Militants in those areas had intended to rise on 5 November 1662 but were forced to delay their plans until 1 January when Tong and his cohorts were seized. On 17 December the deputy lieutenants in Bristol announced to Secretary Bennet that they had discovered some of these plotters and were undertaking a full investigation. The basic outline, corroborated by testimony from both Bristol and Ilchester in Somerset, included the usual references to Ludlow's role as well as to a surreptitious meeting of the Rump in London. The conspiracy was to have been activated at Whitehall with an attempt to seize the king and force him to declare (according to one witness) for Presbyterianism; others wanted to execute Charles. There was opposition too against bishops and the hearth tax. The conspirators claimed that throughout England they had 40,000 supporters, of whom 2,000 were in Somersetshire and another 600 or 700 in Bristol. Among the latter were 300 horse. Ludlow was reputedly the commander, working with an officer corps of 200, fifty of whom were in Bristol. The deputy lieutenants, however, were unable to learn the identity of the ringleaders.[1]

Officials discovered a link between radicals in Bristol and London when they seized a letter to Thomas Wilde, an apothecary's servant, from Captain John Gregory, "a tall man, black visage and a blemish in one of his eyes." Gregory, who had served under Colonel Nathaniel Rich and had taken part in Lambert's rising, was now using the alias Henry Harte and living in Southwark as a leather dresser. Calling for Gregory's arrest, the deputy lieutenants of Bristol accused him of being "the person that hath been Imployed from tyme to tyme to Engage all the disaffected persons in these parts."[2] Gregory worked closely with a man named (Daniel?) Dale, the agent for Somersetshire. Gregory's letter noted the execution of Tong, Phillips, Stubbs, and Gibbs, but dealt mostly with money matters. The message, however, apparently had an ulterior meaning, for it referred to "friends that have to do in the businesse," assurances of funds, and a hope that nothing rash would be undertaken. "My Cossen Hart att the Court is angry with you and the rest of his Cossen Creditors" and desires that they as well as Wilde "will be wise and still."[3] According to Wilde, Gregory claimed the plot was directed by a committee of former members of the Rump Parliament that met in the London area and had appointed Ludlow as its general. Although Gregory was incarcerated in the Tower, he told his wife Katharine not to fear: At an hour's notice his friends would have 500 "sword men that had vowed to kill the King" and would take their revenge on Albemarle by putting him into an iron cage "sett upon Paules church," where they could watch him starve. These militants, who reputedly met in St. Martin's Lane, Clerkenwell, Old Street, and Moorfields, included Captain Hoskew (alias Thomas), who once served Cromwell, Mr. Longland, a tobacconist in St. Martin's Lane, and a goldsmith named Symmons. Imprisoned in the Gatehouse at Westminster, Katharine Gregory gave the authorities contradictory and sometimes bizarre-sounding information (including allegations of bigamy), perhaps to under-mine the case against her husband. Symmons may have been in touch with radicals in Ireland, for in early March he told Mrs. Gregory to be of good comfort and expect her husband's imminent release because the war had already begun in Ireland.[4] As it happened, of course, the Dublin plotters were betrayed on the 4th and there was no rebellion, but Symmons presumably had known of their plans.

Other London radicals were reportedly preparing to assassinate the king sometime prior to Lady Day (25 March). On 28 December Captain Robert Seabrooke of North Crawley, Buckinghamshire, a Baptist, was overheard saying that Captain Randolph Holmes, a Barnet innkeeper, would pay two London tradesmen "to throwe two hand granadoes" into the royal coach. The money was allegedly contributed by William Fosket (or Fosquet), a known fanatic, Ralph Greenwood, and Ralph Ansloe (or Anslow), all of whom were from North Crawley, the baker Thomas Harman of Sherrington, and John Carter, a Newport Pagnell innkeeper. Although the authorities took the precaution of arresting the suspects, Holmes himself was released on bond on 9 January.[5]

The task of ferreting out real conspiracy was complicated by the multitude of malicious and false allegations, the practical effect of which was to inure officials to reports of plotting. On the eve of the Derwentdale conspiracy, for example, there were various assertions of designs in northern England. One of these involved a letter found in late December indicating that Sir Philip Musgrave would be "betrayed" on 1 January and that militants would take control of Carlisle. A second case entailed an allegation by the carrier George Barrow (or Darrow), formerly of Warrington, Lancashire, and now of Liverpool, who claimed that he was offered a lieutenant's com-mission and 28s. a week to serve in the rebel forces. The proposition, he averred, had been made by the Presbyterian Robert Yates, the ejected rector of Warrington, John Naylor, Richard Worrall, and a kiltmaker named Robert Cutchitt. The earl of Derby arrested the four, who disclaimed knowledge of Barrow.[6]

More serious because of the personages involved was the so-called Lascelles plot. In December 1662 Thomas Procter of Warsill (near Ripon) in the West Riding showed Captain Francis Driffield of Easingwold a letter he claimed to have found in the house of John Fewster (or Foster) in the same village while searching for counterfeit currency. Reputedly from Francis Wood of Dacre Banks, the letter conveyed the author's love to Driffield, his brothers Christopher and Stephen, and any others who would "stand up to quitt themselves like men that we may eradicate King and Bishops." The writer explained that he had recently been in York with his brother Matthew to discuss the plot, and that the two of them were prepared to supply fifty horse. Altogether "tenn thousand good horse will root out this Jeroboam & his posterity & I would have us grind that Traytor Monke . . . to powder for his perfidious Treachery." It was, he said, incumbent on them to cut off "that posterity which keeps us all in bondage & slavery[,] & [the] old Queen . . . shall be burnt for her former Idolitrys."[7] Procter claimed to have found a second letter (apparently PRO SP 29/65/89) addressed to Fewster, this time from Simon Ratheg (alias Trotter) of Biggin, in which it was noted that "our businesse failed in 17 places. . . . Now you know what is to bee done against candlemas day." After remarking that Thomas Dickenson, a former alderman of York, and Richard Cholmeley had enlisted to serve with Colonel Francis Lascelles (or Lassels), a member of the regicide court, the author inquired if the Driffield brothers had joined and were "redye in armes and will stand firme that wee may fall on Yeorke with readynes," ideally with 3,000 men.[8]

When Procter was arrested, he appealed for release on bail in order to learn more information, claiming that the allegations against him were the lies of those he had uncovered in the midst of treason. He subsequently argued that he had learned of the rising from Jonathan Kendall of Warsill, who said it was scheduled for 20 February and involved militants in the Bradford area. Among the officers implicated were Luke Robinson, a former M. P., republican, and friend of the Quakers, Colonel Lascelles, Captain William Oddie, and Captain Harrison. Procter asserted that he too had been offered a position as an officer. Lord Fauconberg ordered the arrest of the accused men, including Captain Matthew Beckwith, Captain Thomas Lascelles of Mount Grace, Major Thomas Strangways, and Captain James Strangways of Pickering, but his men could not find some of the other suspects. Kendall and Simon Ratheg testified that

Procter and his father Henry were evil men, that the elder Procter had been in Parliament's service in the civil war era, and that his son had had a quarrel with Francis and Matthew Wood of Dacre Banks, both of whom he accused of plotting.[9] Fauconberg concluded that the information of Procter was malicious, that Francis Driffield and Fewster were persons of good reputation, and that "there is no cause of the least apprehension from theese Parts." Sir Thomas Gower concurred that "there is no danger, and though it caryed a fowle face at first sight and gave just cause of apprehension, yet it will prove a meere Fanfara. . . . There is no designe at hand in this Country."[10] The Lascelles plot, though but a fabrication of Procter, was to prove significant because it helped persuade officials that the north was quiet in early 1663 when in fact it was not.

Another incident occurred in Hampshire in February 1663 when an unknown party tried to implicate Moore Fauntleroy, a known dissident who had fought in the army under the Rump and had more recently been imprisoned when enough weapons were found in his house to arm thirty or forty men. A letter to Fauntleroy from one "Jo. K." was found in a box along a lane by the daughter of a Farnham, Surrey man, but the attempt to frame Fauntleroy, apparently by a personal enemy, almost failed when the girl delivered the note to him rather than the magistrates. The author averred that Ludlow would give Fauntleroy whatever he desired in return for his support of a rising scheduled for the 18th. "They will flie before us as chaff with the winde." Some 40,000 men were supposedly engaged to take Guildford, Portsmouth, and the west. The letter ended with an appeal to Fauntleroy not to betray the conspirators if he were apprehended. Fauntleroy, however, turned the letter over to Sir John Norton, a deputy lieutenant, who was convinced Fauntleroy did so only because the note was discovered before it reached him. Regarding Fauntleroy as a dangerous man who might have been involved in the recent plotting, the king directed the deputy lieutenants either to commit him or to require him to take the oaths and post a bond for peaceful behavior.[11]

The government had no relief from the continued reports of radical threats and alleged designs. Often the reports amounted to nothing more than accusations of seditious and inflammatory language, such as calling the king a bastard and Monck a traitor. However, on 30 January, a day to commemorate Charles I's execution, the disaffected in York insisted on opening their shops as a show of defiance, while in London, "least that Blood should not sinke the Regicides deepe enough, the day was ushered in & entertained with seditious practizes against his Sacred Majesty, &c: & by whom acted? but by the Ingratefull, & remorselese persecutors of his late Royall ffather." It was difficult for the government to gauge the depth of sentiment such demonstrations represented. The previous month the king had concluded that although there were still factious spirits in London "who make it their businesse to endeavour disturbances," they were inconsiderable both in numbers and in status.[12]

The problem was complicated by ongoing difficulties with the Nonconformists, some of whose activities were regarded as serious threats to the peace and even treasonable. The ejected vicar of St. Mary's, Reading, the Presbyterian Christopher Fowler, caused a stir by holding unlawful meetings in his home that some thought were nothing more than "Religious Musters of his Party" to promote rebellion. An informer warned Bennet in January 1663 about enemies of the king in Southwark, especially John Crodacot, the ejected chaplain of St. Saviour's who consulted regularly with Colonel Marsh and Captain (Daniel?) How, and Joseph Caryl, the ejected rector of St. Magnus, London, who was accused of preaching treason. So many were arrested in Southwark for attending conventicles that a warrant had to be issued the same month to release all Nonconformists in Newgate except those believed to be "dangerously seditious & seducers of others."[13] There was some suspicion the previous month that a 900-member congregation that met in Duke's Place near Bishopsgate and was associated with the Fifth Monarchist Nathaniel Strange, had sent one of its members, John Seddon (or Sedan) to Lancashire to recruit militants for a rising. Seddon admitted that he had attended the meetings of Thomas Venner. Nonconformists in the northeast were also worrisome. Sir Philip Musgrave observed to Williamson that he had "never found the nonconformist[s] in thes parts so impudent and publick in their meetings since the tyme they had a King as at this present." From Newcastle there was a report that "there is such a sp[iri]t of Contumacy & disobedience not to be softened," at least in part because the busiest pastors are those who were "the most spitefull & active against our late gracious soveraigne."[14]

One of the most difficult ministers proved to be Edward Bagshaw, the ejected vicar of Ambrosden, Oxfordshire, who accompanied the earl of Anglesey to Ireland in 1662 as his chaplain. Officials were worried because his services attracted various ex-officers, including Colonel Jerome Sankey. After he returned to England in September, he complained that many ministers had been ejected, that the king was concerned only with his mistresses while the country was run by the queen and "her Caball," and that Catholicism was on the rise. Reportedly he also insisted that the Long Parliament had never legally dissolved itself and was therefore still the lawful authority, and that the king was "but a trustee for the People." Nevertheless, he proclaimed his loyalty to Charles II, but insisted that the state had no power to enforce indifferent matters in religion. After a warrant for his arrest and the seizure of his papers was issued on 30 December, he was committed to the Tower in January for treasonable practices.[15]

Bagshaw made his religious views known in several publications, including *The Great Question Concerning Things Indifferent in Religious Worship* (1660), in which he denied the right of a Christian magistrate to impose *adiaphora* (such as the surplice or the sign of the cross in baptism), for these had become occasions of superstition. These impositions led to "the certain decay of the growth of Religion as to its inward Purity" and to a decline in the security of the throne.[16] In *Signes of the Times: or Prognosticks of Future Judgements* (1662), Bagshaw proclaimed that "our National sinnes are . . . great and crying." Judgment was imminent because godly ministers had been imprisoned or silenced, and those responsible would meet sudden, unexpected death.[17] There is no proof that Bagshaw intended his warning to be taken in anything more than a spiritual context, but it would not be difficult for susceptible readers to act on his message, which made it a province for official concern. Charles himself insisted on interrogating Bagshaw when Roger L'Estrange found a suspicious paper entitled "Mr. Davis's Case" in his possession.[18] That the king personally concerned himself with individual dissidents such as Bagshaw as well as purported conspiracies reveals the extent of the state's concern with the radical threat. But how many alleged plots could the authorities investigate without being dulled by the repetitious and often untrustworthy reports?

## The Road to Derwentdale

On 22 March 1663 the authorities received their first substantial report concerning the conspiracy that was underway in the country, especially in the north. This came in the form of a confession by the Baptist John Ellerington (or Etherington), a former servant of the widow of Sir Claudius Forster of Blanchland, Northumberland. Claiming to be troubled in conscience by the conspiracy, Ellerington sought the help of Lady Mallory, who sent him to John Cosin, bishop of Durham.[19]

Since at least the summer of 1661, Cosin had been tracking the movements of three prominent northern radicals: Lieutenant-Colonel Paul Hobson, formerly deputy governor of Newcastle and a militia commissioner for county Durham, the Fifth Monarchist John Joplin (or Jopling), a Durham jailer who once served under Hobson as a cornet, and Captain Thomas Gower (or Goare), a probable co-founder with Hobson of the Particular Baptist church in Newcastle. Hobson had been arrested and briefly imprisoned by Cosin in August 1661. Hobson, Joplin, and possibly Gower came from London to Durham that November, but fled back to the capital to avoid interrogation by the deputy lieutenants. Hobson was arrested in the spring of 1662 but was soon released on bond. "Neither I nor no honest man can expect our liberty or lives one hour," complained Joplin, adding that "the beast doth not only war but rage. The prisons are full, & the cryes of the oppressed goes up to the ears of the Lord mightily."[20] On 7 November Cosin asked Sir Gilbert Gerard to instigate a speedy and secret search for Hobson and Gower, "two of the most dangerous fellowes in all the North," because, he claimed, they were communicating with the Tong plotters. Some of their correspondence, using "charecters & a form of shorthand of their own invention," was intercepted. According to the bishop's information, they were staying with Thomas Lomes in Lothbury, London. The same day warrants were issued and executed for the arrest of Lomes, Hobson, and Gower, but the latter eluded capture.[21] In his capacity as lord lieutenant, Cosin issued a warrant for Joplin's arrest on the 15th. Upon his refusal to enter a bond for peaceful behavior and take the oath of allegiance, Joplin was imprisoned until the next sessions, during which time he took advantage of a negligent jailer to have his private papers delivered to his cell; there he burned them. In conjunction, moreover, with certain imprisoned Quakers, he sent a written attack on one of the assize judges to London for publication. Hobson and Lomes were bonded on 17 November, but Joplin had to wait until March. Although Hobson and Gower stayed in London, after his release Joplin returned to the north, where he rejoined the Derwentdale conspirators.[22]

According to Ellerington's account, the dissidents—bonded together by their oath of secrecy—had been meeting during the previous six months at Muggleswick Park, Durham. They intended to rebel against the government primarily because it denied them liberty of conscience. Resolving to overthrow bishops, deans, and parish clergy as well as to murder any gentry who opposed them, they schemed "to breake all organs," burn the Book of Common

Prayer, and seize more weapons and money in Durham. The most improbable part of Ellerington's story was his assertion that the Catholics would join the "thousands" of Congregationalists and Baptists who had already engaged. The insurrection was originally set for Lady Day (25 March), but was postponed a month or two to see if Parliament would provide "Indulgence to tender con- sciences."[23]

Although Cosin was skeptical of Ellerington's charges, he ordered the militia to apprehend the accused. By the 30th, only nine had been arrested, but others fled, probably to Northumberland or Scotland. The accused "stiffely" denied the charges. Those initially named as plotters were apparently members of the Baptist church at Derwentdale, an offshoot of the Hexham congregation. The accused included the pastor, John Ward, John Joplin of Foxhole, Captain George Gower (possibly Thomas Gower's brother), Captain Doffen, Lewis Frost of South Shields, and the mechanick preachers Cuthbert and Michael Coatesworth (or Coatsworth). Ellerington subsequently implicated four members of the gentry, Sir Henry Witherington, Edward Fenwick of Stanton, the Presbyterian Timothy Whittingham of Holmside, and Captain Thomas Lilburne of Sunderland, but only the latter two were imprisoned, and they were freed after three months of incarceration.[24]

Far from being nothing more than the lies of an unscrupulous informer, as Maurice Ashley argues, Ellerington's account provided the government with enough information to begin unraveling the tangled threads of conspiracy that finally culminated in risings that autumn. To be sure, Ellerington was only a minor functionary who carried conspiratorial letters between Joplin and Captain Mitford of Mitford, Northumberland, and between Joplin, Captain Doe, and other dissidents in Durham on the one hand, and agents in Ipswich who were in contact with radicals abroad, probably in the Nether- lands. Moreover, Ellerington confessed that in 1662 he had trans- ported arms from the Ipswich agents to the north. His usefulness as a spy was compromised by the suspicion with which he was hence- forth regarded by other dissidents. At one point, Anthony Pearson, under-sheriff of Durham, warned him against informing because the rebels would hang him if they prevailed. They even offered him £200 to leave the country, though he unsuccessfully demanded twice that amount. A year later he provided additional information pertinent to the autumn risings, including testimony about one of the key conspirators, John Atkinson "the stockinger." Ironically, Atkinson was in London at the time of Ellerington's confession, allegedly trying to reconstitute a revolutionary council to help plan the insurrection.[25]

## Frustrated Hopes and Rising Tensions

The decision of the Derwentdale radicals to postpone their uprising must have been based in part on their unpreparedness, but they were also willing to wait in the expectation that efforts to provide relief from the Act of Uniformity might bear fruit. One of the Presbyterian leaders, Edmund Calamy, had been released from prison in January, and about a month later was summoned by the king along with Thomas Manton, William Bates, and possibly Richard Baxter. There was some discussion of a restoration to their livings in return for their support of a royal indulgence, but nothing concrete came of the meeting. Nevertheless, there was still hope of either an indulgence or at least comprehension in the established church for the Presbyterians, though such expectations were dampened by hostility in the House of Commons as well as among the prelates. Although the king's hope of an indulgence was frustrated, numerous Nonconformists were discharged from prison, including several hundred Quakers in such places as Southwark, Horsham, and Salisbury.[26]

The intensification of efforts to track radical activities in 1663 may have been due in part to a desire to buttress the opposition to an indulgence by depicting Nonconformists as intrepid revolutionaries. Nor could the government afford to turn a blind eye to extremists in light of disclosures connected with the Tong, Dublin, and Derwentdale conspiracies. It was imperative to measure the pulse of the radical community at home and abroad on a regular basis in order to frustrate new plots.

On 27 March the government received fresh information on the exile community in the Netherlands by interrogating two recent returnees, William Mawtsley, who had fought under Colonel Robert Duckenfield, and the Congregationalist George Thorne, the ejected rector of Radipole, Dorset. Thorne in particular had information concerning Desborough, Kelsey, Ellison, Nathaniel Mather, and Dr. Edward Richardson. The latter, a key figure in the northern conspiracy, apparently sneaked back into England about this time, for he was actively plotting in the north throughout the spring. In a matter of weeks the government issued a proclamation (dated 21 April) ordering thirteen of the exiles to return to England by 22 July on pain of being declared traitors. Desborough, Kelsey, and Richardson were on the list, as were three men wanted in connection with the

Tong plot—Cole, Spurway, and Edward Radden—and a former member of the regicide court, John Phelps.[27]

In England there was a steady stream of arrests on suspicion of treason and related charges throughout the spring and summer. Among the malcontents in the Tower were the agitator Michael Gunning in March, Colonel Robert Overton in May, the Tong plotter George Elton and John Dodington in July, and Paul Hobson in August.[28] A number of Elton's papers were seized, most of which revealed only his millenarian convictions. One letter noted that Captain William Leeving (or Leving) was in town and that Elton hoped to see him; Leeving was a key figure in the plotting that led to the northern rising. Elton, who was but one of several links between the Tong and northern plots, was convicted of treason at the Old Bailey in December.[29]

More enigmatical was the case of Richard White, imprisoned in the Tower for treason on 19 May because of seditious correspondence that the magistrates intercepted. Written in cipher, the crucial letter was sent by one James Smart (possibly an alias) to White's brother Ignatius in Brussels. Smart had expected to have all of Ireland under his command by mid-May, though this obviously had not occurred. Limerick, Cork, and Youghal were secure, he claimed, but there would be no rising until the authorities were lulled into complacency. In the meantime Smart intended to go to Oxfordshire and Devonshire to confer with supporters, and then to London on 6 June. He claimed to have 6,000 foot and 4,000 horse, but required another 4,000 weapons. His followers purportedly included 150 of the king's regiment and 60 of Albemarle's, and their plan called for the assassination of Charles and the duke of York. Edward Whalley supposedly had a list of those who had been recruited, though he was in fact hiding in New England. The implausibility of the scheme is underscored by the fact that the conspirators claimed to enjoy the support of the king of Spain. The letter ends with the date and the name of Ludlow, which was enough to make Orrery suspect Edmund Ludlow of being the author. Although it is possible that the letters were no more than an attempt to frame the White brothers, it is perhaps more plausible that the radicals, who knew some of their letters were being intercepted, deliberately tried to mislead the authorities with excessive estimates of their strength, the myth of Spanish support, and reinforcement of the rumors of Ludlow's presence in the isles.[30] In the Public Record Office there is a set of notes that were probably made when Richard White was examined. They indicate that Ludlow was supposed to be in London, Whalley and Goffe in Brussels, Lisle and William Cawley in Normandy, Oliver St. John in Paris, and the regicide Thomas Challoner (who had died in Zeeland in 1661) in Yorkshire. The notes also contain a suggestion that the house of John Thurloe, Cromwell's secretary of state, be searched and that Thurloe himself be examined if he could be found.[31]

A number of other dissidents attracted the government's attention in this period, thus diverting officials from focusing on the northern conspiracy. In late March they searched for arms and seditious papers at the houses of Major-General William Boteler (or Butler) of Oatlands Park and Major John Doberon (or Dambrun) at Weybridge. The men were detained only briefly, even though Boteler was allegedly a supporter of Samuel Bagley, rector of Haselbeech, Northants. Bagley not only called the king a bastard and threatened to cut off his head but warned that "if Lambert did not ryse & take downe the Cavaleers there would bee noe dealeing with them."[32] Among the others in trouble were ex-officers such as Captain Richard Walton (who served under Sir Anthony Ashley Cooper) and Captain Richard Edwards, members of the gentry such as Sir James Harrington (cousin of the political theorist) and Sir Anthony Morgan, and Nonconformist ministers such as Stephen Charnock (wanted in connection with the Dublin plot) and the General Baptist Stephen Dagnal (jailed for riot and unlawful assembly).[33]

"They tell me," wrote one of Willimson's informants, that their "business goes on apace." There was enough apparent threat to keep the government occupied. Fearing a plot to surprise Windsor Castle, Bennet directed Lord Mordaunt to imprison and interrogate suspicious persons. From Sherborne came word in late May that a rising was imminent in Dorset and Somerset, "at which tyme they will easely suppresse the Cavaliers And then doe what they list." That warning was conveyed to the M. P. John Fitzjames. The mood in London was such that even Pepys was concerned as he noted "the ill temper of the City at this time, either to religion in general or to the King."[34]

In late May authorities in Manchester learned of dissident activity that appeared very serious to them. The ex-soldier Matthew Moreton of Ingleton, Staffordshire, reported a plot to officials after John Walhouse of Hatherton, formerly an adjutant to Lambert, had tried to enlist him. Using the watchword, "the Sword Hewes before the sith mowes," the rebels proposed to revolt in all three kingdoms. Allegedly some 40,000 to 50,000 had already enlisted, including "all or most of the Ould Parliament Party." Moreover, "the old Irish

Souldiers were listed under Ormond for a Colour & . . . they would shortly make him a poore Ormond." Copies of a declaration had reportedly been printed in Edinburgh. Their grievances were at heart religious and economic: hostility to the bishops and apprehension that a third of the estates of those who had fought against the crown would be forfeited.[35] Walhouse erroneously insisted that a party of rebels had already taken up arms in Ireland and that Colonel Jerome Sankey (or Zanchy) had been killed. During the course of the ensuing investigation Sir Brian Broughton learned of "a grande Committee" of some fifteen to seventeen ex-officers who met at Wolverhampton on market days. Among them were Captain Peter Backhouse (who had served under Sir Arthur Haselrig), Captain Thomas Gent, Lieutenant John Daniell, and Colonel Thomas Crompton, former governor of Stafford. They were in communication with malcontents in Scotland, from which Gent returned in early July, and Ireland, where the unnamed messenger was a man who had led troops from Lichfield to aid Lambert at Edgehill in the spring of 1660. They apparently had the support of John Reynolds, the ejected minister of Wolverhampton.[36] The threat had to be taken seriously because an official count determined that 1,128 men in the Stafford area alone had borne arms against the king in the past and many continued to carry weapons. The dissidents, whatever their number, were scared off by the investigation, and by 20 July one of Broughton's informers was convinced that there was no longer any danger.[37] The Wolverhampton group may have been affiliated with the northern conspirators, who were already actively plotting, for one of the latter, Colonel Henry Danvers, had strong Stafford associations.

Other reports of dissidents may likewise reflect activity that was part of the preparations for the autumn insurrection. The informer Peter Crabb's discovery of an alleged scheme to assassinate the king and royal family was probably baseless, but an unnamed informant of Sir Jordan Crosland had unearthed more reliable intelligence pertaining to preparations for a revolt in Ireland, Scotland, and England, particularly the north, the west, and London, including the possibility of arson at Whitehall. The informant told of private committees collecting funds "for the Lords worke" and of the conviction of militants that they would "gaine the heavenly Crowne in Jerusalem" if they destroyed Charles II.[38] There were also ominous reports from Kent not only of the usual conventicles but also of large groups of armed horse and foot rendezvousing at Egerton and Canterbury. Nonconformists at Waltham and Reculver were armed and organized, and Colonels William Kenrick, Edward Scott, and Robert Gibbon were behaving suspiciously. Intercepted correspondence even indicated possible dissident activity on the Isle of Man.[39]

The government's problem with illegal behavior in the country was intensified by the foolhardy attempt of the earl of Bristol to impeach Clarendon of treason on 10 July 1663. Although a Catholic, Digby became something of a hero to many Nonconformists by his futile assault on the man who symbolized the repression of religious dissent. On the one hand the London mob drank to Bristol's health, while on the other, as one contemporary observed, "the Sectaries, especially the Anabaptists met more confidently than before; the recusants likewise splendidly apparelled." In the days that followed, the government received reports of the scheming that was to culminate in the northern rising in the autumn. Against this background Charles prorogued Parliament on 27 July with a request that members assist the judges in curtailing conventicles.[40] The threat to the chancellor, the upsurge of Nonconformist activity, and the renewed reports of plotting succeeded in temporarily turning the king away from his desire to procure an indulgence.

The mood of the Nonconformists was perhaps best reflected in an intercepted letter to Lady Vane which opined that "all things grow darker, but at evening time it will be light." The writer added that "in the midst of fears & dangers, we remain in peace & safety though not without many alarms and warnings." However, there were more than warnings, for periodically the magistrates raided the conventicles. One of Bennet's informers, Peter Crabb, urged him in early August to move against a meeting house at Petty France in the City where thirty or forty commissioned officers were present. A few days later approximately a hundred sectaries were arrested in Southwark. Outside London the story was essentially the same, though there was a complaint from the Theobalds area that "noe persons in the least question" the Nonconformists when they meet.[41] At the Dorchester assizes those who spoke at conventicles were fined forty marks and their auditors twenty, while two Quakers were imprisoned for life after they were convicted of a praemunire. In Leicestershire the deputy lieutenants conscientiously suppressed illegal meetings and apprehended the Congregationalist Matthew Clark, the ejected rector of Narborough and former chaplain to Colonel Francis Hacker, who ministered to a congregation of some 300, which included ex-Cromwellian officers. They also arrested Lieutenant Inge, in whose house a Baptist conventicle met. Sixteen Quakers were arrested at Market Lavington in Wiltshire, though a group of mostly female sectaries who met "in a riotous manner" at Donhead St. Andrew was not bothered.[42]

Although the government issued a proclamation on 22 August concerning the enforcement of the statutes governing church attendance, there are ample indications of defiance by Nonconformists. At Hull the Presbyterians continued to meet, though one observer predicted that "ere long they will be at a non-plus." Sir Philip Musgrave grumbled that the Quakers in the north were insolent and met weekly in congregations of 200 or more. Thirty-three imprisoned Friends in Ilchester politely petitioned the king for relief, but the oft-persecuted Charles Bayly (or Baily) threatened from his prison in Bristol that "the Whirlwinde of the Lord God is a Coming over the Nation & wrath is ready to be poured forth upon all the Workers of Iniquitie"; not even the king would be exempt.[43] The imminence of judgment was reiterated to the Friends by Josiah Cole, while on his deathbed Henry Jessey called on God to destroy the earthly powers with the aid of his people. Perhaps as many as 5,000, described by an informer as "a strange Medley of *Phanatiques*," attended his funeral in a grand demonstration of Nonconformist strength. John Belcher's Fifth Monarchist congregation planned to meet in London in late September, claimed Crabb, "to conclude upon the tyme when to finish the Lords worke."[44]

Sectarian unrest at Chichester led to an investigation in which the magistrates found evidence of a possible conspiracy. Although some Nonconformists had been imprisoned, contempt of the surplice and Book of Common Prayer was so intense that others disrupted a service in the parish church. The trained bands were dispatched to keep order in September. Among the Nonconformists were probably those who met at nearby Kingston, Sussex, to hear the Presbyterian John Peachy (or Peachie), the ejected vicar of St. Paul's, Walden, Hertfordshire, preach. Late in the previous year agents of this group had offered to procure the release of a cutler from a Chichester jail if he would provide them with a hundred weapons by Christmas. The authorities in fact confiscated two barrels of gunpowder, and Peachy's creditors seized weapons enough to arm sixty men. The principal agents in the scheme included the agitators John Oglander, Christopher Nevill, and Peter Evans.[45]

Alarmed by Nonconformist unrest and the earliest reports of the northern conspiracy, the government tightened security, primarily by urging the lord lieutenants to get the militia in order. Special attention was to be paid to walled towns, and the horse were to be used as necessary to disperse conventicles. Only five percent of the militia were normally to be on duty at any given time—a number the deputy lieutenants of Cumberland and Westmorland (where the total number of militia was only 600) thought woefully inadequate. Under the circumstances the king also rescinded his order to reduce the forces at Chepstow Castle. The radicals were encouraged by the unpreparedness of the state's forces, as Sir Brian Broughton reminded Williamson in August. One of Broughton's scouts picked up information that the English in Ireland, fearing the confiscation of their lands, intended to rebel in conjunction with the Scots and then invade England, where "they looke upon the kings forces as inconsiderable."[46] The uprising, however, came neither in Ireland nor in Scotland that autumn but in the northern shires.

## The Northern Risings: Interpreting the Evidence

Thanks in particular to the perseverence of Sir Thomas Gower, by the autumn the government was well informed about the general plans of the conspirators. Yet the state's efforts to deal with the militants were complicated by two related problems: the difficulty of sifting through informers' reports to cull out reliable data, and finding sufficient documentation of conspiratorial activity to procure convictions in a court of law. The latter problem was compounded by the fact that much of the testimony came from informers, whose usefulness terminated as soon as they testified. The alternative the government sometimes pursued allowed plotting to go forward, in the expectation that a rising could be quashed at the last minute by timely arrests of key personnel and the effective use of military units. On the whole, this strategy proved to be effective despite the state's inability to root out, once and for all, the core of ex-Cromwellian officers and men responsible for fomenting much of the sedition.

The incessant rumors of plots as well as the actual conspiracies that characterized the early 1660s had a numbing effect, particularly on Charles II. "The continual discourse of plots and insurrections," Clarendon observed, "had so wearied the king, that he even resolved to give no more countenance to any such informations, nor to trouble himself with inquiry into them." In part this was also due to Charles' desire to avoid the criticism leveled against the Cromwellian government of contriving plots in order to justify imprisoning its enemies. Thus the king paid no heed to the original reports of the northern conspiracy until they began to come together from several places, with specifics as to time and place, and included accusations against persons of substance. In the aftermath of the risings and the intensive investigation that ensued, he informed Parliament in March 1664 that "we are not yet at the Bottom of that Business." In Charles' mind the northern conspiracy was an outgrowth of the Nonsuch House plot, about which he had informed Parliament more than two years earlier. At the core of both conspiracies were alleged revolutionary councils in London that communicated with extremists in the counties.[47]

The king was not alone in his initial reluctance to accept the reality of the northern plot. To stifle the doubts of the skeptical, *The Newes* ran a story on 12 November 1663 announcing that the plot involved "the wary and Malicious Reason of the Best Heads in the Faction." Nonetheless, as late as 28 November many people in the northeast were still unconvinced that the design was genuine.[48] It is, then, little wonder that historians have developed sharply conflicting interpretations of what happened. Less than two weeks after the northern rebels rose, *The Intelligencer* carried a report that the disaffected were trying to convince the people that there had been no plot. One of the many charges hurled at Clarendon after his fall was George Wither's accusation that he had contrived the northern conspiracy himself. Ludlow expectedly saw the design as yet another government excuse to punish its critics, with "the design of subverting the rights and liberties of the nation." Whig historians such as James Ralph essentially followed this interpretation. While admitting the reality of a rising, Ralph insisted that it was only the work of Levellers, disbanded officers, and desperate enthusiasts, all men of mean condition. Such an exercise in futility, he contended, should have made the government scornful rather than apprehensive. Such was the judgment in more recent times of Maurice Ashley and James Walker, the latter specifically endorsing the Whig view that the conspirators were nothing more than "a band of isolated fanatics."[49]

In sharp contrast, other historians, including Bishop Parker, have regarded the northern conspiracy as a serious threat. To Parker (as to Secretary Bennet) it was "a wider flame" of the Dublin plot earlier in the year. Although the risings themselves were indisputably nothing more than an "almost pitiable failure," Wilbur Cortez Abbott justifiably argued that the information received by the government was "too precise and trustworthy to be neglected." A similar view was advanced by Henry Gee and C. E. Whiting, both of whom were impressed by the danger and the widespread nature of the design.[50] The rebels did in fact have contacts in both Scotland and the Netherlands, as well as a network in England that stretched from the north to London. That so much effort produced such inept risings in October was the result of not only the ineffectual leadership and organization of the radicals but also the government's use of strategic arrests and spies as well as its military superiority. Never were the rebel leaders able to muster more than a tiny fraction of the men they so lavishly promised in their recruiting, and the inevitable result was dispirited forces when the risings finally got under way.

## Rebel Councils

The origins of the northern conspiracy are rooted in the radical dissent that gave rise to the Tong plot. "The Originall," as one of Bennet's correspondents remarked, was the great ejection of ministers, "uppon which in the winter followinge it was pretended the Papists would rise and destroy the godly party; then in the next Springe it was divulged that the Act of Indemnitye would be repealed."[51] Religious freedom for Protestants, anger over taxes, resentment toward the Cavalier Parliament, disgust with the immorality of the court, hostility toward Catholics, and bitterness over the treatment of ejected clergy fired a determination to revive the Good Old Cause.

The initial planning was underway by October 1662, the month the state first learned of the Tong cabal.[52] That design, in fact, seems to have been an early and ill-conceived prototype for the more advanced conspiracy of 1663. Not only did the Tong and northern plots share the idea of a revolutionary council, but there is evidence that the London committee for the northern conspiracy was actually revived from the remnants of the Tong council. The ex-soldier John Atkinson, "the stockinger" of Askrigg, Yorkshire, came to London in March 1663, presumably on behalf of the northern plotters, to establish contact with the London council. Its members, he thought, had included not only Tong (now dead) but his allies Thomas (or William) Cole, Captain Spurway, and Nathaniel Strange, as well as Major Richard Salway and Henry Neville. Sir Thomas Gower had essentially the same information from one of his informers by 12 October 1663.[53] The link between the two plots is further substantiated by testimony from Edward Riggs in Rotterdam that Spurway, who had ties to dissidents in Nottinghamshire, was present at a meeting of the northern cabal at the Spa (Harrogate) in Yorkshire. Moreover, Cole, a republican who was very active among the exiles, not only shipped weapons to England in 1663 but returned to further the plot.[54] Thus the government's failure to apprehend all the principal Tong conspirators enabled the escapees to participate in the reorganized design.

The decision to plan another insurrection was probably made independently of the Tong conspirators by radicals in the north, who recruited the surviving Tong extremists. According to Captain Robert Atkinson of Mallerstang, Westmorland, the plot was conceived in February 1663, though in fact its roots were even older. Atkinson, a Presbyterian in his forties, had served under John Hewson in Ireland and as governor of Appleby Castle. After the Restoration, Sir Philip Musgrave employed him as an informer until he was dismissed because of his perfidy. He was recruited to the conspiracy by Captain Spencer and Sergeant Richard Richardson of Crosby Garrett, Westmorland. They claimed to have learned of the plot from Daniel Jackson, former chaplain to Colonel Roger Sawrey, under whom they had served in Scotland.[55] Atkinson initially refused to participate, citing the "unreasonable governments" between Oliver Cromwell's death and the return of the monarchy. After six weeks, however, he agreed to join, persuaded that "the whole Officers of the Army & other considerable Gentlemen" were engaged. Although Spencer and Richardson did not have a copy of the declaration of principles, they insisted that Jackson had read it to them, and that it promised religious liberty. Atkinson acknowledged that he was also persuaded to enlist by various Quakers who were engaged. He was then sent to confer with Dr. Edward Richardson at the Spa (Harrogate) about the necessary details, and became one of the principal conspirators. Although his family lived at Ripon, Richardson practiced medicine at the Spa as a cover for the plot in which he was the dominant figure. Sometimes called "the Anabaptist dean of Ripon," he had been ejected as minister at Ripon in 1660 and was licensed by the College of Physicians two years later.[56]

The determination to establish contact with the London council was made by Richardson and his principal accomplices. The council was rather loosely structured with a membership that fluctuated in accordance with the presence of leading radicals in London. The Yorkshireman Richard Walters, brother of Lieutenant-Colonel (or Major) Robert Walters of Cundall, Yorkshire, gave the state a list of council members following his arrest, but the list is definitely spurious and was probably intended to throw off the authorities. It included Neville, Salway, Colonel John Hutchinson, Oliver St. John, John Wildman, Bulstrode Whitelocke, and a Mr. Lowther.[57] At one time or another in 1663, those who did sit on the council included Colonel Thomas Blood, who returned from a brief sojourn in the

Netherlands after the collapse of the Dublin plot, Captain John Lockyer, Blood's friend and an alleged member of the Tong council, Captain Roger Jones (alias 'Mene Tekel'), Captain Samuel Wise, Major Lee, a suspect in an alleged northern plot the previous summer, and Captain Edward Cary (alias Carew), a Fifth Monarchist whose extremist activities extended into the 1680s. This list is similar to John Atkinson's 1665 roll, which included Blood, Lockyer, Jones, and Cary as well as Nathaniel Strange, Colonel Dalton, and Spurway (alias Frost).[58]

There is also evidence to link the Dublin and northern conspiracies. When dissidents met in Durham on 12 March 1663, they took an oath of secrecy and sent communications to radicals in London and the west. The oath was a "Sacramentall engagement, or vow, not only of secrecy, but also to destroy without mercy all those who did oppose" the rebels, especially Albemarle, Buckingham, the leading Privy Councillors, and Sir Richard Browne.[59] The dissidents at Derwentdale on whom John Ellerington informed ten days later were undoubtedly an affiliate of this group. On 16 April the northern conspirators dispatched an agent named Crowder[60] to Liverpool to confer with an agitator from Dublin and "settle a correspondence between the partyes." The latter may have been John Robinson (alias John Walker) of Blacklea, near Dublin, an agent whom Bennet later discovered knew "*the bottom*" of the northern plot. Another agent dispatched to the northern schemers by the dissidents in Ireland was Theodore Parkinson. There was also a meeting at Coley, near Halifax, in April at which representatives from Lancashire, including Major Peter Crispe (or Crisp) and Thomas Jollie (or Jolly), were present.[61]

Dr. Richardson drafted their declaration, which had to be submitted to the council in London before being revised, apparently several times, in part because some of the sectaries wanted firmer assurances of religious freedom. The Presbyterians, who were concerned essentially with "a preaching Ministry," objected to radical demands for the rule of King Jesus. Cornet George Denham had to draft a second declaration to meet Quaker demands.[62] Richardson's declaration, entitled *A Door of Hope Opened in the Valley of Achor for the Mourners in Sion out of the North*, catalogued the major ills that plagued the kingdom: (1) daily blasphemy; (2) the wickedness countenanced by the authorities—much of it expressed in plays—including adultery, inebriety, swearing, and stealing; (3) the idolatrous worship of the Church of England and persecution of the saints; (4) the unjust suffering of alleged plotters who were the victims of entrapment; (5)

unemployment, decay of trade, the excise, customs taxes, the poll and hearth taxes, subsidies, and benevolences; (6) the increase of papists. According to the declaration, Christians could use all lawful means, including violence, to defend their lives, liberties, and estates, even to overthrow temporal kingdoms, which must fall before the kingdom of God can be established. They proclaimed themselves ready to hazard their lives "for the reviveing of the good ould Cause." Better to "dye like men, then live worse then slaves." They were willing to accept either a monarchy or a commonwealth as long as it was reformed. Included among their goals was a reformation of ecclesiastical polity in conformity with the Bible and the example of the "best" Reformed churches, and the termination of "Episcopal devotions," which left people in ignorance. Their aim was global in nature, extending ultimately to the destruction of the papacy and the Turks, of Gog and Magog.[63] Similar global concerns had been expressed earlier by both the Quakers and the Fifth Monarchists.

Planning for the insurrection was carried out in a series of meetings that extended into the early autumn. Until his arrest in August, the key figure in these sessions was Dr. Richardson. In mid-May he met with the two Atkinsons, John and Robert, Captain John Mason, Lieutenant-Colonel Robert Walters, and Cornets George Denham and Robert Cooke. Walters had been recruited on the understanding that he would command Colonel Lilburne's old regiment if it could be reconstituted.[64] It was not until 30 May, however, that Richardson's cabal decided to strike at York, a mission that they calculated would require 500 "resolved" men. Among those present at this meeting, held at the Spa (Harrogate), were Robert Atkinson, John Ward, and several Scottish agents, including Sir Duncan Campbell. The Scottish representatives were entertained at the home of the clothier Richard Oldroyd, "the Devill" of Dewsbury, a former member of Lambert's regiment.[65]

On 9 June the rebels met again at the Spa under cover of taking the waters. Among those joining Richardson were Mason, the Congregationalist minister Jeremiah Marsden, who had served briefly as lecturer at Kendal in 1659, Isaac Balm (or Balme) of Batley, Lieutenant-Colonel John Beckwith, and the Doncaster agitator Henry North. Captain William Leeving announced that the Durham radicals would provide 200 cavalrymen commanded by former Cromwellian officers, including Captain Robert Hutton.[66] The rebel leaders expected ammunition to arrive at Bridlington from the Netherlands, and counted on support from their friends in the navy. The plan called for extremists in London to seize the king and the dukes of York and Albemarle; the Tower would be betrayed. In general, there was hope that if a small number began the work, "innumerable would apeare all over England."[67]

Crucial news from London was conveyed to the 15 July meeting at Pannal, south of Harrogate, by Captain Roger Jones (alias Rogers) on behalf of the London council. London dissidents, he said, would rise only if the royal Guards could be lured away from the city: "If a Considerable body of horse could bee gotten into a body, and to march towards London the Citty would affoord great forces." However, Major Joshua Greathead, who had served under Lambert and was scheduled to command the rebels in the West Riding, opposed this idea on the grounds that loyalists in the north would attack their families and relations while the rebels were marching on London.[68] Jones brought with him a revised copy of the declaration, which Richardson read to a group that included John Atkinson, Robert Atkins, a salter from Leeds, Joseph Crowder, Simon (or Simeon) Butler of Bingley, Yorkshire, Thomas Fletcher, and William Mason of Gainsborough.[69] Robert Atkinson objected to that part of the declaration calling for the restoration of the Rump and urged instead that the Long Parliament be reconstituted as it had been in 1642. The others agreed.[70]

Attendance at these meetings fluctuated. This was due partly to the expanding base of the conspiracy and partly to the fact that some of the conspirators periodically carried messages to cohorts in other areas. Among the others who were involved in these meetings were Captain Thomas Oates (or Otis) of Morley, Yorkshire, who had an estate worth more than £300 per annum, and Timothy Butler, who was in charge of a cache of some 200 weapons in Thames Street, London. In an effort to preserve secrecy, the location of the meetings varied throughout the summer; in addition to Harrogate and Pannal, the dissidents convened at Doncaster, Boroughbridge, and Leeds.[71]

Unknown to the conspirators, the government had already breached their security. On 21 July a royalist observed that the malcontents were "numerous, & monstrous, malapert, & full of venome & revenge." He recommended that the lord lieutenant of the West Riding arrest their leaders or "wee shall undoubtedly have a new war." But the first hard evidence did not come until the 24th, when an unnamed informant warned that in a matter of days there would be a rebellion in the northern counties involving the Quakers and disbanded officers and soldiers. Although Fairfax allegedly would lead the rebels, "noe considerable men will joine with them unless they prosper."[72] The following day the same informant reported that the rising had been delayed until the declaration could be printed. Although some rebels claimed to have 20,000 horse and 30,000 foot, including some from Lancashire and Cheshire, the informer thought this "business will prove but a Bubble and will come to nothing." According to Lieutenant-Colonel Walters, other malcontents reckoned that they could count on 12,000 horse, and hoped that Lambert or Ludlow would command them. Some consideration was even given to an attempt to liberate Lambert so he could take up command.[73]

After some deliberation, the rebels set 6 August as the date for their revolt in order to coincide with the assizes at York, when leading gentry could be more easily seized. Simultaneous uprisings were planned for Durham, Newcastle, Berwick, Leeds, and Westmorland. Arms and ammunition would be brought in by a collier at Shields, east of Newcastle. When Major Greathead's objections to scheduling the rising for assize week went unheeded , he secretly switched sides and became an informer for Sir Thomas Gower.[74] The latter subsequently remarked to Bennet that Greathead was "sensible of his duty, and being one of the last that departed from it, was the first that returned." Unfortunately for the government, Greathead knew little of the revolutionary council in London. When he and Colonel Smithson told Gower of the conspiracy, the latter instructed them "to dissemble till they had drawn in all the friends they could to joine with them, and then to give evidence against them." In effect, they were to entrap dissidents. The loss of Greathead alone would have proved fatal to the rebels, given his access to so much of the planning, but there were other problems as well. Not the least of these was a personal rivalry between Captains Hutton and John Mason of South Shields, Durham, "about the command in chief."[75]

Before 1 August a group of ex-Cromwellian officers and Fifth Monarchists (including Bradford and Gregory, both ex-officers) met at Hatfield in the West Riding, at Doncaster, in the Isle of Axholme, and elsewhere in the moors, though most of their activity was near Durham. Some came from as far as Lincolnshire, Nottinghamshire, and Derbyshire. Meetings were scheduled in Lancashire, Yorkshire, and Cheshire for the final week in August. At Sunderland a collier brought in a load of concealed weapons. Quakers were recruited by Baptists "to ioyne in outward things to spirituall good," though they refused to use "carnall weapons."[76]

As the evidence mounted, Gower warned Albemarle on the 3rd

that there were 1,500 men in the northern counties, disciplined and accustomed to victory, who were on the verge of attempting what fewer than forty Tong plotters had recently tried in London. "This sort of people . . . follow the Fancyes of Anabaptism and the dreams of those who presently expect to be sharers in a fifth monarchy." Moreover, he added, they had the support of a party in Scotland. He personally kept special surveillance on Sir James McDowel, formerly a colonel of horse in the duke of Hamilton's army and an M. P. from Scotland in the Cromwellian era.[77]

The government could wait no longer. On 3 August Colonel Freschville was ordered to secure York with troops of horse and foot, while Buckingham, in his capacity as lord lieutenant of the West Riding, was dispatched from London with additional forces. Sensing that it was an opportune time to attack, Paul Hobson sent a coded message from London to John Joplin in Durham, urging the rebels to ambush Buckingham and then march on the capital. Joplin passed the message to Dr. Richardson, and a council of rebel chieftains, consisting of Richardson, Captain Jones, Robert Atkinson, Major Greathead, and Hobson's messenger, hurriedly convened at Pannal. Richardson pressed Greathead to act, but the major retorted that his men would not fight as long as trained bands were quartered in the Leeds area. Once they were gone, he promised to raise 500 horse and as many foot, though as Gower's agent he was clearly stalling for time until the authorities could act. The rebels' mood was positive as they discussed the likelihood of winning over many in Albemarle's regiment, some of the Life Guards, and the city of London itself as their forces approached it. When the meeting was concluded, Jones left to take command of rebel units in Durham.[78]

Before the week was over, disaster struck for the rebels. Gower moved first to arrest Sir James McDowel, Dr. Richardson, and an unnamed third person who identified himself as an "intelligencer" from London. Richardson, accused of conniving with Joseph Helling (or Hiller), a Quaker known to Gower for his "ill designes," was detained in a private house at York, but he soon escaped and fled to the Netherlands. By the 8th, approximately a hundred of "the chiefe designers, and old officers" had been arrested and taken to York. Gower craftily had them charged with frequenting conventicles rather than seditious plotting, thus concealing his knowledge of the conspiracy. The accused were forced to provide security and then freed. Among those apprehended were six men with ample arms and money who had apparently been recruiting in the West Riding. Small parties of armed men were also spotted riding through

Bramham Moor.[79] Acting on orders from London, the deputy lieutenants of Westmorland and Cumberland made special efforts to secure dangerous persons and prevent illegal meetings, and provisions were made to exercise a company of the militia's foot each week.[80]

Failing to recognize what was happening, the rebels were not dissuaded by either the arrests or the increased military preparations. John Atkinson was even convinced that as a result of the publicity generated by the discovery of the plot "their number was mightilly augmented in the South & that many men of great Estate were come into them." One of Bennet's correspondents warned that the danger from the north and west had not abated, though fear of betrayal made the radicals more cautious. According to this informant, the dissidents had sent for Ludlow, but "others" would advise him "not [to] come as yet."[81] Ludlow's own account of the rebellion does not, however, support this claim.

## Farnley Wood, Kaber Rigg, and Woodham Moor

Within a matter of days after Gower's crackdown, the rebel council in the north convened again, this time at the house of David Lumbey (or Lumby) near Leeds. Both Atkinsons were present along with Joseph Crowder, Simon and Timothy Butler, Edward Wilkinson of Hunslet, Yorkshire, and William Parker. Joplin had returned from London and was conferring with Captain Jones, but neither was at this meeting.[82] According to Robert Atkinson, the Lumbey group made the momentous decision to press for a general insurrection rather than one restricted to the north. Messengers were accordingly dispatched to London, to those areas of Yorkshire "where their interest lay," to Joplin in Durham, and to Colonels John Birch and John Shuttleworth and Major Robinson in Lancashire. A decision was also made to place Major William Hobart in command of rebel forces in Leicestershire. The conspirators were hopeful of taking Carlisle and Appleby Castle as well as getting the support of 7,000 men and 500 "watermen" in London.[83]

A week later the rebels met again, this time at the skinner William Cotton's house in Leeds.[84] Apparently only two of those present at the Lumbey session, John Atkinson and Simon Butler, were there, but they were joined by the old stalwarts William Leeving, Captain Thomas Oates, and the minister Jeremiah Marsden. With them were Christopher Dawson (alias John Mann) of Leeds, who subsequently conveyed letters from the London council to Robert Atkinson, the

Durham messenger George Rumford (or Rumfitt), Richard Wilson, and three agents from the south.[85] The latter brought word that Captain Mason had obtained assurances from dissidents in western England and southern Wales to rise at the appropriate time. Gloucester would be the responsibility of the regicide Thomas Wogan, but this presupposed his escape from York Tower where he was being held. Glamorgan radicals would be led by Prichard—presumably Richard Prichard, a militant supporter of the Baptist preacher Jenkin Jones—and those in Herefordshire by Bridstock Harford, former militia commissioner, member of the county committee, and sequestrator—a dissident known for his "Sawcy Seditious Discourse."[86]

The failure of the rebels to rise on 6 August or the decision to broaden the insurrection apparently caused more internal dissension, for a meeting at Stank House, Kirkby Sigston (a residence of the Lascelles family), was necessary in order "to reconcile and unite the dissentinge sectes." The two Atkinsons, Rumford, Greathead, John Joplin of Foxholes, Robert Joplin, and Robinson were among those attending.[87] Robert Joplin, nephew of the Durham jailer John Joplin, served as their liaison with the Scots. Because his uncle was watched so closely, he was sometimes used as a messenger and had some contact with the revolutionary council in London. Another of Joplin's messengers was the youthful Eleanor Simcox. John Joplin himself served as treasurer for the northern conspirators. Among those to whom he distributed funds were Sir Nicholas Cole (£800) and Colonel John Tempest (£500), both of whom were nominal royalists who accepted bribes to treat dissidents leniently. Charles Carr, who had earlier gone to Ireland to meet with dissidents, was in Scotland in early September in connection with the rising.[88]

No later than 2 September[89] the northern rebels sent Marsden and Thomas Palmer to London to confer with the council. Throughout the summer Marsden had been particularly active on behalf of the conspiracy, meeting several times in Lancashire with Lieutenant-Colonel John Wigan, with agents from Wales and Ireland at Liverpool, with Scottish representatives at Dewsbury in the West Riding, and with dissidents in eastern England such as William Mason and Captain Salmon, Jr. En route to London he and Palmer conferred with the principal conspirators in Derbyshire at the home of Captain Woolhouse and stayed with Captain Lockyer at Skegby, Notts. Also present was John Atkinson, who was not party to the discussions, though he accompanied Marsden and Palmer to London. From the capital Marsden wrote several letters "in dark expressions" to his allies in Yorkshire informing them of progress in the west and promising to return with a new date for the insurrection. By the end of September he was back in the north with word that the rising would occur on 12 October. Some problems had been encountered in London with the Fifth Monarchists. Nathaniel Strange had told John Atkinson that his people could not "join with a mixt multitude[,] part of them being fifth Monarchy Men," though they promised to rebel independently. Marsden had more success, reporting on his return to the north that he had had "much ado to get the ffith Monarchy men together to join with us," but that in the end they finally acquiesced.[90]

In the meantime Gower busily studied reports about radical movements. On 24 September he warned the bishop of Durham that the plotters intended to seize him and his money along with his dean and chapter and any gentry who opposed them. At this point his information indicated that they had 300 horse and enough foot soldiers for the attack on Newcastle. Yet he complained to Williamson on the 26th that the gentry in the West Riding had precipitously arrested some of the fanatics using intelligence provided by Greathead, thereby jeopardizing his safety as well as his access to the inner circles of the cabal. It was still too early, he insisted, to call out the trained bands. A report to Bennet the following day indicated that the rebels claimed to have 10,000 men "fitt for warr" in the four northern counties, though they would not rise "unles they have the Alarum from some of the other kingdomes," or the opportunity to take advantage of a digression caused by factional dispute at court or a foreign war.[91]

On 28 September Gower acquired the essential outline of the latest plan from no less than three informers, of whom the most important was undoubtedly Major Greathead. Gower and three fellow deputy lieutenants subsequently said of him that he "hath really and effectually contributed very much to the discovery of the late plott."[92] By the end of the month, however, the radicals suspected him of being an informer. Gower seemed unconcerned: "I have more strings to the bow, nor shall he be the single witnesse." The other key informants at this crucial juncture seem to have been Colonel Smithson, who had supported Monck in 1660, and Joseph Strangways, who reported to Sir Roger Langley. John Ellerington was still providing intelligence to officials, though he was not close to the rebels' inner circle.[93] A case has also been made against Paul Hobson as an informer. After the authorities intercepted one of his coded letters to John Joplin on 18 August, he was imprisoned in the

Tower. To save his neck, according to Robert Atkinson, at the king's behest Hobson "had frequent & constant converse with the Trators makeing it his bussiness to involve soe many as possible." This was also Mason's opinion. A scant two weeks earlier, however, Atkinson had given out a different story, testifying that Hobson "confessed he had undertaken to discover to his Majestie any plott against him but that he played double, and did (indeed) advance the designe by all means possible."[94] Given the fact that Hobson was kept in prison for several years, begging to be exiled, he had probably been a double agent. Atkinson's change of story may have been an attempt to help Hobson by making the government think he had truly betrayed his fellow extremists.

As officials pieced together the story in late September, they knew that the risings were scheduled for 12 October, supposedly in every county. Colonel John Pearson was to attack Whitehall and apprehend the dukes of York and Albemarle, the lord chancellor, and the lord treasurer. To secure the Trent and the Severn, Nottingham and Gloucester would be taken. Scarborough, as Walters later confessed, could not be surprised, but the rebels hoped to capture both York and Hull, the latter by sending 500 men at night in flat-bottomed boats. Boston would be fortified in order to receive ammunition and supplies from the Netherlands, and if possible Newcastle and Tynemouth would be seized to facilitate communications with Scotland. There was even some talk of a "great force" from the Netherlands landing at Bridlington. Command in the west would go to Ludlow, who could expect 8,000 men in Dorset, Somerset, and Wiltshire. Large numbers of recruits would also be available in Berkshire, Sussex, Surrey, Essex, and Suffolk. In London, however, the disaffected "were awed by the King's guards and Auxiliarys," and would not rise until these troops left London to quell disturbances in the shires. Not only did the rebels allegedly have agents in France, Scotland, and the Netherlands, but they also had the backing of "many persons of great account, and members of Parliament [who were] engaged in the conspiracy."[95] This version was obviously based in part on hearsay gathered by the informers, who must themselves have been as gullible as the recruits the rebels hoped to enlist.

The exaggerations notwithstanding, there was an unmistakable kernel of truth in the account that Gower and others had pieced together. There were, for instance, definite links with radical exiles in the Netherlands, not least because Dr. Edward Richardson was now in their midst, along with the Tong plotters Richard Tyler, Cole, and Spurway. Bennet's primary source of information about the exile community was Edward Riggs, the ex-Tong plotter, who received a stipend of £40 per annum for his efforts. By late August, he had acquired information that the dissidents expected to act soon in all three kingdoms. Cole, who was seen with Tyler in Rotterdam, was caught shipping approximately a thousand pistols and carbines from Amsterdam the same month. According to Tyler, who was also smuggling weapons, Cole "speakes hye, & feares not what the King of England can doe to him." Two Congregationalist ministers, Richard Lawrence of Yarmouth, ejected as rector of Trunch with Swafield, Norfolk, in 1660, and George Thorne of Weymouth, ejected as rector of Radipole, Dorset, in 1662, were in Rotterdam throughout the summer enlisting support for the design. Referring to the Apocalypse, both men believed that the three and a half year period in which the witnesses were slain would be over in October, "& then the people of god will live & the ould cause." Lawrence had left for Yarmouth by 4 September, when Thorne was preparing to return to Weymouth.[96]

Another dissident who may have returned briefly to England was the regicide Sir Michael Livesey, who had reportedly been with Desborough at Arnhem in early September. On the 10th the magistrates interrogated a John Lockyer, who was accused of accompanying Livesey from Mardike to Plymouth. Lockyer, who claimed to be a boatswain from Colchester, had allegedly called the bishops rogues and bragged that "the King should not have lived tyll August was out, but he should not live this month out." The possibility that Livesey had indeed returned to England in the company of Captain Lockyer is intriguing but incapable of proof. In any event, at month's end Riggs reported that Livesey was in Arnhem along with Desborough and Colonel (or Major) Thomas White, while Cole, Kelsey, and Cornet George Joyce were in Rotterdam. The omnipresent Ludlow was reportedly in the company of Colonel Dewey at Amsterdam, Haarlem, and Arnhem. In the meantime the arms shipments continued, especially to Scotland.[97]

Dr. Richardson, who spent his time at Rotterdam and Amsterdam practicing medicine, was conversing "with all the discontented English." His presence thoroughly frustrated Downing, who begged Clarendon to ask the king to send a formal request to have Richardson banned from the country. Jan De Witt, Grand Pensionary of the United Provinces, adamantly refused, however, to sanction Richardson's arrest and extradition to England. By December Downing was trying to recruit two or three "resolute" men to kidnap Richardson, but nothing came of the plan.[98]

The situation in England moved toward a climax in late September and early October. Rebel agents met in London at month's end to discuss rising as early as 3 October, but this proved unworkable. Meetings were then scheduled in the West and North Ridings. Perhaps because three Scots were seized at Ripon, apparently as agents in the conspiracy, there was still some uncertainty in rebel ranks: "At present their designes are at a stand, and attend some directions out of the South."[99]

The meeting in the West Riding took place at Isaac Balm's house in Gildersome, southwest of Leeds, on 6 or 7 October. Those present included Greathead, John Atkinson, Robert Atkins, Simon Butler, Joseph Crowder, Thomas Oates, the Durham representative George Rumford, Robert Nicholson, William Cotton, Thomas Calton of Charley, Leicestershire (a recruiter in Derbyshire), John Nettleton and William Childrey representing Knaresborough and the Dales, an agent named Taylor sent from Westmorland by Captain Robert Atkinson, Isaac Balm, Marsden, and agitators from other counties. Jones was still in Durham preparing his men. After telling the Gildersome group that the insurrection was set for the 12th, Marsden urged them to proceed "vigorously, and assured [them] that God was with them."[100] Calton, who had been sent by Captain Lockyer and other rebel leaders in Derbyshire and Nottinghamshire, told the group that they could expect "great assistance" from those counties as well as Lincolnshire and Leicestershire. Lockyer himself would bring two troops from Nottinghamshire. The head of the party in that county (as well as Staffordshire) was purportedly Major John Gladman, aided by Captain James Wright, a Presbyterian of Shirland Park, Derby. In the north they hoped to capture Skipton and Tynemouth Castles, Durham, Newcastle, York, and Hull, as well as Boston, Lincolnshire. They hoped as well to seize £3,000 from the bishop of Durham's treasury and additional funds from the capture of excise and subsidy monies.[101]

On 9 October the ineptness of the radical organization was underscored when a messenger from the London council, Cornet Daniel Carey, who had once served in the parliamentary army under Anthony Buller, arrived in Yorkshire with instructions to delay the rebellion two weeks "for that a great party newly came in would ingage effectually, if they could have that time to provide." There was also some division among the dissidents in London that necessitated a delay. Oates and Marsden, however, retorted that it was too late to retract the orders to rise.[102]

In the face of the rumors about the impending revolt that were spreading among the landed class, there was renewed concern about the state of the militia and the "Implacable Bitter Spirit" of the dissidents, but no panic.[103] The guards at Durham and Chester were alerted, and Colonels Robert Duckenfield and Thomas Croxton and Captain Benjamin Croxton were secured in Chester Castle by the 5th.[104] Deputy lieutenants in the north directed loyalists to stand ready to suppress a revolt on the 12th, and the militia was called out in the West Riding, Cheshire, and Lancashire, though not the North and East Ridings for fear of alerting the radicals that they had been discovered.[105] Because intelligence reports indicated that there would be simultaneous risings in the west, the guard was doubled at Gloucester, and both volunteers and militia were alerted in Gloucestershire, Herefordshire, and Monmouthshire. Bristol too was reinforced with extra guards, and 140 suspected persons were arrested and weapons seized. Elsewhere special guards were posted and the trained bands alerted.[106]

In a preemptive strike, the state arrested some of the "principall officers and Agitators" on the 10th, among them Greathead (in an attempt to preserve his cover as long as possible), Captain Thomas Lascelles, Robert Walters, Denham, Robinson, and more than eighty others. One of the leading Lancashire dissidents, Colonel Roger Sawrey, was indicted on 6 October for violating the Elizabethan statute against conventicles (35 Eliz. I, c. 1).[107]

A satisfied Gower reported to Bennet that "almost all the Leaders of the Fanatiques are seized. . . . I am still of the same opinion as formerly that there is no present danger, notwithstanding the late advertisements . . . from my selfe and others." Three of his informers assured him that the design had been "layed aside." Colonel Freschville similarly reported to Bennet and Williamson the same day that there had been a false alarm and that all was quiet. Bennet himself was relatively unconcerned as he awaited these reports, convinced that Yorkshire was probably overly prepared for trouble. Only Buckingham was fully cognizant that an insurrection was imminent: "I am persuaded they will make some attempt, since the same intelligence is brought to us from soe many severall hands," especially Smithson.[108]

Buckingham ordered the militia to rendezvous near Pontefract and Ferrybridge, southeast of Leeds. Sir George Savile's regiment of foot, Sir Edward Wroth's troop from Oxford's regiment, and the duke's own troop of volunteers provided him with at least 1,000 men. Deputy lieutenants in the North Riding similarly directed their units to muster on the 12th. Buckingham correctly surmised that the mobilization of the trained bands initially gave the rebels pause, but they resolved to continue with their insurrection.[109]

Disaster, however, dogged the rebels to the end. Heavy rains and flooding, which might have been effectively utilized to disguise their various rendezvous, instead seem to have discouraged the recruits from turning out. Furthermore, units in the North Riding and Westmorland were spotted on the 10th, presumably having taken up arms too early.[110]

The plan called for rebel units to act on the night of 12–13 October. A rendezvous was scheduled at Topcliffe Bridge, from which the rebels—with "Freedome" as their watchword—would march to Northallerton to seize weapons. This area was chosen for a rendezvous because of the many ex-officers and soldiers in this region. At Northallerton command would be assumed by Lieutenant-Colonel Walters, aided by Denham, Cooke, John Atkinson, Robinson, and others. Their goal was the capture of York, but failing that they were to march to Leeds. They expected half of the militia to defect to them. Although Lord Darcy reported that 300 horse had gathered at Northallerton, in fact this phase of the insurrection came virtually to naught. Some rebels, including Charles Carr and William Childrey, were at Topcliffe, but they were far fewer than the number expected. Several parties of horse were also spotted in the Tadcaster area, between York and Leeds.[111]

Captain Thomas Oates gathered a contingent of perhaps fifty men at Farnley Wood, near Leeds, but some of them had no weapons and soon dispersed. The others rode north to Bradford Moor, but before morning became discouraged and scattered. This was a far cry from the 1,200 horse and dragoons that had been expected, some from Bradford (under the command of Henry Bradshaw), Leeds, and Skipton. Wilkinson, Lumbey, Simon Butler, the Crowders, and John Nettleton were among those at Farnley Wood.[112]

In Westmorland, Captain Robert Atkinson, astride a white horse and armed with pistols, gathered a small group of about twenty horse and possibly some foot at Kirkby Stephen, southeast of Appleby. Atkinson's brother-in-law, Captain Robert Waller of Mallerstang, Sergeant Richardson, Thomas Wharton, and Atkinson's nephew, John Waller, a Durham yeoman (formerly of Mallerstang), were among those present, as were some Quakers. Their plans called for an attack on the jail at Appleby to release the prisoners, the seizure of the excise funds in the town, and the capture of Sir Philip Musgrave at Hartley. The password was "God be with us." Atkinson exhorted the men that Philip Lord Wharton, Fairfax, and

Manchester supported the rebellion, and two messengers from the Leeds area rode in with news that the Yorkshire rebels were rising that night. Atkinson had also been assured by John Joplin of an extra troop of horse from Durham, though it failed to materialize. Atkinson and Waller marched their men to Kaber Rigg, expecting to meet a contingent from Kendal, but a company of militia in that town prevented them from acting. The two captains had intended to rendezvous at Northallerton with Walters, but with so few men in their ranks they decided about 1 A.M. to send their followers home. "I advised them to returne to their owne habitations," said Atkinson, "and sit quietly." The recruits left "discontently," despite assurances that they were safe because they had done nothing wrong. Although this unit was to have been reinforced by as many as 800 horse from Scotland, they too failed to arrive. There is, however, a report from Sir Brian Broughton indicating that rebels from Ireland were landed by eighteen barks, but they fled into Scotland when the risings collapsed.[113]

Under the leadership of Captain Roger Jones, other rebels gathered at Findon Hill and Woodham Moor in Durham. Captain William Carter, Timothy Whittington, a gentleman worth £400 per annum, and George Marshal, who lived near Ripon, were among those involved. These men were supposed to join forces with the Westmorland group but failed to do so.[114] Throughout the north, news of the risings was met not only with resolve and judicious concern, but also quiet confidence. At least in part this was due to the government's access to superior manpower. Buckingham's forces alone badly outnumbered all the extremists who rose, and in addition Lord Belasyse was quick to offer the duke an additional 1,000 foot and 300 horse. The king approved Buckingham's plan to defend York itself with two regiments of foot, one from the militia and the other of volunteers. On the 20th, a bare week after the insurrection, Bennet notified Buckingham that the king wanted the militia dismissed unless he thought otherwise. Because of the expense, the duke had done so as soon as the rebels were dispersed. The king himself had been confident enough to deny Buckingham's request, issued on the eve of the risings, for authority to raise a regiment of horse in an emergency.[115]

Newspaper accounts of the rebellion reflect the government's concern to assure the population that all was in hand. A story filed from Newcastle on the 17th reported the insurrection, but added that "we take these Stories to be rather Prudentiall Hints to provide for the worst, then Substantiall Grounds for any Apprehension of

Disturbance, or Disorder." The same issue carried a report from
Preston, Lancashire, that there was no apparent danger and accused
the fanatics of fanning the alarms. From Nottingham, which was
supposed to have been one of the centers of the conspiracy, came
word that talk of a rising had "spent it self so long in Noise, without
any likelihood of effect."[116] But the papers also carried a steady
stream of reports about militia activities and the arrest of suspected
rebels that reflected the government's protracted repression of the
militants.

## Investigation and Suppression

Although the government's initial reaction to the insurrection was
one of relative confidence, as its investigation began to substantiate
how widespread the conspiracy was, its concern deepened. On 14
October Gower reported to Bennet that his spies could see no signs
of a rising, though he arrested two rebel messengers, Cotton and
Fletcher, who were carrying "papers of ill consequence" and a key to
the rebels' cipher. In Newcastle and Somerset the Nonconformists
suspended their meetings in order to avoid suspicion. It was quiet too
in London, where dissidents believed that the northern rebels had
acted rashly. Lord Fauconberg probably reflected the views of many
in the political nation when he echoed the judgment of his informant
that "there can be no plot Considerable at this time." So calm did
things appear in early November that Pepys concluded that "the
spirits of the old Parliament-soldier[s] are so quiet and contented
with God's providences, that the King is safer from any evil meant
him by them, a thousand times more then from his own discontented
Cavalier[s]."[117]

But already the mood began to shift as the dissidents recovered
their courage and officials gathered evidence of the extent of the
conspiracy. After conferring with Buckingham at York, Belasyse—
convinced that the plot was indeed universal—pressed the king to
provide "an adition off standing Tropes as may secure the government against thes Treasonable plotts." On 3 November Bennet
admitted to Ormond that "we find the grounds of the Plot further
laid than we conceiv'd at first."[118] Nearly a month after the risings Sir
Philip Musgrave was surprised that "every day we fynde out more
Persons to have been at the meeting" at Kirkby Stephen and Kaber
Rigg. On 24 November Bennet explained to Ormond that the
government was now convinced that the design extended far beyond
northern England, and that the rebels were in contact with dissidents

in all of the kingdoms, a conclusion subsequently reached by the judges who tried the rebels. Walters, the key witness, testified that the conspiracy involved all three kingdoms and was originally to have begun in Ireland. Ormond was directed to review the examinations of the Dublin plotters for possible links to the northern conspiracy, and Bennet instructed Buckingham to interrogate suspects carefully. Although there might be insufficient evidence to procure convictions, the government at least wanted enough proof "to vindicate us from the Malice that may probably accuse us of having been affraid without cause, but also keep the Country in a disposition to secure themselves."[119]

Concern was also increased by renewed radical activity. A party of armed horsemen led by Colonel Thomas Birch was seen near Keighley heading toward Skipton on the night of 30 October. Sir Roger Bradshaigh was ordered to seize and disperse them; his troop was kept busy for the next two years searching for weapons and suspected plotters.[120] Some of the conspirators were reportedly still scheming in early November to rise in western Cheshire. Others met at Wolverhampton, Staffordshire, where they maintained contact with cohorts in the north. Radicals in the Newcastle area were hoping for another chance to revolt, and there was intelligence from Staffordshire that the Fifth Monarchists would take up arms in early December.[121]

The continued reports of radical activity, coming closely on the heels of the insurrection and coupled with the unfolding story of the conspiracy, necessitated vigilant security measures throughout the autumn. In part this entailed the apprehension of suspected radicals, whether implicated in the northern risings or not. In Cumberland Musgrave secured "some of the most dangerous of the old army," and at Newcastle twenty-seven dissidents were arrested in late October and forced to post bonds for peaceful behavior.[122] In some places the radicals were disarmed, though Sir Roger Bradshaigh complained that he met with little success in the Wigan area because "all but fooles hide close."[123] Special efforts were made to ensure that key cities, such as Bristol, Hull, York, and Canterbury were secured. The militia not only had to ensure security in the immediate aftermath of the risings but subsequently was called on to maintain order, as at Rochester, Kent, in early November, and in Westmorland when Captain Robert Atkinson escaped and allegedly threatened to release his colleagues and wreak vengeance on loyalist gentry.[124]

Because of both the plotting and the continued resort to conventicles, the Privy Council ordered the lords lieutenant on 2 November to put the militia into a "useful posture." The state of the militia was such that volunteers had to be used in times of emergency, as in the Midlands in October and Westmorland in November. Musgrave complained that some Westmorland companies had no weapons, some no knowledge of how to use those they did have, and some no commissioned officers. In Monmouthshire the number of militia was so paltry that Lord Herbert could not keep more than fifteen on duty, hence he urged Charles to maintain a garrison in Chepstow Castle and even promised to pay part of the cost himself.[125] Complaining about "how naked & unpreparied wee are heer," one of Williamson's correspondents in Cornwall stressed the militia's weakness. Bradshaigh, however, remarked in December that the Lancashire militia was "soe well setld" that there was sufficient leisure for recreation. Nevertheless, in the face of repeated complaints about the militia's unreadiness, it is little wonder that the crown eventually expressed a desire for a professional army. The earl of Peterborough went so far as to argue that the militia is a "useless and a dangerous constitution" which teaches "the use of armes unto more Ennemies then friends, it discontents the people very much and at the same time gives them severall occasions to discharge it."[126] Charles' English subjects were unwilling to shoulder the responsibility for a reliable and efficient militia. That the radicals were unable to take advantage of this weakness is eloquent testimony to their ineptitude.

Throughout 1664 the authorities, spearheaded by Gower, pieced together evidence suggesting a network of "agitators" that extended throughout some twenty-five counties, London, and Wales. Expectedly, the largest contingents were in the north, especially Yorkshire, where fifty men were named. Among them were nine clergymen, twenty-seven ex-officers, and the M. P. William Stockdale. The lists include many very prominent radicals, though in most instances the state had insufficient evidence of complicity to consider prosecution.[127]

The dragnet brought in substantial numbers of suspects but failed to trap some of the key personnel in the conspiracy. Dr. Richardson had fled in August, and Tyler, Spurway, Cole, and Henry Danvers (who "left some agents and silenced ministers to carrie on the busines" in Leicestershire) were likewise in the Netherlands, safely beyond the government's reach. It took the magistrates as much as six to eight months to capture such rebels as Timothy Butler, Thomas Calton, John Joplin of Durham, Robert Joplin, John

Atkinson (who "colored his Face" and pretended to be a laborer in county Durham), Roger Jones (who fled by ship to London), William Mason, George Rumford, John Waller, and John Ward.[128] There is no clearer indication of the importance attached by the government to the investigation than the fact that arrests continued throughout the decade and into the next. In March 1671 Gower urged Williamson to try or preferably pardon five suspects committed as recently as the previous summer. One of the last to be accused, the soldier Joseph Midgeley (arrested in 1670), was described in 1671 as sickly, in need of charity, and imprisoned without trial.[129]

As late as 1667, warrants for the arrest of Dr. Richardson, Roger Jones, Lockyer, Wise, Marsden, Simon and Timothy Butler, Cary (alias Carew), Spurway, Lee, Blood, Wilkinson, Dawson, Ralph Alexander, and Henry Danvers were issued at the request of the informer William Leeving, who had agreed to testify against them for their role in the 1663 conspiracy. A warrant was also issued for Lumbey. Wise and Timothy Butler had been incarcerated in 1664, but were now wanted again. A warrant was issued on 7 March 1667 to convey Jones, John Joplin, and John Atkinson from the Tower to York. When officials tried to transfer Mason there in August, however, Blood, Timothy Butler, Lockyer, and others rescued him.[130]

Several of the rebels escaped from custody, though one—William Leeving—did so with the connivance of the authorities after he promised to spy on his former confederates, including Blood. The alternative was probably hanging, for the state had two witnesses against him.[131] Despite having posted a bond, Captain Robert Atkinson absconded on the eve of his interrogation, leading to rumors among the prisoners at Appleby that he would rescue them on the night of 7 or 8 November. Instead he used Sir Thomas Braithwaite of Burnside and Richard Braithwaite as intermediaries in an attempt to procure a pardon in return for his confession. Following an interview with the king, he provided substantial information about the design.[132] Captain John Mason initially eluded his pursuers but was captured in Newark upon Trent, Nottinghamshire, on 15 November 1663. In early July 1664 he escaped from Clifford's Tower, leaving behind a written protestation of his innocence: "I looked upon the thing as sinfull, and did upon the first heareing, conclude . . . Itt would be Blasted not blessed of the Lord." The proclamation of 27 July calling for his apprehension also named Edward Cary, though Daniel Carey was probably the person intended, for he had escaped from a royal messenger.[133]

Many of those who died for their involvement in the insurrection were of little import in the radical underground. The difficulty of obtaining the necessary two witnesses for an act of treason, the willingness of some leaders to confess in return for their lives, and the flight of others saved some of the principals from the hangman's noose. Most of the trials were held at York between January and April 1664, with Sir Christopher Turner, baron of the Exchequer, and Sir John Keeling and Sir John Archer, justices of Common Pleas, presiding. The deputy lieutenants, sensitive to local feelings, persuaded Buckingham to hold the trials in the north, for otherwise "the Country will thinke . . . [the rebels] are unjustly condemned, if they bee removd from hence where theyr freinds & neighbors may witnesse how they are dealt with." There was also a desire for the punishment to be administered locally as a warning to others and to avoid the expense of bringing witnesses to London.[134]

In early January twenty-one rebels were sentenced to be hanged, drawn, and quartered, three of them at Northallerton. Seven of the twenty-one had played important roles in the conspiracy. At least six of them—George Denham, "the Grand Agitator," Robert Atkins, Thomas Oates, William Cotton, John Nettleton, and Richard Wilson—had been involved in the planning councils. Cotton, Oates, Nettleton, and Atkins had been at the crucial Gildersome meeting in early October, and Oates had joined Marsden in refusing to delay the rising at the request of the London council. In addition, Oates (who confessed) had been a commanding officer at Farnley Wood. Denham had worked on a scheme to seize horses and weapons from Viscount Fauconberg, lord lieutenant of the North Riding, and Lord Fairfax of Gilling, and to secure their prisoners in Skipton Castle.[135] A conspirator condemned at York in August 1664, Richard Oldroyd, had hosted Scottish agents in the spring. An additional three men were also sentenced to death at Appleby, one of whom was Captain Robert Waller, an officer at Kaber Rigg. Some of the condemned breathed defiance to the last: Denham used "Horrible Extravagancies" in his trial and Cotton boasted that he valued his life no more than the judge did his handkerchief. Apart from Oldroyd (who died on 13 August), those condemned at York were executed on 16 January, those at Allerton on 19 January, and those at Appleby on 28 March. Two heads of the York conspirators were sent to Doncaster and two to Northallerton for public display; the rest were affixed to the poles on the gates at York and Allerton (where the heads blew down in a storm, narrowly missing pedestrians). Despite his confession, Robert Atkinson was executed in August 1664, having angered the authorities by the inconsistencies in his testimony, his insolence, and his willingness to "be hanged [rather] then come to the barr to be witness against any man."[136]

Altogether the state put at least twenty-six men to death for their participation in the northern conspiracy. At least two others committed suicide rather than face trial: George Blackburne, a wealthy clothier from Huddersfield in the West Riding who thought that "the Gentry were insupportable to the People," and John Robinson of Worsall. Yet indictment was by no means a guarantee of conviction, notwithstanding the state's efforts to disqualify dissidents from serving on the juries.[137] Nine men, including Robert Cooke, who had been involved in a mid-May planning session and was charged with misprision, were acquitted on 13 January, as were others in subsequent trials. To be sure, the state had problems finding two witnesses for each of the accused, but there were also "defects" in the formal examinations.[138] There were instances too of rebels receiving pardons despite the king's initial desire that they be treated severely. Among them were Joseph Crowder and William Childrey, both of whom were at the Gildersome meeting. Leonard Fletcher was acquitted solely on the grounds of his age and poor health. In general, such clemency as there was proved to be popular among the citizenry. One sympathizer warned that "innocent blood cryes loud against those that shed it." Some of the sympathy for the convicted stemmed from the conviction that they had been recruited by the very men who testified against them.[139]

The fate of the other principals is worth noting. The state could not obtain a conviction against John Joplin of Durham (who was nevertheless held in confinement); of the three possible witnesses, Leeving could not testify without destroying his cover, and John Waller testified only to what Joplin had told him, which the jury (including several of Joplin's friends) found insufficient. Hobson remained in prison without a trial until 1665, when he was released on condition that he leave the country, though death seems to have intervened sometime before June 1666. John Atkinson, Thomas Calton, Charles Carr, Evan Price (a Manchester clothworker who served as a messenger), and Robert Walters probably saved their lives by confessing. Blood and Lockyer eluded arrest, enabling them, with the help of Timothy Butler, to free Mason before he could be tried in 1667. According to Blood's earliest biographer, he had had a change of heart before the risings, had adopted the alias Ayliff, and had taken up the practice of medicine in Romford, Essex.[140]

Of the leading ministers involved, Palmer, Thorne, and Jollie were imprisoned for relatively short periods, while the Baptist Periam (or Peregrine) Corney of Leeds was executed at York in January 1664. Corney had been recruited with appeals against the perfidy of Monck as well as prelates whose "throats was soe wide and their bellies soe Large, that the whole Substance of the Nation was too Little to Suffice them." In his trial he defended himself with the maxim, "Faithful and true are those which follow the Lamb." The Fifth Monarchist James Fisher, who had been ejected as vicar of Sheffield in 1660 and had allegedly promised to recruit eighty men for the risings, managed to elude arrest, was cited in a royal proclamation, and was finally apprehended in early 1665.[141] One of the principal leaders, Jeremiah Marsden, was still at large in early March 1664 (using the alias Ralphson), though his wife was trying to negotiate a pardon in return for his confession. Some arrangement was apparently worked out, though he was a wanted man again in 1667. Various other clergymen, such as Vavasor Powell, John Cromwell (who was believed to have provided horses for the rebels), Philip Henry, Richard Steele, and five of the Nonconformists in Dorchester were arrested in connection with the conspiracy, but were soon freed for lack of evidence.[142]

The most prominent radicals arrested were Henry Neville, Colonel John Hutchinson, and Major Richard Salway. Neville adamantly professed his innocence, but admitted coming to London in June (with a license) and staying a fortnight. He denied knowledge of a revolutionary council or communication with disaffected persons, including Hutchinson. The government had little more than hearsay evidence against him, including a charge that he predicted a new Parliament by March 1664 in which he would sit. The State Papers (29/88/53) contain a reformer's plan for a Parliament composed of 300 representatives from the three kingdoms that may be linked to Neville.[143] Salway too professed his ignorance concerning a council, denied corresponding with Neville and Hutchinson, and insisted he had no knowledge of the plot: "I was perfectly inocent and know nothing of that matter, nor of any person in any wit concerned therin." He acknowledged only innocent visits in October to such places as Warwick, Kidderminster, Throckmorton, and Richards Castle.[144] Although Hutchinson also made similar denials about plotting and corresponding, even denying that he had been asked to concur in the conspiracy, the state was dubious, especially when he refused to provide assurances for his peaceful behavior. In 1664 Hutchinson was transferred from the Tower to Sandown Castle in Kent, where he died the same year.[145]

The highest ranking person suspected of involvement was Philip Lord Wharton, friend of many Nonconformist clergy and supporter of Bristol in his struggle with Clarendon. Captain Robert Atkinson accused Wharton, with "divers of great quality and consideration"—including Fairfax, Manchester, and Sir John Lawson—of knowledge of the plot; the latter three repudiated it. Wharton had just made a trip to the north, purportedly for business reasons. The investigation of him was discreet, though his estate agent in the north, the Congregationalist minister John Gunter (ejected as curate of Whittlebury, Green's Norton, Northamptonshire, in 1662), was required to provide security for his appearance should the government decide to interrogate Wharton. Richard Walters too claimed that Wharton was involved because Cornet Denham had contacted him, but Walters also averred that Wharton was too cunning to be caught. Wharton himself remarked that Atkinson "knew little [but] only was to command . . . a troop," though he acknowledged that John Atkinson "knows much." On the basis of this remark Wharton's biographer suggests that he may not have been telling the whole truth when he professed innocence, but there is no reliable evidence to link him to the conspiracy. Of Wharton's improbable involvement, Gower aptly noted "how little he could gett, and how much he might loose."[146]

In the north several persons of regional prominence were arrested, one of whom was the M. P. William Stockdale of Bilton Park, "a hott headed young fellow" and "an Errant Republican." He was the brother-in-law of Lieutenant-Colonel Walters, one of the rebel chieftains. Stockdale was acquitted of a charge of misprision of treason, though he allegedly failed to inform authorities of the conspiracy after hearing Ralph Rymer senior of Brafferton, Yorkshire, announce the date of the rising. This must have been galling to the magistrates, for after the younger Rymer and Richard Nelson consulted with Stockdale, they retracted their confessions; Nelson was subsequently acquitted. Described by the earl of Anglesey as "a kind of fifth monarchy man," Rymer had an estate worth some £400 per annum, and had been involved in raising funds to aid Nonconformist clergy. Having foolishly attempted to recruit Colonel Smithson through a letter, he was tried and found guilty of treason at York in January 1664 and executed. His son, Ralph Jr., was convicted of misprision of treason.[147] A friend of Thomas Jollie, Captain John Hodgson of Coley Hall in the West Riding, who had once fought under Cromwell and Lambert, was accused of the same offense for not revealing his knowledge of the plot. Although he was found guilty, a bribe to the clerk of assizes obtained him a pardon. Another gentleman, Christopher Hodgson of Gargrave, Yorkshire, was briefly imprisoned for the same offense.[148]

At Carlisle, Captain Cuthbert Studholme, a shopkeeper who had allegedly threatened to assassinate Charles in 1660, was incarcerated on charges that he was the rebel leader in that town, and would betray it to his allies with the aid of members of its garrison. Robert Atkinson claimed that he met with Studholme in July or August 1663. However, there was insufficient evidence for conviction.[149] The other leading Cumberland dissident, Major Timothy Scarthe (or Skaife), who once served under Robert Overton, was also arrested.[150]

Despite the usual assumption that Quakers in the Restoration era were pacifists, evidence pertaining to the risings indicates Quaker involvement. This was, of course, a flagrant repudiation of the advice that George Fox had given his followers in 1659 in the context of Sir George Booth's rebellion. Friends at that time were exhorted to "keep out of plots and bustling and the arm of the flesh, for all these are amongst Adam's sons in the Fall, where they are destroying men's lives like dogs and beasts and swine." Those who fight, he averred, are beyond the pale of Christ's kingdom. When Fox learned of the northern conspiracy, he declared "against all plots and plotters both public and private," and reissued his 1659 declaration. But in the north some Quakers were of a different mind.[151]

Evidence of Quaker involvement was strongest in the northwest. Sir Philip Musgrave remarked to Williamson in November 1663 that "the Quakers have had a deep hand in this plott for in all examinations Wee Meet with them."[152] In the ensuing weeks the justices of the peace dispatched agents to Quaker meetings, particularly in Westmorland, because so many Friends had allegedly been engaged in the design. At one time Richardson had intimated to Walters that he expected to have the support of no less than 1,000 Quakers. Quakers had been especially utilized as messengers, either because their itinerant preaching provided a convenient cover or because some were willing to help in some way short of shedding blood.[153] The two messengers, one of whom was Reginald (or Richard) Faucett of Orton, who assured Robert Atkinson and Robert Waller of aid from Joplin's confederates were Quakers in the guise of woolmen. Ralph Robinson of Cockerton, Durham, who was subsequently pardoned, testified that he received word concerning the time of the insurrection from the Quaker Thomas Randall. Likewise, it was the Quaker Thomas Wright of Castlethwaite, south of Kirkby Stephen, who told John Waller of the plan. Another Friend, Thomas Wharton of Orton, a friend of Faucett's, was heavily involved, having met on one occasion with Dr. Richardson, who told Wharton of the London council. Wharton was supposed to organize troops in his area (west of Kirkby Stephen), but on the night of the rising he showed up with only a single unarmed man.[154] The Quaker Joseph Helling (or Hiller), while a prisoner at Durham, wrote to Richardson in early June 1663 to tell him of the favorable conjunction of the stars and suggest that the 24th was a good day to rebel if preparations were completed. A Quaker widow, Judith Oates, provided a horse to one of the rebels on the day of the rising. George Whitehead and Edward Smith, both Friends, were imprisoned for suspected complicity in the plot, though the former at least was surely innocent.[155] Thus by 1663 Quaker leaders had not yet persuaded some of their followers that conspiracy and fighting were wrong; the militancy of the 1650s lived on, especially in the north.

## Aftershocks

Feelings among royalists were decidedly mixed in the aftermath of the risings. Blaming the recurring conspiracies on the Baptists and Fifth Monarchists, Albemarle was smugly certain that they could never pose a serious threat to the kingdom. Sir William Morice was of like mind, and expressed satisfaction that the militia was now "so well setled" that malignants could never inflame the country into a major rebellion. The continued failures of the radicals, concluded the earl of Southampton, would finally cure them of their seditious ways.[156]

Others, however, recognized the depth of the popular discontent and pressed for remedial measures. The dean of Carlisle, Dr. Guy Carleton, insisted that the militia was too scattered to be of much use, and that the trained bands would melt away if the rebels succeeded in kidnapping the lord and deputy lieutenants. To increase security he proposed a permanent guard of fifty to sixty horsemen in the bishopric of Durham, the assignment of a party of soldiers to Raby Castle to ensure its availability as a rendezvous for loyalists, and the imprisonment of leading dissidents in Tynemouth Castle where they could not correspond with radicals abroad. One of the most penetrating indictments of royalist failure came from the earl of Peterborough, who castigated loyalists for failing to "take the care we should, to improve, either the affections, or the reverence of men." He deplored corruption among those who governed, bishops who were uninformed, and chancellors who were remiss in fulfilling their responsibilities. Instead of sneering at the dissidents, Peterborough gave them their due as "sober[,] vigilant and very industrious." It was essential, one of Joseph Williamson's correspondents wrote, to review the management of royal and ecclesiastical affairs, for the troubles of the 1640s and 1650s "sprang from the remiseness of inferior governors."[157]

The immediate effect of the failed insurrection on many dissidents was a spirit of caution and even a distrust of each other, "having been so lately bitten, by the Exemplary Conversion of Diverse of their own Party, in whom they reposed even their highest confidence." But for the most part the disaffected remained defiant. There was bitterness toward those who had betrayed their trust as well as enmity toward those who served as the instruments of royal repression. With respect to the Restoration regime, "they are now more scornifull & hy then Ever they were." The unsigned letter of one radical damned Sir Thomas Gower for shedding innocent blood and compared the rule of Charles II with the "evil Spirit of . . . [the] corrupt & degenerate Monarchy [of the Roman Emperor Tiberius] in all its murderous & undooing Circumstances." A letter thought to be the work of John Williams, chaplain to Colonel Jerome Sankey in 1659, bemoaned the fact that the northern rebels had been "too hasty," but expressed hope that in the future the saints would once again take up the sword.[158]

Symbolic acts of defiance continued. There were more reports of malcontents who defiantly opened their shops at Christmas 1663 and on the anniversary of Charles I's execution the following month. On Christmas night the Presbyterian Nathaniel Barry, ejected as vicar of St. Mary's, Dover, in 1660, reportedly preached rebellion in a Dover brewer's house. At Poole in Dorset, sectarian shipmasters commandeered the parish church to enable their sailors to make new sails. Cheshire radicals castigated the government for its tyranny, and one warned that within a few years everyone would side with Colonel Croxton or be hanged.[159]

The failure of the risings did not quell the plotting. As early as 26 October 1663, those who had not been arrested were "debating about a fresh adventure upon any terms, but the hope of miraculous successe beinge the chiefest argument nothing was agreed." Information obtained by Sir Brian Broughton in January 1664 indicated that malcontents in Warwickshire were searching for officers to lead a new rebellion, which they thought feasible if their allies in Scotland, Ireland, and the south would take up arms. They were already communicating with confederates in Nottinghamshire. Other intel-

ligence noted that a group of radicals associated with Colonel Henry
Danvers, Major John Breman (still in prison), Captain John Toomes,
and Cornet George Joyce (in Rotterdam) hoped to raise a rebel force
by pretending to enlist volunteers to fight the Turks. Danvers,
disguised with a long beard and rural dress, was spotted conferring
with the Congregationalist minister Anthony Palmer in London.
There was concern in February about an unidentified party of forty
to fifty horse marching at night in the Doncaster area, though
nothing came of it.[160]

More serious was the ability of the radicals to use the Netherlands
as a base of operations and refuge. At most the government could
hope for some idea of radical movements abroad through the reports
of spies such as Edward Riggs, the ex-radical, and Colonel Joseph
Bampfield. Riggs, with advance knowledge of the northern conspiracy, had informed Bennet that Thomas Cole, Thomas Kelsey,
Captain Spurway, Major Thomas White, and others were involved.
The Scots, he said, were transporting weapons to their homeland and
Richard Tyler was shipping arms to Mr. Mansfield in London; they
were carried at one point by Jacob Davison in the *King David*.
Major Breman admitted knowing of weapons brought into En-
gland from both the Netherlands and New England.[161] One of the
key figures in the illicit arms trade was Sydrach Lester, master of the
*Magdalen*, based in Poole. A man of about forty, he made regular
trips between Holland and Southampton and the Isle of Wight. He
had reportedly castigated the king as "a whoremaster Rogue" and
had hoped for a captaincy in the rebel forces. He worked closely with
Cole, a former Southampton merchant, and also had contacts with
Joyce as well as English Quakers. Officials finally arrested Lester in
December on the Isle of Wight, but he escaped almost immediately,
and, aided by Cole, returned to Holland.[162]

There was a fairly regular correspondence between the exiles and
their allies in Scotland and England. Relations were close between
William Bridge's Congregational church at Great Yarmouth and the
exiles, with Richard Lawrence "frequently" serving as one of the
principal contacts. George Thorne performed the same function for
Weymouth Nonconformists. There was also contact between the
exiles and dissidents in Aylesbury, Buckinghamshire; the latter
group knew John Atkinson the hosier and was disturbed by his
arrest. The Presbyterian Robert Stirling and Gilby Carr's friend
James Buchanan returned to Scotland in December, presumably
with news concerning the exiles. Carr himself, as well as Henry
Danvers, had arrived in Holland by early November.[163] Others

followed to escape punishment for their part in the northern rebellion. They arrived daily, said Riggs in late January. Among them were Thorne and Captains Hannibal Vyvyan, James Wright, Stringer, and Spurway. Desborough, Kelsey, and Cole urged the new arrivals to seek safety in Arnhem. Their hope now was an apocalyptic faith that "before the yeare 1666 the beast will be destroyed." Tyler, however, was still shipping arms, hoping for "a resurrection of the good old cause," and threatening to kill any person who sent word of his activities to England. English officials were especially interested in apprehending Tyler (alias Richard Taylor), not only because of his arms smuggling but also because of his knowledge about Captain George Elton (still in the Tower) and his work in England on behalf of the northern conspiracy, especially in the west with Captain Rose, in Suffolk, and in Nottinghamshire with Captain Spurway.[164]

The government was even more anxious to nab Dr. Edward Richardson. From Delft he went to Rotterdam, but officials there refused him permission to stay even while denying an English request for extradition. Moving to Amsterdam, Richardson became involved in publishing an English edition of *A Voice Crying in Babylon*, for which he wrote an epistle that was "full of Sedition." One of Bennet's agents met with him in March and finally persuaded him to confess. In retrospect, Richardson thought that if the conspirators had "had a good Leader . . . he beleeved their buysenesse had taken stronger."[165] He insisted, however, that the plot extended only from Durham to Nottinghamshire, apart from two agents in London, Paul Hobson (alias Dr. Love) and an unimportant Baptist tradesman. He admitted drafting the declaration, adding that a second had been written by Denham, principally on behalf of the Quakers. Because this confession contradicts so much other evidence, it is virtually certain that Richardson was deliberately revealing only enough of the conspiracy to alleviate pressures on his family in England. He finally found some peace by purchasing citizenship in 1664 at Haarlem, where he preached in the English church and enjoyed the modest support of the burgomasters.[166]

The fact that most of the exiles as well as the northern conspirators were Nonconformists underscored the state's dilemma over the conventicles. Passage of the Conventicle Act, which had provoked serious division in Parliament in 1663, was possible in May 1664 because of the risings. Ironically, prosecution of Nonconformists, apart perhaps from Quakers (of whom there were 463 in prison in early 1663), was generally declining before the rebellion, at least in the quarter sessions.[167] In October Williamson and Henry Muddiman received reports that in the last quarter sessions the number of Nonconformists indicted was one in Somersetshire, no more than four in Norfolk (though 200 were prosecuted in the commissary court at Yarmouth for not taking the sacrament of the Lord's supper), none in Northumberland, and no more than twenty in Herefordshire (where about 130 Catholics were indicted). "Many" Nonconformists were indicted in Wiltshire, but they included Catholics as well as Protestants.[168]

The decline in indictments does not reflect a decrease in conventicling. A London reformer recorded forty-two illegal services in the City between 18 January and 9 April 1663. Magistrates in Somersetshire opted not to disrupt conventicles in Taunton and Bridgwater because of the king's desire for indulgence. One conventicle near Bridgwater attracted approximately 1,000 persons, some of whom told magistrates that they "would loose their Lives rather then the Parson." A Bristol conventicle drew some 300 persons, and there was one of nearly comparable proportions at Burton-on-Trent, Staffs.[169] The size and frequency of conventicles in 1663 point to both a bolder spirit and the growing acceptance of toleration among some royalists.

For certain Nonconformists, conditions were not improving rapidly enough, and it was these who resorted to conspiracies against the regime. One of Williamson's correspondents complained from Hereford on 12 October that this "Wild Distracted Generation of People . . . doe still persevere in their Phanaticke Humor, . . . openinge afresh the Wounds of an almost Ruined Kingdome." Fifth Monarchists in the Watford area were preaching on behalf of the Good Old Cause, while some Nonconformists were predicting in the autumn that before long they would be preaching more publicly. Just as "the sunne showne so hott uppon some people that they went out with their bowes & arrowes to shoote at [it]," preached the fiery Congregationalist George Cokayne, so the government shot at the people of God for preaching the gospel so freely.[170] Such themes could only induce hostility in those of a different persuasion.

The crackdown that resulted from the northern risings brought renewed repression for Nonconformists. In Bristol, for example, conventicles were raided and the preachers jailed. The militia disrupted an illegal religious meeting on the Somerset estate of Colonel William Stroud, to which he responded by trying to incite the troops to mutiny. An attempt to break up a conventicle of about eighty persons in Dorchester led to violence when the Nonconformists stormed out with pikes, staves, and other weapons to assault the soldiers. But the work went on as arrests were made throughout the kingdom.[171]

The northern risings, which were intended to establish godly rule and religious freedom for Protestants, set the stage for the passage of new legislation that further curtailed that freedom. Furthermore, by acting precipitously, the rebels destroyed any chance that a more widespread and organized insurrection might have achieved some success. Given the shakiness of the militia, the rebels failed because they lacked effective leadership, sufficient weapons (despite the supplies from the Netherlands and New England), reliable and secret lines of communication, and internal security. The weakness of the militia, the deep dissatisfaction among dissidents with the regime, and the huge number of ex-officers and troops from which to recruit were not enough to guarantee success. When the state used the reports of informers such as Greathead and Smithson to instigate a preemptive strike, the rebels' plans were doomed in 1663. For the Nonconformist community especially, the cost could not be measured solely by the loss of more than two dozen lives, the imprisonment of many more, and the flight of some into exile. No less important was the hardening of attitudes in the political nation that intensified the legal persecution of dissent. This was the real tragedy of the northern risings.

# 7

# "Yet One Warning More"

## THE RADICAL PRESS

Radical literature was the handmaiden of political and religious dissent. The connection between the press and radical political activity was particularly apparent in those conspiracies, such as the Tong and northern plots, which planned to distribute printed manifestos detailing rebel aims. The Tong plotters also intended to use printed copies of a letter proclaiming a popish plot as a cover for taking up arms. Beyond this, however, unlicensed publications played a major role in fanning the flames of discontent and encouraging the dissidents. The millenarian message that was so common in many of these publications offered solace as well as inspiration to those who suffered at the hands of the Stuart state. Although the government made serious efforts to quash the radical press and control the dissemination of news, in the end they were only marginally effective. Nevertheless, such efforts underscore the importance of the printed word in the political and religious struggles of the Restoration era.

## The Radical Press at the Restoration

Censorship of the press, the bane of Levellers and sectaries, had been lifted in the 1640s, only to be restored the following decade. Edward Waterhouse spoke for many moderates when he complained in 1653 that "there are too many, whose rapes on the innocency of paper, make the Press almost execrable."[1] That view was shared by Charles

207

II as well as the Convention. The pamphlets prejudicial to royalist interests that were dispersed in the City and around Whitehall on a summer morning in 1660 may have been a factor in the king's decision in July to have the Privy Council suppress libelous and seditious materials. The previous month the House of Commons asked Charles to call in and burn John Goodwin's *The Obstructours of Justice* (1649) and John Milton's *Pro Populo Anglicano Defensio* (1650) and *Eikonoklastes* (1649). Proclamations followed, and in September copies of the books were burned by the common hangman at the Sessions House in the Old Bailey.[2]

The tone for many of the works that subsequently appeared from the underground presses was set in a book probably published in January or February 1660, *Plain English to His Excellencie the Lord General Monck, and the Officers of the Army.* In his appeal for Monck to prevent a Stuart restoration, the anonymous author condemned the Stuarts for oppressing the church and the people, recalled the bloody massacre of Protestants in Ireland, and justified the execution of Charles I. That monarch was blamed for scorning parliaments, enslaving the Scots, indulging papists, wrongfully sacrificing English blood against the French, and betraying the Huguenots. The motto of true Englishmen, he argued, must be *exit tyrannus*. Surmising that the author was probably Milton or Marchamont Nedham, Roger L'Estrange deplored the pamphlet as a seditious affront to Christianity and nature, though the work of "no *Fool*."[3]

Nedham was in fact the author of the anonymously published *News from Brussels*, which appeared around April. Having served Cromwell prominently as a propagandist, Nedham fled to Amsterdam at the Restoration, then made his peace with the new regime, was pardoned, and returned to London. His *News*, cast in the form of a satirical letter from a royalist pen, depicted the Presbyterians as supporters of the Stuart monarchy through fear of the sectaries. Eventually, the royalists would turn on them, for "a Roundhead is a Roundhead; black and white Devils all alike to us." The pretended author was made to exhort other royalists to "use all art to make them take the halter tamely," and to buy up arms in recognition of the fact that monarchists could not "safely ferry while the Fleet's Phanatique." The prickly sarcasm was aimed at royalist and Presbyterian alike.[4]

Opponents of the Restoration were quick to dip into their sixteenth-century arsenal for literary weapons. When the government learned in early June that the London bookseller Joshua Kirkton was printing an English translation of George Buchanan's

*History of Scotland* and *De Jure Regni apud Scotos*, both of which were deemed injurious to the monarchy and the Stuart family, the Council ordered the seizure of all copies.[5] *The Judgement of Foraign Divines as Well from Geneva as Other Parts, Touching the Discipline, Liturgie, and Ceremonies of the Church of England*, which appeared the same year, reprinted three items of particular interest to religious dissidents. The first was an October 1547 letter from Theodore Beza and seventeen others to English Protestants criticizing episcopal appointment of clergy, the clerical garb of the Church of England, the sign of the cross in baptism, baptism by midwives, and kneeling at the Lord's supper. A second letter to English Protestants, which came from John Craig and his Reformed colleagues in Scotland, likewise found fault with traditional ministerial dress. The final piece was Calvin's letter to John Knox and William Whittingham acknowledging the presence of "many tolerable foolish things" in the Book of Common Prayer.

Many of these themes appeared in George Gillespie's *A Dispute Against the English-Popish Ceremonies, Obtruded upon the Church of Scotland*. A substantive work of 366 pages, its theme was the indictment that "the rotten dreggs of Popery, which were never purged away from *England* and *Ireland*, and having once been spewed out with detestation, are licked up again in *Scotland*." Gillespie denied Charles the right to introduce any innovations into the church or issue any ecclesiastical laws without the free consent of the clergy. Christians, he insisted, are bound to obey only those things prescribed in Scripture, which excludes ceremonies and other indifferent things. Moreover the rites the king was endeavoring to impose were deplored by Gillespie as superstitious monuments to past idolatry that hindered edification and fostered popery. Consequently, they could not be accepted in the name of either peace or unity. Gillespie's book escaped the fate of two other publications, Sir Archibald Johnston's *Causes of the Lords Wrath Against Scotland* (1653) and Samuel Rutherford's *Lex, Rex* (1644), which were burned at the market cross in Edinburgh on 16 October.[6]

The underground press contributed to the process of making martyrs out of the regicides. *The Speeches and Prayers* of Harrison, Carew, Cook, Peter, Scott, Clement, Scrope, Jones, Axtell, and Hacker were published, according to an anonymous editor, "to let all see the riches of grace magnified in those servants of Christ" and to demonstrate that they were faithful to his cause.[7]

Three radical works appeared in November, probably about the same time as *The Speeches and Prayers* of the regicides. Of these, *The*

*Common-Prayer Book Unmask'd* purported to be "newly reprinted," possibly to throw the authorities off the track or to create the impression of historical precedent. Beginning with the premise that the Book of Common Prayer was derived entirely from the Catholic mass, the author anathematized it as "a rank Imposter in Gods worship, and . . . a violent intruder in the house of God." There was no call for revolution, but there was a summons to adhere to the Solemn League and Covenant as well as to the May 1641 Protestation. As loyalty to king and country is the divinely commanded wall of polity, so undefiled religion, according to the author, is the foundation and rock of loyalty.[8]

From Worcester jail, the Quaker Daniel Baker wrote *Yet One Warning More, to Thee O England*, ostensibly to save the king as well as his subjects. With the voice of a prophet, Baker gave notice that a sword was "coming upon all thy *High Places*, and upon thy *Idols*." Governors, lawyers, teachers, and pastors had lost the key of knowledge. He decried both the "*long robed black Rabbies* and *Doctors*" and the "many hasty, subtil, and deceitful, self-willed, drunken Pilats, who would not suffer the right Helmsman to stear the course." There was condemnation too for the cruel, oppressive prisons in which the saints suffered. Baker lamented an England that ignored both divine mercy and judgment, and cried: "O *England, England, England*, what hast thou done? Wilt thou not yet be warned?"[9]

Although the government was concerned with the potentially seditious activities of the sectaries, there was as yet no opportunity to deal with sectarian publications of a strictly religious nature. The Convention too, caught up in political matters and containing a large number of Presbyterian moderates, displayed virtually no interest in purely religious diatribes. It was, however, sensitive to overtly political works, such as *The Long Parliament Revived*, published under the pseudonym of Thomas Phillips, gentleman. The author, the merchant William Drake, appeared before the House of Commons on 17 November. Three days later the members resolved that the book was seditious for arguing that the Long Parliament had never been legally dissolved, and that the English people "have no reason to hold themselves safe in their Lives, Liberties, and Estates, till it have made provision in that behalf, and it be legally dissolved." Drake was subsequently impeached, though the House of Lords failed to act. Drake acknowledged his authorship, and his work was burned by the common hangman.[10]

Members were alerted to other possibly seditious pamphlets when a press corrector, Thomas Philpott of Snowhill, London, wrote to them urging that the Solemn League and Covenant be maintained. From an examination of Philpott they learned of the *Animadversions on a Book Entitled Inquisitions for the Blood of Our Late Sovereign*, which was printed by Robert White in Warwick Lane, and *The Discovery of the Poor Man's Plot for the Saving of the Nation*, printed by Mr. Mattershatt near Doctors' Commons.[11]

Two other works from the underground press in 1660 deserve notice. *The Valley of Achor* was, according to a conservative critic, written by John Rhye, a former Leveller and Agitator, though he eventually spied on the Levellers for Cromwell. In 1660 he was arrested while carrying a radical manuscript to a printer and incarcerated in the Tower by Secretary Nicholas. In *The Valley of Achor* Rhye argued for a mixed constitution and the legitimacy of deposing tyrannical princes. Charles I was blamed for the bloodshed in Ireland, and those who defended his cause in the civil wars were denounced as rebels. Rhye defended the regicide court and the Solemn League and Covenant, but insisted that the Convention was illegally constituted. Like other radicals he was hostile to Monck.[12]

The notorious *Mirabilis Annus* tracts of 1661–62 were foreshadowed by Henry Jessey's *The Lords Loud Call to England*, published for two of the most influential men involved in the underground press, Livewell Chapman and Francis Smith. Less political than the *Mirabilis Annus* tracts, Jessey's Book amassed reports of natural occurrences (e.g., an earthquake in France, a whirlwind in Leicestershire), accounts of sudden deaths of the saints' enemies, and natural oddities (a large number of toads in Gloucestershire). Jessey also included accounts of the recent ejections at Oxford University and of the troubles experienced by such sectaries as Carnsew Helme and Vavasor Powell.[13]

## *A Phoenix*, Portents, and Prodigies

Throughout 1661 the dissidents continued to use the press to indict the government, particularly for its religious policy, to which the magistrates responded with more and more arrests. During the first week in January, John Tombes (probably not the Baptist minister of Worcestershire of that name), Humfrey Beeland, and Richard Woodward were imprisoned at Warwick for dispensing "scandalous" and seditious books. A month later the Presbyterian firebrand Zachary Crofton went to the Tower for publishing his views that the Solemn League and Covenant still bound Christians to seek reform and oppose prelacy, though not to rebel. Crofton's book, *Berith*

*Anti-Baal,* which defended the Solemn League and Covenant and attacked John Gauden's defense of episcopacy, also led to the arrest of the stationer Ralph Smith, who claimed that the book had been printed in his name while he was ill.[14]

Officials demonstrated a growing interest in Quaker publications in 1661. While confiscating weapons and securing discontented persons in Hampshire in the context of Venner's uprising, magistrates seized a bundle of books from Ambrose Rigge, "a pernicious fellow" who was arrested along with Josiah Cole. Copies of their works were sent to Nicholas for examination. An order of the king-in-council dated 21 August directed that a parcel of books seized en route from London to a Chester Quaker be delivered to the bishop of Chester or his ordinary for investigation. If they proved to be scandalous or dangerous, the bishop was to burn them in public. Three months later the Council commanded that books confiscated from the Quaker Robert Wilson (arrested on 2 October) be burned by the common hangman because they were seditious and blasphemous. Among them were Quaker catechisms and *Englands Sad Estate & Condition Lamented* (1661). They went up in flames in St. Martin's le Grand and the Palace Yard at Westminster on 25 and 26 November respectively.[15]

When magistrates burned the Covenant earlier in the year, dissidents responded with *A Phoenix: or, the Solemn League and Covenant.* Reminding the people that Charles himself had taken the Covenant in Scotland, the tract included a summary of Edmund Calamy's 1646 sermon on 2 Timothy 3:3, *The Great Danger of Covenant-Refusing.* According to the title page, the tract was published in Edinburgh, but in fact was printed in London in May. Livewell Chapman, Giles Calvert, and Thomas Brewster compiled the work, which was printed by Simon Dover and Thomas Creake (in an edition of 2,000 he said), and stitched by George Thresher, a freeman of the Stationers' Company. Thresher delivered copies to the stationer Francis Tytan (or Tilam) and others for 13d. apiece. Creake himself provided 660 copies each to Chapman, Calvert, and Brewster, and six copies were sent to Richard Moore in Bristol. Calvert, Creake, and Thresher went to prison, thanks to the efforts of Roger L'Estrange, but Chapman, who apparently fled, was not arrested until March 1663. In the course of the search for Chapman, there was a report that Thomas Tillam and Christopher Pooley, who had been arrested after their return from Germany, knew his whereabouts.[16]

When L'Estrange tracked down those responsible for *A Phoenix,* he discovered *Mirabilis Annus, or the Year of Prodigies and Wonders*. Once again, his seditious "Confederates" were responsible. Calvert claimed not to know who composed the book, but thought he, Chapman, or Brewster had ordered Creake to print it. A thousand copies of the first sheet were delivered to Thresher for binding as soon as the other sheets were ready. Although Calvert, Creake, and Thresher were in prison, Calvert's wife Elizabeth, secretly working in conjunction with Francis Smith, managed to print the book. Too late, the government issued a warrant for Smith's arrest on 15 August; he was apprehended with copies of *Mirabilis Annus* under his cloak as well as in his house. In his defense he appealed to the Magna Carta and cited the tyrannical treatment accorded to Richard Empson and Edmund Dudley by Henry VIII's government.[17] Methodically, the authorities tracked down those involved with the book, finally nabbing Elizabeth Calvert during the first week in October. Hugh Chamberlain admitted that he had received a copy of the book from Mrs. Hester, a gentlewoman, and had delivered it to William Howard, son of Lord Escrick. Copies went to the Leicester bookseller Francis Ward and Stephen Lincoln from Nathan Brookes of London at a cost of 16d. each.[18]

By late November Nicholas was struggling to ascertain the authorship of *Mirabilis Annus*. On the 27th, warrants were issued for the arrest of Henry Jessey, Ralph Butter, and Nathaniel Crabb. Examined two weeks later, Jessey confessed that about a year ago he had discussed prodigies at his brother's house in Soper Lane with Francis Smith and Henry Danvers. He also admitted exchanging prodigies with the Congregationalist George Cokayne and receiving a copy of *Mirabilis Annus*, but he refused to identify his source. Jessey was an obvious suspect because he had published his *Scripture-Calender* every year from 1645 to 1661. In his last edition he had calculated that there had been forty-seven changes in the English government since 1640, which he interpreted as the fulfilment of God's promise to "overturn, overturn, overturn."[19] Jessey acknowledged that he had given a sheet containing prodigies to a Mr. Stanbridge in November 1660, and that another sheet had been found in his house when he was arrested by Monck's men the following month. But Jessey came no closer to admitting the authorship of *Mirabilis Annus* than confessing that the book's account of Major Orde's death came from one of his sheets. Nor did Smith confess authorship, insisting that he had not read the book.[20] Because Jessey was in prison when *Mirabilis Annus Secundus* appeared in 1662, a more likely author was Cokayne or Danvers.

The intent of *Mirabilis Annus* was obvious at the outset: The day of calamity is at hand for persecutors of the church, as witnessed by signs and prodigies of the kind that signified the overthrow of the Pharaoh and his Egyptian subjects. Although God "hath suffered this year so many *hundreds*, if not *thousands* of our able godly, *preaching Ministers* to be *removed into corners*, yet the defect of their Ministry hath been *eminently* supplied by the *Lords* immediate preaching to us from *Heaven*, in the great and wonderful works of his Providence." Such works or signs demonstrate the imminent end of the world "and that God is now making hast *to consummate* his *whole* work in the earth." Although he wrote of Belshazzar, the author was really thinking of Charles II when he interpreted "mene tekel"—the words on the wall in Daniel 5:25—as a rebuke to the debauchery of the king, his concubines, and his associates, as well as a declaration of the sudden termination of the kingdom.[21]

Some of the prodigies had obvious political connotations. The supposed appearance near Hertford of two suns that were soon covered by clouds was interpreted to mean the fall of great men as well as the end of innovations in religion. A Worcester woman was said to be stricken speechless for drinking to the king's health and cursing the fanatics; four days later she was dead. There were accounts too of those who rejoiced in the deaths of regicides: One gentleman suffered a convulsion, while an Eastcheap poulterer was bitten by a dog. The litany of prodigies assaulted the imagination: skies filled with beasts and armies, churches and reapers, multiple moons and rainbows. Frogs and toads rained down from the heavens, but in Devonshire it was white ash. Red spiders marched in serried ranks at Bury St. Edmunds, while six horses drew a coach up and down a Yorkshire river.[22]

Many of the prodigies were given unmistakable religious meanings, always slanted against the Church of England. At Magdalen College, Oxford, the devil appeared in the likeness of a bishop, whereas at Canterbury Cathedral two hogs interrupted the prebends in the midst of their devotions. Tales of mishaps were intended as warnings, such as the story of an Essex minister who was killed by a fall from his horse after baptizing a child with the sign of the cross. Those who imprisoned sectaries near Carmarthen were supposedly stricken with a fatal sickness. When a Leicestershire minister refused to read the Book of Common Prayer, the gentleman who took his place was dead within a week. There was a special message for clerics who pondered conformity: A Norfolk Presbyterian who conformed was stricken twice in the pulpit and had to be carried from the church.[23] In response to such stories, loyalists jeered. A story in the *Kingdomes Intelligencer* gave a blanket condemnation of these prodigies as "bottomless Fictions," but sectaries seem to have thought otherwise. The ejected master of the Savoy, William Hooke, referred to the stories in *Mirabilis Annus* as "the Judgements of God remarkeably executed upon sundry within this yeare & halfe."[24]

The sequel, *Mirabilis Annus Secundus*, appeared in 1662. Simon Dover, who helped print the original, testified that year that copies of *Mirabilis Annus* were printed by Roger Laghorn at Mr. Bell's, near Christ Church, Newgate. This may have been a reference to the sequel. In any case, copies of *Mirabilis Annus Secundus* were discovered in the house of Richard Moone, a Bristol bookseller, in October 1663, along with a letter to him from Thomas Brewster containing mysterious expressions that Moone would not explain to authorities. Brewster's letter also mentioned Thomas Ewins (or Ewens), whom Sir John Knight called "the most daungerous Anabaptist . . . that ever Lived."[25]

The epistle to the sequel observed that some had responded to *Mirabilis Annus* with assertions that the prodigies were not only false but seditious. On the contrary, the author insisted, the intent was never to stir up sedition—which was repugnant to Scripture—but repentance. The most interesting feature of the new collection is the discussion of unexplained troop movements. Apparently apparitions, if not deliberate falsifications, they were reported near Montgomery in Wales (December 1661), near Worksop in Nottinghamshire (January 1662), in the Dorchester area (June 1662), and near Sir George Booth's home in Lancashire later that year.[26] Once again, there were stories describing the punishment of those who persecuted or mocked the godly and of ministers who forsook their ideals by conforming. Visions filled the air with castles, a red gallows, armies fighting and marching, a man's head on a white cross, and an inverted steeple. There was even a vision of the Tower and city of London burning, an idea embodied in some of the subsequent plots. The most gruesome tale recounted how two debauched men became ill (one died) after broiling and eating Sir John Barkstead's liver in an alehouse.[27]

The strong interest in prodigies among radicals, which was also characteristic of the 1650s, reflects both their belief in the providential ordering of the universe by God and their conviction that such extraordinary events were in fact divine revelations to the people of the gross sinfulness of the Restoration regime in particular and of the masses in general. Thus the prodigies were in effect a striking form of propaganda, a means of conveying seditious or spiritually judgmental messages short of overt action. There was no apparent intent for the most part to use the prodigies as a covert call to arms, but rather to persuade people of the validity of the radical claims against the state. In a sense they were also the response of the dissidents to excessive and unsubstantiated charges by some royalists of rampant plotting, for the prodigies demonstrated divine disapproval of the government.

Radical publications triggered proposals for better control of the press in July 1661. One plan called for a surveyor of the press to have authority to search for and confiscate all unlawful books and papers, as well as to license books with the approval of the archbishop of Canterbury and the secretaries of state. A second proposal called for twelve members of the Stationers' Company to have the authority to prosecute printers of seditious or schismatical works. This plan also urged a reduction in the number of printers. It was not until May 1662, however, that Parliament drew on these ideas by legislating (in the bishop of Derry's words) "the cut off [of] one of the schismatic's and rebels' best prop[s] and engine[s], the press, by securing and fencing it from bold, impudent pens." The new act imposed censorship by requiring printers to obtain licenses from a secretary of state (for history and politics) and the archbishop of Canterbury or the bishop of London (for religion and philosophy). Renewed periodically, the act remained in force until 1679.[28]

## L'Estrange's Campaign Against Dissident Printers and Publishers

To curtail the publication of inflammatory material, Roger L'Estrange was appointed surveyor of the press in February 1662. On the 24th, Nicholas issued him a warrant to search for and seize all seditious material, including pictures, manuscripts, and books, and to arrest the authors, printers, and publishers. Nicholas, however, refused his request for a general search warrant because of its dubious legality.[29] L'Estrange struck the same day by searching the house of the printer John Hayes. There he unearthed a veritable library of dissident literature that included works of Edward Bagshaw, *Mirabilis Annus*, *A Narrative of . . . John James*, *The Speeches and Prayers* of the regicides, *The Grand Debate* (1661) at the Savoy Conference, *The Traitors Claim* (1661), *A Triall of the English Liturgy* (1643), *A Petition for Peace* (1642), and George Wither's *An Improve-*

*ment of Imprisonment* (1661), *Speculum Speculativum* (1661), and *A Triple Paradox* (1661).[30]

The difficulty of stopping the flow of radical material is reflected in a proposal dated 24 February to curtail the dissemination of libels. The object was to crack down on those who claimed that they possessed such matter only because they found it in the street or because it was left on their premises by persons unknown. This was particularly a problem in coffeehouses and among printers who relied on such material to make a living. According to the proposal, "the principall, and professed Dealers in them [seditious works], are observed to be some certain Stationers, & Coffee-men and that a great part of their profit depends upon this kinde of Trade." To solve the problem, it was suggested that the government give persons finding such material a specified amount of time to surrender it to the magistrates without divulging the contents to others. Clauses to this effect, according to the proposal, should be inserted into the licenses of stationers and proprietors of coffee houses.[31]

In early 1662 the campaign to curtail dissident literature extended as far as Jersey and Bristol. Magistrates seized over one hundred books in French from a Quaker who had come to Jersey intent on spreading the Friends' message. In February Thomas Brewster was arrested at the Bristol fair with a trunk full of suspicious material in his possession. The same month the London printer (Robert?) White was accused of hoping that the Cavalier Parliament was about to adjourn, never to meet again. He also spoke irreverently of the bishops and church government, and warned the king to beware lest death catch him unprepared. The House of Commons took special notice of one radical pamphlet, George Wither's *Vox Populi*. Wither was taken from Newgate on 24 March to appear before the House. The M.P.s committed him to the Tower for composing his allegedly seditious libel, a critique of the Convention Parliament, which remained unpublished until 1880.[32]

The Presbyterian Thomas Watson, rector of St. Stephen, Walbrook launched a more oblique attack in April. In Παραμυθιον: *or a Word of Comfort for the Church of God*, he offered the solace of the "tender care of God towards his Church Militant," which was threatened by "the rage of the enemy." God, he prophesied, would either make his adversaries friendly to the church or turn them against each other. England's hope, according to Watson, was the "sober and considerable party in the Land" that had proclaimed its "dissent, and openly protested against the scandalous actings of others."[33] Although ejected in August, Watson was not punished for this indirect assault on the Restoration regime.

The great ejection spurred radical writers and printers to renewed activity. In late August 1662 William Marshall published the High Commission's examination of the Elizabethan Separatists Henry Barrow, John Greenwood, and John Penry, clearly intending to evoke the image of parallel persecutions. Early the following month the Venetian resident noted that seditious libels against the government and the king had recently been disseminated urging the people to remain loyal to the Solemn League and Covenant. These pamphlets highlighted such grievances as heavy impositions and decaying trade while calling for new demonstrations.[34] Secretary Nicholas responded on the 18th by ordering a search of printing houses and suspicious places for libels and unlicensed pamphlets, and the detention of their publishers. On the 27th officials discovered a secret press in a garden shed located in an alley running off Charterhouse Lane, but the printers escaped. A fresh warrant was issued on 28 October to continue the search.[35]

By early November the government was focusing its attention on *The Panther-prophecy, or, a Premonition to All People, of Sad Calamities and Miseries Like to Befall These Islands* The informers Peter Crabb and Simon Wilcox hoped to find the author, Owen Lloyd, who had associated with the Fifth Monarchist John Rogers in 1653–54, and the printer, Simon Dover. Lloyd's prophecy was a four-pronged assault on a soldier, a lawyer, a citizen with a bag of gold, and a cleric in a canonical gown and surplice. In the end, the panther, whose rise to power they applauded, destroyed them: "We for partaking of her Sins, must partake of her Judgements." As they tried to flee with arrows "thick Shot into their Backs," the poor emerged from the woods, the prisons were thrown open, and the people cried, "the Lord Reigns, let the Earth rejoyce." Then the City was torched.[36] The prophecy was clearly pregnant with meaning for radicals.

The same month, officials seized 103 copies of dissident publications, of which the largest number were fifty-one copies of *A Compleat Collection of Farewel Sermons* by thirty-one ejected ministers. Thirty-five copies of William Dyer's innocuous but evangelical *Christs Famous Titles* (not formally published until 1663) were confiscated, along with six copies of Sir Henry Finch's *Law, or a Discourse Thereof* (1661), and four of *Voyce out of the Wilderness Crying* (1651). There were also copies of Sir Henry Vane's *A Retired Mans Meditations*, John Archer's *The Personall Reigne of Christ upon Earth*, *The Judgment of the Old Nonconformists* (1662), and the speeches and prayers of the regicides. Material on the regicides had a ready market and was sometimes sold door to door. In January 1663 Thomas Leach, a printer in Shoe Lane, testified that his wife had purchased an account of the regicides' trials at their door, and he himself was preparing to print a narrative of the trials when he was arrested.[37]

The authorities had only limited success tracking down those responsible for disseminating the radical material. In June 1662 Nicholas placed a fishmonger named Chandler under surveillance for dispensing copies of *The Wise Virgins*. That autumn Francis Cruse, formerly an officer in Okey's regiment and now of Hoxton, Middlesex, was apprehended for handing out tracts in the London area that confuted the Book of Common Prayer as "nothing but Blasphemie & Poperie." If civil war erupted again, he boasted that he would give no quarter to royalists.[38] In December John Batty of Cripplegate had to post a bond of £300 in which he promised not to receive or distribute seditious books or libels, and the same month Elizabeth Evans was taken into custody for dispensing seditious publications. Although Giles Calvert had posted a £500 bond in November to stop publishing seditious material, a warrant was issued the next month to keep him a close prisoner in the Tower; however it was never executed, and Calvert died in 1663.[39]

As L'Estrange intensified his campaign against the radical press, the printers targeted for detention were Thomas Brewster, who was arrested in Bristol in February 1663, Livewell Chapman, Thomas Creake, who had published part of *Mirabilis Annus*, Thomas Leach, Thomas Johnson, John Downes, Joseph Cranford, William Gilbertson, and a Mr. Twinning (Twyn?), who had printed Vane's *An Epistle General* (1662). Chapman proved to be elusive: Warrants for his arrest had to be issued in March and again in April, but he insisted on his innocence. John Streater, who had been a suspect in the Presbyterian plot, was arrested in March and forced to promise not to print anything seditious, treasonable, or heretical.[40]

Utilizing a warrant from Secretary Bennet dated 7 April 1663 empowering him to search for seditious manuscripts and publications, L'Estrange discovered *A Short Surveigh of the Grand Case of the Present Ministry* (1663). The probable authors included Matthew Darby, ejected curate of Plaxtol, Wrotham, Kent, Onesiphorus Rood, ejected curate of Tothill Fields Chapel, Westminster, and Stephen Charnock, who had ties to the Dublin plotters. In essence, they argued that it was lawful to restrain a king who became tyrannical but not to resist him. However, they also asserted that one could take up arms in the king's name against the king's person or those he commissioned, a thesis common in the civil war period. They acknowledged a limited royal prerogative in religion, but insisted that "Church-men . . . [can] scrue the Prerogative of the King beyond its due pitch, and the proportion of *Englands* Constitution." They refused, moreover, to repudiate the Solemn League and Covenant, which in their view did not derogate from royal authority.[41]

L'Estrange also discovered twenty to thirty reams of paper that were being used to print copies of the 1662 farewell sermons. Warrants were issued on 23 and 24 June for the arrest of two of those responsible, Peter Lillicrap (or Lillicraft) and his wife. Further investigation revealed that John Heydon (alias Ayton), who wrote books about Rosicrucian tenets, had brought Lillicrap a manuscript containing treasonable passages, including an attack on the king as a tyrant. Lillicrap's wife persuaded her husband not to print it despite Heydon's willingness to strike the offensive passages. Heydon eventually petitioned Bennet for his release, admitting that he had intended to print "the prisoner's papers in a book"; he was bonded on 21 August.[42] At the end of June, magistrates also arrested Elizabeth Calvert and imprisoned her in the Gatehouse at Westminster for delivering unlawful books purchased by her recently deceased husband Giles. She was bonded on 24 July and shortly thereafter returned to her work with the underground press.[43]

There was less difficulty with the press in Ireland, although in the aftermath of the Dublin conspiracy Ormond and his Council had to issue a proclamation on 26 June 1663 for the destruction of an inflammatory book. Entitled *A Collection of Some of the Murthers and Massacres Committed on the Irish Since the 23rd of October, 1641* (1662), the author ("S.R.") dealt harshly with the government of Charles I. The mayor of Dublin was ordered to have the common hangman burn copies in public.[44]

As part of his counteroffensive against the radical printers, L'Estrange published his own *Considerations and Proposals in Order to the Regulation of the Press* in June 1663. Charging that the spirit of scandal, malice, and hypocrisy that caused the civil war still reigned in many, thus threatening the life and dignity of the king, L'Estrange violently attacked dissident printers. He reckoned that since the Restoration, a hundred schismatical pamphlets against episcopacy and the Book of Common Prayer had been printed or reprinted, many of them accusing Charles of popery. The press was castigated for canonizing the regicides and for printing nearly 30,000 copies of the Nonconformists' farewell sermons, whose alleged intent was to encourage the people to rebel. Altogether, he charged (with exaggeration), hundreds of thousands of *"Seditious Papers"* had been published and those responsible left unpunished. Incensed that persons of means usually escaped punishment, he charged that scarcely one in five of those arrested were interrogated by a secretary of state.[45]

L'Estrange's *Considerations and Proposals* specifically cited both printers and booksellers as well as publications he deemed objectionable. Among the former were Thomas Brewster, Simon Dover, Livewell Chapman, Elizabeth and Giles Calvert, Henry Bridges, and Thomas Creake. Many of the books he deplored had been published in the 1640s and 1650s, but he also included such works of the early 1660s as the speeches of the regicides, *Plain English to His Excellencie, A Phoenix, Mirabilis Annus,* Thomas Watson's *Word of Comfort, A Short Surveigh,* Edward Bagshaw's *The Great Question,* and Edmund Calamy's sermon, *Eli Trembling for Fear of the Ark.*[46]

To suppress the radical press L'Estrange proposed substantive rewards for persons who discovered unlawful publications, more severe penalties for printers and publishers who issued them, and the suppression of all books that justified regicide, denied Charles II's regal title, libeled the royal family, promoted rebellion, asserted the sovereignty of Parliament or people, defended the Solemn League and Covenant, countenanced the separation of the king's person from his office, or denied the royal supremacy in matters ecclesiastical. It was even necessary to suppress old books advocating similar ideas, for *"Knox* will do the business as sure as *Baxter,* and *Calamy."* Furthermore, some of the older works "strike *homer* to the *Capacity* and *Humour* of the Multitude," that is, are easier for the people to understand. L'Estrange also called for a reduction in the number of presses, masters, apprentices, and journeymen, with mandatory government inspection and licensing. Henceforth he wanted every work to carry the printer's name and an end to the practice of antedating publications. Those who printed or sold books overseas that dishonored the government should be required to answer charges in England or be penalized and banned from corresponding with anyone in the home country. Finally, six surveyors should be appointed by those responsible for licensing books in order to oversee the press.[47]

With Bennet's support, L'Estrange was appointed to the new office of Surveyor of the Imprimery and Printing-press in August. He subsequently offered a reward of 40s. for information about illegal presses, and £5 for the actual discovery of unlawful or seditious books. There were additional bounties of 10s. for exposing an unlicensed book and 5s. for turning in the seller of such a publication. L'Estrange's powers over the printed word were further enhanced when he replaced Sir John Berkenhead as editor of *Mercurius Publicus* in August. Henceforth he put out two newspapers, *The Intelligencer* (published Mondays) and *The Newes* (published Thursdays). Until he stepped down in January 1666, L'Estrange used these publications in his war against malcontents.[48]

The third issue of *The Intelligencer*, which appeared on 14 September 1663, carried a story paralleling attacks on the government in the early 1640s with those of the early 1660s: "Those very *Screws*, and *Engines*, that overturn'd the *Late Government*, are now Apply'd, (and by the very same hands too) to the Subversion of *This*." After citing the publication of the farewell sermons as proof of an appeal to the rabble, the story revealed a real coup in the campaign against the radical press—receipt of a manuscript copy of a work justifying the execution of Charles I. The manuscript praised the Elizabethan Separatists John Penry and Henry Barrow for their assault on the prelates and superstition. More importantly, the author cited the precedent of Eglon's assassination by Ehud (Judges 3) as a lawful remedy for those who suffered under the Stuart government. Not until 12 October, however, could L'Estrange announce to his readers that the intended printer of this manuscript, John Twyn, had been caught in the act.[49]

In the early hours of the morning of 7 October, L'Estrange and his men raided Twyn's shop in Cloth Fair. After spending nearly thirty minutes to gain access, they found approximately 1,000 printed sheets of the offending manuscript. They broke the formes and carried most of the sheets away. Some, however, had already been delivered to Elizabeth Calvert's maid, a woman named Evans (possibly the Elizabeth Evans arrested for dispersing seditious literature in 1662); both fled before L'Estrange could arrest them. Twyn subsequently confessed that he received the manuscript from Evans. The work was entitled *A Treatise of the Execution of Justice; Wherein Is Clearly Proved, That the Execution of Judgment and Justice, Is as Well the Peoples as the Magistrates Duty, and If the Magistrates Pervert Judgement, the People Are Bound by the Law of God to Execute Judgement without Them and upon Them*. The heart of the work is unmistakable in its meaning: "The Lord doth command his Saints to take a two edged Sword in their hands to execute the judgements written in his Word upon wicked Kings." Scripture thus not only allowed but mandated active resistance against tyrants. The work had been scheduled for publication on 12 October 1663, the day of the northern insurrection.[50]

The investigation that ensued disclosed a good deal about the underground press. One of the major discoveries was Twyn's admission that he had printed *Mene Tekel; or the Downfal of Tyranny.* Anthony à Wood attributed this book to John Owen, though neither style nor content support such a claim. Nor is it likely that the informer who named John Goodwin as the writer was correct, for Goodwin's interests were essentially religious. The author was probably Captain Roger Jones, who once served in Colonel Ralph Cobbett's regiment in Scotland and refused to support Monck when the latter declared for Parliament. Jones, who was often called "Mene Tekel," was one of the leaders of the northern conspiracy.[51]

In *Mene Tekel* Jones asserts the principle that the people have the right to choose their governors with a view to both their own good and the glory of God. "Royal Primogeniture alone, without the Peoples Consent, is no rightful Title to the Government." To deny popular election was to violate natural law. Nor was Jones willing to grant the king the right to appoint judges and magistrates, a practice he deemed responsible for the people's oppression. Instead magistrates must be the servants of the people and not "exercise Lordship" over them in contravention of their liberties. Even members of Parliament were the people's servants, trustees to make laws for the common good. There was condemnation too for the clergy who usurped popular authority, but support for godly ministers who suffered unjustly.

In the tradition of John Ponet, John Knox, Christopher Goodman, and John Milton, Jones lashed out against tyranny, whether by king or by magistrates, which is "most superlative Treason, and transcendent Rebellion." A king who ruled despotically forfeited his right to rule and had no claim on the obedience of his people. The right of citizens to resist was not merely passive in nature or limited to lesser magistrates, for every person had the right to defy "any great and unsufferable Evil, which may be offered to the Life, Liberty or Estate, of himself or others."[52]

The search for Elizabeth Calvert (a warrant for whose arrest was issued on 12 October) took L'Estrange into the heart of the underground press network. An examination of Richard Moone, the Bristol bookseller who had sold copies of *Mirabilis Annus Secundus* and with whom Calvert had dealings, dealt in part with a letter from Thomas Brewster containing a mysterious reference to "the Athenian" and the comment that "the Lord is gooing on in his worke." When Brewster's associate Simon Dover, who had been involved in printing *A Phoenix* and *Mirabilis Annus*, was arrested in mid-October, the magistrates found a copy of *Murther Will Out* as well as an unlicensed Quaker pamphlet. Suspicious that *Murther Will Out* had been printed in Ireland, Bennet ordered Ormond to investigate; "at least 'tis certain the Instruction and Composure of it came from thence." Others, however, suspected that the author was Paul Hobson.[53]

A warrant for Brewster's arrest was issued on 30 October and he was detained the same day. Calvert too was in custody by month's end, though Evans, her maid, remained at large. In October L'Estrange and his men also raided the house of the binder Nathan Brookes, who had been involved with *Mirabilis Annus*. Initially denied entrance, someone finally gave L'Estrange a copy of the speeches of the regicides John Barkstead, Miles Corbet, and John Okey, but others tried in vain to burn some 200 copies of John Goodwin's *Prelatique Preachers None of Christ's Teachers* on the second floor of the adjoining house.[54] Goodwin's book tried to dissuade people from attending services conducted by episcopally ordained clergy, castigated "the Idolatrous madness of the Common-Prayer-Book-worship," deplored episcopacy as "that plant of bitterness," and urged the saints to continue worshipping in their own congregations, though more circumspectly than usual. In addition to confiscating copies of this work, L'Estrange found Brookes' record of the delivery of the regicides' speeches and other illegal pamphlets, some of which had gone to Henry Mortlock. As the net tightened, Livewell Chapman was accused of seditious practices and returned to prison on 24 November.[55]

The state tried Twyn, Dover, Brewster, and Brookes at the Old Bailey in February 1664. Accused of printing *A Treatise of the Execution of Justice* and therefore of traitorously imagining and intending the death of the king, Twyn was convicted of high treason. Asked by the condemned man to intervene on his behalf, Chief Justice Hyde retorted: "I would not intercede for my own father in this case." Twyn was executed at Smithfield on 24 February.[56]

Indicted for having *The Speeches and Prayers of John Barkstead, John Okey, and Miles Corbet* printed and for selling copies, Brewster pleaded not guilty. However, Thomas Creake testified that Brewster and Giles Calvert had paid him and that he had printed 3,000 copies of the first thirty-six folios. Chapman too, he said, had asked him to print *The Speeches*. This was essentially the same group responsible for printing *A Phoenix* in 1661, for which Brewster was now belatedly indicted. Although sheets of *The Speeches* were found in Dover's house by L'Estrange, he denied printing them. Brookes was charged with stitching the sheets. Brewster, Dover, and Brookes were found guilty of a seditious misdemeanor, fined, pilloried, and imprisoned at the king's pleasure. Weakened by the punishment, Brewster and Dover died in April, and one of them was honored by a crowd of more than 3,000 mourners at his funeral.[57]

The author of *An Exact Narrative* of these trials, who was probably L'Estrange himself, calculated that since the return of Charles over 300 treasonous and schismatic books and pamphlets had been published. They alone, he argued, substantiated the existence of "a Settled, Formal Plot against His Sacred Majesty." There was more merit in his contention that *A Treatise of the Execution of Justice* was linked to the northern conspirators. "It bears," he asserted in *The Intelligencer*, "the very Image of the Conspirators *Declaration*," though this was probably because the rebel leaders had read it than of common authorship.[58] Roger Jones was probably influenced by *A Treatise* in writing *Mene Tekel*. There is, moreover, a strong possibility that it was Jones who commissioned Twyn to print *A Treatise* as justification for the impending insurrection. There is in any event no doubt that the government was fully aware of the link between the radical press and the rebels. Speaking for the prosecution in the trial of Brewster, Sergeant Morton declared: "Raising of Tumults is the more Masculine, and Printing and Dispersing Seditious books, is the Feminine part of every Rebellion." The dissidents too appreciated the power of the printed word. Undeterred by Twyn's execution, they printed copies of *Mene Tekel* at Rotterdam in Dutch as well as English. "Now the *Press* and the *Pen* is beginning as hot a War upon us," said Bennet in January 1664, "as if they intended speedily to follow it with the *Sword*."[59] They did indeed.

# Afterword

Beneath the relatively placid surface of the Restoration the radical underground preserved the revolutionary ideology of the preceding decades. Measured against their own goals—the establishment of a godly republican government, the overthrow of prelacy, the acceptance of religious toleration, and to a lesser degree the reduction of taxes and the suppression of Catholicism—the radicals failed in the 1660s. Instead of fostering freedom and toleration, they sparked repression. Their persistent scheming played into the hands of their opponents by providing a rationale for the Clarendon Code. The actions of the militants made it possible for advocates of an exclusive settlement to cast the opprobrium of sedition on even moderate Nonconformists, creating a legacy of distrust that lasted to 1689 and beyond.

Historians have generally ignored the continuation of radical activities after 1660. Those who see the events of the 1640s and 1650s as an untidy hiatus in the otherwise progressive development of English history have no motive to pursue the study of a revolutionary tradition that refused to perish. Moreover, the interpretation of the post-1660 period as the beginning of a new era, more closely tied to the eighteenth century than to the pre-1640 years, is averse to acknowledging the continuity of a radical tradition. The radical activities of the 1660s and beyond are a salutary warning against an excessive emphasis on periodization.

Still motivated by the radical ideals of the 1640s and 1650s, and encouraged by the continuing publications of the radical press, dissidents demonstrated a surprising resiliency in the 1660s. The failure of Lambert in 1660 and Venner in 1661, the crushing of the Dublin plot before the conspirators could rebel, and the collapse of the inept northern risings in 1663 did not destroy the hopes of the militants. These defeats, however, did force them to look to the Netherlands for deliverance. There the exile community, bolstered by new refugees who fled when the northern insurrection failed, increasingly placed its hope in an Anglo-Dutch war. That story, however, belongs to the sequel to the present study.

The radical underground had a demonstrable impact on the government of Charles II. Considerable time was spent gathering and evaluating information. The task was compounded by the difficulty of distinguishing between genuine militants on the one hand and peaceful Nonconformists and ex-military men on the other. Every conventicle or social gathering of these people was a potential cause of concern. Moreover, the continued use of millenarian imagery, with its potential political overtones, made the speech of dissidents, no matter how peaceful, suspect. The government thus had to sift through the reports from magistrates and informers in order to identify genuine threats. It would be easy to fault the authorities for too readily giving credence to allegations of conspiracy, but it was manifestly safer to err on the side of caution than to gamble that reports of plotting were spurious. From the historian's perspective it is not hard to discount the radical threat, for there was no successful rebellion against Charles II. But his officials obviously had no such assurances and consequently had to maintain constant vigilance.

Ongoing radical activity forced the government to continue and expand the intelligence system created in the 1650s, and increased funding was appropriated for it in the early years of Charles' regime. But the network of spies was impaired both by the need of informers to report radical activity in order to justify their fees, and by the utilization of unsavory persons whose motives were often personal and unprofessional.

In attempting to repress radical activity, the state indisputably inflicted wrongs on the innocent. Guiltless persons were repeatedly detained in castles and prisons and their weapons arbitrarily seized. The government was not always insensitive to the law, and was normally scrupulous, for example, in bringing treason charges only if it could produce the necessary two witnesses. But it was not averse to moving prisoners from jail to jail in order to impede their legal rights, or to ordering ex-officers out of the London area at every supposed emergency, or to sweeping arrests of suspicious persons in the face of an alleged conspiracy. Ultimately, the backlash against such actions helped pave the way for the enactment of further *habeas corpus* legislation in 1679.

Although the radicals failed to attain their aims, their legacy was nevertheless significant. Their dedication to the principles of a government bound by law, their abhorrence of arbitrary rule whether in church or state, their commitment to religious freedom for Protestants, and their insistence on the right to publish their views were ideals that gradually won acceptance. At root, the radical cause did not die, although some of its more parochial or unenlightened goals—rule by a godly elite and suppression of Catholicism—mercifully did. But in its broadest principles—government under law, freedom, and toleration—it ultimately triumphed. Viewed in this light, their experience of defeat was only temporary.

# Abbreviations

| | |
|---|---|
| Abbott, *Blood* | Wilbur Cortez Abbott, *Colonel Thomas Blood, Crown-Stealer* (1911), reprinted in *Conflicts with Oblivion* (2nd ed.; Cambridge: Harvard University Press, 1935) |
| Abbott, "Conspiracy" | Wilbur Cortez Abbott, "English Conspiracy and Dissent, 1660–1674" *AHR* 14 (1908–1909): 503–28, 696–722 |
| Adair | Patrick Adair, *A True Narrative of the Rise and Progress of the Presbyterian Church in Ireland (1623–1670)*, ed. W. D. Killen (Belfast: C. Aitchison, 1866) |
| *AHR* | *American Historical Review* |
| Ashley, *Wildman* | Maurice Ashley, *John Wildman: Plotter and Postmaster: A Study of the English Republican Movement in the Seventeenth Century* (New Haven: Yale University Press, 1947) |
| *BDBR* | *Biographical Dictionary of British Radicals in the Seventeenth Century*, ed. Richard L. Greaves and Robert Zaller, 3 vols. (Brighton: Harvester Press, 1982–84) |
| BL | British Library |
| Bodl. | Bodleian Library, Oxford |
| Burnet | Gilbert Burnet, *History of His Own Time* (new ed.; London: William Smith, 1838) |
| Capp, *FMM* | B. S. Capp, *The Fifth Monarchy Men: A Study in Seventeenth-Century English Millenarianism* (London: Faber and Faber, 1972) |
| Carte | Thomas Carte, *An History of the Life of James Duke of Ormonde*, 2 vols. (London: J. Bettenham, 1736) |
| *CCSP* | *Calendar of the Clarendon State Papers Preserved in the Bodleian Library*, vol. 5: 1660–1726, ed. F. J. Routledge (Oxford: Clarendon Press, 1970) |

231

| | |
|---|---|
| CH | Huntington Library, San Marino, Calif. |
| *CJ* | *Journals of the House of Commons 1547–1714*, 17 vols. (1742 ff.) |
| *CMHS* | *Collections of the Massachusetts Historical Society* |
| Cobbett | William Cobbett, *Cobbett's Parliamentary History of England*, vol. 4 (London: R. Bagshaw, 1808) |
| Cosin | John Cosin, *The Correspondence of John Cosin, D.D., Lord Bishop of Durham*, Surtees Society, vol. 55 (1872) |
| *CR* | A. G. Matthews, *Calamy Revised* (Oxford: Clarendon Press, 1934) |
| Crosby | Thomas Crosby, *The History of the English Baptists*, 4 vols. (London: For the Author, 1738–40) |
| *CSPD* | *Calendar of State Papers, Domestic Series, 1603–1714* |
| *CSPI* | *Calendar of State Papers Relating to Ireland* |
| *CSPV* | *Calendar of State Papers . . . Venice* |
| DCY | *Depositions from the Castle of York, Relating to Offences Committed in the Northern Counties in the Seventeenth Century*, ed. J. Raine, Surtees Society, vol. 40 (1861) |
| *EHR* | *English Historical Review* |
| Evelyn | *The Diary of John Evelyn*, ed. E. S. de Beer, 6 vols. (Oxford: Clarendon Press, 1955) |
| Firth & Davies | Charles Firth and Godfrey Davies, *The Regimental History of Cromwell's Army*, 2 vols. (Oxford: Clarendon Press, 1940) |
| Greaves, *Saints and Rebels* | Richard L. Greaves, *Saints and Rebels: Seven Nonconformists in Stuart England* (Macon, Ga.: Mercer University Press, 1985) |
| Heath | [James Heath], *A Brief Chronicle of All the Chief Actions So Fatally Falling Out in These Three Kingdoms* (London, 1662) |
| Henry | Philip Henry, *Diaries and Letters of Philip Henry*, ed. Matthew Henry Lee (London: Kegan Paul, Trench & Co., 1882) |
| *HMC* | *Historical Manuscripts Commission, Reports* |
| Hodgson | John Hodgson, *Original Memoirs* (Edinburgh: Arch. Constable; London: John Murray, 1806) |
| *Int.* | *Intelligencer* |
| *JEH* | *Journal of Ecclesiastical History* |
| Kennet | White Kennet, *An Historical Register and Chronicle of English Affairs* (London: Charles Marsh, 1744) |
| *KI* | *Kingdomes Intelligencer* |
| Latimer, *Annals* | John Latimer, *The Annals of Bristol in the Seventeenth Century* (Bristol: William George's Sons, 1900) |
| Lister | T. H. Lister, *Life and Administration of Edward, First Earl of Clarendon*, 3 vols. (London: Longman, 1837) |
| *LJ* | *Journals of the House of Lords* (1767 ff.) |

| | |
|---|---|
| Ludlow, *Memoirs* | *The Memoirs of Edmund Ludlow*, ed. C. H. Firth (Oxford: Clarendon Press, 1894) |
| Ludlow, "Voyce" | Edmund Ludlow, "A Voyce from the Watch Tower," Bodleian Eng. Hist. MS c. 487 |
| Ludlow, *Voyce* | Edmund Ludlow, *A Voyce from the Watch Tower Part Five: 1660–1662*, ed. A. B. Worden, Camden Society, 4th ser., vol. 21 (London, 1978) |
| *MCR* | *Middlesex County Records*, ed. John Cordy Jeaffreson, 4 vols. (London: Middlesex County Records Society, 1886–1892) |
| *Misc. Aul.* | Thomas Brown, *Miscellanea Aulica* (London: J. Hartley, Rob. Gibson, & Tho. Hodgson, 1702) |
| *MP* | *Mercurius Publicus* |
| *NCR* | *Nottinghamshire County Records*, ed. H. Hampton Copnall (Nottingham: Henry B. Saxton, 1915) |
| Nicoll | John Nicoll, *A Diary of Public Transactions and Other Occurrences, Chiefly in Scotland*, Bannatyne Club, vol. 52 (Edinburgh, 1836) |
| *NRR* | *Quarter Sessions Records*, ed. J. C. Atkinson, North Riding Record Society, vol. 6 (London: Printed for the Society, 1888) |
| *Orm. Coll.* | *A Collection of Original Letters and Papers . . . from the Duke of Ormonde's Papers*, ed. Thomas Carte, 2 vols. (London: Society for the Encouragement of Learning, 1739) |
| *Orrery Coll.* | *A Collection of the State Letters of . . . Roger Boyle, the First Earl of Orrery*, ed. Thomas Morrice, 2 vols. (Dublin: George Faulkner, 1743) |
| Parker, *History* | Samuel Parker, *History of His Own Time*, trans. Thomas Newlin (London: Charles Rivington, 1727) |
| Pepys | Samuel Pepys, *The Diary of Samuel Pepys*, ed. Robert Latham and William Matthews, 9 vols. (Berkeley and Los Angeles: University of California Press, 1970–75) |
| *PI* | *Parliamentary Intelligencer* |
| PRO SP | Public Record Office (London), State Papers |
| Reresby | *Memoirs of Sir John Reresby*, ed. Andrew Browning (Glasgow: Jackson, Son, & Co., 1936) |
| Schwoerer | Lois G. Schwoerer, *"No Standing Armies!": The Antiarmy Ideology in Seventeenth-Century England* (Baltimore and London: The Johns Hopkins University Press, 1974) |
| *Som. Tr.* | W. Scott, ed., *Collection of Scarce and Valuable Tracts . . . of the Late Lord Somers*, 13 vols. (1809–15) |
| Sprunger | Keith L. Sprunger, *Dutch Puritanism* (Leiden: E. J. Brill, 1982) |
| *ST* | W. Cobbett, T. B. Howell, et al., *Cobbett's Complete Collection of State Trials and Proceedings*, 34 vols. (London: R. Bagshaw, 1809–28) |
| Strype | John Strype, *A Survey of the Cities of London and Westminster* (London: A. Churchill, et al., 1720) |

STT                                 Stowe Collection, Temple Correspondence, Huntington
                                    Library

*TRHS*                              *Transactions of the Royal Historical Society*

Turner                              *Original Records of Early Nonconformity*, ed. G. Lyon
                                    Turner, 3 vols. (London: T. Fisher Unwin, 1911–14)

Walker, "Secret Service"            James Walker, "The Secret Service Under Charles II and
                                    James II, " *TRHS*, 4th ser. (1932), 15:211–35

Walker, "Yorkshire Plot"            James Walker, "The Yorkshire Plot, 1663," *Yorkshire
                                    Archaeological Journal*, 31 (1934): 348–59

Watts                               Michael R. Watts, *The Dissenters: From the Reformation to the
                                    French Revolution* (Oxford: Clarendon Press, 1978)

Whiting                             C. E. Whiting, *Studies in English Puritanism from the Resto-
                                    ration to the Revolution, 1660–1688* (London: Society for
                                    Promoting Christian Knowledge, 1931)

Wodrow                              Robert Wodrow, *The History of the Sufferings of the Church
                                    of Scotland from the Restoration to the Revolution*, ed. Robert
                                    Burns, 4 vols. (Glasgow: Blackie, Fullarton, & Co., 1829)

# NOTES

## Notes to Introduction

1. Christopher Hill, *The World Turned Upside Down* (New York: Viking Press, 1972), p. 306. Cf. Hill's Curti Lectures, *Some Intellectual Consequences of the English Revolution* (Madison: University of Wisconsin Press, 1980).
2. Hill, *The World Turned Upside Down*, p. 308.
3. J. C. Davis, "Radicalism in a Traditional Society: The Evaluation of Radical Thought in the English Commonwealth 1649–1660," *History of Political Thought* 3 (Summer 1982): 203. Cf. Hill's cogent defense of the use of modern terminology in *The Experience of Defeat: Milton and Some Contemporaries* (New York: Viking Press, 1984), pp. 25–26.
4. *BDBR*, 1:viii.
5. Davis, "Radicalism," pp. 201–13.
6. C. H. Firth, *Cromwell's Army* (4th ed.; London: Methuen & Co., 1962), pp. 34–35. The calculation of the number of officers in 1659 was made by Dr. Paul H. Hardacre, Research Scholar at the Huntington Library, based primarily on "A Brief View of the Public Revenue, Both Certain and Casual," presented to the House of Commons on 7 April 1659. It is printed in *The Parliamentary or Constitutional History of England from the Earliest Times to the Restoration of Charles II*, 24 vols. (London, 1751–63), 21:326–37. In Ireland there were 557 officers in December 1660. Bodl. Carte MSS 68, fol. 156$^r$.
7. Schwoerer, pp. 74–75.
8. Ibid., pp. 77, 81.
9. PRO SP 29/56/109; 29/58/73.
10. Turner, 3:732–36.
11. The geographical location of Nonconformists in the early eighteenth century can be ascertained with fairly good accuracy, but there is less certainty for the preceding half century. See Watts, chap. 4, appendix, and tables 1–3, 6–13.
12. Greaves, *Saints and Rebels*, chap. 3.

13. Turner, 3:732–36.

14. Watts, p. 160; Turner, 3:732–36.

15. Capp, *FMM*, p. 82.

16. Hugh Barbour, *The Quakers in Puritan England* (New Haven: Yale University Press, 1964), pp. 83–86; William C. Braithwaite, *The Second Period of Quakerism* (London: Macmillan and Co., 1919), p. 9.

17. D. G. Hey, "The Pattern of Nonconformity in South Yorkshire, 1660–1851," *Northern History* 8 (1973): 89.

18. Schwoerer, pp. 76, 82.

19. Walker, "Secret Service," pp. 212–15. The total amount spent on all intelligence activities between midsummer 1660 and October 1662 was £1,480 9s. 6d. BL Egerton MSS 2543, fols. 115$^r$–116$^r$. As an ambassador to the Netherlands, Sir William Temple expended funds for informers to spy on the exiles. BL Add. MSS 22,920, fol. 194$^r$.

20. *CSPD 1661–62*, p. 154; PRO SP 29/61/153.

21. Walker, "Secret Service," p. 222.

22. PRO SP 29/63/111.

23. Carte, 2:324.

24. *Munster Paralleld in the Late Massacres Committed by the Fifth Monarchists* (London, 1661).

25. Adair.

26. Thomas Long, *A Compendious History of All the Popish & Fanatical Plots and Conspiracies Against the Established Government in Church & State, in England, Scotland, and Ireland* (London, 1684).

27. Burnet. A thoroughly Presbyterian perspective is provided by James Stuart and James Stirling in *Naphtali, or the Wrestlings of the Church of Scotland for the Kingdom of Christ* ([Edinburgh], 1667).

28. Parker, *History*, p. 6.

29. James Ralph, *The History of England*, 2 vols. (London: Daniel Browne, 1744–46), 1:97.

30. Abbott, "Conspiracy."

31. Abbott, *Blood*.

32. Ashley, *Wildman*.

33. Champlin Burrage, "The Fifth Monarchy Insurrections," *EHR* 25 (October 1910): 722–47; Capp, *FMM*.

34. Henry Gee, "The Derwentdale Plot, 1663," *TRHS*, 3rd ser., 11 (1917): 125–42; Walker, "Yorkshire Plot."

35. Walker, "Secret Service."

36. Charles Sanford Terry, *The Pentland Rising & Rullion Green* (Glasgow: James MacLehose and Sons, 1905); M. Sidgwick, "The Pentland Rising and the Battle of Rullion Green," *Scottish Historical Review* 3 (July 1906): 449–52; James King Hewison, *The Convenanters: A History of the Church in Scotland from the Reformation to the Revolution*, 2 vols. (Glasgow: John Smith and Son, 1908); Ian B. Cowan, *The Scottish Covenanters 1660–1688* (London: Victor Gollancz, 1976).

37. Thomas Babington Macaulay, *The History of England from the Accession of James the Second*, 5 vols. (London: Longman, Brown, Green, Longmans, and Roberts, 1858–61), 1:155.

38. Richard Lodge, *The History of England from the Restoration to the Death of William III, 1660–1702*, vol. 8 of *The Political History of England*, ed. William Hunt and Reginald L. Poole (London: Longmans, Green, 1910), pp. 1, 3–4.

39. J. R. Jones, *Country and Court: England, 1658–1714* (Cambridge: Harvard University Press, 1979), pp. 138–39.

40. J. P. Kenyon, *Stuart England* (Harmondsworth, Middlesex, and New York: Penguin Books, 1978), p. 185.

## Notes to Chapter 1

1. Pepys, 1:122, 129.
2. *CSPV 1659–61*, p. 136; *CSPD 1660–61*, pp. 184–85. Cf. Godfrey Davies, *The Restoration of Charles II 1658–1660* (San Marino, Calif.: Huntington Library, 1955), p. 355.
3. PRO SP 29/8/69 (Capt. Henry Clare); 29/10/119; 29/440/13; *MCR*, 3:303–304.
4. *DCY*, pp. 84, 94; PRO SP 29/10/47; *MCR*, 3:309, 310.
5. *MCR*, 3:305, 309–10, 316; *DCY*, p. 84.
6. PRO SP 29/7/145; *DCY*, p. 83.
7. *MP* 38 (13–20 September 1660), p. 608; *NCR*, p. 108; *MCR*, 3:303–307, 309, 311–12, 314.
8. *MCR*, 3:304, 306, 317.
9. *CSPD 1660–61*, p. 69; PRO SP 29/10/47; *CSPD 1655–56*, pp. 102, 464.
10. PRO SP 29/47/76.
11. *DCY*, p. 86; PRO SP 29/29/4.
12. Ludlow, *Voyce*, p. 200; PRO SP 29/14/74; *MCR*, 3:303.
13. Pepys, 4:372; *DCY*, p. 84; PRO SP 29/29/4; 29/45/27.
14. *DCY*, p. 85; PRO SP 29/24/42; 29/24/104; *MCR*, 3:304–305; *NRR*, 6:33.
15. *DCY*, pp. 88, 94; *NRR*, 6:42–43.
16. PRO SP 29/1/57; *MCR*, 3:311; *DCY*, p. 84.
17. PRO SP 29/3/4; 29/5/19; *HMC* 25, *Le Fleming*, p. 26.
18. PRO SP 29/7/83; *BDBR*.
19. *LJ*, 11:175; *MP* 40 (27 September–4 October 1660), p. 626; *BDBR*.
20. *DCY*, p. 83; *CR*.
21. *KI* (18–25 March 1661), p. 192; "Extracts," in *The Note Book of the Rev. Thomas Jolly A.D. 1671–1693*, ed. Henry Fishwick (Manchester: Chetham Society, new ser., vol. 33, 1894), p. 131; *MCR*, 3:306–307 (cf. 308–309). Day, still in the Gatehouse prison in Nov. 1661, condemned Charles for not fulfilling the promises he made in the Declaration of Breda. Day refused to accept anyone but Christ as head of the church. PRO SP 29/44/54.
22. *HMC* 55, *Var. Coll.*, 1:143, 322; Kennet, p. 324.
23. PRO SP 29/18/22; 29/30/32; Kennet, p. 543.
24. *CCSP*, 5:53; PRO SP 29/24/29; Adis, *A Fanatic's Address*, in *Som. Tr.*, 7:261, 263.
25. Crosby, 2:19–26; PRO SP 29/21/99; 29/21/98; 29/21/107; 29/21/87; Kennet, p. 155; Watts, p. 222.
26. Kennet, pp. 114–15; *CSPV 1659–61*, pp. 134, 138, 139.
27. Pepys, 1:111; Heath, p. 64.
28. Kennet, p. 116, says that one troop was involved, but Davies, *Restoration*, p. 335, says none were.
29. *CSPV 1659–61*, p. 140; Kennet, p. 116.
30. Heath, p. 64; Kennet, p. 118.
31. Davies, *Restoration*, p. 336.
32. *CSPV 1659–61*, pp. 141–42; Strype, 1:91; Kennet, pp. 119–20; Davies, *Restoration*, p. 336. Davies' surmise that Henry Clare was captured is erroneous; cf. PRO SP 29/8/69.
33. *Orm. Coll.*, 2:333; Kennet, p. 116.
34. Pepys, 1:109, 115; *Orm. Coll.*, 2:334; CH STT 1081 (Martin Holbeach).
35. *MCR*, 3:304; *DCY*, p. 93; *CCSP*, 5:9, 11, 18.
36. *CSPV 1659–61*, pp. 141–42; *MP* 19 (3–10 May 1660), pp. 289–90; Crosby, 2:28.
37. *CSPV 1659–61*, p. 135; PRO SP 29/4/98; 29/8/155.
38. PRO SP 29/8/27.
39. PRO SP 29/8/188; Kennet, p. 246; *Correspondence of the Family of Hatton*, ed. Edward Maunde Thompson, Camden Society, n.s., 22–23 (1878), 1:20; *CCSP*, 5:16.

40. *MP* 20 (10–17 May 1660), p. 310; PRO SP 29/1/56; Nicoll, p. 285.

41. *MP* 20 (10–17 May 1660), pp. 310, 312; *CSPV 1659–61*, p. 146.

42. *MP* 19 (3–10 May 1660), p. 292; *HMC* 4, *Fifth Report*, Appendix, Part I, p. 150.

43. PRO SP 29/5/97; 29/8/69; *PI* (25 June–2 July 1660), p. 431. An undated document in the State Papers, provisionally placed under 1661, probably belongs to the summer of 1660. It contains a note to the effect that Jenkins "is said to have a Designe upon the Kings person." John Mainwaring of Deptford is also listed as a dangerous person. PRO SP 29/47/74.

44. PRO SP 29/8/180; 29/11/87. The others present were John Greenwood, Josias Stanfield, John Lumme, and William Croft.

45. *BDBR*, s. v. Smallwood; PRO SP 29/192/112; Hodgson, p. 175.

46. PRO SP 29/8/180; 29/11/87; Hodgson, pp.166–69, 172–75; *DCY*, pp. 86–87.

47. *CSPV 1659–61*, p. 179; *HMC* 4, *Fifth Report*, Appendix, Part I, p. 168; PRO SP 29/4/18; *MP* 29 (12–19 July 1660), p. 480.

48. PRO SP 29/7/132; 29/43/23. Information provided by a Southwark combmaker in October probably had little foundation. A prisoner in the White Lion, he claimed, had told him of a conspiracy to surprise the king on his trip to Portsmouth, though a planned uprising in London had to be postponed. Ludlow, he heard, was in Gloucester. From Captain Beaker's wife, he confessed, he had learned that an insurrection was imminent. PRO SP 29/18/64.

49. Davies, *Restoration*, p. 348; 12 Car. II, c. 11.

50. PRO SP 29/16/24. Among those in the congregation were two naval captains, Richard Potter and (Robert?) Taylor. The latter may have been the Robert Taylor who commanded the *Raven* in 1653.

51. PRO SP 29/18/58; *HMC* 4, *Fifth Report*, Appendix, Part I, p. 174.

52. *CSPD 1660–61*, pp. 312–13, 316; PRO SP 29/19/26; 29/24/42; William Sedgwick, *Animadversions upon a Book Entituled Inquisition for the Blood of Our Late Soveraign* (London, 1661), p. 257.

53. *Notes Which Passed at Meetings of the Privy Council Between Charles II and the Earl of Clarendon, 1660–1667*, ed. W. D. Macray (London: Nichols and Sons, 1896), p. 29.

54. Ludlow, *Voyce*, p. 188; PRO SP 29/14/6; *PI* (3–10 September 1660), p. 592; *HMC* 4, *Fifth Report*, Appendix, Part I, p. 168; *HMC* 43, *Fifteenth Report*, Appendix, Part VII, p. 92; PRO SP 29/16/53; *MP* 39 (20–27 September 1660), p. 603.

55. Maurice Ashley, *Cromwell's Generals* (New York: St. Martin's Press, 1955), p. 229; Ludlow, *Voyce*, pp. 154, 195–96; *CSPV 1659–61*, p. 176; C. H. Firth, "Thomas Scot's Account of His Actions as Intelligencer During the Commonwealth," *EHR* 12 (January 1897): 116–17; *HMC* 4, *Fifth Report*, Appendix, Part I, p. 153.

56. PRO SP 29/24/51; 29/26/33; 29/24/16.

57. *CSPD 1670*, p. 645; PRO SP 29/16/113.

58. *CSPD 1660–61*, p. 457; CH STT 524.

59. PRO SP 29/19/18; Latimer, *Annals*, pp. 300–301.

60. PRO SP 29/9/42; Schwoerer, pp. 72, 76 n. 20, 83.

61. *CSPD 1660–61*, p. 305; *CSPV 1659–61*, p. 204; PRO SP 29/28/13.

62. *CSPD 1655–56*, p. 61; Firth & Davies, p. 717; *HMC* 4, *Fifth Report*, Appendix, Part I, p. 201; *MP* 51 (13–20 December 1660), pp. 810–11; *PI* (10–17 December 1660), p. 823.

63. *HMC* 4, *Fifth Report*, Appendix, Part I, pp. 158, 201. Cf. *Munster Paralleld in the Late Massacres Committed by the Fifth Monarchists* (London, 1661), pp. 29–32.

64. PRO SP 29/23/106.

65. *HMC* 4, *Fifth Report*, Appendix, Part I, p. 158; PRO SP 29/23/106.

66. PRO SP 29/23/107, 108, 127.

67. *PI* (10–17 December 1660), pp. 823–24; *PI* (17–24 December 1660), p. 827; Kennet, p. 328; Pepys, 1:318–19.

68. *MP* 51 (13–20 December 1660), p. 824; 53 (20–27 December 1660), p. 840; 54 (27 December 1660–3 January 1661), p. 856 (mispr. 846); Nicoll, pp. 309–10, 312; *PI* (17–24 December 1660), pp. 827–28, 832; *PI* (24–31 December 1660), p. 833; *KI* (31 December 1660–7 January 1661), p. 8. Parker says that Abraham Holmes was arrested too. *History*, p. 9. Among the others arrested were Lieutenant-Colonel William Farley (who had served under Herbert Morley), and Majors Lewis Audley and Francis Mercer. The junior officers included Captains Edward Jones, John Smith, Samuel Lynn, Thomas Middleton, John Shovell (or Shewell), Robert Shaw, Henry Hatsell, and Brandon.

69. PRO SP 29/23/128, 129, 130; *PI* (24–31 December 1660), pp. 833–34; Nicoll, p. 312; *MP* 53 (20–27 December 1660), p. 840; *CSPV 1659–61*, p. 230.

70. PRO SP 29/28/28, 28.1. Gray allegedly said that the king would not reign long and that all ministers were rogues who "kept the 5th part of the nation to themselves." In six months none would be left in England. He also claimed to have enough arms to supply a hundred men. PRO SP 29/28/28.2.

71. PRO SP 29/24/55. Major Edmund Rolfe, who had been released from Newgate prison in November, was reported to be en route toward Theobald Park (where he had property) with a "dangerous" sectary named Barrington (of Cheshunt, Hertfordshire). PRO SP 29/28/37. Rolfe was subsequently said to be a friend of a Mr. Tasweks, who had been arrested. PRO SP 29/47/69.

72. PRO SP 29/24/64; 29/23/87; 29/24/8; *HMC* 4, *Fifth Report*, Appendix, Part I, p. 201.

73. PRO SP 29/23/71, 71.2, 73.1; Lister, 3:116–17.

74. *HMC* 4, *Fifth Report*, Appendix, Part I, p. 201; PRO SP 29/23/87; Ludlow, *Voyce*, pp. 276–77; Ludlow, *Memoirs*, 2:330. Cf. Nicoll, p. 313.

75. *CSPD 1660–61*, p. 415; *PI* (10–17 December 1660), p. 824; *CSPV 1659–61*, pp. 229, 235; Nicoll, p. 310; Kennet, pp. 352–53.

76. Abbott, "Conspiracy," 14:503–504; Ashley, *Wildman*, p. 163.

77. PRO SP 29/24/4, 7, 43, 70; Ludlow, *Voyce*, pp. 275–77.

78. Ashley, *Wildman*, p. 163. Cf. *CSPD 1660–61*, p. 415.

79. See Chapter 2.

80. PRO SP 29/24/66, 67, 68; *CSPD 1660–61*, p. 426.

81. There were supposedly another 2,500 men in the north and 2,500 in the west, which made Ludlow scoff. *Memoirs*, 2:329; *Voyce*, pp. 276–77.

82. *LJ*, 11:237.

83. This was the period in which Richard Rogers, an ex-soldier, was trying to recruit men to go to Flanders to form an antiroyalist army. According to one witness against him, he asserted that if the "late" plot had succeeded, he would have been £40 per annum richer. PRO SP 29/24/51; *CSPD 1660–61*, p. 466.

84. *CSPD 1660–61*, p. 425; cf. p. 420.

85. PRO SP 29/24/6; *HMC* 4, *Fifth Report*, Appendix, Part I, p. 201. Cf. *CSPV 1659–61*, p. 230.

86. Christopher Hill, *The World Turned Upside Down* (New York: Viking Press, 1972), pp. 59–64. While Powell was in prison, the high sheriff of Cardiganshire, Morgan Herbert, refused to impanel a jury to hear a case involving riot and murder that occurred at Lampeter when Charles was proclaimed king. Misdemeanor charges were brought against Herbert, who had been appointed to his office by Cromwell. PRO SP 29/4/99. For Powell's political behavior see Geoffrey F. Nuttall, *The Welsh Saints 1640–1660* (Cardiff: University of Wales Press, 1957), pp. 50–51.

87. R. Tudur Jones, "The Sufferings of Vavasor," *Welsh Baptist Studies*, ed. Mansel John (n. p.: South Wales Baptist College, 1976), pp. 77–78; PRO SP 29/7/146.

88. PRO SP 29/8/29, 29.1, 29.2 The assistants were Edward Rogers, Nicholas Carter, Richard Prichard, and Arthur Smallman.

89. PRO SP 29/8/29.2; Jones, "The Sufferings of Vavasor," pp. 79–80.

90. PRO SP 29/8/47.

91. PRO SP 29/8/47; Jones, "The Sufferings of Vavasor," pp. 79–80. Those jailed at Bala included Owen Lewis, Hugh Evans, Owen Humphrey, Thomas Ellis, and Richard Jones.

92. PRO SP 29/8/105, 105.1.

93. Kennet, pp. 241–242.

94. PRO SP 29/29/15, 15.1, 15.2; *HMC* 13, *Tenth Report*, Appendix, Part IV, pp. 395–96.

95. Another factor that contributed to the relative calm was the work of Hugh Lloyd as bishop of Llandaff. A native Welshman, he appointed clergy to their home parishes to improve their relations with the laity and thus enhance their efforts to re-establish the episcopalian church. John R. Guy, "The Significance of Indigenous Clergy in the Welsh Church at the Restoration," in *Religion and National Identity*, ed. Stuart Mews, Studies in Church History, 18 (Oxford: Basil Blackwell, 1982), p. 342.

96. *MP* 23 (31 May–7 June 1660), p. 357; *MP* 26 (21–28 June 1660), p. 416.

97. *CSPI 1660–62*, p. 16; Kennet, p. 197; David W. Miller, *Queen's Rebels: Ulster Loyalism in Historical Perspective* (Dublin: Barnes and Noble, 1978), p. 21.

98. Bodl. Carte MSS 45, fols. 38$^r$, 44$^r$.

99. PRO SP 63/304/27; *MP* 43 (18–25 October 1660), p. 688; *PI* (22–29 October 1660), p. 696.

100. PRO SP 63/304/45, 71. Among the others who were arrested were Colonel Richard Lehunt, Captain Lehunt, and Major Greene.

101. PRO SP 63/304/36; 63/305/116.

102. *CSPI 1660–62*, pp. 115–16, 128–29; Bodl. Carte MSS 45, fol. 43$^4$. Taylor complained to Clarendon that some of the dissidents had threatened to kill him. Ibid., fol. 38$^r$.

103. *PI* (3–10 December 1660), p. 796; *CSPI 1660–62*, pp. 128–29.

104. F. D. Dow, *Cromwellian Scotland 1651–1660* (Edinburgh: John Donald, 1979), p. 268; I. M Green, *The Re-Establishment of the Church of England 1660–1663* (Oxford: Oxford University Press, 1978), p. 15.

105. *CSPV 1659–61*, p. 173: *MP* 30 (19–26 July 1660), p. 470. A Captain Kiffin, formerly a collector in Ayrshire, was imprisoned in Edinburgh Castle in July. *MP* 32 (2–9 August 1660), p. 503.

106. *PI* (26 August–3 September 1660), p. 564; *MP* 36 (30 August–6 September 1660), p. 563; Wodrow, 1:66–71; Nicoll. p. 298. The others were Alexander Moncrief, minister of Scone, John Semple, minister of Carsfairn, Thomas Ramsay, pastor at Mordington, Gilbert Hall from Kirkliston, John Scott of Oxnam, George Nairn, minister at Burntisland, John Murray, pastor of Methven, and James Kirkco, laird of Sundiwell in Nithsdale. Wodrow adds Andrew Hay, ruling elder of Craignethan, near Lanark.

107. Dow, *Cromwellian Scotland*, p. 269; *PI* (26 August–3 September 1660), pp. 565–66.

108. *MP* 39 (20–27 September 1660), p. 623; Nicoll, pp. 300–303, 306; Wodrow, 1:79; William C. Braithwaite, *The Beginnings of Quakerism* (London: Macmillan and Co., 1923), p. 350.

109. *BDBR*, s.v. Gilby Carr; Nicoll, p. 303. Purves had been chief clerk of the Exchequer.

110. Julia Buckroyd, "The Resolutioners and the Scottish Nobility in the Early Months of 1660," in *Church, Society, and Politics*, ed. Derek Baker, Studies in Church History, 12 (Oxford: Basil Blackwell, 1975), pp. 245–52.

111. *CSPD 1660–61*, p. 308

## Notes to Chapter 2

1. John Tillinghast, *Mr. Tillinghasts Eight Last Sermons* (London, 1655), p. 68; anon., *Certain Quaeres Humbly Presented in Way of Petition* (London, 1648), p. 4.

2. *Certain Quaeres*, p. 8; E. J. Hobsbawm, *Primitive Rebels: Studies in Archaic Forms of Social Movement in the 19th and 20th Centuries* (New York: W. W. Norton & Company, 1965), pp. 57–58.

3. Sir Richard Baker, *A Chronicle of the Kings of England* (7th ed.; London, 1679), p. 735; *CSPV 1659–61*, p. 239; *ST*, 6:110–11; *MP* 1 (3–10 January 1661), p. 12.

4. *KI* (7–14 January 1661), pp. 19–20; Burnet, p. 105; Edward Hyde, Earl of Clarendon, "The Continuation of the Life of Edward Hyde Earl of Clarendon," *ad cal. The History of the Rebellion and Civil Wars in England* (Oxford: at the University Press, 1843), p. 1033; *A Door of Hope* (London, 1661), *passim*; *MP* 1 (3–10 January 1661), p. 13.

5. *ST*, 6:111; *Munster Paralleld in the Late Massacres Committed by the Fifth Monarchists* (London, 1661), π6ᵛ; PRO SP 29/28/42; Pepys, 2:11; Heath, p. 66 (mispr. 56).

6. Clarendon, "Continuation," p. 1033; *KI* (7–14 January 1661), pp. 21–22; *MP* 1 (3–10 January 1661), pp. 13–14; Evelyn, 3:266.

7. *MP* 1 (3–10 January 1661), p. 15; *KI* (7–14 January 1661), p. 22; Pepys, 2:8.

8. *KI* (7–14 January 1661), pp. 23–24; (14–21 January 1661), pp. 43–44; *MP* 1 (3–10 January 1661), pp. 15–16; *ST*, 6:111; PRO SP 29/28/42; Evelyn, 3:266–67; Nicoll, pp. 318–20; Baker, *Chronicle*, p. 735. See also Champlin Burrage, "The Fifth Monarchy Insurrections," *EHR* 25 (October 1910): 740–43. There are discrepancies in the various accounts of the uprising.

9. PRO SP 29/28/42; *MP* 1 (3–10 January 1661), p. 16; Pepys, 2:9–10; Victor S. Sutch, *Gilbert Sheldon: Architect of Anglican Survival, 1640–1675* (The Hague: Martinus Nijhoff, 1973), p. 77.

10. *CSPD 1660–61*, p. 470; *MP* 2 (10–17 January 1661), pp. 23–24.

11. According to Edward Gower, another Fifth Monarchist—wearing only a shirt— turned himself in at the Sessions House, claiming he "had done execution upon the Lord's enemies, and desired he might suffer with his brethren." *HMC* 4, *Fifth Report*, Appendix, Part I, p. 201.

12. *MP* 2 (10–17 January 1661), p. 32; PRO SP 29/28/42.

13. *MP* 3 (17–24 January 1661), pp. 34, 38, 39; *ST*, 6:112–13; Heath, p. 473; *KI* (21–28 January 1661), pp. 57–58; Kennet, p. 363; Reresby, pp. 36–37. Those executed on the 21st were Jonas Allen, William Ashton, William Corbet, John Elston, Stephen Fall, John Gardiner, Leonard Gowler, Thomas Harris, and John Tod (or Dod). Reprieves were given to John Pym, Robert Brierly, and John Smith.

14. PRO SP 63/306/11.1; *CSPV 1659–61*, p. 240; *MP* 2 (10–17 January 1661), p. 31; *KI* (21–28 January 1661), p. 49. For Culmer see Greaves, *Saints and Rebels*, chap. 2.

15. *MP* 2 (10–17 January 1661), pp. 22–23, 31–32; *MCR*, 3:310; *KI* (7–14 January 1661), p. 26; (14–21 January 1661), pp. 33–34, 39; PRO SP 29/31/78; 29/61/152; *CSPV 1659–61*, p. 242.

16. PRO SP 29/28/84. There was also a report on the 12th that the Baptists would rise that night in conjunction with the Fifth Monarchists. *CSPD 1660–61*, p. 471.

17. *MP* 4 (24–31 January 1661), p. 62; *KI* (28 January–4 February 1661), p. 70; Parker, *History*, p. 14.

18. PRO SP 29/28/40; Parker, *History*, pp. 14–15; *MP* 2 (10–17 January 1661), pp. 17–18, 30–31; *KI* (14–21 January 1661), pp. 34, 37–38.

19. *KI* (14–21 January 1661), p. 37; *MP* 2 (10–17 January 1661), p. 30; Thomas Ellwood, *The History of the Life of Thomas Ellwood*, ed. C. G. Crump (London: Methuen, 1900), p. 56; George Fox, *Narrative Papers of George Fox*, ed. Henry J. Cadbury (Richmond, Ind.: Friends United Press, 1972), p. 179: PRO SP

29/28/56; 29/29/104. The arrested men who had served with Creed were Captain Turner, a Baptist; Captain Foxe, a Congregationalist "teacher"; Lieutenant Thomas Juice, and William Clare, clerk to Creed's regiment. Two other officers were arrested: Captain Taylor and Lieutenant Richard Bunston.

20. CH HA 8528; HA 9805; PRO SP 29/28/87, 90.

21. PRO SP 29/29/16, 16.1, 16.2; *CSPD 1660–61*, pp. 516–17; *KI* (21–28 January 1661), pp. 61–62; *MP* 4 (24–31 January 1661), pp. 53–54; *CSPD 1661–62*, p. 185.

22. CH STT 718, 719; STT 2174; *KI* (14–21 January 1661), p. 38; *MP* 2 (10–17 January 1661), p. 31; PRO SP 29/28/58.

23. PRO SP 29/28/45, 45.1, 99.

24. PRO SP 29/28/50, 87; 29/29/48; *KI* (21–28 January 1661), p. 59; *MP* 4 (24–31 January 1661), p. 52.

25. *Munster Paralleld*, π5$^r$; Nicoll, p. 320; Kennet, p. 364; *CCSP*, 5:76.

26. *CSPV 1659–61*, p. 244; Henry, pp. 75, 77.

27. James Ralph, *The History of England*, 2 vols. (London: Daniel Browne, 1744–46), 1:35; Ludlow, *Voyce*, p. 282; *CSPD 1660–61*, pp. 475–76.

28. Schwoerer, pp. 72–73, 79, 81; *CSPD 1660–61*, p. 470; *CSPV 1659–61*, p. 255; *KI* (18–25 February 1661), pp. 113–16.

29. *HMC 71, Finch*, 1:130; *HMC 4, Fifth Report*, Appendix, Part I, p. 170.

30. *CSPD 1660–61*, p. 476; PRO SP 29/46/5.1. Cf. Ludlow, *Voyce*, pp. 278–79.

31. PRO SP 63/308/p. 16. Cf. PRO SP 63/306/12.

32. *A Renuntiation and Declaration of the Ministers of Congregational Churches and Publick Preachers* (London, 1661), pp. 1–4, 8–9.

33. Whiting, pp. 101–105; Kennet, p. 383.

34. Crosby, 2:65, 98–114; PRO SP 29/30/60. Cf. John Bunyan, "A Relation of the Imprisonment of Mr. John Bunyan," *ad cal. Grace Abounding to the Chief of Sinners*, ed. Roger Sharrock (Oxford: Clarendon Press, 1962), pp. 121–24. Between August 1661 and March 1662, Bunyan used the liberty given to him by his jailor to visit London. His enemies accused him of going there to "plot and raise division, and make insurrection." Ibid., p. 130.

35. Ellwood, *History*, p. 55; George Fox, et al., *A Declaration from the Harmles & Innocent People of God, Called Quakers* (London, 1661), pp. 3–5, 8. As one might expect, there were a number of public attacks on Venner's rising, including Thomas Ellis' *The Traytors Unveiled in a Brief and True Account of That Horrid and Bloody Design* (1661), *An Advertisement as Touching the Fanaticks Late Conspiracy* (1661), and *Munster Paralleld*.

36. Whiting, p. 101; Watts, p. 223; Henry, *Diaries*, p. 76; PRO SP 29/28/86; 29/32/69, 139.

37. PRO SP 29/29/12; Kennet, pp. 364, 371. Cf. *HMC 31, Thirteenth Report*, Appendix, Part IV, p. 237.

38. PRO SP 29/31/24; 29/32/139; 29/56/134; *HMC 71, Finch*, 1:101; Frank Bate, *The Declaration of Indulgence 1672* (London: University Press of Liverpool by Archibald Constable and Co., 1908), p. 17; *CSPD 1660–61*, p. 587.

39. *KI* (7–14 January 1661), p. 32; PRO SP 29/30/56; *MCR*, 3:311–12 (cf. pp. 310, 313); *CSPD 1660–61*, p. 515. Martindale was detained for his refusal; cf. *CR*, s.v.

40. BL Egerton MSS 2543, fols. 24$^r$, 25$^v$; PRO SP 29/34/2. For conventicles in the London area in June and July see *MCR*, 3:313–14, 323.

41. *LJ*, 11:242–43.

42. CH STT 895 (cf. STT 721); PRO SP 29/40/84.

43. PRO SP 29/40/91; 29/42/38; *BDBR*, s.v. Belcher, Cf. Bodl. Clarendon MSS 75, fol. 191$^{r-v}$

44. PRO SP 29/41/28, 28.1, 39; 29/42/36.1.

45. PRO SP 29/43/57; 29/44/4; *CSPD 1661–62*, p. 162.

46. PRO SP 29/43/57, 69, 107, 130.

47. PRO SP 29/43/46; 29/44/137; *CSPD 1661–62*, p. 205.

48. PRO SP 29/41/49; 29/42/38; 29/44/69.

49. Robert S. Bosher, *The Making of the Restoration Settlement* (New York: Oxford University Press, 1951), p. 238; PRO SP 29/40/42, 86.

50. PRO SP 29/42/21, 37; 29/43/2, 106, 117.

51. PRO SP 29/43/38, 68, 84, 85, 108; *CR*, p. 35.

52. PRO SP 29/43/32; 29/44/2, 136.

53. Ralph, *History*, 1:51.

54. *A Narrative of the Apprehending, Commitment, Arraignment, Condemnation, and Execution of John James* (London, 1662), *passim; KI* 48 (18–25 November 1661), pp. 737–38; 49 (25 November–2 December 1661), p. 739; *MP* 47 (14–28 November 1661), pp. 727, 752; *CSPV 1661–64*, p. 76; John James, *The Speech and Declaration of John James* (1661); Crosby, 2:166–71; Whiting, pp. 108–109.

55. *MP* 4 (24–31 January 1661), pp. 62–64; *KI* (28 January–4 February 1661), pp. 71–72; Parker, *History*, pp. 15–16.

56. PRO SP 29/30/52, 59; 29/446/15; 63/308/p. 20; BL Egerton MSS 2543, fols. 28$^r$, 30$^r$. In September the bodies of twenty radicals were removed from Westminster Abbey and all but one buried in a pit outside St. Margaret's. Bodl. Clarendon MSS 75, fol. 186$^r$.

57. Pepys, 2:57; *CSPD 1660–61*, pp. 538–41; *CSPV 1659–61*, p. 275; *CCSP*, 5:89–90; Ludlow, *Voyce*, p. 285; *HMC* 4, *Fifth Report*, Appendix, Part I, p. 181; BL Egerton MSS 2543, fols. 35$^r$, 36$^r$; Douglas R. Lacey, *Dissent and Parliamentary Politics in England, 1661–1689* (New Brunswick, N. J.: Rutgers University Press, 1969), pp. 29–30. Cf. Sutch, *Sheldon*, p. 78. Fowke was definitely a Presbyterian; the religious loyalties of the other three are tentative. Cf. Lacey, pp. 416, 419, 448–49.

58. PRO SP 29/47/70, 71. On 18 April Gladman was bonded for good behavior. PRO SP 29/34/70. Nicholas ordered the release of Allen and Courtney from the Gatehouse and Vernon from Newgate on 19 June, but gave them fifteen days to leave England. *CSPD 1661–62*, p. 12. Allen and Courtney were still in the Gatehouse on 5 October. PRO SP 29/43/23.

59. *CSPD 1660–61*, pp. 567–68.

60. *CSPD 1660–61*, p. 526; PRO SP 29/34/50, 71, 73.

61. PRO SP 29/34/67, 68; 29/43/25, 26.

62. PRO SP 29/34/84; *CSPD 1660–61*, p. 572.

63. *HMC* 71, *Finch*, 1:116–17; *Correspondence of the Family of Hatton*, ed. Edward Maunde Thompson, Camden Society, n.s., 22–23 (1878), 1:22; *HMC* 38, *Fourteenth Report*, Appendix, Part IX, p. 280.

64. *CSPV 1661–64*, p. 40; PRO SP 29/41/8; 29/446/40. Another list from about this time recorded the names of officers such as Gladman and Packer who still had their horses. The list also included the names of fourteen inns in Holborn where a large number of horses were kept. PRO SP 29/47/70.

65. *DCY*, p. 88; PRO SP 29/41/29; 29/42/1; CH HA 3146. Cf. PRO SP 29/41/32, 61.

66. PRO SP 29/40/37, 42; 29/41/2.

67. PRO SP 29/40/101, 102. For Fitch see also PRO SP 29/42/40; he was reportedly a close associate of Jacob Willett of St. Lawrence Lane. John Lowry of Cambridge sat in the Long Parliament.

68. PRO SP 29/41/17, 56; 29/43/61.

69. PRO SP 29/42/38.

70. *CSPV 1661–64*, p. 52; PRO SP 29/43/1; *CSPD 1661–62*, p. 103; *MP* 37 (12–19 September 1661), p. 581; *HMC* 78, *Hastings*, 4:116.

71. Pepys, 2:204; PRO SP 29/43/89, 97, 98, 99.

72. PRO SP 29/43/89; *CSPV 1661–64*, pp. 63–64.

73. PRO SP 29/43/130, 135.

74. *CSPV 1661–64*, p. 66; *HMC* 22, *Eleventh Report*, Appendix, Part VII, p. 3; *CSPD 1661–62*, pp. 123–24; BL Egerton MSS 2618, fol. 102$^r$.

75. *HMC* 78, *Hastings*, 4:116; *MP* 42 (17–24 October 1661), p. 672; 44 (24–31 October 1661), p. 680; *KI* 43 (21–28 October 1661), pp. 680–81, 688; *CMHS*, 8:180; Kennet, p. 566; *Som. Tr.*, 7:532, 537; PRO SP 29/43/89, 132, 133. Colonels Leonard Lytcott and Thomas Rede, and Majors John Gladman and Haynes were also arrested. Captains John Chaffin and William Newman, Captain John Mason, and a Colonel or Major Henry Wansey were apprehended shortly thereafter.

76. *KI* 44 (28 October–4 November 1661), pp. 696, 704; *MP* 45 (31 October–7 November 1661), p. 796; PRO SP 29/43/122, 122.1, 122.2; 29/44/2.1, 2.2.

77. PRO SP 29/44/39, 40.

78. PRO SP 29/44/39.3, 39.4; Arthur John Hawkes, *Sir Roger Bradshaigh of Haigh* (Manchester: Lancashire and Cheshire Antiquarian Society, 1945), p. 28.

79. For Sparry, Osland, and the Baxters see *CR*, s.vv.

80. PRO SP 29/44/39.2.

81. PRO SP 29/44/39.1.

82. PRO SP 29/44/61.

83. PRO SP 29/44/45, 91.

84. *MP* 47 (14–28 November 1661), p. 751; PRO SP 29/44/82.

85. Andrew Yarranton (or Yarrington), *A Full Discovery of the First Presbyterian Sham-Plot* (London, 1681), pp. 4–5; Ashley, *Wildman*, pp. 172–75. Yarrington's book was printed by Francis Smith.

86. Yarranton, *A Full Discovery*, p. 6; PRO SP 29/44/62. Among the others who were arrested were Dr. Jackson of Kidderminster, Simon Moor, ejected from Worcester Cathedral in 1660, Jarvis Bryan, ejected rector of Old Swinford, Worcestershire, Henry Baldwin, George Wilson, John Vicars, and Mr. Mekine, all of Worcester.

87. Yarranton, *A Full Discovery*, p. 8.

88. Ibid., pp. 9–11.

89. *HMC* 78, *Hastings*, 4:119; PRO SP 29/44/83, 90, 90.1, 92.

90. Cobbett, 4:224–25; *CSPD 1661–62*, pp. 144, 161, 178; CH STT 896. Richard Mayor of St. Paul's, Covent Garden, thought the cashiered men would cause more mischief away from the City than in it. *MCR*, 3:317.

91. Yarranton, *A Full Discovery*, pp. 12–15; *CSPD 1661–62*, pp. 383, 385, 398; PRO SP 29/56/96.

92. Ludlow, *Voyce*, p. 292.

93. Cf. Ashley, *Wildman*, pp. 174–75.

94. Ashley, *Wildman*, pp. 175–76; *CSPD 1661–62*, p. 196; Samuel Palmer, *The Nonconformist's Memorial*, 2 vols. (London: W. Harris, 1775), 1:30–31.

95. *CSPD 1661–62*, pp. 196–97; *HMC* 22, *Eleventh Report*, Appendix, Part VII, p. 3; *MP* 47 (14–28 November 1661), p. 752.

96. BL Egerton MSS 2543, fols. 65$^r$–66$^v$; Ashley, *Wildman*, pp. 178–80.

97. *HMC* 71, *Finch*, 1:173. Cf. *CSPD 1661–62*, p. 168.

98. Kennet, pp. 576–77; *LJ*, 11:355.

99. Cobbett, 4:226–27; *KI* 52 (16–23 December 1661), p. 790; *HMC* 27, *Twelfth Report*, Appendix, Part IX, p. 51; Kennet, pp. 576–77; *CSPV 1661–64*, p. 91.

100. Kennet, p. 602; Ashley, *Wildman*, pp. 181–82; Parker, *History*, pp. 19–20.

101. Ludlow, *Voyce*, p. 291; PRO SP 29/293/46; Ashley, *Wildman*, pp. 183–84.

102. *CSPV 1661–64*, p. 106; *CMHS*, 8:181–82; Kennet, p. 602; Pepys, 3:15 (cf. 2:225, where he was dubious about the plot as early as 1 December); Cobbett, 4:224–28.

103. PRO SP 29/44/135.

104. PRO SP 29/44/133, 134.
105. PRO SP 29/44/20, 47, 84.
106. *CSPD 1661–62*, p. 154; PRO SP 29/40/43; 29/44/101, 101.1. For Hobson see Greaves, *Saints and Rebels*, chap. 5.
107. *CSPD 1661–62*, p. 169; PRO SP 29/45/29.
108. *CSPD 1661–62*, pp. 196, 236.
109. PRO SP 29/24/44; *Remarkable Passages in the Life of William Kiffin*, ed. William Orme (London: Burton and Smith, 1823), pp. 28–32; Whiting, pp. 100–101. In late 1661 or early 1662 Kiffin was also falsely accused of hiring two men to assassinate Charles II. Whiting, pp. 110–11.
110. Ludlow, *Voyce*, p. 291.
111. Ashley, *Wildman*, pp. 156–58; *CSPD 1661–62*, p. 56; PRO SP 29/23/71.2; 29/24/112; 29/34/71.
112. *CSPD 1661–62*, pp. 55–56; Ashley, *Wildman*, pp. 168–71; PRO SP 29/43/123.
113. PRO SP 29/45/29; 29/49/71; 29/54/27.
114. PRO SP 29/34/57; *CSPD 1661–62*, p. 241; *CCSP*, 5:206–207.
115. *CSPD 1663–64*, pp. 145–46, 149.

## Notes to Chapter 3

1. PRO SP 29/57/123.
2. *DCY*, p. 94: *NRR*, 6:58; (cf. *MCR*, 3:326); PRO SP 29/58/17.
3. PRO SP 29/57/25.
4. *CSPD 1661–62*, p. 248; PRO SP 29/52/130, 131, 132.
5. PRO SP 29/50/8, 8.1, 8.2, 8.3.
6. *CSPD 1661–62*, pp. 253, 268; *HMC* 33, *Lonsdale*, p. 89; Capp, *FMM*, p. 209.
7. *CSPD 1661–62*, p. 385; *MCR*, 3:321.
8. PRO SP 29/54/75; *CSPI 1660–62*, pp. 549–50.
9. PRO SP 29/49/93, 104.
10. PRO SP 29/50/3; 29/51/32; 29/52/2.
11. *MP* 16 (17–24 April 1662), pp. 241–46; *CSPD 1661–62*, p. 346; Ludlow, *Voyce*, pp. 302–303; *HMC* 78, *Hastings*, 4:130–31.
12. PRO SP 29/56/8; Ludlow, *Voyce*, pp. 312–13; *KI* 24 (9–16 June 1662), p. 384; William Riley Parker, *Milton: A Biography*, 2 vols. (Oxford; Clarendon Press, 1968), 1:582.
13. PRO SP 29/66/39; 29/89/31.
14. PRO SP 29/88/56; *DCY*, p. 95.
15. Max Beloff, *Public Order and Popular Disturbances 1660–1714* (London: Frank Cass & Co., 1938), p. 35; *DCY*, p. 94; Kennet, p. 767.
16. *Letters Addressed to the Earl of Lauderdale*, ed. Osmund Airy, Camden Society, n.s., 31 (1883), p. 16; *HMC* 51, *Popham*, p. 190.
17. PRO SP 29/58/53; *CSPD 1661–62*, p. 481.
18. PRO SP 29/54/72; *CSPD 1661–62*, pp. 437–38; *MCR*, 3:327.
19. *KI* 2 (6–13 January 1662), pp. 15–16.
20. *CSPD 1660–61*, pp. 550–51, 583. Cf. PRO SP 29/44/66.
21. He served in this capacity from June 1661 to September 1662, and again from September 1663 to July 1665. *CCSP*, 5:175, n. 3.
22. Burnet, p. 136; Walker, "Secret Service," pp. 218–19.
23. *CCSP*, 5:107, 117; Ralph C. H. Catterall, "Sir George Downing and the Regicides," *AHR* 17 (January 1912): 274.
24. Lister, 3:155; Catterall, "Downing," 17:271, 274; *CCSP*, 5:140; Ludlow, *Memoirs*, 2:330. According to Ludlow, Barkstead, Dixwell, Okey, and Walton were made burgesses at Hanau.
25. *CCSP*, 5:153, 156.

26. *CCSP*, 5:104; PRO SP 29/41/1; Lister 3:155.

27. *CCSP*, 5:113–14; PRO SP 29/50/51; Sprunger, pp. 407–408.

28. Lister, 3:155; *CCSP*, 5:172, 196.

29. *CCSP*, 5:196–97, 200; Ludlow, *Voyce*, p. 299; Catterall, "Downing," 17:280–84; PRO SP 29/52/96; *HMC* 22, *Eleventh Report*, Appendix, Part VII, p. 4; *MP* 16 (17–24 April 1662), pp. 241–46; *CSPV 1661–64*, p. 138; BL Egerton MSS 2538, fols. 37ʳ–38ʳ.

30. *CCSP*, 5:202, 253, 258 (cf. 268); *CMHS*, 8:215.

31. William Steven, *The History of the Scottish Church, Rotterdam* (Edinburgh: Waugh and Innes; Rotterdam: Vander Meer and Verbruggen, 1832), pp. 53–54.

32. Ludlow, *Voyce*, p. 192; Ludlow, *Memoirs*, 2:336–37, 343–44.

33. Walker, "Secret Service," p. 234, n. 2; Blair Worden, "Edmund Ludlow: The Puritan and the Whig," *Times Literary Supplement* (7 January 1977), p. 15; Worden, intro. to Ludlow, *Voyce*, p. 10; Ludlow, *Voyce*, pp. 309–10; Parker, *History*, p. 10.

34. PRO SP 29/41/1.

35. *HMC* 78, *Hastings*, 4:129–30; PRO SP 29/448/18; *CSPV 1661–64*, p. 158; J. J. Jusserand, *A French Ambassador at the Court of Charles the Second: Le Comte de Cominges from His Unpublished Correspondence* (New York: G. P. Putnam's Sons; London: T. Fisher Unwin, 1892), pp. 116, 196.

36. Kennet, pp. 723, 740; *CCSP*, 5:248.

37. PRO SP 29/57/122.1; *CMHS*, 8:197.

38. PRO SP 29/52/30; Kennet, p. 612; *CR*, s.v. Henry Field; *CSPD 1661–62*, pp. 295, 372. The fine was later remitted and Parsons was released on 11 September 1662. *CR*, s.v. Andrew Parsons.

39. PRO SP 29/56/1, 17; PRO SP 29/57/122; *CR*, s. v. Elias Pledger.

40. *CSPD 1661–62*, p. 376; *LJ*, 11:476.

41. *CCSP*, 5:225; Pepys, 3:92. By October 1662 Packer and Gladman had been transferred to Dublin Castle. BL Egerton MSS 2538, fol. 150ʳ.

42. Firth & Davies, p. 404; PRO SP 29/53/98.

43. PRO SP 29/56/6; *CSPD 1661–62*, pp. 398, 400, 416, 428, 434; *KI* 26 (23–30 June 1662), p. 406.

44. PRO SP 29/54/60; 29/56/1; 29/57/24; Firth & Davies, pp. 691–97.

45. PRO SP 29/56/22; *CSPD 1661–62*, p. 400; *MCR*, 3:321–25, 327.

46. PRO SP 29/51/15; 29/56/48, 77.

47. PRO SP 29/49/115; *KI* 13 (24–31 March 1662), p. 189; Kennet, p. 647.

48. *HMC* 78, *Hastings*, 4:133–34; *KI* 28 (7–14 July 1662), pp. 447–48.

49. *CSPD 1661–62*, p. 431; *NRR*, 6:57; *CCSP*, 5:253, 265–66.

50. "Letters of Early Friends," *The Friends' Library*, ed. William Evans and Thomas Evans, vol. 11 (Philadelphia: Joseph Rakestraw, 1847), p. 361. Cf. *Episcopal Visitation Book for the Archdeaconry of Buckingham, 1662*, ed. E. R. C. Brinkworth, Buckinghamshire Record Society, 7 (Bedford: Sidney Press, 1947), pp. 2–3.

51. Ludlow, *Voyce*, p. 274; George Fox, *The Journal of George Fox*, ed. John L. Nickalls (Cambridge: at the University Press, 1952), p. 439; Pepys, 3:165; *KI* (4–11 August 1662), p. 529.

52. *CSPD 1661–62*, pp. 404, 411; PRO SP 29/56/64, 100; 29/57/15.

53. PRO SP 29/56/86, 86.1; *CSPD 1661–62*, pp. 404, 421, 423; *CSPV 1661–64*, p. 161. A jail list dated 22 June 1662 noted that thirty-nine Fifth Monarchists were in jail in Surrey. PRO SP 29/56/91.

54. PRO SP 29/57/42, 42.1, 87.1.

55. PRO SP 29/57/57, 72, 78, 79, 87; Bodl. Carte MSS 47, fols. 340ᵛ, 345ʳ, 351ʳ. Colonel Robert Russell was jailed at Salisbury for wearing his sword in defiance of a royal proclamation, but he probably had no connection with the alleged Taunton conspirators. PRO SP 29/57/84.

56. PRO SP 29/57/85, 87; 29/58/16. Cf. PRO SP 29/58/16.1; Latimer, *Annals*, pp. 316–17. John Woodman was jailed at Winchester in August on charges of treason and sedition. The government was also searching for three other Hampshire men: Robert Read of Cholderton, John Drake of Amport, and Mr. Moody of Little Ann. *CSPD 1661–62*, p. 466.

57. Bodl. Carte MSS 47, fols. 343$^{r-v}$, 347$^v$; PRO SP 29/57/142; Arthur John Hawkes, *Sir Roger Bradshaigh of Haigh* (Manchester: Lancashire and Cheshire Antiquarian Society, 1945), p. 27. On 4 August Clarendon ordered that suspicious persons in Coventry be secured. Northampton subsequently directed Sir Henry Jones to search the houses of a dozen recently discharged magistrates for weapons and papers. *CCSP*, 5:247, 255.

58. PRO SP 29/57/70, 70.1. In an apparent case of mistaken identity, authorities at Newcastle-upon-Tyne examined John Hollys, a former corporal of foot in Haselrig's regiment, who denied knowledge of a plot and professed loyalty to the established church. *HMC* 55, *Var. Coll.*, 2:117.

59. PRO SP 29/57/111, 119; 29/58/32; *CCSP*, 5:254. The archbishop of York reported on 13 August that a letter from "an agent" to "Our Presbyterian Primate B" had been intercepted, though it contained nothing of substance. "B" himself had recently arrived in York. *CCSP*, 5:253.

60. BL Egerton MSS 2543, fol. 92$^r$; *CSPD 1661–62*, p. 442; *The Twysden Lieutenancy Papers, 1583–1668*, ed. Gladys Scott Thomson, Kent Archaeological Society, Records Branch, 10 (Ashford: Headley Brothers, 1926), pp. 39–40; PRO SP 29/58/72.

61. Nicholas, cited in Bosher, *Restoration Settlement*, p. 266; *HMC* 55, *Var.Coll.*, 2:117–18. Cf. *HMC* 71, *Finch*, 1:206. But Dean Guy informed Williamson on 27 August that the "fanatics" were boldly speaking treason, asserting that their time of deliverance was at hand. Guy pleaded that the government disarm them, for "we are as . . . negligent to prevent any danger as if we were all of their partie." PRO SP 29/58/83.

62. *KI* 34 (18–25 August 1662), p. 554; PRO SP 29/58/59; *CMHS*, 8:202; Pepys, 3:169.

63. *CR*, pp. xii–xiv; Watts, p. 219; I. M. Green, *The Re-Establishment of the Church of England 1660–1663* (Oxford: Oxford University Press, 1978), chap. 8.

64. Pepys, 3:178; *CMHS*, 8:201; *KI* 34 (18–25 August 1662), p. 562; *MP* 34 (21–28 August 1662), p. 570.

65. *CSPV 1661–64*, p. 185; *CMHS*, 8:205; Robert S. Bosher, *The Making of the Restoration Settlement: The Influence of the Laudians 1649–1662* (New York: Oxford University Press, 1951), p. 266, n. 2; Pepys, 3:210; Bodl. Carte MSS 47, fols. 361$^v$, 365$^{r-v}$. Nicholas attributed the rumors of plotting to the Presbyterians, who allegedly hoped to instigate the other Nonconformists to rebel and thus prompt the king to offer an indulgence to the Presbyterians. Bodl. Carte MSS 47, fol. 359$^v$.

66. *HMC* 78, *Hastings*, 4:136. On 16 July two men testified that former Lieutenant Robert Carter, a Baptist and a costermonger in Thames Street, indicated that a rising was imminent. PRO SP 29/57/66. Another ex-soldier, the distiller John Tomes, was arrested about the same time. PRO SP 29/61/6.

67. PRO SP 29/65/85; 29/66/40. A warrant for the arrest of Captain Richard Williams for treasonable designs was issued on 16 August. *CSPD 1661–62*, p. 461.

68. Evelyn, 3:331; *CSPD 1661–62*, p. 488; *KI* 35 (25 August–1 September 1662), pp. 563, 564, 570; *KI* 36 (1–8 September 1662), pp. 585–86, 589.

69. *KI* 36 (1–8 September 1662), p. 582; Bosher, *Restoration Settlement*, pp. 267–68.

70. Henry Newcome, *The Diary of the Rev. Henry Newcome*, ed. Thomas Heywood, Chetham Society, o.s., 18 (Manchester, 1849), p. 115; PRO SP 29/61/46, 46.1.

71. *MCR*, 3:329, 330; PRO SP 29/65/65, 65.1.

72. *KI* 40 (29 September–6 October 1662), p. 664; PRO SP 29/61/119; Ward, quoted in Allan Brockett, *Nonconformity in Exeter 1650–1875* (Manchester: Manchester University Press for the University of Exeter, 1962), p. 23.

73. Pepys, 3:183; PRO SP 29/61/120; 29/62/68, 110; 29/66/14; *KI* 45 (3–10 November 1662), p. 715.

74. "Letters of Early Friends," pp. 359–60; Thomas Ellwood, *The History of the Life of Thomas Ellwood*, ed. C. G. Crump (London: Methuen and Co., 1900), pp. 91–92; David Masson, *The Life of John Milton*, 6 vols. (New York: Macmillan, 1880), 6:471; *CSPD 1661–62*, p. 541.

75. *NRR*, 6:61–62, 67–68; PRO SP 29/61/118; 29/63/70; Kennet, pp. 782, 836; *KI* 49 (1–8 December 1662), p. 789; *CSPD 1661–62*, p. 466.

76. Kennet, p. 764; PRO SP 29/64/58.

77. *KI* 36 (1–8 September 1662), p. 586; *CCSP*, 5:278–79.

## Notes to Chapter 4

1. Raymond C. Mensing, Jr., *Toleration and Parliament 1660–1719* (Washington, D.C.: University Press of America, 1979), p. 71; *CCSP*, 5:267; *CSPD 1661–62*, pp. 477, 487. With Baynes (or Baines) was jailed one Angel of Southwark on the same charge. *CSPD 1661–62*, p. 477.

2. *CSPV 1661–64*, p. 187; PRO SP 29/59/23, 23.1.

3. *KI* 40 (29 September–6 October 1662), pp. 665–66; Kennet, p. 783; *CSPD 1661–62*, pp. 499, 500.

4. *MCR*, 3:327; PRO SP 29/61/161; *CSPD 1660–85 Addenda*, p. 94. Cf. PRO SP 29/63/105.

5. PRO SP 29/62/86, 108; 29/64/68–71; Pepys, 3:255.

6. *MCR*, 3:328; Pepys, 3:266–67; PRO SP 29/63/72; 29/64/18–19; *CSPD 1661–62*, p. 572.

7. PRO SP 29/61/35; Arthur John Hawkes, *Sir Roger Bradshaigh of Haigh* (Manchester: Lancashire and Cheshire Antiquarian Society, 1945), p. 28.

8. PRO SP 29/61/96; 29/66/38; *CSPD 1660–85 Addenda*, p. 94; *HMC 55, Var. Coll.*, 1:144–45. At Hull, Colquitt hired only former Cromwellian soldiers as under-officers in the customs office, raising suspicions that there was "some designe upon the Garrison." PRO SP 29/62/121.

9. *CSPD 1661–62*, p. 504; PRO SP 29/61/25, 26, 79, 112. Cf. PRO SP 29/61/93; Bodl. Carte MSS 47, fol. 387$^{r-v}$.

10. Pepys, 3:240.

11. PRO SP 29/62/9.1–4. In May 1663 John Eyre urged Secretary Bennet to have Buckle and Trehearne tried in London as an example to potential plotters in Wiltshire. PRO SP 29/74/17. PRO SP 29/82/102 is erroneously dated; it was written about the same time as this letter.

12. Ludlow, "Voyce," pp. 942–43, 1117; Ludlow, *Memoirs*, 2:341; James Ralph, *The History of England*, 2 vols. (London: Daniel Browne, 1744–46), 1:83; Ashley, *Wildman*, p. 190.

13. Parker, *History*, p. 63; Abbott, "Conspiracy," p. 515.

14. *HMC 50, Heathcote*, p. 48.

15. Anthony Wood, *Athenae Oxonienses, an Exact History*, ed. Philip Bliss, 4 vols. (London: P. C. and J. Rivington et al., 1813–20), 3:801–802; [William Hill], *A Brief Narrative of That Stupendious Tragedie* (London, 1662), sig. A3$^v$; Ashley, *Wildman*, pp. 189–90.

16. PRO SP 29/62/58; *CR*, s.v. Edward Riggs; *CSPD 1661–62*, p. 530; Walker, "Secret Service," p. 224.

17. PRO SP 29/65/10; Hill, *Narrative*, sig. A2$^{r-v}$, A3$^v$ –B1$^r$; Ashley, *Wildman*, p. 190.

18. Hill, *Narrative*, sigs. B1$^{r-v}$, B4$^{r}$.
19. Ibid., sigs. B1$^{v}$–B2$^{r}$, p. 46; PRO SP 29/66/36. Arthur Brown (or Browne) was captain of the *London* in 1653. William Laird Clowes, *The Royal Navy: A History*, 7 vols. (London: Sampson Low, Marston and Company, 1897–1903), 2:187. Goodwin was imprisoned on suspicion of corresponding with Ludlow. PRO SP 29/68/133.
20. PRO SP 29/66/36. Phillips' brother was a minister in Buckinghamshire. *KI* 52 (22–29 December 1662), pp. 839–40. Richard Tyler had a brother, probably William Tyler, a Baptist ironmonger in London, who was imprisoned in the Tower and was believed to be part of the plot from the beginning. PRO SP 29/66/25, 36; *HMC* 22, *Eleventh Report*, Appendix, Part VII, p. 5.
21. Hill, *Narrative*, sig. B2$^{r}$, p. 15; *KI* 50 (8–15 December 1662), pp. 804–806; PRO SP 29/65/10.
22. Hill, *Narrative*, p. 33; *KI* 50 (8–15 December 1662), pp. 804–806. According to the Venetian resident, the Presbyterians were willing to supply funds if the sectaries "started the work." *CSPV 1661–64*, p. 212. There is, however, no reliable evidence for this assertion.
23. Hill, *Narrative*, sig. B2$^{r}$; anon., *A True and Exact Relation of the Araignment, Tryal, and Condemnation* (London, 1662), p. 17; PRO SP 29/72/61; *CSPD 1661–62*, p. 548. According to Phillips, Tong's contacts at Windsor consisted of a captain, two sergeants, and a gunner. Hill, *Narrative*, p. 37. In addition to Sergeant Seabrooke, officials interrogated Sergeant Sprigg. PRO SP 29/62/89.
24. A congregation in Blackfriars reputedly supplied pistols. *True Relation*, p. 7.
25. Hill, *Narrative*, sigs. B2$^{r}$–B3$^{r}$; PRO SP 29/65/39; 29/448/40; *CSPD 1661–62*, pp. 555, 574.
26. Hill, *Narrative*, sig. B2$^{r-v}$; PRO SP 29/66/36.
27. Hill, *Narrative*, sig. B3$^{r}$; *True Relation*, pp. 7, 11, 17–18.
28. *True Relation*, p. 10; Hill, *Narrative*, sig. B3$^{r-v}$. When Elton was finally examined in July 1663, he denied having seen Strange in the previous year and a half or knowing Sallers and Phillips. He did, however, admit that he had seen Tong several times. PRO SP 29/76/35.
29. Hill, *Narrative*, sig. B3$^{v}$; Thomas Long, *A Compendious History of All the Popish & Fanatical Plots and Conspiracies* (London, 1684), p. 133. According to the *Kingdomes Intelligencer*, over 5,000 copies of the letter were actually dispersed. *KI* 50 (8–15 December 1662), pp. 804–806. Bishop Parker, however, claims that there were 5,000 copies in London alone, ready for distribution on the eve of the rising. Parker, *History*, pp. 58–60.
30. Hill, *Narrative*, pp. 12–13. Cf. Long, *History*, p. 134. There is a Yoxford in Suffolk.
31. Parker, *History*, p. 60; Hill, *Narrative*, p. 41.
32. Hill, *Narrative*, sigs. B3$^{v}$–B4$^{r}$. Brown was now a shoemaker in the Strand. Ibid., p. 13.
33. *True Relation*, p. 12; Hill, *Narrative*, sig. B4$^{r-v}$, p. 25.
34. *True Relation*, p. 14; PRO SP 29/62/21, 24; Hill, *Narrative*, pp. 30–31. A Captain Foster had served in the Tower Regiment in the 1650s. Firth & Davies, p. 515.
35. *True Relation*, p. 17. Cf. PRO SP 29/62/20–24.
36. PRO SP 29/65/5, 12; 29/66/36; 29/67/85.
37. *True Relation*, pp. 10, 12, 14; Hill, *Narrative*, pp. 26, 36; PRO SP 29/64/73; 29/66/36. As late as 24 November Sir John Robinson learned that if the king had reviewed these troops, "hee had been endanger'd by some treacherous shott from amongst my Soldiers." PRO SP 29/63/65.
38. Hill, *Narrative*, sig. B2$^{r-v}$, pp. 14, 26, 28; *True Relation*, pp. 6, 14; *KI* 50 (8–15 December 1662), pp. 804–806; PRO SP 29/62/27; 29/64/73.
39. *True Relation*, pp. 11, 14, 16; Hill, *Narrative*, sig. B3$^{r}$, pp. 7, 24, 37, 47; *KI* 50

(8–15 December 1662), pp. 804–806; 45 (3–10 November 1662), pp. 711–12; PRO SP 29/66/36.

40. *KI* 50 (8–15 December 1662), pp. 804–806; Hill, *Narrative*, p. 46.

41. *True Relation*, pp. 6, 15, 16; *KI* 50 (8–15 December 1662), pp. 804–806; Hill, *Narrative*, pp. 14, 34, 39; Parker, *History*, pp. 62–63. A similar declaration had allegedly been prepared by a group of plotters who intended to restore the commonwealth, confirm the Interregnum sales of crown and ecclesiastical lands, establish liberty of conscience, and overturn the hearth tax. According to the informer A. Bradley, he learned of the design from Charles Hooker in July, but the rising was postponed because the declaration was not ready. By October it had been completed, and the rebels were said to have 1,400 or 1,500 horse and a war chest of £30,000. Reportedly among the rebel leaders were Colonels Edward Rossiter and John Birch. This account may have been a variation of the rumors circulating about the Tong plot. PRO SP 29/66/41.

42. The others who were arrested included Sergeant Sprigg, Lieutenant Harrison, the gunner Thomas Roberts, and John Phillips, all at Windsor, and White "the Cane man," Captain Foster, Richard Tyler, John Baker, and Elton's acquaintance John Webb, who admitted hearing about the council. Hill, *Narrative*, sig. B4ᵛ; PRO SP 29/62/89; 29/66/36; 29/67/1; Capp, *FMM*, p. 267; *HMC* 22, *Eleventh Report*, Appendix, Part VII, p. 5; *CSPD 1661–62*, pp. 540, 591. Webb was identified as a Baptist or Fifth Monarchist. PRO SP 29/66/36. Harrison, Sprigg, Roberts, and Phillips were discharged on 14 November. *HMC* 22, *Eleventh Report*, Appendix, Part VII, p. 5. Thomas Seabrooke's wife Elizabeth appealed for the release of her husband and his brother Silas around April 1663. PRO SP 29/72/62.

43. *CSPD 1661–62*, pp. 532, 552, 564, 606; PRO SP 29/62/29.

44. Hill, *Narrative*, p. 41. Cf. *HMC* 6, *Seventh Report*, Appendix, Part I, p. 463, which reports rioting in the Sherborne area.

45. PRO SP 29/61/91, 97; Pepys, 3:236; *True Relation*, p. 9.

46. PRO SP 29/62/16, 19; *KI* 13 (23–30 March 1663), p. 197. The four arrested by 2 November were John Lambert, Walter Stone, Thomas Gill, and a Mr. Bartlet. A Captain Cloke was also apprehended. PRO SP 29/62/16.

47. Hill, *Narrative*, sig. B2ʳ⁻ᵛ, pp. 37, 42; *True Relation*, pp. 7, 15, 16; PRO SP 29/62/3, 18, 30; *KI* 50 (8–15 December 1662), pp. 804–806.

48. *True Relation*, pp. 15–16; Hill, *Narrative*, pp. 35, 41; PRO SP 29/62/14. At Chard the aldermen refused to take the oath of allegiance, prompting the mayor to urge Charles to revoke the charter, "there being not honest men enough in the towne to carry on the government." PRO SP 29/62/4.

49. *True Relation*, p. 15; Hill, *Narrative*, p. 32; PRO SP 29/66/36. A Mr. Smith of Northampton and a Mr. Elose of Chesterfield, Derby, were also reportedly involved. Hill, *Narrative*, p. 35.

50. PRO SP 29/62/34. From Carlisle Christopher Musgrave also reported on the 3rd that letters from William Troughton of London to John Woods had been intercepted bearing postscripts in strange characters. PRO SP 29/62/33.

51. *CSPD 1661–62*, p. 405; PRO SP 29/61/35; *CSPV 1661–64*, pp. 209, 214; *HMC* 6, *Seventh Report*, Appendix, Part I, p. 463.

52. PRO SP 29/63/19, 56, 56.1–5. Cf. *CSPD 1661–62*, pp. 546, 551.

53. PRO SP 29/63/60, 61. Cf. 29/64/66. According to Kenrick's wife, the colonel went to London on 24 October to account for his actions to Nicholas and had not returned by the 8th. However, some seamen at Whitstable, near Canterbury, reported seeing him there. PRO SP 29/62/80. On 25 November Sir Robert Harley was certain that Ludlow was in the Dover area. *HMC* 29, *Portland*, 3:270.

54. *CSPD 1661–62*, pp. 568, 571, 579; *1663–64*, p. 37; PRO SP 29/63/62, 83; 29/64/65.

55. Hill, *Narrative*, pp. 3, 52, 55, 57; *KI* 50 (8–15 December 1662), pp. 804–806; *ST*, 6:240–41, 246, 248; *True Relation*, pp. 13, 20.

56. *MP* 51 (18–25 December 1662), p. 838; *KI* 52 (22–29 December 1662), pp. 839–40; *CSPD 1661–62*, p. 602. As a prisoner, Thomas Ellwood was repulsed by the sight of the hangman parboiling the heads in bay salt and cumin to prevent putrefaction and keep the birds away. Ellwood, *History*, pp. 114–15. According to Nicholas, numerous dissidents decided to emigrate in the aftermath of the executions. Bodl. Carte MSS 47, fol. 385[r].

57. *HMC* 6, *Seventh Report*, Appendix, Part I, p. 463; PRO SP 29/64/73; 29/65/11. Johnston was imprisoned in the Gatehouse on the 16th and transferred to the Tower the following day on suspicion of treason. *CSPD 1661–62*, pp. 592, 595.

58. PRO SP 29/64/73; 29/65/6; 29/67/123.

59. PRO SP 29/65/9. A warrant for Caitness' arrest was issued on 17 December. *CSPD 1661–62*, p. 595.

60. PRO SP 29/65/8, 9, 10.

61. *CR*, s.v. James Forbes; PRO SP 29/65/10; Sprunger, pp. 256, 260. Johnston also accused the Quaker Cornet Billing of being a dangerous man. Ludlow, he said, had been in Kent as well as at the house in Gray's Inn Lane of Cromwell's former chaplain Francis Johnson, a friend of the Congregationalist minister Joshua Sprigge. Sprigge or Vane's widow might, said Johnston, know Ludlow's whereabouts. Johnston admitted knowing the regicides Goffe and Whalley, but not well. PRO SP 29/65/8, 9; 29/67/51.

62. PRO SP 29/65/8. A warrant for Lawry's arrest was issued on 17 December, but he was bonded three days later for £500. He was imprisoned in the Gatehouse at Westminster on 27 December on a charge of treasonable correspondence, and remained in jail for months. PRO SP 29/65/27; *CSPD 1661–62*, p. 595; *1663–64*, p. 27.

63. PRO SP 29/65/8, 11, 26; 29/67/51, 121; *CSPD 1661–62*, p. 592; *1663–64*, p. 27.

64. PRO SP 29/65/9; 29/67/51, 121.1; 29/68/6.

65. PRO SP 29/67/51, 52; 29/68/6, 40. Lawry used the alias Kedman. PRO SP 29/67/120. Lady Warriston also corresponded with Lady Vane. PRO SP 29/67/54.

66. PRO SP 29/65/11; 29/67/51; 29/68/6, 9. MacGuire was in Rotterdam by 27 December. PRO SP 29/86/66. Johnston also provided information against the Scottish Quaker Andrew Robinson, an associate of Lawry's, who carried seditious papers between Edinburgh and London; the bookseller Giles Calvert, from whom Johnston purchased books; Captain Luke Williams, a Baptist and "a furious forward man"; Captain Joseph Sabberton (or Saberton), the earl of Pembroke's steward, who was angry because he lost lands valued at £300 to £400 per annum; Major Hebron of Walton-on-Thames; David Anderson, a Scotsman who had been ejected as vicar of the same town and who was linked to Edward Calamy; and the Congregationalist George Griffith. Johnston also pointed to a group of women whose husbands were prominent radicals: Mrs. William Cawley, Mrs. Edmund Ludlow, Mrs. William Goffe, and Mrs. Edward Whalley. Cawley's wife was living with her brother, a brewer named Ford, in Red Cross Street. PRO SP 29/67/50, 54.1, 120. In January 1663 Carr was with Simpson and MacGuire in Leyden. PRO SP 29/67/54.1.

67. PRO SP 29/67/8, 108; 29/68/6; *CSPV 1661–64*, p. 231; *KI* 5 (26 January–2 February 1663), pp. 65, 80. Ashley erroneously states that Wariston was seized at Rouen in June. *Wildman*, p. 191.

68. PRO SP 29/67/123, 143; 29/68/6; *HMC* 22, *Eleventh Report*, Appendix, Part VII, p. 5; *KI* 25 (15–22 June 1663), pp. 385–86; 31 (27 July–3 August 1663), p. 498; BL Add. MSS 23,119, fol. 79[r]; Bodl. Carte MSS 34, fols. 399[r]–402[r]. In January

the authorities intercepted a letter from William Shaw to Scooler. They also stopped and searched the Irish mail. PRO SP 29/67/37.

69. A warrant for Gibbs' arrest had been issued on 9 January. *CSPD 1663–64*, p. 7 (cf. p. 16); *KI* 4 (19–26 January 1663), p. 50.

70. Arrested with Gibbs and Pardoe were Gibbs' apprentice John Lock and Thomas Freeman, both of whom were Gibbs' intended trustees. *KI* 3 (12–19 January 1663), pp. 45–46; *CSPD 1663–64*, p. 13.

71. *KI* 8 (16–23 February 1663), pp. 127, 148; *MP* 8 (19–26 February 1663), p. 124. Firth's supposition that Baker was reprieved is erroneous. Ludlow, *Memoirs*, 2:342, n. 1.

72. *CSPD 1663–64*, p. 51; Hill, *Narrative*, pp. 32–33; PRO SP 29/76/34; *HMC* 22, *Eleventh Report*, Appendix, Part VII, p. 6; *KI* 28 (6–13 July 1663), pp. 436–37; *CMHS*, 8:215. Elton was also allegedly involved. Hill, *Narrative*, pp. 32–33.

73. *CSPD 1663–64*, pp. 2, 15, 16, 20. Cf. PRO SP 29/73/44. Ferguson was released in May 1663. PRO SP 29/73/45; *CSPD 1663–64*, p. 135.

74. Ludlow, *Memoirs*, 2:342; *CSPV 1661–64*, p. 232 (cf. p. 209).

75. PRO SP 29/62/27. Cf. SP 29/66/36.

76. In December 1661 the lieutenant of Chepstow Castle urged Lord Herbert to arrange for the destruction of a "strong wall" around a house overlooking the castle. It had been built "with an ill Designe" by Lieutenant-Colonel Edward Massey during the civil war. PRO SP 29/45/73.

77. *CSPD 1661–62*, pp. 423–24, 434–35, 454, 505. In November a recent bridge over the river at Canterbury was taken down for security reasons because it led through a breach in the town walls. PRO SP 29/62/80.

78. PRO SP 29/57/78; *CSPD 1661–62*, pp. 505, 511.

79. *HMC* 43, *Fifteenth Report*, Appendix, Part VII, p. 93.

80. Cf. Schwoerer, p. 89.

81. *HMC* 71, *Finch*, 1:206; *CSPD 1661–62*, pp. 483, 495, 509; PRO SP 29/61/58.

82. *CSPD 1661–62*, pp. 490, 525; Latimer, *Annals*, p. 317; PRO SP 29/62/84. In contrast, the Sussex militia was reportedly in good shape. BL Egerton MSS 2538, fol. 184$^r$.

83. CH STT 897; STT 8540; *HMC* 78, *Hastings*, 4:219–20; Reresby, p. 43; PRO SP 29/62/6.

84. PRO SP 29/62/6, 35, 44.

85. *KI* 48 (24 November–1 December 1662), p. 772; Kennet, pp. 830, 833; *MP* 45 (6–13 November 1662), p. 733; PRO SP 29/62/67; *KI* 47 (17–24 November 1662), p. 758.

86. Walker, "Secret Service," p. 229; PRO SP 29/62/1, 82, 90; *CSPD 1661–62*, p. 581.

87. Oliver Heywood, *Life of John Angier of Denton: Together with Angier's Diary*, ed. Ernest Axon, Chetham Society, n.s., 97 (Manchester, 1937), p. 127; Bodl. Carte MSS 47, fol. 359$^r$; George R. Abernathy, Jr., "Clarendon and the Declaration of Indulgence," *JEH* 11 (April 1960); 63; Victor S. Sutch, *Gilbert Sheldon: Architect of Anglican Survival* (The Hague: Martinus Nijhoff, 1973), pp. 86–87; *CCSP*, 5:266.

88. PRO SP 29/67/46.

89. PRO SP 29/65/54; Schwoerer, p. 82; *CSPD 1661–62*, pp. 490, 594–95; Cosin, 2:101–102.

90. *CJ*, 8:440, 442–43, 451; Cobbett, 4:260–63; Abernathy, *JEH*, 11:68–69 (correcting Keith Feiling, "Clarendon and the Act of Uniformity, 1662–3," *EHR* 44 [April 1929]:290); I. M. Green, *The Re-Establishment of the Church of England 1660–1663* (Oxford: Oxford University Press, 1978), pp. 220–21; *HMC* 25, *Le Fleming*, p. 30.

## Notes to Chapter 5

1. David Ogg, *England in the Reign of Charles II* (2nd ed.; London, Oxford, New York: Oxford University Press, 1972), p. 171.
2. Ibid., p. 173; J. C. Beckett, *A Short History of Ireland: From Earliest Times to the Present Day* (6th ed.; London: Hutchinson, 1979), pp. 79–80.
3. PRO SP 63/306/20.
4. St. John D. Seymour, *The Puritans in Ireland 1647–1661* (Oxford: Clarendon Press, 1912), pp. 200–201; J. C. Beckett, *Confrontations: Studies in Irish History* (Totowa, N. J.: Rowman and Littlefield, 1972), p. 81.
5. PRO SP 63/306/1; *HMC* 78, *Hastings*, 4:110.
6. PRO SP 63/306/72.
7. *HMC* 78, *Hastings*, 4:104, 110. Ormond, however was willing to consider some toleration for Congregationalists. Ibid., p. 134.
8. Ibid., pp. 110–11, 114, 128.
9. *The Rawdon Papers*, ed. Edward Berwick (London: John Nichols and Son, 1819), pp. 167–68; *CCSP*, 5:281; Seymour, *Puritans*, p. 197. Cf. Bodl. Carte MSS 45, fol. 458ʳ.
10. *CCSP*, 5:208, 213; *CSPI 1660–62*, p. 426.
11. *CCSP*, 5:281; *HMC* 78, *Hastings*, 4:134; PRO SP 63/306/72; *CSPI 1663–65*, pp. 312–13. Cf. *CSPI 1661–64*, p. 191.
12. PRO SP 63/306/72; 63/308/p. 25.
13. PRO SP 63/308/p. 65; *CSPI 1663–65*, p. 490; *CSPI 1660–62*, p. 423.
14. *HMC* 78, *Hastings*, 4:117, 121; *CSPI 1660–62*, pp. 643–44; PRO SP 63/313/31.
15. *CSPI 1660–62*, p. 437; *KI* 49 (25 November–2 December 1661), pp. 741–43.
16. *KI* 50 (2–9 December 1661), pp. 759–60; 52 (16–23 December 1661), p. 770; *MP* 50 (5–12 December 1661), p. 768; *HMC* 78, *Hastings*, 4:121; *CCSP*, 5:275–76.
17. PRO SP 29/56/19, 78. Cf. Bodl. Carte MSS 45, fol. 117ʳ; 68, fol. 548ʳ.
18. *KI* 47 (17–24 November 1662), pp. 743–44.
19. *CCSP*, 5:294, 298; PRO SP 63/313/33; 63/312/pp. 19–20.
20. PRO SP 63/313/33; *CCSP*, 5:296–97.
21. Parker, *History*, pp. 68–69; *CSPI 1669–70*, p. 454; *HMC* 36, *Ormonde*, o.s., 2:251.
22. Carte, 2:262.
23. PRO SP 63/313/54, 61, 81, 170; *CCSP*, 5:300.
24. PRO SP 63/313/59, 81, 82; *CSPI 1669–70*, p. 446; *CCSP*, 5:302. One of those arrested was (George?) Ayres, against whom there was only one witness. *CCSP* 5:301–302. Another was Captain Thomas Browne. Bodl. Carte MSS 68, fol. 570ʳ.
25. *CCSP*, 5:306; PRO SP 63/313/76, 164.
26. PRO SP 63/313/76; *CCSP*, 5:308–309. Cf. Pepys, 4:100.
27. *Orrery Coll.*, 11:132; *CCSP*, 5:310. An investigation by the bishop of Cork failed to turn up sufficient evidence to arrest anyone in his diocese in connection with the March plot. Bodl. Carte MSS 45, fol. 135ʳ.
28. Bodl. Carte MSS 34, fol. 674ʳ; PRO SP 63/313/132. Cf. SP 63/314/16.
29. PRO SP 63/313/132.
30. *CR*, s.v. Stephen Charnock; PRO SP 63/313/137.
31. PRO SP 63/313/156; Bodl. Carte MSS 68, fol. 580ʳ.
32. *HMC* 7, *Eighth Report*, Appendix, Part I, pp. 623–24; Carter, 2:267–68; Bodl. Carte MSS 68, fol. 572ʳ.
33. PRO SP 63/313/187. The two men from Trim were Ford and Lawrence.
34. PRO SP 63/313/64, 187, 227; *The Horrid Conspiracie of Such Impenitent Traytors as Intended a New Rebellion in the Kingdom of Ireland* (London, 1663), pp. 3–6; *CSPI 1669–70*, pp. 454–55; Carte, 2:268–69); *CCSP*, 5:314.
35. *HMC* 36, *Ormonde*, o.s., 2:251; Bodl. Carte MSS 68, fol. 564ʳ⁻ᵛ; PRO SP 63/313/64; *KI* 24 (8–15 June 1663), p. 376. Cf. PRO SP 63/313/173. Alden says that the

postponement was only for four days, at which time the rebels would rise throughout the kingdom. *HMC* 36, *Ormonde*, o.s., 2:252.

36. PRO SP 63/313/170, 173, 187; 63/309/pp. 103–104; Bodl. Carte MSS 68, fols. 558ʳ, 559ʳ, 572ʳ. Cf. *Orrery Coll.*, 1:134.

37. PRO SP 63/313/164, 165.

38. *CSPI 1669–70*, pp. 453–54; *KI* 23 (1–8 June 1663), pp. 353–55. Ludlow, "Voyce," p. 1135. The troopers were Thomas Ball of Dublin, Robert Davies, John Biddell, John Smullen, John Griffin, and William Bradford. The others were John Foulke (or Fouke, Foulks), son of the colonel of the same name who had once served as governor of Drogheda, James Tanner, the innkeeper Andrew Sturges, William Dodd, a clerk in the discriminator's office, Stephen Radford, Abraham Langton of Dublin, William Bayley, and Samuel Fann (or Farr).

39. PRO SP 63/309/pp. 105–106; Bodl. Carte MSS 68, fols. 560ʳ, 561ʳ; *KI* 23 (1–8 June 1663), pp. 353–55. The other officers were Colonel Daniel Abbott, Lieutenant-Colonel William More (or Moor), Majors Henry Jones and Alexander Staples, and Lieutenants John Ruxton and Richard De la Rock. The others were the Dublin brewer John Chamberlain and John Fook, Esq., recently of county Louth. Among those subsequently arrested were Captains Abraham Hoare and Robert or Richard Holt. PRO SP 63/314/142. Fook was arrested on 24 May, Jones on the 25th, Abbott and De la Rock on the 26th, and Abel Warren on the 30th. A warrant was also issued on the 23rd for the arrest of Colonel William Moore and Captain Abraham Hood. Carte MSS 68, fol. 568ʳ. Moore was arrested the next day. Ibid. 68, fol. 570ʳ.

40. *HMC* 71, *Finch*, 1:263; PRO SP 63/313/211, 225, 227, 243.

41. PRO SP 63/313/182, 225.

42. Carte, 2:262. According to Vernon, five of the six members were Presbyterians, and the sixth was a Congregationalist. PRO SP 63/313/227.

43. Parker, *History*, p. 75.

44. Carte (2:267) suggests that the rebel soldiers, unable to have Ludlow as their commander, wanted Sir Theophilus Jones or Colonel Shapcote.

45. *HMC* 36, *Ormonde*, o.s., 2:252–53.

46. PRO SP 63/313/187, 387; Adair, p. 272; William Thomas Latimer, *A History of the Irish Presbyterians* (2nd ed.; Belfast; James Cleeland and William Mullan, 1902), pp. 137, 139.

47. PRO SP 63/313/187; 63/314/142.

48. PRO SP 63/313/187; 63/314/142; Carte, 2:266.

49. PRO SP 63/313/168, 187; 63/314/142; Bodl. Carte MSS 68, fol. 566ʳ.

50. PRO SP 63/313/187; Carte, 2:267 Ludlow, *Memoirs*, 2:443. Edward Warren apparently had three brothers: Abel, William, and John. Cf. *BDBR*, s.v. Edward Warren.

51. Alden deprecates Blood's role, saying he was only an agent who ran errands. It is probable that although Blood conceived the plot, he had to share power with others, especially the M. P.s who supported the design. *HMC* 36, *Ormonde*, o.s., 2:252.

52. Carte, 2:269; PRO SP 63/313/207, 209.1–3, 220, 220.1; Parker, *History*, p. 72; *Misc. Aul.*, p. 291. Carr's wife presented testimony in June from magistrates in Rotterdam that he had been there the preceding six months, but witnesses placed him in Ulster on 23 May. PRO SP 63/314/9; *Misc. Aul.*, p. 291.

53. *KI* 25 (15–22 June 1663), p. 386; *CCSP*, 5:317; *CSPI 1669–70*, pp. 476–77; *CSPI 1666–69*, pp. 591–92; *CSPI 1663–65*, pp. 303, 322; Richard Bagwell, *Ireland Under the Stuarts and During the Interregnum*, 3 vols. (London: Longmans, Green, and Co., 1906–1916), 3:38; *HMC* 63, *Egmont*, 2:12. Bodl. Carte MSS 35, fols. 425ʳ⁻ᵛ, 429ʳ; ibid. 47, fol. 193ʳ. There was only sufficient evidence against Shapcote, Boyd, Hoare, and Holt to try them for misprision. Of the two witnesses

against Staples for high treason, one (John Hart) refused to take an oath in court. Bodl. Carte MSS 68, fol. 572$^r$.

54. *CSPI 1663–65*, p. 691; *CSPI 1666–69*, pp. 106–107, 150; *CSPI 1669–70*, pp. 26, 53, 57.
55. PRO SP 63/313/207, 219; *CCSP*, 5:325.
56. PRO SP 63/313/217, 243, 245, 249; *KI* 27 (29 June–6 July 1663), p. 240 (which erroneously gives the date as 24 June).
57. PRO SP 63/313/200; 63/314/2.
58. *KI* 28 (6–13 July 1663), pp. 436, 451–52; 29 (13–20 July 1663), pp. 442–43; PRO SP 63/313/197, 200; 63/314/7, 11. Shapcote and Boyd were tried in September. *Int.* 4 (21 September 1663), p. 27.
59. PRO SP 63/314/24; Bodl. Carte MSS 68, fols. 574$^{r-v}$, 576$^r$–578$^r$.
60. PRO SP 63/314/17, 24, 30; *CCSP*, 5:320–21; *MP* 30 (23–30 July 1663), pp. 480–82; *KI* 30 (20–27 July 1663), p. 471; 31 (27 July–3 August 1663), p. 484–85.
61. PRO SP 63/314/12.
62. *CSPI 1663–65*, p. 294; *HMC* 7, *Eighth Report*, Appendix, Part I, p. 502; *Int.* 14 (30 November 1663), pp. 105–107; James Seaton Reid, *History of the Presbyterian Church in Ireland*, 3 vols. (new ed.; Belfast: William Mullan, 1867), 2:299, n. 7; R. H., "Remarks on the Life and Death of the Famed Mr. Blood," *Som. Tr.*, 8:439–40. According to one account, Lecky changed clothes with his wife in order to escape, but was captured when he left his hiding place in search of beer. PRO SP 29/84/20.
63. PRO SP 63/313/225, 231; *HMC* 36, *Ormonde*, o.s., 2:253.
64. Carte, 2:323–24; Parker, *History*, pp. 75–77; *CSPI 1666–69*, pp. 707–708; Walker, "Secret Service," pp. 217, 224–25. Cf. PRO SP 29/79/7.
65. PRO SP 63/313/166, 167, 176, 186, 192.
66. *KI* 24 (8–15 June 1663), p. 376; PRO SP 63/313/192. Cf. *CCSP*, 5:316.
67. PRO SP 63/313/192; Reid, *History*, 2:298, n. 6; *CSPI 1669–70*, p. 547; *CSPI 1663–65*, pp. 659–60; *Int.* 94 (20 November 1665), p. 1151; *Oxford Gazette* 1 (16 November 1665); 3 (7 December 1665), p. 18; 4 (23–27 November 1665); *CCSP*, 5:515.
68. PRO SP 63/313/168, 247; *Misc. Aul.*, pp. 286–87.
69. PRO SP 29/75/105, 108; 63/312/p. 146.
70. Cf. Carte, 2:259, 266–67.
71. PRO SP 63/313/168, 169, 186.
72. PRO SP 63/313/182, 219, 246.
73. PRO SP 63/313/233; 63/314/59; Carte, 2:271; *CSPD 1663–64*, pp. 255, 267, 288.
74. PRO SP 63/312/p. 102; 63/313/217; *CSPI 1663–65*, p. 344.
75. PRO SP 63/313/226, 233, 245; *Misc. Aul.*, p. 289; *Orrery Coll.*, 1:139; *HMC* 20, *Eleventh Report*, Appendix, Part V, p. 11.
76. *CSPI 1663–65*, pp. 299–300; *HMC* 36, *Ormonde*, n.s., 3:125–26; Bodl. Carte MSS 68, fols. 594$^r$, 595$^r$.
77. *Misc. Aul.*, p. 329; PRO SP 63/313/168; *CCSP*, 5:503; *Orrery Coll.*, 1:171, 192–93.
78. *CSPI 1663–65*, pp. 312–13.
79. *HMC* 36, *Ormonde*, n.s., 3:57–58; PRO SP 63/313/245; *Misc. Aul.*, pp. 292–93.
80. PRO SP 63/309/pp. 123–25; 63/314/5, 20; Bodl. Carte MSS 68, fols. 596$^r$, 597$^r$; ibid. 80, fol. 679$^r$.
81. *Misc. Aul.*, p. 297; PRO SP 63/312/p. 145; 63/314/59.
82. Adair, pp. 274–76, 281; Latimer, *History*, p. 138. The twelve ministers arrested in Antrim were the Presbyterians William Keyes of Belfast, Thomas Hall of Larne, John Douglas of Broughshane, Robert Hamilton of Killead, James Cunningham of Antrim, John Cowthard (or Couthart) of Drumal, John Shaw of Ahoghill, James Shaw of Carnmoney, and Robert Hogsyard (or Hogsyeard) of Ballyrashane, the Baptist Andrew White, and the Congregationalist Timothy Taylor.

Hall and John and James Shaw left Ireland when given the chance, and Massereene intervened on behalf of Cunningham. By November 1663, Keyes had been sent to Galway and Cowthard to Athlone; Hamilton and Cunningham were in prison at Carrickfergus; White had been transplanted to England, and Hall, Douglas, Hogsyard, the Shaws, and Hugh Wilson to Scotland; and Taylor had been licensed (with Patrick Adair and others) to stay in his home in Ireland. Bodl. Carte MSS 45, fol. 465$^r$. Cf. ibid. 45, fol. 446$^r$.

83. Adair, pp. 277–79, 283; Latimer, *History*, pp. 138–39; Reid, *History*, 2:302, n. 12. The Presbyterians from Down who were jailed were William Richardson of Killyleagh, John Greg, John Drysdale (or Drisdaile) of Portaferry, Gilbert Ramsay (or Ramsey) of Bangor, James Gordon of Comber, Alexander Hutcheson (or Hutchinson) of Saintfield, and Andrew Stewart. Four other Ulster ministers were arrested by 7 August 1663; John Craigheid, James Wallis, John Hamilton, and Robert Wilson. Bodl. Carte MSS 45, fol. 145$^r$. Cf. the complaint of Bishop Jeremy Taylor in June: ibid. 45, fol. 141$^r$.

84. See, for example, PRO SP 63/313/167, 172, 174, 175, 198, 221.

85. Bagwell, *Ireland*, 3:35; *BDBR*, s.v. Daniel Abbott; *Orm. Coll.*, 1:160–61.

86. PRO SP 29/92/94; 29/94/35.

87. *HMC* 78, *Hastings*, 2:365–66; *CSPI 1663–65* pp. 454–55, 459.

## Notes to Chapter 6

1. PRO SP 29/65/16, 19, 20, 33, 33.1–3, 34. The Bristol dissidents allegedly included Captain Morse, William Cole, Henry Ford, James North, Mr. Wilcox, and an apothecary's servant named Thomas Wilde (or Wild); John Elliott and Thomas Hayes were among the Somerset militants.

2. PRO SP 29/65/63, 63.1; 29/67/25; 29/86/20.3. Firth and Davies' assertion that Gregory "was long a prisoner for his part in Lambert's rising" appears to be an error. Firth & Davies, p. 163.

3. PRO SP 29/65/63.1; 29/86/20, 20.2–4.

4. PRO SP 29/69/48–50, 63, 64; 29/86/20.3; *CSPD 1663–64*, p. 74.

5. PRO SP 29/65/66; 29/67/3, 10; *CSPD 1663–64*, pp. 2, 7. PRO SP 29/90/28 and 41 are wrongly catalogued; they belong to 1663, not 1664.

6. PRO SP 29/65/57; 29/67/22, 22.1, 83, 84, 84.1; Henry, p. 129.

7. PRO SP 29/67/7.1.

8. PRO SP 29/65/89.

9. PRO SP 29/67/12, 74, 82.

10. PRO SP 29/67/68, 112, 113.

11. PRO SP 29/68/35, 35.1–4, 48.1; *CSPD 1663–64*, p. 52.

12. PRO SP 29/65/15; 29/67/105; 29/86/43; *CMHS*, 8:213.

13. PRO SP 29/67/39, 45, 73, 90.

14. PRO SP 29/64/38, 38.1, 39; 29/67/36; Lister, 3:230–31; *CMHS*, 8:213.

15. PRO SP 29/61/121; *CSPD 1661–62*, p. 606; *CSPD 1663–64*, p. 14; Bodl. Carte MSS 47, fols. 367$^r$, 460$^r$–461$^r$. A warrant for Bagshaw's transfer to Southsea Castle was issued on 31 March 1664. *CSPD 1663–64*, p. 536.

16. Edward Bagshaw, *The Great Question Concerning Things Indifferent in Religious Worship* (London, 1660), pp. 2, 13, 16.

17. Bagshaw, *Signes of the Times: or Prognosticks of Future Judgements* (London, 1662), sig. A4$^r$, pp. 12–13.

18. *CR*, s.v.

19. PRO SP 29/70/56.

20. PRO SP 29/63/34.1.

21. PRO SP 29/62/71; 29/63/34.1; Cosin, 2:98; *CSPD 1661–62*, p. 549.

22. *KI* 48 (24 November–1 December 1662), p. 774; PRO SP 29/63/2, 3; 29/70/58; Cosin, 2:104.

23. PRO SP 29/70/13. Cf. BL Add. MSS 33,770, fol. 71$^{r-v}$; Robert Surtees, *The History and Antiquities of the County Palatine of Durham*, 4 vols. (London: J. Nichols and Son, 1816–20), 2:391.

24. BL Add. MSS 33,770, fol. 37$^{r}$; PRO SP 29/70/58; 29/96/70.1; Walker, "Yorkshire Plot," p. 351; Surtees, *Durham*, 2:389. Witherington's son and servant got their revenge in mid-1665 when they imprisoned Ellerington on a charge of trespass. PRO SP 29/127/33.

25. Ashley, *Wildman*, pp. 192–93; PRO SP 29/96/69; 29/97/33.1; 29/98/4; 29/115/36.1. The offer to Ellerington was made by Lewis Frost, Edward Fenwick, Captain Edward Shepperdson, and others. PRO SP 29/97/33.1.

26. Greaves, *Saints and Rebels*, chap. 1; PRO SP 29/67/133; 29/68/75, 75.1; 29/69/5, 33. Nevertheless, the arrest of Quakers continued. PRO SP 29/69/13; *CMHS*, 8:213.

27. PRO SP 29/70/38; *CMHS*, 8:215 (which refers to Thomas Cole of Southampton; this appears to be William Cole of the same city).

28. *CSPD 1663–64*, pp. 77, 193, 194, 204, 244, 245; *HMC* 22, *Eleventh Report*, Appendix, Part VII, p. 6; PRO SP 29/74/58; 29/90/112. Gunning was an agitator in London and Southwark. PRO SP 29/88/62.

29. PRO SP 29/76/33.2–3, 33.7; *CSPD 1663–64*, p. 371. Cf. PRO SP 29/109/63.

30. *CSPD 1663–64*, p. 144; PRO SP 29/73/12, 12.1–2; 29/74/32; *CCSP*, 5:309.

31. PRO SP 29/74/4. Whiting suggests that this episode was part of the northern conspiracy. C. E. Whiting, "The Great Plot of 1663," *Durham University Journal* 22 (March 1920): 159. This undocumented article is very unreliable.

32. *CSPD 1663–64*, p. 83; PRO SP 29/70/46; 29/88/44.

33. *CSPD 1663–64*, pp. 98, 161, 163, 175; PRO SP 29/71/77; 29/75/98; 29/77/26. Cf. *CSPD 1663–64*, pp. 179, 202, 211, 250, 258; *CCSP*, 5:317; *HMC* 22, *Eleventh Report*, Appendix, Part VII, pp. 6–7.

34. PRO SP 29/70/49; 29/72/73; 29/74/38; Pepys, 4:163.

35. PRO SP 29/74/48, 48.2; 29/75/115. Cf. 29/75/54, 54.1.

36. PRO SP 29/74/48.2, 66; 29/75/115; 29/76/46. Cf. *CR*, s.v. John Reynolds.

37. PRO SP 29/74/66, 66.2; 29/76/46; 29/77/28. A tally in August 1662 turned up 1,329 names. PRO SP 29/58/73.

38. PRO SP 29/75/11; 63/313/224.

39. PRO SP 29/75/99, 100, 106, 106.1, 107, 109; 29/77/7. Cf. SP 29/75/85, 85.1–4.

40. Frank Bate, *The Declaration of Indulgence 1672* (London: University Press of Liverpool, 1908), p. 40; Abbott, "Conspiracy," pp. 520–21.

41. PRO SP 29/76/55; 29/78/43, 93; Pepys, 4:271.

42. PRO SP 29/78/80; CH HA 8542, 8543; *HMC* 55, *Var. Coll.*, 1:145.

43. *CSPD 1663–64*, pp. 249–50; PRO SP 29/79/60, 90; 29/80/19, 20.

44. PRO SP 29/80/100, 101; *Newes* 2 (10 September 1663), p. 16.

45. PRO SP 29/80/99; 29/81/2. Cf. *CSPV 1661–64*, p. 265.

46. *HMC* 19, *Townshend*, p. 26; *HMC* 43, *Fifteenth Report*, Appendix, Part VII, pp. 96–97; PRO SP 29/78/109; 29/79/103 (cf. 29/448/96); *CSPD 1663–64*, p. 283.

47. Edward Hyde, earl of Clarendon, "The Continuation of the Life of Edward Earl of Clarendon," *ad cal. The History of the Rebellion and Civil Wars in England* (Oxford: Oxford University Press, 1843), p. 1114; *LJ*, 11:582.

48. *Newes* 11 (12 November 1663), pp. 82–83; *Int.* 15 (7 December 1663), pp. 114–15.

49. *Int.* 9 (26 October 1663), pp. 67–68; [George Wither], *Vox & Lacrimae Anglorum* (1668), p. 13; Ludlow, *Memoirs*, 2:376; James Ralph, *The History of England*, 2 vols. (London: Daniel Browne, 1744–46), 1:98; Ashley, *Wildman*, pp. 192–96; Walker, "Yorkshire Plot," p. 358. Cf. Francis Nicholson, "The Kaber Rigg Plot,

1663," *Transactions of the Cumberland & Westmorland Antiquarian & Archaeological Society*, new ser., 11 (1911): 232.

50. Parker, *History*, pp. 77–82; *Misc. Aul.*, pp. 319–20; Abbott, "Conspiracy," pp. 521–25; Henry Gee, "The Derwentdale Plot, 1663," *TRHS*, 3rd ser., 11 (1917): 125, 132; Gee, "A Durham and Newcastle Plot in 1663," *Archaeologia Aeliana*, 3rd ser., 14 (1917): 146; Whiting, "Great Plot," pp. 157, 159.

51. PRO SP 29/103/60.

52. PRO SP 29/70/13; 29/103/60; *Newes* 4 (14 January 1664), p. 40 (which records the claim of Robert Walters that planning began about October 1662).

53. PRO SP 29/81/77; 29/86/69; 29/97/98; 29/115/38. The committee is discussed later in this section.

54. PRO SP 29/85/2; 29/92/26; 29/107/89; *Int.* 1 (31 August 1663), p. 6; Parker, *History*, p. 66.

55. PRO SP 29/90/95; 29/95/111; 29/98/91; 29/102/73; *DCY*, p. 103; Firth & Davies, p. 480. Sergeant Richardson was later described as a captain. *CSPD 1663–64*, p. 347.

56. PRO SP 29/93/9; 29/98/91. Richardson (M.A., Emmanuel College, Cambridge) was admitted as an extra-licentiate of the College of Physicians on 10 November 1662. William Munk, *The Roll of the Royal College of Physicians of London*, 3 vols. (2nd ed.; London: Royal College of Physicians, 1878), 1:307.

57. BL Add. MSS 33,770, fols. 33ᵛ, 34ᵛ; PRO SP 29/86/70. When pressed, Edward Richardson allegedly told Robert Atkinson that the council included Ludlow, Goffe, Salway, "and others of Great Estates," though Atkinson at this point was trying to mislead his interrogators. PRO SP 29/98/91. According to Walters, in the summer of 1663 the council moved to Oxforshire to be closer to Salway. BL Add. MSS 33,770, fol. 34ᵛ.

58. *Som. Tr.*, 8:441; PRO SP 29/97/97; 29/115/36.1, 38. John Lockyer is at times erroneously referred to as Nicholas or Michael Lockyer. Cf., for example, *CSPD 1663–64*, p. 334; *Int.* 12 (16 November 1663), pp. 89–90; PRO SP 29/121/132 (for Cary, alias Carew). Atkinson once carried a message from Jones to Spurway and Cary. PRO SP 29/115/38.

59. PRO SP 29/84/64.

60. Joseph Crowder, an active conspirator, is probably the agent involved, though Joshua and Timothy Crowder were government witnesses in the January 1664 treason trials. *Newes* 4 (14 Janury 1664), p. 40.

61. PRO SP 29/81/77; 29/94/101; 29/97/98; 29/115/38; *Misc. Aul.*, p. 345; *CCSP*, 5:343; Bodl. Carte MSS 46, fol. 174ᵛ. Richardson told Walters that Colonel Sankey "miss'd of his design upon Dublin." There is, however, no hard evidence to link Sankey to the Dublin plot. BL Add. MSS 33,770, fol. 35ᵛ.

62. PRO SP 29/94/64.1; 29/96/112; 29/97/63; 29/98/91; Bodl. Carte MSS 81, fol. 197ʳ; BL Add. MSS 33,770, fols. 5ᵛ, 6ʳ⁻ᵛ (which indicates that the declaration was sent to Captain Roger Jones in London), 8ʳ, 28ʳ, 33ʳ, 37ᵛ, 38ʳ. The declaration apparently went to London for approval at least twice. Once it was carried by John Atkinson and once by Roger Jones. Nathaniel Strange was one of those who saw it. PRO SP 29/97/98; 29/115/38.

63. BL Add. MSS 38,856, fols. 79ʳ–80ʳ. Cf. Evan Price, *Eye-Salve for England* (London, 1667), pp. 4–6; PRO SP 29/84/64; *Som. Tr.*, 8:441.

64. PRO SP 29/81/77; BL Add. MSS 33,770, fol. 33ʳ. Cooke had served under Captain Thomas Lilburne. BL Add. MSS 33,770, fols. 2ᵛ, 3ʳ (where he is identified as a captain).

65. PRO SP 29/80/137; 29/98/1; 29/100/53; *CMHS*, 8:214; *DCY*, p. 108.

66. PRO SP 29/85/103; 29/95/13; 29/97/98; 29/99/110.1; cf. 29/96/33; BL Add. MSS 33,770, fol. 29ᵛ; Bodl. Clarendon MSS 75, fol. 447ᵛ. The date is erroneously given as 11 June in SP 29/81/77.

67. PRO SP 29/97/98. According to an anonymous report, by late June Paul Hobson or his wife had given a copy of the declaration to the king. Hobson supposedly then told a rebel messenger what had been done and urged the rebels to rise by 10 August. There is no reliable evidence to support such an unlikely occurrence. PRO SP 29/97/63.

68. Walker, "Yorkshire Plot," p. 352; PRO SP 29/82/108; 29/98/91; BL Add. MSS 33,770, fol. 3$^v$.

69. PRO SP 29/82/108; 29/97/98; 29/99/110.1; BL Add. MSS 33,770, fol. 47$^r$; Bodl. Clarendon MSS 75, fol. 447$^v$. This Thomas Fletcher is not to be confused with the Thomas Fletcher imprisoned in June 1662 for supplying papers to Sir Robert Wallop in the Tower. PRO SP 29/74/58; 29/192/90; 29/202/83; 29/217/34. Robert Atkins was recruited by Marsden, Robert Atkinson, and Dr. Edward Richardson. SP 29/93/20.1. One of those in Scotland who corresponded with the northern radicals was Captain Hume. PRO SP 29/167/5, 5.1.

70. PRO SP 29/98/91.

71. PRO SP 29/93/11; 29/95/113; 29/97/98; 29/99/110.1; 29/115/36.1, 38; Reresby, p. 47; Bodl. Clarendon MSS 75, fol. 447$^v$. Oates was recruited by Greathead. BL Add. MSS 33,770, fol. 6$^{r-v}$.

72. PRO SP 29/77/29, 50. According to subsequent testimony, one of Fairfax's servants was approached by William Hurd just before Buckingham arrived in Yorkshire; Hurd wanted to ascertain whether Fairfax would join the rebels. He of course did not. DCY, p. 119. Walters subsequently confessed that the plotters had hoped for Fairfax's help, "but they judged him a Man not to be meddled with & that he would discover all if he should be spoke to in it." BL Add. MSS 33,770, fol. 35$^v$.

73. PRO SP 29/77/51; Newes 4 (14 January 1664), p. 40; BL Add. MSS 33,770, fol. 34$^v$.

74. PRO SP 29/81/77; 29/82/47; 29/83/42. Lewis Frost of Durham was responsible for bringing weapons by ship from London. Robert Atkins' wife was also apparently involved in procuring gunpowder. BL Add. MSS 33,770, fols. 15$^v$–16$^r$, 34$^r$; cf. fol. 23$^v$.

75. PRO SP 29/83/42; 29/95/113; Reresby, p. 47; Bodl. Clarendon MSS 81, fol. 59$^r$.

76. PRO SP 29/78/6; 29/82/47.

77. PRO SP 29/78/16.

78. CSPD 1663–64, p. 226; PRO SP 29/93/9; 29/95/113; 29/98/80, 91; BL Add. MSS 33,770, fol. 9$^r$.

79. PRO SP 29/78/52, 53, 63, 71; 29/81/77. For other recruiting in August see SP 29/103/124, 124.1–2.

80. HMC 25, Le Fleming, p. 31; cf. p. 30. See also Arthur John Hawkes, Sir Roger Bradshaigh of Haigh (Manchester: Lancashire and Cheshire Antiquarian Society, 1945), pp. 28–29, for preparations in Lancashire.

81. PRO SP 29/78/81. BL Add. MSS 33,770, fol. 32$^r$. There is no reliable evidence for Whiting's suggestion that Ludlow may have made one or more secret visits to England. "Great Plot," p. 156–57.

82. PRO SP 29/78/71; 29/81/77; 29/97/98; 29/99/110.1.

83. PRO SP 29/93/9; 29/98/131; John Angier, "Diary," ad cal. Oliver Heywood, Life of John Angier of Denton, ed. Ernest Axon (Manchester: Chetham Society, n.s., vol. 97, 1937), pp. 131–32.

84. There is some confusion in the evidence as to the dating and sequence of the next two meetings. Gower's papers record a meeting at Stank House on 18 August, a Tuesday. (PRO SP 29/81/77). However John and Robert Atkinson's testimony indicates that a week after the Lumbey meeting the rebels gathered on a Tuesday at Leeds, and that the Stank House meeting followed at a later date. (SP 29/93/11; 29/97/98; cf. 29/99/110.1). Jeremiah Marsden attended the Leeds

meeting and then left no later than 2 September for London, not returning to the north until late September; he was not at the Stank House. This makes a suggested date of 20 September for the Leeds meeing (SP 29/80/140) virtually impossible. The gathering at Leeds probably occurred on Tuesday, 18 August, the date Gower erroneously recorded for the Stank House meeting.

85. PRO SP 29/93/11; 29/97/98; 29/99/110.l; Bodl. Carte MSS 81, fol. 218ʳ.

86. PRO SP 29/80/140; *BDBR*, s.v. Thomas Wogan; *Misc. Aul.*, p. 324.

87. PRO SP 29/80/139; 29/81/77; 29/82/107; 29/93/11; 29/97/98; 29/99/110.1; 29/115/38.

88. PRO SP 29/82/108; 29/103/10; 29/109/61; BL Add. MSS 33,770, fol. 3ʳ⁻ᵛ.

89. One source says they went in August. PRO SP 29/85/103.

90. PRO SP 29/81/77; 29/85/103; 29/92/58.1; 29/97/98; 29/103/59; 29/115/38; 29/117/66; BL Add. MSS 33,770, fols. 7ᵛ, 11ʳ, 31ʳ.

91. PRO SP 29/80/107, 114, 115.

92. PRO SP 29/83/51.1. Cf. SP 29/83/51. Greathead was rewarded with £100 in December 1663, and the right to the excise farm in Yorkshire when the present farm expired. In May 1665 the king wanted him to have the excise farm in Suffolk. PRO SP 29/86/46; *CSPD 1663–64*, p. 383; *CSPD 1664–65*, p. 366.

93. PRO SP 29/80/122; 29/83/12; 29/96/69, 70; *Newes* 4 (14 January 1664), pp. 38–39; Walker, "Yorkshire Plot," p. 353.

94. PRO SP 29/82/106 (erroneously dated 1662); 29/84/64; 29/85/51; 29/96/112; 29/98/80. According to Walters, Richardson too had distrusted Hobson. BL Add. MSS 33,770, fol 35ʳ.

95. PRO SP 29/81/77; BL Add. MSS 33,770, fol. 26ʳ.

96. Walker, "Secret Service," p. 216; PRO SP 29/79/99; 29/80/17, 18; *Int.* 1 (31 August 1663), p. 6.

97. PRO SP 29/80/17, 109; 29/82/16. 1–2.

98. PRO SP 29/84/65, 65.1; *CCSP*, 5:346, 350, 353–54; Lister, 3:262–63.

99. PRO SP 29/80/121, 122. There was some talk of a plan to surprise London when the new term began by having some 5,000 rebels enter the City in the guise of petitioners; their task would have been the seizure of the Tower. BL Add. MSS 33,770, fol. 20ʳ.

100. PRO SP 29/85/103; 29/97/98; 29/99/21, 110.1; 29/101/29.1; 29/103/59; BL Add. MSS 33,770, fols. 6ᵛ, 10ʳ. John Atkinson confessed that the group met on 6 October at Pannal and the following day at Gildersome. SP 29/97/98.

101. PRO SP 29/92/58.1; 29/101/29.1, 33.1; 29/103/59; BL Add. MSS 33,770, fols. 6ᵛ, 7ᵛ, 8ʳ, 9ʳ⁻ᵛ, 34ʳ. Lockyer helped raise necessary funds. SP 29/115/38. Charles Carr of Pannal subsequently confessed that "there was a Banke of money at London to maintaine the Warr." SP 29/86/69; cf. *Misc. Aul.*, p. 310; *Int.* 5 (18 January 1664), p. 42. Ralph Rymer offered similar testimony. BL Add. MSS 33,770, fol. 32ᵛ. Presbyterians and Baptists contributed the funds. SP 29/82/37.2. There were also funds at Leeds. BL Add. MSS 33,770. fol. 27ᵛ.

102. PRO SP 29/81/77; 29/82/54; 29/85/102, 103; BL Add. MSS 33,770, fols. 8ʳ, 10ʳ, 11ʳ.

103. PRO SP 29/81/7, 8, 15, 19, 58, 69; *Newes* 7 (15 October 1663), p. 54.

104. PRO SP 29/80/110; 29/81/17, 57. Cf. SP 29/82/51. Duckenfield's brother, Major John Duckenfield, returned from Ireland in early October, but the magistrates failed to apprehend him as he passed through Cheshire en route to London. SP 29/81/75.

105. *HMC 33, Lonsdale*, p. 93; PRO SP 29/81/44.1, 44, 45, 53, 60, 61.1, 62, 63, 79, 81; *HMC 29, Portland*, 2:144; *Int.* 8 (19 October 1663), pp. 62–63.

106. PRO SP 29/81/57, 65, 71, 74, 80, 92, 96, 99; 29/82/88; Walker, "Yorkshire Plot," p. 355. At Bristol the general alarm remained in effect the rest of the year. *Int.* 18 (28 December 1663), p. 138.

107. PRO SP 29/81/60, 77; *Int.* 8 (19 October 1663), p. 60, Cf. SP 29/97/98. Sawrey was freed on bond in May 1664. SP 29/98/57. Even the minister Philip Henry was arrested and interrogated. Henry, pp. 148–49.

108. PRO SP 29/81/53, 54, 55, 61, 70.1; *Misc. Aul.* p. 302.

109. PRO SP 29/81/70, 70.1; Reresby, pp. 47–48. According to Colonel Freschville, however, Buckingham had 2,000 foot and 900 horse. SP 29/81/66.

110. PRO SP 29/81/61; 29/83/111.1; *Int.* 9 (26 October 1663), pp. 1–2.

111. PRO SP 29/81/77, 84, 111, 112 132; 29/98/131; *Int.* 9 (26 October 1663), p. 66; 27 (4 April 1664), p. 224; BL Add. MSS 25,463, fol. 168$^r$; 33,770, fols. 2$^r$, 35$^v$. Eighty armed horsemen were spotted at Carlton, not far from Topcliffe. SP 29/81/106. One early report indicated that Smithson would command at Northallerton. SP 29/81/84. At one time, plans called for Walters to command the North Riding and Greathead the West Riding. SP 29/98/91. According to Denham, forty or fifty horse were actually expected at Northallerton, though they were supposed to have been reinforced by another fifty from Durham. Another source indicated that as many as 800 horse and dragoons were expected. BL Add. MSS 33,770, fol. 6$^v$.

112. PRO SP 29/81/77, 83, 131; 29/82/37.1; *DCY*, pp. 111–12; BL Add. MSS 25,463, fols. 167$^r$–169$^v$; 33,770, fols. 6$^v$–7$^v$, 12$^v$, 17$^v$, 27$^v$, 47$^v$. Several rebels claimed that only 25 or 30 showed up, but other estimates ranged from 150 to 300. Two lists of rebels indicate 20 and 29 names respectively; when combined, 25 persons are mentioned. They were joined by 11 others from the Holbeck-Leeds area. BL Add. MS 25,463, fol. 167$^{r-v}$; 33,770, fol. 47$^v$. A later newspaper report claimed that the rebels were scared away by the militia. *Newes* 9 (29 October 1663), p. 66. The ejected minister of Holbeck, the Presbyterian Robert Armitage, was accused of supporting the rebels. BL Add. MSS 33,770, fols. 24$^v$ –25$^r$.

113. *DCY*, pp. 102–108; PRO SP 29/83/46, 80.1–2; 29/84/28.2; 29/86/19; 29/93/10; 29/94/116; 29/95/1, 2; 29/98/91; Bodl. Carte MSS 81, fol. 222$^r$; Gilbert Burton, *The Life of Sir Philip Musgrave, Bart.* (Carlisle: Samuel Jefferson, 1840), p. 42. Again, estimates of the number at Kaber Rigg differ. The number of horse is fairly constant at nineteen or twenty, but Atkinson's nephew, John Waller, claimed that the *total* number of rebels was only seventeen. *DCY*, p. 107. A claim that there were fifty foot at Kaber Rigg appears to be erroneous.

114. PRO SP 29/82/37.2; 29/143/37; *DCY*, pp. 110–11. Mason was also supposed to have commanded the Durham rebels. Bodl. Carte MSS 81, fol. 211$^r$.

115. *HMC* 29, *Portland*, 2:144; PRO SP 29/81/82, 100; 29/82/37; *Misc. Aul.*, pp. 303, 307–308. Perhaps deliberately intending to mislead, the *Newes* announced that Belasyse had only 200 men to offer Buckingham. *Newes* 8 (22 October 1663), p. 60.

116. *Newes* 8 (22 October 1663), pp. 58–59, 62.

117. PRO SP 29/81/91, 97, 130; 29/83/48; *Misc. Aul.*, p. 305; Pepys, 4:374; Bodl. Carte MSS 46, fol. 98$^r$. Cf. SP 29/82/85, 86.

118. PRO SP 29/82/26; *Misc. Aul.*, pp. 319–20.

119. PRO SP 29/83/55; *Misc. Aul.*, pp. 308–309, 327; Bodl. Carte MSS 46, fols. 108$^r$, 116$^v$, 146$^v$; 81, fol. 197$^r$. Cf. SP 29/84/13; *Misc. Aul.*, pp. 318–19. On 14 and 16 November Musgrave arrested fifty suspicious persons in Cumberland. Nicholson, "Plot," pp. 218–19.

120. *Int.* 11 (9 November 1663), p. 82; *Newes* 11 (12 November 1663), p. 82; 12 (19 November 1663), p. 91; Hawkes, *Bradshaigh*, pp. 29–30. The rebels sighted in the Keighley area were dispersed by 10 November. *Int.* 12 (16 November 1663), p. 91.

121. PRO SP 29/83/13, 46; 29/84/23; *Newes* 12 (19 November 1663), pp. 91–92. Cf. SP 29/81/129.

122. PRO SP 29/82/87, 103. Cf. SP 29/81/93; 29/82/7, 16; 29/83/69, 81; *Newes* 8 (22 October 1663), pp. 58–59.

123. PRO SP 29/84/27. Cf. SP 29/83/57; 29/85/10; *Newes* 11 (12 November 1663), p. 82.

124. *Newes* 8 (22 October 1663), pp. 60–61, 84; PRO SP 29/82/88; 29/83/98; *Int.* 16 (14 December 1663), pp. 121–22; 18 (28 December 1663), p. 138. Cf. SP 29/81/91, 98; 29/82/52, 81; *Newes* 8 (22 October 1663), pp. 58–61; *Int.* 10 (2 November 1663), pp. 74–75.

125. PRO SP 29/83/7, 55, 56, 111; 29/84/103; *Int.* 10 (2 November 1663), pp. 74–75.

126. PRO SP 29/81/94; 29/84/67; 29/85/49.

127. PRO SP 29/81/77 (which mentions messengers to two more counties, Essex and Oxfordshire); 29/94/64.1; 29/99/110.1, 169; 29/107/29; Bodl. Clarendon MSS 75, fol. 447$^{r-v}$ (which refers to more than a hundred agitators).

128. PRO SP 29/83/47; 29/85/48; 29/97/18; 29/99/21, 110; 29/100/119; 29/103/49.1; 29/105/116; 29/143/37; *Int.* 21 (20 March 1665), p. 184; *Newes* 34 (28 April 1664), p. 280; *CSPD 1663–64*, p. 331; 1664–65, p. 255.

129. PRO SP 29/288/102; 29/290/108. Philip Wild of Derbyshire was sentenced to death at the Derby assizes in March 1665 for recruiting troops, but he was pardoned in June. SP 29/115/56, 57, 58, 58.1; 29/125/56, 56.1; *CSPD 1664–65*, p. 448.

130. PRO SP 29/192/90, 137; 29/193/22; 29/211/126; *CSPD 1666–67*, pp. 546, 551; *CSPD 1667*, p. 369.

131. PRO SP 29/97/20.1; 29/99/72, 142, 155; *Int.* 11 (9 November 1663), p. 81.

132. PRO SP 29/82/103; 29/83/54, 80.1, 98; 29/91/11, 21, 68; 29/93/17, 40 40.1–6; 29/99/120; *HMC* 25, *Le Fleming*, p. 31.

133. PRO SP 29/82/109; 29/100/27, 119; *Int.* 13 (23 November 1663), pp. 97–98; *CSPD 1663–64*, pp. 360–61, 652–53; *Newes* 56 (14 July 1664), pp. 449–50. The proclamation names Edward Carey, but numerous other documents indicate that David Carey was meant. Cf. *CSPD 1663–64*, pp. 389, 393, 454, 495–96.

134. PRO SP 29/82/37, 37.3; 29/91/81; *Int.* 16 (14 December 1663), p. 121.

135. PRO SP 29/90/95; *Newes* 4 (14 January 1664), p. 40; *CMHS*, 8:215; Bodl. Carte MSS 81, fol. 220$^r$.

136. *Newes* 4 (14 January 1664), pp. 39–40; 6 (21 January 1664), p. 55; 8 (28 January 1664), p. 72; 26 (31 March 1664), p. 215; 66 (18 August 1664), p. 536; *DCY*, p. xix; PRO SP 29/80/140; 29/91/4; 29/98/91; 29/102/33; *Int.* 5 (18 January 1664), pp. 43–45; 7 (25 January 1664), p. 63; 25 (28 March 1664), pp. 206–207; CH HA 10, 657; *HMC* 25, *Le Fleming*, p. 32; Bodl. Carte MSS 81, fols. 197$^r$–198$^r$; BL Add. MSS 33,770, fol 48$^r$; S. J. Chadwick, "The Farnley Wood Plot," *Publications of the Thoresby Society* 15 (1909): 125: Nicholson, "Plot," p. 225. In the end, Atkinson was given a reprieve, but it arrived too late.

137. *Int.* 11 (9 November 1663), p. 82; *Newes* 11 (12 November 1663), pp. 81–82; PRO SP 29/83/47; 29/90/8. The jurors, according to Colonel Freschville, were all "gentlemen of quality." SP 29/90/25. Blackburne's son was also arrested. There were a number of instances where fathers and sons were involved.

138. *Int.* 5 (18 January 1664), p. 45; 29 (11 April 1664), p. 240; 65 (15 August 1664), p. 528; PRO SP 29/82/109; 29/90/25; 29/93/91; *CSPD 1663–64*, p. 493.

139. *Misc. Aul.*, p. 306; *Int.* 29 (11 April 1664), p. 240; 63 (8 August 1664), p. 512; 65 (15 August 1664), p. 528; PRO SP 29/90/74; 29/91/99; *CSPV 1664–66*, p. 16; Bodl. Carte MSS 81, fol. 220$^r$. Bennet too argued that the state needed to make many examples of the rebels. Bodl. Carte MSS 46, fol. 136$^r$. As late as c. 1685 the bitterness in the north was such that one anonymous writer blamed the entire rebellion on Sir John Armitage and John Peples of Dewsbury, who, he said, used Greathead to seduce others to conspire against the state. Chadwick, "Plot," p. 124.

140. PRO SP 29/101/29; 29/103/110, 110.1; *CSPD 1664–65*, pp 94, 255; Walker, "Yorkshire Plot," p. 358; Greaves, *Saints and Rebels*, chap. 5; *Int.* 5 (18 January 1664), p. 42; *DCY*, p. xix; *Som. Tr.*, 8:441.

141. PRO SP 29/84/70; 29/93/10; *Newes* 4 (14 January 1664), pp. 34–35; *CR*, s.v. James Fisher; *Int.* 12 (16 November 1663), pp. 89–90; BL Add. MSS 33,770, fols. 8ʳ, 22ᵛ.

142. PRO SP 29/82/110; 29/85/103; 29/88/58; 29/92/96; 29/94/4; 29/100/24; 29/107/99; 29/154/118; Parker, *History*, pp. 80–81; BL Add. MSS 33,770, fol. 27ᵛ; Thomas Richards, *Wales Under the Penal Code (1662–1687)* (London: National Eisteddfod Association, 1925), pp. 3, 79. Richard Walters accused a Nonconformist minister named Leaver of Durham of complicity, but the charge cannot be substantiated. This would be Henry or Robert Leaver. SP 29/86/68; *CR*, s.vv.

143. *Misc. Aul.*, p. 320; *HMC 22, Eleventh Report*, Appendix, Part VII, p. 6; PRO SP 29/82/74; 29/83/66; 29/88/53; 29/90/112.

144. PRO SP 29/82/76; 29/83/10; 29/84/22, 85; 29/90/112; *Misc. Aul.*, p. 320.

145. PRO SP 29/80/139; 29/82/58; 29/83/37; 29/86/70; 29/90/112; 29/92/58.1; 29/95/16; 29/97/83, 84; *CSPD 1663–64*, pp. 314, 555, 579, 662; BL Add. MSS 33,770, fol. 10ᵛ. Robert Nicholson, citing Denham as his authority, dubiously claimed that Colonel Matthew Alured was involved and had £20,000 to pay the insurgents. BL Add. MSS 33,770, fol. 31ʳ.

146. PRO SP 29/82/44; 29/84/64; 29/86/70; 29/93/11; *CSPD 1663–64*, p. 352; Bodl. Carte MSS 81, fols. 197ᵛ, 199ʳ, 201ʳ⁻ᵛ, 203ʳ⁻ᵛ; BL Add. MSS 33,770, fols. 7ʳ⁻ᵛ, 31ʳ, 34ᵛ; *CR*, s.v. John Gunter; G. F. Jones, *Saw-Pit Wharton: The Political Career from 1640 to 1691 of Philip, Fourth Lord Wharton* (Sydney: Sydney University Press, 1967), pp. 201–207, 211–12. Cf. *DCY*, p. 108. Wharton had an agent at the trials to provide him with an account of the proceedings. Carte MSS 81, fols. 218ʳ–219ʳ.

147. *Misc. Aul.*, pp. 310, 317, 323; PRO SP 29/82/109, 109.1; 29/84/64; 29/85/51; 29/86/70; 29/99/110; Walker, "Yorkshire Plot," p. 356; *HMC 36, Ormonde*, n.s., 3:140; *Int.* 5 (18 January 1664), p. 43; 29 (11 April 1664), p. 240; 65 (15 August 1664), p. 528; *DCY*, p. xix; BL Add. MSS 33,770, fol. 28ᵛ. Walters tried to help Stockdale by testifying that the latter tried to dissuade him from participating in the rebellion. BL Add. MSS 33,770, fol. 36ʳ. Clarendon described Rymer as "a sullen man." Hyde, "Continuation," p. 1114.

148. Hodgson, pp. 181–93; *Int.* 65 (15 August 1664), p. 528; Walker, "Yorkshire Plot," p. 357; PRO SP 29/94/101 (cf. 29/80/139; 29/82/42); *DCY*, p. 115. The gentleman Anthony Garforth, who claimed he saw the declaration, got off with a fine of £20. *DCY*, p. 126.

149. PRO SP 29/84/64, 89; 29/92/12; 29/93/11; 29/95/1; 29/96/112; 29/101/35; *DCY*, p. 108; Walker, "Yorkshire Plot," pp. 357–58.

150. PRO SP 29/99/110; *DCY*, pp. 110–11.

151. George Fox, *The Journal of George Fox*, ed. John L. Nickalls (Cambridge: Cambridge University Press, 1952), pp. 357, 452. Cf. *HMC 25, Le Fleming*, p. 32.

152. PRO SP 29/84/28. Cf. *Int.* 8 (19 October 1663), pp. 59–60; *Newes* 14 (3 December 1663), p. 106; SP 29/84/28.1; 29/92/2; 29/107/29.

153. PRO SP 29/83/54; 29/85/85; 29/92/12; 29/98/80; BL Add. MSS 33,770, fols. 33ʳ, 34ᵛ.

154. PRO SP 29/82/37.2; 29/84/28.2; 29/91/99; 29/95/112; 29/96/112; 29/97/18.1; 29/98/91; BL Add. MSS 33,770, fol. 31ᵛ (as "Matthew" Robinson); *DCY*, pp. 107–108, 110–11. The Quaker Richard Robinson of Countersett in the West Riding, a neighbor of John Atkinson, also knew Dr. Richardson, but claimed not to have spoken to him for seven years. SP 29/83/84.

155. PRO SP 29/82/105; 29/100/60; BL Add. MSS 33,770, fols. 10ʳ, 13ʳ; Richards, *Wales*, p. 58.

156. *HMC* 71, *Finch*, 1:294–95, 297–98, 299.

157. PRO SP 29/86/18.1; 29/93/64; 29/94/52. The correspondent was J. Bentham.

158. PRO SP 29/83/8; 29/85/15, 18.1, 111; *Newes* 16 (25 February 1664), p. 130. Cf. SP 29/85/18; 29/86/83, 95.

159. PRO SP 29/86/71, 87; 29/90/23; 29/91/57; *Newes* 10 (4 February 1664), p. 88.

160. PRO SP 29/82/47; 29/90/101; 29/91/100; 29/92/38. Cf. *CSPV 1661–64*, p. 274; SP 29//86/18.1.

161. PRO SP 29/80/17, 18; 29/81/46; 29/83/28; 29/85/71; 29/88/74, 91; 29/91/20; 29/92/26; 29/107/89. Among those also named by Riggs were Richard Lawrence, George Thorne, Colonel Thomas Fitch, Captain (Benjamin?) Groome, and the Arian sectary John Knowles. In March 1664 government agents seized forty-eight musket barrels and seven pistols when the *Anne and Speedwell* arrived from Dunkirk. The sender is unkown. SP 29/95/13.

162. PRO SP 29/84/66, 90; 29/85/2, 6, 43, 50, 109; 29/86/47.1, 47.3; 29/91/57; 29/107/89. Cf. SP 29/86/47, 47.2.

163. PRO SP 29/81/46; 29/82/80; 29/83/28; 29/84/30; 29/85/71; 29/86/66; 29/90/45; *CCSP*, 5:384. In December Carr contemplated accepting command of a regiment in Germany. SP 29/86/66.

164. PRO SP 29/85/31; 29/91/79; 29/92/26, 74; 29/96/96; 29/107/89; *CSPD 1663–64*, p. 572.

165. *CCSP*, 5:367; PRO SP 29/83/47; 29/94/18, 112; *CSPD 1663–64*, p. 465.

166. PRO SP 29/94/112; (cf. 29/94/100); Sprunger, p. 414.

167. *HMC* 50, *Heathcote*, p. 127; PRO SP 29/67/155.1. Cf. *KI* 34 (17–24 August 1663), p. 545.

168. PRO SP 29/81/65, 71, 74, 80, 99; 29/82/2 (which indicates none were indicted in Norfolk).

169. PRO SP 29/71/48; 29/72/12, 12.1; 29/81/16; A. G. Matthews, *The Congregational Churches of Staffordshire* (London: Congregational Union of England and Wales, [1924]), pp. 61–62. Cf. *MCR*, 3:332, 334.

170. PRO SP 29/81/65; 29/82/106; 29/91/22.

171. Latimer, *Annals*, p. 325; PRO SP 29/83/53, 60; 29/90/54; 29/92/42; 29/93/8; 29/94/45; (cf. 29/94/126); *Int.* 17 (29 February 1664), p. 17; *Newes* 18 (3 March 1664), p. 152; *CSPD 1663–64*, p. 468.

## Notes to Chapter 7

1. John Lilburne, *Englands Birth-Right Justified* [1645], p. 10; [John Hall], *An Humble Motion to the Parliament of England* (London, 1649), p. 30; Edward Waterhouse, *An Humble Apologie for Learning and Learned Men* (London, 1653), p. 2.

2. *HMC* 78, *Hastings*, 2:140; Kennet, pp. 180–81, 189–90, 206, 230; *CSPD 1660–61*, p. 189; *PI* (3–10 September 1660), p. 589; *MP* 37 (6–13 September 1660), p. 578.

3. [Roger L'Estrange], *Treason Arraigned, in Answer to Plain English* (London, 1660), pp. 2, 4, 5.

4. Kennet, p. 117; Joseph Frank, *Cromwell's Press Agent* (Lanham, Md.: University Press of America, 1980), p. 143; [Marchamont Nedham], *News from Brussels* (1660), pp. 4, 6, 7, 8. Mr. Price, the customer of Dover, was accused of publishing a "scandalous" pamphlet against Charles II. PRO SP 29/9/45.

5. Kennet, p. 176.

6. George Gillespie, *A Dispute Against the English-Popish Ceremonies* ([Edinburgh], 1660), pp. 5, 11–12, 77–80, 82–84, 115–48, 159–92, 235, 258–59, 269; Nicoll, p. 304.

7. *The Speeches and Prayers of Major General Harrison . . .* ([London], 1660), sig. A2ᵛ.

8. *The Common Prayer-Book Unmasked* (1660), sig. A2$^r$, pp. 1, 58–61.

9. D[aniel] B[aker], *Yet One Warning More, to Thee O England* (London, 1660), pp. 1, 4, 7, 12, 23, 29.

10. *ST*, 5:1363–70; *MP* 47 (15–22 November 1660), p. 760; *PI* (19–28 November 1660), p. 763; Kennet, p. 325; [William Drake], *The Long Parliament Revived* (London, 1661), p. 4.

11. PRO SP 29/24/105. Philpott matriculated at Trinity College, Cambridge, in 1628, and graduated B.A. in 1632–33 and M.A. in 1636. J. Venn and J. A. Venn, comps., *Alumni Cantabrigienses*, 4 vols. (Cambridge, 1922–27), 3:357.

12. The principal themes of *The Valley of Achor* are reprinted in *Munster Paralleld*, pp. 8–22.

13. For Jessey, Chapman, and Smith see *BDBR*, s.vv.

14. *Warwick County Records: Quarter Sessions Order Book Easter, 1657, to Epiphany, 1665*, ed. S. C. Ratcliff and H. C. Johnson (Warwick: L. Edgar Stephens, 1938), p. 143; Kennet, p. 375; PRO SP 29/34/64. Smith was also the publisher in 1661 of Crofton's *A Serious Review of Presbyters*, the second edition of Ἀναληψις ανελυφθη. *The Fastning*, and the fourth edition of Ἀναλιψις, *or Saint Peters Bonds Abide*. The authorities also had Peter Cole, a printer in Cornhill, under surveillance. Among the works he sold were *The Rise and Ruin of the Stuarts* and *The Presbyterians Petition*. BL Egerton MSS 2543, fol. 27$^r$.

15. PRO SP 29/28/57; 29/43/23; Kennet, p. 524; *KI* 49 (25 November–2 December 1661), p. 743; *CSPV 1661–64*, p. 76; Kennet, p. 637. Wing does not list any books by Cole.

16. *CSPD 1661–62*, p. 23; PRO SP 29/75/117; 29/446/40; George Kitchin, *Sir Roger L'Estrange* (London: Kegan Paul, Trench, Trübner & Co., 1913), pp. 112–13. As late as February 1663 Peter Bodvile was questioned concerning the distribution of *A Phoenix* as well as the regicide speeches and the account of Vane's trial. PRO SP 29/68/88.

17. *CSPD 1661–62*, p. 23; PRO SP 29/41/40; 29/43/23; 29/45/74; 29/75/117; Kitchin, *L'Estrange*, pp. 113–14.

18. *CSPD 1661–62*, p. 106; PRO SP 29/41/41, 42; 29/43/8, 9; cf. 29/43/30, 31.

19. *CSPD 1661–62*, p. 159; Bernard Capp, *English Almanacs 1500–1800: Astrology and the Popular Press* (Ithaca, N.Y.: Cornell University Press, 1979), pp. 171–72. Because almanacs often contained "divers scandalous untruths and Treasonable assertions," printing or publishing them without license was prohibited beginning 25 September 1660. PRO SP 29/16/60.

20. PRO SP 29/45/28; 29/49/14.

21. Anon., ΕΝΙΑΥΤΟΣ ΤΕΡΑΣΤΙΟΣ. *Mirabilis Annus, or the Year of Prodigies and Wonders* ([London], 1661), sigs. A2$^v$, A3$^v$, A4$^v$.

22. Ibid., pp. 1–2, 6, 18–19, 23, 25, 29–30, 41–42, 51, 56, 69, 76, 79.

23. Ibid., pp. 46–47, 50, 62, 65–66, 70–71. Ludlow was a firm believer in prodigies. Cf. "Voyce," pp. 1061, 1073–74, 1140, 1147.

24. *KI* 42 (14–21 October 1661), p. 671; *CMHS*, 8:178.

25. PRO SP 29/56/135; 29/81/73.

26. *Mirabilis Annus Secundus* ([London], 1662), sigs. A3$^v$, A4$^{r-v}$, pp. 48–51, 66–67.

27. Ibid., pp. 1–3, 6–8, 11, 24–25, 27–31, 35–36, 40–41, 74–88. See also *Mirabilis Annus Secundus: or the Second Part of the Second Years Prodigies* (1662).

28. *CSPD 1661–62*, pp. 44–45; *HMC* 78, *Hastings*, 4:133; 14 Car. II, c. 33, *Statutes of the Realm*, 5:428–33; P. W. Thomas, *Sir John Berkenhead 1617–1679* (Oxford: Clarendon Press, 1969), p. 210.

29. Kitchin, *L'Estrange*, p. 82; PRO SP 29/51/6, 9; Thomas, *Berkenhead*, p. 223; J. B. Williams, "The Notebooks and Letters of News of the Restoration," *EHR* 23 (April 1908); 261.

30. PRO SP 29/51/8. *The Traitors Claim* argued that regicides who had surrendered

themselves in response to a proclamation "penned in a stile of Clemency" could not be justly executed.

31. PRO SP 29/51/10.1.
32. *KI* 5 (27 January–3 February 1662), p. 70; Kitchin, *L'Estrange*, p. 116; PRO SP 29/51/5; 29/68/4; *CSPD 1663–64*, p. 43; *HMC* 22, *Eleventh Report*, Appendix, Part VII, p. 4; *HMC* 43, *Fifteenth Report*, Appendix, Part VII, p. 93.
33. Thomas Watson, Παραμυθιον: *or a Word of Comfort for the Church of God* (London, 1662), sig. A4ʳ, pp. 10, 37.
34. Kennet, p. 748; *CSPV 1661–64*, p. 190–91.
35. *CSPD 1661–62*, pp. 492, 493, 529; *KI* 40 (29 September–6 October 1662), pp. 664–65; Kennet, p. 788; PRO SP 29/61/109.
36. PRO SP 29/62/36; Whiting, p. 551; Owen Lloyd, *The Panther-prophecy, or, a Premonition to All People, of Sad Calamities and Miseries Like to Befall These Islands* ([London], 1662), pp. 1–6.
37. PRO SP 29/62/37; 29/67/30.
38. *CSPD 1661–62*, pp. 405, 504, 508, 554; PRO SP 29/61/1.
39. PRO SP 29/65/90; *CSPD 1661–62*, p. 589; *BDBR*, s.v. Giles Calvert.
40. PRO SP 29/67/161; 29/68/4; 29/70/24; 29/72/60; *CSPD 1663–64*, pp. 71, 77, 101.
41. *CSPD 1663–64*, p. 101: *A Short Surveigh of the Grand Case of the Present Ministry* (London, 1663), pp. 21, 27, 40–44; PRO SP 29/88/75; Roger L'Estrange, *Considerations and Proposals in Order to the Regulation of the Press* (London, 1663), sig. a4ʳ.
42. L'Estrange, *Considerations*, sig. a4ʳ; *CSPD 1663–64*, pp. 179–80, 246; PRO SP 29/77/37; 29/78/37–40; 29/79/9; Whiting, pp. 309–10. The printer Richard Hodgkinson and the stationer Robert Cutler were released on 1 August. *CSPD 1663–64*, p. 225. The stationer Henry Marsh was bonded on 24 September. PRO SP 29/80/108.
43. PRO SP 29/76/29, 30, 80; 29/77/49.
44. PRO SP 63/309/pp. 121–22.
45. L'Estrange, *Considerations*, sigs. A2ᵛ, A3ʳ–A5ʳ.
46. Ibid., pp. 11–23.
47. Ibid., pp. 2–4, 8–10, 24–30. For further reform proposals see PRO SP 29/88/132; *A Brief Discourse Concerning Printing and Printers* (London, 1663).
48. David Masson, *The Life of John Milton*, 6 vols. (London: Macmillan, 1880), 6:328–30; Thomas, *Berkenhead*, p. 225.
49. *Int.* 3 (14 September 1663), pp. 23–24; 7 (12 October 1663), pp. 49–50.
50. *An Exact Narrative of the Tryal and Condemnation of John Twyn* (London, 1664), sig. A2ᵛ, pp. 12–27; *Newes* 6 (8 October 1663), pp. 47–48; PRO SP 29/88/76 (p. 30).
51. William Orme, *Memoirs of the Life, Writings, and Religious Connexions, of John Owen* (London: T. Hamilton, 1820), p. 387. W. Carew Hazlitt, *Third and Final Series of Bibliographical Collections and Notes on Early English Literature 1474–1700* (London: Bernard Quaritch, 1887), p. 129; *Int.* 12 (16 November 1663), p. 91; Firth & Davies, pp. 473–74.
52. *Mene Tekel; or, the Downfal of Tyranny* (1663), pp. 5, 8, 10, 26, 39, 41, 66, 70–82.
53. *CSPD 1663–64*, p. 295; PRO SP 29/81/73.1; *Exact Narrative*, p. 61; *Misc. Aul.*, pp. 305–306; *HMC* 36, *Ormonde*, n.s., 3:91. Copies of *Murther Will Out* were also found in York. *Exact Narrative*, p. 61.
54. *CSPD 1663–64*, p. 311; PRO SP 29/43/21; 29/83/15; *Exact Narrative*, pp 66–67.
55. [John Goodwin], *Prelatique Preachers None of Christ's Teachers* (London, 1663), pp. 1, 33, 68; *Exact Narrative*, pp. 66–67; *CSPD 1663–64*, p. 349.
56. *Exact Narrative*, pp. 2–3, 33–35; *CSPV 1661–64*, p. 288. Twyn was a widower with four small children. *CSPD 1641–43*, p. 427 (misdated). *ST*, 6:513–14 is a reprint of the *Exact Narrative*.
57. *Exact Narrative*, pp. 5–7, 36–60, 64, 72–73; *Newes* 16 (25 February 1664), p. 136;

34 (28 April 1664), p. 273. Cf. PRO SP 29/97/80. In connection with the trials, Elizabeth Calvert was interrogated concerning the author and printer of *Mene Tekel* and *The Speeches*. Authorities were looking for 500 or 600 missing copies of one of the works. PRO SP 29/92/10. Dover's wife Joan insisted on her husband's innocence. PRO SP 29/85/44.

58. *Exact Narrative*, sigs. A2ᵛ, A3ᵛ; *Int.* 15 (22 February 1664), p. 128.
59. *Exact Narrative*, p. 50; *CCSP*, 5:465; *Misc. Aul.*, p. 335. Cf. *Int.* 27 (4 April 1664), pp. 217–18.

# Suggestions
## For Further Reading

The following suggestions are limited to secondary sources and are not intended to constitute a comprehensive bibliography. Additional material may be found in the notes.

The only modern attempt to survey the radical underground was undertaken by Wilbur Cortez Abbott, "English Conspiracy and Dissent, 1660–1674," *American Historical Review* 14 (1908–1909): 503–28, 696–722. In *Public Order and Popular Disturbances 1660–1714* (London: Frank Cass & Co., 1938), Max Beloff provides a useful context but has little to say about radical activity. Several of the conspiracies have been singled out for treatment: see, for example, Henry Gee, "The Derwentdale Plot, 1663," *Transactions of the Royal Historical Society*, 3rd ser., 11 (1917): 125–42; James Walker, "The Yorkshire Plot, 1663," *Yorkshire Archaeological Journal* 31 (1934): 348–59; and for Venner's rising, Champlin Burrage, "The Fifth Monarchy Insurrections," *English Historical Review* 25 (October 1910): 722–47. For the Fifth Monarchists in general the indispensable work is B. S. Capp's superb *The Fifth Monarchy Men: A Study in Seventeenth-Century Millenarianism* (London: Faber and Faber, 1972). The same author's *English Almanacs 1500–1800: Astrology and the Popular Press* (Ithaca, N.Y.: Cornell University Press, 1979) is helpful.

There is an abundance of good material on Restoration religion, including an overview of the Nonconformists by Michael R. Watts, *The Dissenters: From the Reformation to the French Revolution* (Oxford: Clarendon Press, 1978). Gerald R. Cragg is good on matters of the spirit though not on political activity: *Puritanism in the Period of the Great Persecution, 1660–88* (Cambridge: Cambridge University Press, 1957). The older work by C. E. Whiting, *Studies in English Puritanism from the Restoration to the Revolution, 1660–1688* (London: Society for Promoting Christian Knowledge, 1931) is still worth consulting, but there is less reason to peruse Harry Grant Plum, *Restoration Puritanism: A Study of the Growth of English Liberty* (Chapel Hill: University of North Carolina Press, 1943). For the restoration of the Church of England, the best places to start are Robert S. Bosher, *The Making of the Restoration Settlement: The*

*Influence of the Laudians 1649–1662* (New York: Oxford University Press, 1951); Victor S. Sutch, *Gilbert Sheldon: Architect of Anglican Survival, 1640–1675* (The Hague: Martinus Nijhoff, 1973); and especially I. M. Green, *The Re-Establishment of the Church of England 1660–1663* (Oxford: Oxford University Press, 1978). For a brief overview, one can refer to Norman Sykes, *From Sheldon to Secker: Aspects of English Church History 1660–1768* (Cambridge: Cambridge University Press, 1959), or, for the Congregationalists, to R. Tudur Jones, *Congregationalism in England 1662–1962* (London: Independent Press, 1962). The Baptist story is recounted by B. R. White, *The English Baptists of the Seventeenth Century* (London: Baptist Historical Society, 1983). There is a biography of one of the great Congregationalist leaders by Peter Toon: *God's Statesman: The Life and Work of John Owen, Pastor, Educator, Theologian* (Exeter: Paternoster Press, 1971). For the Quakers the pre-1660 period is well covered in Hugh Barbour's *The Quakers in Puritan England* (New Haven and London: Yale University Press, 1964). For the period after 1660 the best work is still William C. Braithwaite, *The Second Period of Quakerism* (2nd ed.; Cambridge: Cambridge University Press, 1961). An introduction to Welsh Nonconformity may be found in Thomas Richards, *Wales Under the Penal Code (1662–1687)* (London: National Eisteddfod Association, 1925). The toleration issue is best approached through Raymond C. Mensing, Jr., *Toleration and Parliament 1660–1719* (Washington, D.C.: University Press of America, 1979), and in more general terms in Douglas R. Lacey, *Dissent and Parliamentary Politics in England 1661–1689* (New Brunswick, N.J.: Rutgers University Press, 1969).

For Scotland the necessary pre-1660 background is superbly discussed by F. D. Dow, *Cromwellian Scotland 1651–1660* (Edinburgh: John Donald Publishers, 1979). For the Scottish church there are very good studies by Ian B. Cowan, *The Scottish Covenanters 1660–1688* (London: Victor Gollancz, 1976); and Julia Buckroyd, *Church and State in Scotland 1660–1681* (Edinburgh: John Donald Publishers, 1980).

The necessary context for the exiles in the Netherlands is provided in Keith Sprunger's excellent study, *Dutch Puritanism* (Leiden: E. J. Brill, 1982). There is also a helpful article by Ralph C. H. Catterall, "Sir George Downing and the Regicides," *American Historical Review* 17 (January 1912): 268–89. There is a useful historical study of Aphra Behn by Angeline Goreau: *Reconstructing Aphra: A Social Biography of Aphra Behn* (New York: Dial Press, 1980). Behn was part of the government's intelligence network, which is briefly surveyed by James Walker, "The Secret Service Under Charles II and James II," *Transactions of the Royal Historical Society*, 4th ser., 5 (1932): 211–35.

The acquisition and control of information is approached from a different perspective by Peter Fraser, *The Intelligence of the Secretaries of State & Their Monopoly of Licensed News 1660–1688* (Cambridge: Cambridge University Press, 1956). There are biographies of the two principal figures in this story: George Kitchin, *Sir Roger L'Estrange* (London: Kegan Paul, Trench, Trübner & Co., 1913); and P. W. Thomas, *Sir John Berkenhead 1617–1679* (Oxford: Clarendon Press, 1969).

There are numerous good political studies of the 1660s, a sampling of which is found in the essays edited by J. R. Jones, *The Restored Monarchy 1660–1688* (Totowa, N.J.: Rowman and Littlefield, 1979). The latter chapters of R. W. Harris, *Clarendon and the English Revolution* (London: Hogarth Press, 1983) are relevant, but there is little on Clarendon's attitude toward the radicals. For political questions pertaining to the military, there is a small classic by Lois G. Schwoerer, *"No Standing Armies!": The*

*Antiarmy Ideology in Seventeenth-Century England* (Baltimore and London: Johns Hopkins University Press, 1974).

In addition to the biographical studies already mentioned, there are others of interest, particularly W. C. Abbott's *Colonel Thomas Blood, Crown-Stealer* (1911), reprinted in *Conflicts with Oblivion* (2nd ed.; Cambridge: Harvard University Press, 1935). Maurice Ashley's study of *John Wildman: Plotter and Postmaster* (New Haven: Yale University Press, 1947) is provocative but undocumented. James Ferguson's life of *Robert Ferguson the Plotter* (Edinburgh: David Douglas, 1887) is of little value for the early 1660s. G. F. Jones's *Saw-Pit Wharton* (Sydney: Sydney University Press, 1967) argues for a close relationship between Philip, fourth Lord Wharton, and the radicals. Unfortunately, Marchamont Nedham had little to do with the radical press in the 1660s, though there is a good biography of him by Joseph Frank: *Cromwell's Press Agent* (Lanham, Md.: University Press of America, 1980). For Milton the best biography is William Riley Parker's classic, *Milton: A Biography*, 2 vols. (Oxford: Clarendon Press, 1968), but for context it is still worth reading David Masson's *The Life of John Milton*, 6 vols. (London: Macmillan, 1880). Milton's place in the radical tradition has been firmly established by Christopher Hill in *Milton and the English Revolution* (New York: Viking Press, 1978). As a sequel to that study, Hill wrote *The Experience of Defeat: Milton and Some Contemporaries* (New York: Viking Press, 1984), much of which deals with the pre-1660 period. For the ideas the radicals continued to espouse after the Restoration, the best study is Hill's *The World Turned Upside Down* (New York: Viking Press, 1972). It is also worth reading the same author's *Some Intellectual Consequences of the English Revolution* (Madison: University of Wisconsin Press, 1980). For biographical studies of Edmund Calamy, Richard Culmer, George Griffith, John Simpson, Henry Danvers, Paul Hobson, and Francis Bampfield, see Richard L. Greaves, *Saints and Rebels: Seven Nonconformists in Stuart England* (Macon, Ga.: Mercer University Press, 1985). Basic biographical data about many of the people in the present book may be found in the *Biographical Dictionary of British Radicals in the Seventeenth Century*, ed. Greaves and Robert Zaller, 3 vols. (Brighton: Harvester Press, 1982–84).

# Index